THE RADICAL BOOKSTORE

The Radical Bookstore

Counterspace for Social Movements

Kimberley Kinder

University of Minnesota Press
Minneapolis
London

Published by the University of Minnesota Press
111 Third Avenue South, Suite 290
Minneapolis, MN 55401-2520
http://www.upress.umn.edu

ISBN 978-1-5179-0917-8 (hc)
ISBN 978-1-5179-0918-5 (pb)

A Cataloging-in-Publication record for this book
is available from the Library of Congress.

UMP LSI

To Cora and Charlotte

Contents

Acknowledgments

I OWE MY BIGGEST DEBT OF GRATITUDE to the booksellers and librarians who graciously agreed to my interview requests. Their informed perspectives and colorful stories provided both raw material and big ideas for this book. These interviewees, whom I cite by name, shared their time despite the pressures of running a business and despite receiving no compensation. This book would not have been possible without their generosity.

When beginning this project, before the scope was fully set, I met with the owners of local independent bookstores in Ann Arbor who graciously discussed my ideas and provided background information on independent bookselling. I later decided to focus exclusively on activist bookstores, so these booksellers are not quoted in the final project. Nevertheless, I appreciate the behind-the-scenes support I received from Crazy Wisdom Bookstore and Tearoom, Aunt Agatha's Mystery Bookshop, Bookbound Bookstore, and Literati Bookstore during my project's most fledgling moments.

Several colleagues helped me refine the ideas for this book. Sarah Knuth provided feedback on the early research proposal. She also gave me much-needed moral support during the research process. Similarly, John Stehlin acted as an informal developmental editor for this project. As a personal favor, he reviewed an early draft, and he offered invaluable feedback and numerous suggestions. Many of his ideas made their way into the final manuscript, and I am grateful for his assistance.

I presented portions of this manuscript to audiences at Columbia University, University of California, Los Angeles, and the University of Miami. The feedback I received from those audiences made the manuscript stronger.

This project also benefited from the editorial support I received from the University of Minnesota Press. Editor Jason Weidemann gave advice and guidance on the project's development from start to finish. I am likewise indebted to the anonymous reviewers who provided invaluable constructive feedback through the University of Minnesota Press's peer review process. To those anonymous reviewers, thank you for your time and support.

Building the Infrastructure of Dissent

WHY AND HOW DO ACTIVISTS construct counterspaces? Is it enough to claim turf by squatting in abandoned buildings and hanging rebellious posters around a proverbial soapbox, or is activist placemaking more complex and multifunctional than that?

One person I asked was Leslie James Pickering. Pickering was a spokesperson for the Earth Liberation Front in the late 1990s when the FBI dubbed it their number one domestic terrorism priority. Today, Pickering is a small business owner in Upstate New York. It may seem like a big leap to go from being a suspected terrorist to running a mom-and-pop shop. But for Pickering, owning a small business is not the end of his activism. It is just the start of a constructivist chapter.

After leaving the Earth Liberation Front in 2002, Pickering moved to Buffalo, New York, and began looking for other ways to make a difference. He "walked around the whole summer just talking to people."[1] On these walks, he asked residents in the "most downtrodden" neighborhoods "what they thought was wrong with Buffalo and how they could change it."

A lack of imagination was the first obstacle to change. "People didn't really have a whole lot of knowledge or hope because they knew very little about how movements for change had fought and struggled in the past." To inspire visionary thinking, Pickering screened documentaries on topics like the Black Panther Party and the Attica Prison Uprising in local libraries and community centers. But when other patrons complained, Pickering says he "ended up getting kicked out" and banned from using city-funded spaces for organizing. "At that point, we realized we needed to have our own space that we couldn't get kicked out of."

Space costs money. Pickering considered starting an activist library, but he needed revenue to sustain it, so he opened a radical bookstore instead. He and his wife bought a house, and in 2011, they founded Burning Books in the converted storefront on the ground floor.

Burning Books is no mere bookstore. Like countless other radical

Bookshelves on casters have been rolled aside to make space for a community event
with Black liberation activists at Burning Books in Buffalo, New York. Photograph by
Leslie James Pickering, 2018; courtesy of Leslie James Pickering.

spaces across the country, Burning Books is a node for organizing. It provides free meeting space for grassroots groups. It stockpiles information
on movements like Occupy, Antifa, and Anonymous. Burning Books
is also a landing pad for international organizers who otherwise bypass
small, struggling cities while traveling to Chicago, San Francisco, and
New York.

This case of using a bookstore as a platform for radical organizing is also an
example of activist placemaking. Activists need a place of their own. Constructing these autonomous spaces involves securing locations, converting buildings, generating revenue, selecting inventory, recruiting speakers,
cultivating relationships, resolving disputes, and coordinating interventions. All of these practices produce activist space and make it useful for
organizing. The rebellious T-shirts and posters on display at places like
Burning Books are only part of the radical space. I mention this because,
in the place-branding literature, scholars often treat symbolic icons as a de-
finitive substrate. Image-making rules the day, and productive forces fade
away. This book challenges these reductive interpretations. Placemaking is

a cultural, economic, and political process, as well as a stylistic one. Furthermore, analyzing activist counterspaces sheds light on the material, regulatory, and discursive work that everyone undertakes when producing distinctive, meaningful, and functional home turf.

In this book, I use examples like Burning Books to think through the constructive aspects of contentious placemaking. I ask how and why activists insert hubs of contentious politics into everyday landscapes of dissent. These durable hubs are not one-off demonstration sites. Instead, they persist 365 days a year between the spikes of public protest. I call this phenomenon "constructive activism," by which I mean the process of building physical spaces that advance political causes in a repeatable way. Constructive activism takes many forms. Some counterspaces are private while others are public. Some last for years and others for decades. Within this mix, this book focuses on the subset of constructed spaces that find a home in retail and that leverage the durability and porosity of retail to advance political causes. This focus also highlights how having autonomous space, instead of relying only on seized or borrowed space, constructs additional opportunities for organizing.

My analysis is based on seventy-seven venues like Burning Books operating across the United States. Burning Books is emblematic of activists nationwide who use print and retail to facilitate dissent. These venues take many forms. They are bookstores, infoshops, libraries, knowledge cafes, community centers, publishing collectives, thrift stores, and art installations in the guise of bookstores. They build on the twentieth-century legacies of Black, feminist, communist, and queer bookstores but reinvent them to reflect updated movement goals and business models. These constructed environments bring people together, stimulate progressive visioning, and facilitate public protest.

Within this mix, some venues have a warm-and-fuzzy "third place"[2] feel, but even the warm and fuzzy ones are social movement hubs that sometimes get raided by the FBI, wiretapped and infiltrated by undercover agents, or attacked by alt-right agitators. Not all progressive counterspaces reach these extremes, but I raise the issue to emphasize that, among the people I interviewed, the point of constructing radical bookstores and libraries is not to make quaint community spaces. On the contrary, the point is to challenge capitalism, imperialism, white privilege, patriarchy, and homophobia in a significant way that poses material threats to existing systems of power.

As another feature, all of the venues I studied are organized around books. I focus on books because my research, work, and life experiences have taught me that reading changes lives. Books, newspapers, pamphlets, and magazines nourish people with ideas. For feminist Carol Seajay, activist publishing not only changed the lives of readers; it also "changed even the lives of the women who didn't read. Because it changed the lives around them."[3] Another reason I focus on books is that selling print commodities helps pay the rent, which makes it easier to maintain radical spaces. Activists sell other things, too, like food, art, and bicycles, but print capitalism in Western culture is a privileged ideological medium. It communicates at a distance, it conveys authority, and it confers legitimacy on progressive ideas.

Print-based movement spaces are also proliferating. Although the New Left wave of activist bookstores declined in the 1990s and 2000s, along with the independent bookselling industry as a whole, this industry is rebounding since 2009. Several factors contribute to this partial resurgence. As one factor, consumer demand for walkable neighborhoods with distinctive identities is reviving interest in community-based retail. As another factor, consumers bored with the doldrums of screen fatigue are searching for tactile spaces with sensual objects they can touch, smell, and hold. A third factor involves the changing emotional role of retail and its emergence as a key landscape for social interactions. New business formats help as well, most notably the rise of retail-nonprofit hybrids. These combined factors are creating new cultural and financial opportunities to use physical bookstores, libraries, and knowledge cafes as platforms for dissent.

One umbrella term for this phenomenon of retail-based activism is "activist entrepreneurship." Historians use this term to describe activists who create businesses as tools for political organizing.[4] Some activist enterprises are retail businesses while others focus on production, distribution, and financing. Activist entrepreneurship is different from corporate social responsibility because the goal is not to use ethics to enhance profits. Instead, activist-entrepreneurs use businesses to support contentious politics.

Print-based movement spaces are one subtype of activist enterprise. In these spaces, activists leverage print capitalism as a social movement tool. These print-based environments exist within a diverse social movement terrain including public streets, private homes, college campuses, service institutions, religious institutions, party offices, and city halls. Constructing movement-oriented retail does not negate the need for these other modes and spaces of organizing. Instead, retail plays a complementary role by absorbing tasks less easily accomplished elsewhere.

Importantly, *radical* bookstores are not the same thing as *independent* bookstores. On the contrary, most independent booksellers, librarians, and publishers are not part of the radical fringe. Saying indies are not radical does not mean they are not socially conscious or politically engaged. Often, they are. Nonradical indies support progressive causes like Buy Local campaigns, free speech protections, and antitrust legislation. However, these reformist interventions are qualitatively different from radical movements to overthrow capitalism or end white supremacy.

Similarly, although I use print-based environments as examples throughout this book, my analysis is not primarily about publishing or bookselling. For scholars interested in those topics, Laura Miller's *Reluctant Capitalists* and Ted Striphas's *Late Age of Print* provide comprehensive analyses of the cultural aspirations and economic pressures in the bookselling industry. John Thompson's *Merchants of Culture* provides a similar analysis of the publishing industry. Huw Osborne's edited volume *Rise of the Modernist Bookshop* provides a historical perspective on early-twentieth-century bookselling, and Andrew Laties's *Rebel Bookseller* offers a noir-style account of capitalism's assault on indie businesses today. Instead of replicating those efforts, I ask different questions. I ask why and how activists construct space for contentious politics, including spaces using print commodities to facilitate activist goals.

In terms of politics, a smattering of examples from interviews and archives illustrates the political goals embedded in movement-oriented spaces. Activists construct storefronts "to shake people up"[5] at Resistencia, "to provoke a line of questioning" at Beyond Repair, "to challenge structures of domination and oppression" at Wooden Shoe, "to incite a dissenting imagination" at City Lights, to provide "the raw material for revolt" at Revolution NYC, "to raise feminist consciousness and have that feminist consciousness turn into political action" at People Called Women, to provide "a community space" for "people being marginalized because of our sexuality or gender identities" at the Bureau of General Services, to have "a free private meeting room" for grassroots organizing at Boneshaker, to be a "fundraising engine" for people experiencing homelessness and living with AIDS at Housing Works, to provide "sanctuary to writers who are exiled and under threat of persecution"[6] at City of Asylum, to do "prison support work and anti-prison work" at Boxcar, "to offset the enormous power" of corporations and governments by amplifying the voices of "ordinary citizens" at the Civic Media Center,[7] and to "demonstrate that the [anarchist] ideals we have politically are possible to translate into the real world" at Red Emma's.[8]

To advance these goals, activist retailers have to comply enough with market dictates and government regulations to keep their spaces open, but after that, they can overlay scores of other contentious practices. Overlay functions are about using space for more than one purpose, for instance by using a room simultaneously as a retail venue, community space, storage room, promotional tool, and logistical base. The overlay dynamics in radical bookstores and libraries echo those found in the urban commons movement. For Patrick Bresnihan and Michael Byrne, "After the film screening, chairs are cleared away to make room for a party; the morning after the party, the space is cleaned up to hold a discussion or writing workshop, which in turn makes way for a baking session."[9] In a similar manner, activists operating bookstores and infoshops rarely maintain single-use storefronts. Instead, they treat space as an enabling resource sustaining many functions through continual repurposing.

However, because of my focus on constructive placemaking, I analyze those overlays from an unconventional perspective. Instead of describing seemingly neutral spaces that accommodate many functions, I show that activists use overlays as constructive tools. These constructive dynamics include designing space to dramatize radical worldviews (chapter 5), governing space to promote equitable interactions (chapter 6), programming space to engender collective caretaking (chapter 7), and mobilizing space to support political demonstrations (chapter 8). Activist retail does not merely accommodate these practices. On the contrary, these practices shape space and give it meaning.

These constructive overlays transform vanilla-box storefronts into progressive counterspaces where people live and promote alternative lifestyles. These revolutionary imaginations embedded within humble settings unmoor people from allegiances to oppressive subjectivities and encourage identification with progressive alternatives. The hope is that, in these constructed environments, people find the homes they've been denied, discover agency they never knew they could possess, and develop alternative vocabularies for understanding politics and personhood. By contributing to these spaces as workers, writers, sojourners, and demonstrators, people live differently, even if only in intermittent bursts.

Participating in Capitalism Involves Tensions, Contradictions, and Shortfalls

That is the grand ambition, but in reality, even as constructive activism gestures toward progressive liberation, movement-oriented businesses are at best "concrete utopias."[10] Concrete utopias are aspirational spaces, imperfect and unfinished. For radical booksellers, the compromises required to build alternatives within real-world constraints thwart aspirational purities. Activists struggle with insufficient financial resources and limited institutional support. Participants clash over political goals and leadership styles. Market discipline seeps in, and legal barriers get in the way. Building utopian visions in stone also freezes ideas in place, which forecloses emerging possibilities, at least for a while.[11]

These contradictions lead to disappointments and failures. Some failures are economic. Working through capitalism is not a smooth process, and tensions invariably arise when antiauthoritarian activists participate in capitalist commodity exchange by selling books and paying rent. Katie Renz aptly summarizes these contradictions in her profile of AK Press.[12] "If they want to continue publishing media essentially centered on undermining an economic system wholly obsessed with screwing folks over to make a buck, they somehow have to participate (money generation) without total acquiescence (exploitation)."[13] Similarly, for activist booksellers, working through retail often requires sacrificing some movement goals to advance others, for instance by selling commodities that activists may not fully support because they need the cash to pay the rent. Participating in real estate introduces additional tensions not only because these spaces are complicit in gentrification but also because municipal licensing and zoning requirements exert normative pressure on how activists can use their spaces.

These economic challenges generate social tensions among activists who disagree about which types of concessions are worthwhile and which types of "oppressors' tools"[14] to deploy. Conflicts arise for other reasons as well. Activists disagree over how much to accommodate "outsiders" who may not (yet) feel comfortable in subcultural spaces and who may not (yet) comply with subcultural codes. Activists also disagree over business

practices, for instance whether queer themes should have a strong presence in Black bookstores, or whether it is ethical to pay workers below
minimum wage if businesses will otherwise crumble. Another challenge
is that activists use businesses not just for outreach but also for discipline,
for instance by making moral claims about how other activists ought to
behave, what they can say, and when they have to leave.

Alongside these economic and social challenges, political tensions arise
as well. Social movements have taken a prefigurative turn in recent decades,
but participants, scholars, and commentators disagree over whether it is
sufficient for a few people to do things differently or whether prefiguration
is better understood as a stepping-stone toward institutional reform. Additionally, a shared commitment against oppression does not mean people
agree about which of the many alternatives to implement instead. These
differences lead to operational disputes, for instance over whether Black
liberation booksellers should support every Black author or only the progressive ones, as well as whether feminist booksellers should reject pornography and sadomasochism as violence against women or reclaim them
as legitimate and liberating sexual choices.

Because of these economic, social, and political tensions, reversing the
usual arrow of co-option is simultaneously hopeful and vulnerable. Instead of subcultures being symbolically incorporated into mainstream
consumer culture,[15] activist-entrepreneurs appropriate publishing and retail as mechanisms for reform. It works to some extent, but it is no pana-
cea. Activist retail does not end capitalism, patriarchy, or white privilege,
and overlay functions do not fully neutralize the external discipline of
the state.

Utopian Dreaming Has Many Benefits

Despite these limitations, constructive activism is a common social movement repertoire. Incompleteness has benefits, not just liabilities. Instead of
assuming the onerous burden of developing robust "replacement ideologies"[16] and full-fledged alternative communities ready to supplant existing
institutions, the fluidity and openness of concrete utopias allow them to
be places of open-ended dreaming and scheming. When people visit nonnormative spaces like progressive bookstores and infoshops, "The opening of a door leads to the opening of books and the opening of ideas."[17] The
worlds encapsulated in radical print and in the counterspaces surrounding

it show that society has been done differently in the past, is currently being done differently elsewhere, and could be done differently here.

Within concrete utopias, radical literature plays an important role in provoking the dissenting imagination. For Guy Baeten, dystopian writing, the critical side of utopian thought, is a powerful political tool for unsettling the status quo because it frees people to question basic social institutions and their unacknowledged pernicious effects. Political novels like George Orwell's *1984* and Margaret Atwood's *The Handmaid's Tale* use hyperbolic portrayals of institutional authority to "give us access to ways of thinking that we had previously not allowed into our consciousness."[18] Nonfiction exposés like Betty Friedan's *The Feminine Mystique* and Noam Chomsky's *Manufacturing Consent* likewise express disenchantment with the most basic elements of American culture. These dystopian critiques transform nebulous feelings of dysphoria into well-defined concepts of oppression with names, contours, and patterns of significance that, once recognized, can be resisted.

Alongside dystopian writing, the more hopeful side of utopian literature expresses yearnings for how society could be done otherwise. For people trapped in invalidating or marginalizing environments, imagining alternatives is an important first step. For Nicholas Thoburn, "Books allow us to believe there is an escape from or alternative to the world."[19] These imagined escapes may be more fiction than fact, but considering possibilities, even if only in the collective imagination, is nonetheless liberating. Utopian thinking provides hope against the odds. It broadens the limits of thinkability. It conjures options when no obvious ones exist. Aspirational visions encourage people to seek alternatives if they can find them, construct alternatives if none are available, and make partial alternatives stronger. For Baeten, this boundary-defying imagining is the process of "thinking and dreaming the materials of new images of the future."[20]

Despite these benefits, constructing concrete counterspaces is not easy, and the perpetual feeling of falling short can lead to frustration and burnout. For David Harvey, extracting utopian dreams "from the dark recesses of our minds and turning them into a political force for change may court the danger of the ultimate frustration of those desires."[21] Despite these disappointments, Harvey nevertheless celebrates the aspirational imagination. "Better that, surely, than giving in . . . and living in craven and supine fear of expressing and pursuing alternative desires at all."[22] An imperfect effect is still an effect that should not be discounted. The print-based movement described in this book happens in real places filled with real people having real experiences that are really different from the norm. Their utopian imaginations work because they signal a conscious intention to act otherwise. Even if a full revolution never arrives, by starting to do things differently now, people discover unanticipated possibilities, which then generate new opportunities for organizing.

Retail Politics Are about Human Connections

Retail spaces are porous spaces. Like other commercial environments, people often think of retail as part of the public realm because so many strangers pass through. In this book, I give special attention to two subgroups of people who cross paths in radical businesses. These two subgroups include the committed activists who manage progressive spaces or regularly spend time there and the newbies who are awakened by what they discover there. Many other groups pass through as well, but the public-facing aspects of commercial settings create opportunities for activists to construct brokering sites where novices and mentors connect.

The process of search and discovery is deeply personal for both groups. Unlike demonstrations, which emphasize strength in numbers, retail politics is about human connections.[23] It is about courting public opinion by connecting one-on-one at the intimate level of memories, worries, and dreams. The goal is political, but the process is personal.

As an example, newcomers often visit activist enterprises during moments of personal crisis. Queer feminist bookstores, for instance, were lifelines for women in the 1970s and 1980s. Lesbians came out to each other in these bookstores, and battered women went there to escape domestic violence.[24] This lifeline dynamic explains why Kit Quan went to Old Wives' Tales to escape unbearable circumstances. For this fifteen-year-old runaway carrying the trauma of homophobia and interpersonal violence, escape was both liberating and dangerous. "I left my family and my culture to live by my political beliefs, but except for the driving forces of anger and hunger, I did not have much backup for my new life."[25] Visiting the queer feminist bookstore, Quan found refuge, camaraderie, and employment, as well as an ideology for reclaiming her personal narrative and reshaping her political future.

According to Lynn Mooney with Women & Children First, this lifeline function "still happens today." Mooney regularly interacts with customers in crisis. When I interviewed her in 2016, she shared several stories from the previous year of people using the bookstore to regroup and heal. One story involved "a man who came in and was asking for certain kinds of books [on] violence against women and trauma. And we got talking. And eventually he started crying. And he told me that his daughter had just been date raped." The customer's distraught wife and child "were at home waiting for him to come back with these materials. And they had specifically sent him here," to the feminist bookstore, because "they knew not only that we'd have the materials, but [also] that it was an OK place for him to be. Because it was hard for him to be out and talking about it." Mooney spent a long time consoling the distressed father. She recommended resources, both in print and in the community, and she offered a compassionate ear. But this interaction was political as much as personal. Instead of only emphasizing self-help for victims, they also discussed the structural nature of rape culture, the need for systemic legal reforms, and the strategies for getting involved.

Conversations like these are common in all activist enterprises and not just the ones emphasizing feminist ethics of care. Print-based counterspaces provide solace not only from patriarchy and misogyny but also from white supremacy, capitalist alienation, Western imperialism, and homophobic trauma. Alongside solace, these spaces provide critical languages for interpreting collective harm. Even with gendered issues like sexual assault, many of Mooney's interactions involve men. Around the same time she consoled the distraught father, she connected with another man who "told me that he'd been sexually molested by a priest as a boy. And then he told me that I was the first person he'd ever told that wasn't a family member." In spaces like these that feel safe enough to disclose sensitive information to strangers, people bond around trauma. Then, once the unspeakable gets expressed, political discussions often ensue.

Conversations like this one within Women & Children First emphasize the deeply emotional aspects of movement-oriented retail. Like a politician leaving the crowded arena to talk with "real people" in the streets, activists construct small businesses in part to create environments that accommodate intimate interactions among strangers. Reading books alone is somewhat helpful, but having physical spaces for face-to-face conversations also facilitates healing. Activist-entrepreneurs do not just sell books. Their stores also bring people together to discuss oppression and enact alternatives. As a subtheme within constructive activism, this book highlights the nurturance work activists perform and the deeply personal and intimate steps they take to make society better, safer, more equitable, and more just.

Print-Based Movement Spaces Combine Place, Text, and Activism

The material for this book comes from a study of print-based movement spaces. Print-based movement spaces are a subtype of constructive activism. I developed the phrase "print-based movement space" as an umbrella term to define activist enterprises combining three elements: place, text, and activism. I used these three elements as selection criteria for my research.

Starting with place, all of the venues I studied had physical locations and not just a digital presence. These locations were "their" locations, not borrowed spaces. They were also "durable" locations intended to last several years or decades, not temporary spaces lasting only a few hours. Most of these durable venues had a digital presence as well, allowed other people to borrow their spaces, and developed occasional pop-ups in satellite locations. Nevertheless, my selection criteria required activists to have a physical, durable, autonomous space as a precondition for inclusion in this study. Additionally, I focused on public-facing spaces where activists use the porosity of retail to interact with large cross sections of the population. This selection criteria included radical bookstores and retail-like infoshops, as well as publishing entities with storefront subcomponents, but it excluded less porous residential and institutional settings, including large movement archives. Institutional archives are valuable, but they function less like public-facing commercial spaces and more like private organizations. In terms of location, 84 percent of the venues I studied were located in storefronts with entrances and windows on the ground floor. The rest were down a floor, up a floor, inside institutions, or in permanent market stalls.

Next, in terms of text, a significant portion of each location was organized around print objects. Print objects include books, as well as other book-like creations such as pamphlets, chapbooks, newspapers, and zines. Activist-entrepreneurs trade in all these formats. Book sales are the most profitable and help pay for space, but activist businesses are not primarily about making a profit. Mainstream culture confers less respect to pamphlets, chapbooks, and zines, and these objects usually have lower profit margins. But these noncorporate, barely commodified publications pluralize public discourse and accommodate nonnormative expression. For many activist-entrepreneurs, these boundary-defying characteristics make book-like objects worthy of inclusion.

Third, in terms of activism, all of the venues I studied had an explicit social justice agenda. It took some trial and error to decide where to draw the admittedly fuzzy line distinguishing radical activism from other forms of nonradical political engagement. In the end, for my purposes, I decided it was not enough for venues to just sell nonnormative commodities or use noncapitalist business practices. Instead, I focused on venues where people approached their businesses primarily as social movement tools. Additionally, I focused on the radical left. Scholars often study causes they support, and my work is no exception.[26] I focused exclusively on progressive causes, like new anarchism and prison abolition, as opposed to alt-right causes, like antiabortion activism and white supremacy. I've made my peace with this selection bias. This book is a labor of love as much as a work of scholarship, and to make the evening hours and time spent away from my children worthwhile, I focus on causes I consider worthwhile.

Although my selection criteria include all three dimensions of place, text, and activism, my analysis focuses primarily on space and how people use constructive placemaking in contentious politics. Other scholars have written about the other two themes. For text, Kristin Hogan's *Feminist Bookstore Movement* and Nicholas Thoburn's *Anti-Book* analyze print objects as tools for organizing. For activism, Doug McAdam et al.'s *Dynamics of Contention* and Charles Tilly's *Contentious Performances* analyze the performative aspects of social movement repertoires. I draw on their scholarship, but I do not replicate their labor. Instead, by focusing on space, this book analyzes why and how activists construct counterspaces enabling contentious politics, as well as the strategic opportunities associated with having porous retail spaces.

Print-Based Movement Spaces Come in Many Stripes

Although my selection criteria required a progressive vision, I did not filter further by movement. For instance, I did not focus exclusively on feminism or anarchism, nor did I write separate chapters for race, class, and gender. Instead, in the spirit of McAdam et al., I use a process-based approach, which "wagers that we can learn more about all [social movements] by comparing their dynamics than by looking at each on its own."[27] Different social movements operate in similar socioeconomic contexts, which is one reason a shared technique can advance many causes. Analyzing the spatial strategies that social movements have in common moves beyond the idiosyncrasies of specific movements to instead foreground the political environment that all progressives inhabit. This contextual, process-based approach shifts the focus from individual actors and subcultures to the institutional opportunity structures these actors mobilize. My analysis of print-based movement spaces contributes to this structural analysis by assessing the financial, cultural, and spatial opportunity structures for advancing movements through retail, as well as the systemic advantages that arise when constructing durable, autonomous spaces organized around print.

Emphasizing commonality does not negate difference, especially when it comes to differential privilege. Within social movement theory, scholars frequently distinguish between movements of "the discontented" and movements of "the deprived."[28] Movements of the discontented focus on lifestyle issues, for instance when lefty professionals chafe against monotonous work environments or when alienated teenagers rebel against suburban norms. Movements of the deprived, by contrast, are less about lifestyles and more about survival. These movements emphasize the social production of poverty and homelessness, the structural oppression of women and queer folk, and the systemic criminalization of people of color.

Issues of discontentment and deprivation overlap, but they should not be conflated. The people involved occupy different strategic positions relative to systems of authority, and these differences constrain opportunities for organizing. Differential privilege explains why white anarchists can more safely engage in direct action campaigns than people of color.[29] It explains why women, whose labor has been devalued for centuries, may prioritize living wages even if it means sacrificing other movement goals.[30] The diverse landscape of print-based movement spaces reflects these distinctions, and I flag those differences throughout this book even as I do not allow them to overshadow the spatial practices that movements share.

Taken together, the radical counterspaces included in this analysis include a cross section of radical bookstores, infoshops, libraries, knowledge cafes, thrift stores, publishing houses, community centers, and art installations in the guise of bookstores. In terms of topics, this landscape includes some still-surviving venues from the 1960s and 1970s dedicated to Black power, feminism, queer liberation, and anticapitalism. It also includes younger venues organized around Latino/a, Chicano/a, and Indigenous peoples movements, as well as new anarchism, political asylum, and prison abolition. These younger venues are often explicitly intersectional, meaning instead of focusing on one issue, such as race or gender, they emphasize interlocking axes of oppression.

Next, in terms of business structure, even though print-based movement spaces use a variety of business models, because society inherits language from the past, most of these spaces are still called bookstores. Their owners and users refer to them as bookstores even though more than half are nonprofits and even though the for-profit venues rely heavily on subscriptions, donations, and crowdfunding. In many cases, activists blend their bookstores with other non-bookstore formats. One non-bookstore format includes libraries, infoshops, and archives selling access to print material without selling objects outright. Another alternative includes media centers and publishing spaces where people produce printed material in addition to selling and archiving it. A third format includes cultural centers and multiyear art installations that look and function like bookstores but get their material and revenue from other sources. Most of the spaces included in this study are creative blends of the above.

Despite belonging to different movements and despite their diverse business formats, I interpret these spaces as part of a shared phenomenon of activists using print and retail to construct movement-oriented environments. By giving myself a consistent set of selection criteria—place, text, and activism—I was able to generate a snapshot of this phenomenon as it existed in 2016. An important caveat, however, is that the fixity of my definition does not imply fixity within the cultural landscape. Activist enterprises are dynamic. Their participants change business models, commodity types, and organizing intensity over time. These changes bring venues in and out of my selection criteria, as well as in and out of the larger social movement scene. Happily, when some venues fade from view, new ones take their place, and contentious energy keeps churning.

Methods of Research and Analysis

When researching this book, I selected a subset of seventy-seven print-based movement spaces for analysis. Geographically, these venues are spread across the United States, which provides a national perspective on this activist repertoire. However, this national framework leaves out the many print-based movement spaces existing in other countries. Similarly, spaces organized around books are similar to non-print-based spaces such as temporary autonomous zones, squatted social centers, and urban commons spaces. For practical reasons, I was unable to include all this diversity in one project. However, I recognize the potential for comparisons, and I encourage other scholars studying other regions and venues to pick up where I leave off.

Temporally, instead of diving into the past, I focused on the present. My initial list included roughly ninety venues that were open when I began the project in 2016. Of those venues, my analysis generated sufficient data for seventy-three of those venues to be meaningfully included in the final study. This list includes a few borderline cases straddling the fuzzy boundary dividing radical activism from nonradical social engagement. I later added an additional four venues that were closed but where I met the key players in other contexts. About a dozen venues included in my sample closed during the two-year data collection phase. A comparable number of new venues replaced them, and I include brief references to some of these upstarts throughout this book. However, I was not able to incorporate new venues into the analysis with the same thoroughness as those on the initial list.

Methodologically, I researched constructive activism in print-based movement spaces by conducting interviews with key players in forty-five venues and by compiling archival-based profiles of sixty-six venues with a partial overlap between the two methods. Thirty-four venues were both interviewed and profiled, eleven were interviewed only, and thirty-two were profiled only.

Conducting interviews as a research method was appropriate in this context given the qualitative nature of my research questions. I completed the forty-five interviews—thirty-nine in person and six by phone—in 2016 and 2017. I used "purposive sampling" to recruit participants. Purposive sampling is well-suited for intensive case studies of cultural phenomena.[31] It is also well-suited for hard-to-find populations,[32] which applied in this instance because activist storefronts are unique and partially camouflaged. During interviews, I followed a "semi-structured" format involving generalized sets of open-ended questions.[33] I solicited information about location, aesthetics, management, programming, and organizing. I also asked about the strengths and weaknesses of using print-based retail as a social movement tool. I asked these questions using a "narrative approach,"[34] which encourages interviewees to share the personal, cultural, and spatial stories associated with their experiences. On average, interviews lasted just over one hour. All interviewees agreed to have their interviews recorded. I transcribed the recordings myself.

Archival work was equally important, especially for older, well-established, or well-known venues. These venues serve as role models for newer upstarts, and archival records provide benchmarks of change over time. References to past events surfaced in interviews as well, but because memory is fallible,[35] archival records offer additional information and important correctives to present-day reminiscences. Archival work is also a respectful way to gather information because people running activist businesses are already stressed trying to keep their ventures afloat. Many activists work without pay, and many have answered reporters' basic questions many times before. Archival research makes use of these public statements without imposing additional burdens on activists' time.

Using archival sources, I compiled extensive profiles of sixty-six venues in 2016 by reviewing both corporate and independent media records from the 1990s onward. To locate this material, I used search engines like LexisNexis for corporate media. Parallel engines like the Alternative Press Index were somewhat useful for indymedia, but word-of-mouth referrals were even more helpful. I located material using generic search terms such as "feminist bookstore," as well as by searching for venues by name, for instance "Women & Children First." Print-based movement spaces often make headlines during moments of political turmoil, and they frequently appear in newspaper descriptions of changing cityscapes. Additionally, activist-entrepreneurs publish their own editorials describing their experiences in industry journals, indymedia magazines, and online webpages. Although these records leave much information uncollected, they preserve something of the history and vibe of activist spaces. As an aside, these archival sources also contain references to activist bookstores that are now closed, as well as references to nonactivist but socially conscious bookstores with tangential connections to key research themes. I occasionally refer to those businesses throughout this book with language indicating their defunct or nonactivist status.

The seventy-seven venues included in the final study are demographically diverse. Activist-entrepreneurs are constantly innovating, which makes categorization difficult. In broad brushstrokes and with apologies for oversimplification, twenty venues focused on anarchism, thirteen on racial and ethnic liberation, ten on anti-imperialism, nine on anticapitalism, nine on feminism, eight on queer liberation, and eight on intersectional antioppression. These venues reflect a range of business structures. Many are for-profit businesses, but about half (48 percent) are wholly or partially nonprofit, about one-third (35 percent) are collectively owned and operated, and about half (51 percent) rely exclusively or primarily on unpaid volunteer labor. The venues also vary in age. At the time my research began, the average number of years in business was twenty-five with the oldest opening in 1953 and the youngest in 2016.

I analyzed transcripts and archives using a "grounded theory" approach, which Michael Burawoy describes as a robust method for using qualitative data for theoretical inquiry. For Burawoy, grounded theory involves an "attempt to make generalizations across different social situations, looking for what they have in common."[36] This approach aligns with my process-oriented framework where the goal of searching for similarities is to analyze social phenomenon "from the standpoint of their *generality*" by treating "each case study as a potential exemplar of some general law or principle that applies across space and time."[37] Another advantage of grounded theory is that, instead of superimposing preexisting normative constructs on top of social phenomenon, the key analytical themes emerge directly from the data. This inductive approach was especially useful because, to analyze crosscutting themes, I had to prevent key concepts from one social movement from excessively coloring similar but nonidentical elements in other movements.[38] In this spirit, rather than imposing research codes on the material in advance, I allowed thematic categories to emerge organically from close readings of transcripts and archives. In 2017, I read these materials, reread them, and read them again looking for recurring themes. I experimentally coded portions of the transcripts and archival records several times to test (and debunk) working hypotheses. These methods were inductive, not statistical.

I eventually decided to analyze constructive activism as a microscale cultural phenomenon embedded within larger urban systems. From that framing, several recurring themes emerged. These themes included the movement-related opportunities activists construct when opening businesses, selecting commodities, choosing locations, designing storefronts, formalizing policies, hosting events, planning protests, and changing formats. In this book, I devote one chapter to each of these themes. This structure also reflects my focus on mechanisms rather than issues. I use examples from many movements to illustrate any given point. Spaces organized around Black liberation, anarchism, feminism, and anticapitalism all put ideas on display. They all facilitate healing, nurture community, and support protests. In searching for generalities across difference, this book emphasizes what movement spaces have in common. I note when certain trends are more prevalent in some venues, for instance the tendency for anarchists to formalize safe space policies or the tendency for nonprofits to eschew electoral politics, but I keep my primary focus on the place-based repertoires that movements share.

Counterspaces Have Many Layers

In the chapters that follow, I use the metonym of counterspace as an organizing theme to analyze the constructed dimensions of activist retail. I ask why activists construct counterspaces in retail settings organized around print. I ask where they are located, why they look the way they do, and how they are regulated. I ask what makes counterspaces useful for community building and how activists use them to support public protests. I also ask how activists interpret a project's end.

I start in chapter 1 by defining "counterspace" and explaining the value of "constructive" counter-placemaking as a social movement repertoire. Although social movement scholars have not always appreciated the significance of space and materiality, the turn to contentious politics creates opportunities to broaden the field's institutional focus to include other social, cultural, and material dynamics. Using the lens of constructive activism, which I borrow and adapt from feminist architectural historians, I argue that ideas alone are not sufficient to sustain movements. People also need concrete infrastructure, including counterspaces where counterpublics manage counterinstitutions organized around counterconducts. These countersystems operate in parallel with normative systems of power, and they offer alternatives when needed at the prefigurative level of everyday practice. Analyzing how and why activists construct these countersystems sheds light on spatial agency and spatial autonomy as assets for organizing.

Next in chapter 2, I define "activist entrepreneurship," and I explain the value of retail environments within the multisite division of activist labor. Activist-entrepreneurs construct retail businesses as social movement tools. Activists use other spaces for organizing as well, including public streets, private homes, and civic settings, but those environments come with externally imposed fees, censorship, and use restrictions. By contrast, movement-oriented retailing generates independent revenue streams, which helps activists maintain autonomous spaces for independent decision-making. The easy accessibility of retail also makes these porous spaces useful for search and discovery. People who are curious about radical ideas but not yet confident enough to join cliquey communities or dangerous protests can browse and explore without having to commit. Additionally, in an era when people are socialized to shop for community, consumers approach retail not only seeking commodities but also seeking camaraderie. Activist-entrepreneurs leverage these trends as tools for autonomy, outreach, and networking.

In chapter 3, I explain the advantages of organizing activist retail around print capitalism, and I assess the potential for activists to continue using bookstore-like formats in the age of corporate superstores and online retailing. Although the history of print capitalism is steeped in oppression, radical publishing also played a significant role in nearly every major progressive social movement during the twentieth century. In addition to disseminating ideas and integrating communities, print in Western culture confers legitimacy. Activists who trade in books benefit from the apparent certification of radical thought. However, activist-entrepreneurs can only leverage these benefits if they can construct financially viable businesses despite the supposed collapse of independent retailing. Ethical consumerism helps a little, the nonprofit turn helps a lot, and entrepreneurial volunteerism is crucial. However, even though capital flows through these circuits, most venues survive as labors of love.

Next in chapter 4, I analyze the locational opportunity structure for building radical businesses, and I explain how gentrification is transforming the social movement landscape. Print-based movement spaces are a predominantly urban phenomenon, and marginalized progressive groups continue to converge in urban environments. Large diverse cities and progressive college towns provide anonymity and critical mass, which are invaluable resources for organizing. The challenge, however, is that cities are expensive. To get around the high cost of urban real estate, activist-entrepreneurs usually open in marginalized neighborhoods and disinvested buildings. Although this strategy worked for much of the twentieth century, gentrification is reducing the supply of these locations. The limited availability of affordable alternatives is one of the most significant barriers to constructive placemaking. To get around this barrier, activist-entrepreneurs are experimenting with new locational strategies, including by tapping into gentrification (a process they are already complicit in), relocating to the suburbs, moving inside cultural institutions, and buying property to stabilize costs. These tactics work, but they come with trade-offs, and I did not find consensus about which trade-offs are worthwhile. Regardless, innovative experimentation is creating a variety of toeholds, which makes it possible for different types of movement spaces to continue operating in the gentrification age.

After reviewing these contextual dynamics, I shift gears and take a deep dive into the internal workings of print-based movement spaces. I start this internal analysis in chapter 5 by studying the visualization techniques activist-entrepreneurs use to dramatize progressive ideas, not only for people who already support radical movements, but also for people who may otherwise avoid them. The visual vocabularies in counterspaces include subcultural codes marking space as feminist, anarchist, queer, or Black. However, because activist-entrepreneurs know people are socialized to avoid information deemed too difficult, too dangerous, or of the wrong sort, activist-entrepreneurs modulate these subcultural codes with a second set of presentation techniques designed to circumvent avoidance impulses. Using a cultural geography approach, I analyze the constructive techniques activists use to make spaces shout, entice, or heal. These visual vocabularies help a greater range of people see the progressive messages on display. Additionally, these findings shed light on the efficacy of visual communication techniques that go beyond claiming turf to also destabilize norms, which is a process that begins with environmental cues even before people read the books on the shelves.

Next in chapter 6, I review the territorial governing dynamics at work in print-based movement spaces. I describe how activist-entrepreneurs use management tasks to construct protective spaces and support non-normative voices. Other studies of counterspaces emphasize secessionist dynamics where people construct bubbles of turf operating separately from the surrounding terrain. Although these separatist dynamics sometimes occur in radical bookstores and libraries, activist-entrepreneurs rarely use countergoverning systems just to escape oppressive systems. Instead, they are much more likely to use their spaces as bridges linking normative and alternative realms. Using the lens of territorial governing, I analyze how administrative practices like safe space policies, open consignment practices, and horizontal management structures help new people navigate counterspaces and help longtime participants speak out to the mainstream. These dynamics shed light on counterspaces as bridges reworking social norms from both sides.

Conversely, in chapter 7, I analyze the opposite perspective by assessing the separatist dynamics of counterspaces, including the role filtering plays in planning for difference. Although urban designers and city planners celebrate universal access as a supposed hallmark of equitable cities, as long as society remains unjust, creating spaces where everyone is present interferes with democratic debate. In the company of strangers who may be oppressors, people withhold vulnerable information to protect themselves from potential harm. By contrast, in filtered environments where opposition groups are likely absent, there is more opportunity for robust debate around risky themes. These debates build common ground, but they can also become conflictual and antagonistic. People who are queer, Black, anarchist, or feminist may not approach these subjectivities from the same perspectives. Constructing filtered-enough spaces where people can let down their guard and speak across some but not all axes of difference facilitates the contentious conversations that help build alliances. Without these spaces, these conversations may easily remain unspoken.

After reviewing the everyday dynamics of contentious politics, I shift gears in chapter 8 by analyzing moments of political upheaval. Other scholars analyze "frontstage" spaces during contentious moments and "backstage" spaces during quiet moments, but they say little about the logistical support radical businesses provide during marches, rallies, and protests. Despite this silence, activists rely on behind-the-scenes spaces when staging dissent. Providing logistical support is risky because it exposes behind-the-scenes spaces to potential backlash from opposition movements and government agencies, which is why many activist-entrepreneurs take defensive steps to protect themselves and their users from surveillance. Activist-entrepreneurs often cannot stop these intrusions, but they can minimize the damage by constructing environments preserving anonymity where organizing leaves no trace behind.

I conclude the book by revisiting questions of durability and by critiquing common misconceptions about what constitutes success. Although provisional tactics are useful, strategic placemaking accommodates longer-term overlay functions, and it generates additional opportunities to capitalize on incremental gains. Nevertheless, durability is not the same as immortality, and the number of years in business should not be the only measure of success. Business analysts often measure success by years open and dollars earned, but activist-entrepreneurs have other goals, and these other goals are sometimes better served by closing and reconfiguring in new forms. Analyzing these closures and reconfigurations broadens the concept of success by attending to the lived experiences making counterspaces meaningful, as well as to the nimble adaptations keeping spaces durable.

In sum, these chapters shed light on the constructive dynamics of radical organizing. They analyze the experiences of activist-entrepreneurs who approach print capitalism as a tool for radical placemaking. They also shed light on the variety of ways activists use spatial agency to construct durable infrastructures for dissent. For activists like Leslie James Pickering with Burning Books, using spatial agency to construct an activist hub—a place of his own where he and his fellow organizers would not get kicked out—was crucial for enabling dissent. I explore these themes in greater detail in the next chapter by more clearly defining constructive activism and the role counter-placemaking plays in facilitating movements for change.

CHAPTER 1

Constructing Places for Contentious Politics

L ILIA ROSAS IS A HISTORY BUFF. Her father was a cook, her mother was a housekeeper, and for a number of years Rosas was an anxious graduate student at the University of Texas at Austin. She was anxious because she was struggling financially. "I had run out of funding as a graduate student." Rosas also struggled existentially. "What I had felt at the time . . . was alone and alienated." Like many first-generation students of color navigating the "ivory tower," Rosas was "becoming brighter [and] smarter" through her educational pursuits even if she did not necessarily "feel connected to those places" of privilege.

When she wasn't in class, Rosas spent time off campus visiting a friend who had an internship with Red Salmon Arts. Red Salmon Arts is a nonprofit organization that, among other things, manages event programming for Resistencia Bookstore. "Because she was there, I would just come visit more often." Like many large universities, UT Austin provides funding for local organizations to hire student interns, and Red Salmon Arts received some of those funds. The director got to know Rosas during her visits. After learning about her struggles, he used UT funding to offer Rosas a part-time paid internship at the bookstore, which eased her money trouble and provided her with mentorship.

Rosas characterized Resistencia as a "movement-oriented bookstore." She described its founder, Raul Salinas, as "an ex-prisoner, a poet, a human rights activist, a filmmaker, a professor, [and] a mentor to many folks, including me." According to newspaper archives, the bookstore began in Seattle in the 1970s when activist squatters constructed a multipurpose social services center in an abandoned school.[1] As part of that occupation, Salinas assembled a Chicano/a movement-oriented bookstore and resource center to "resist cultural imposition, illiteracy and the obscuring of our literature."[2] When Salinas moved to Austin a few years later, he rebirthed Resistencia with the same activist mission, but this time it was a formal business with an official license and a commercial lease.

The community room and display area at Resistencia Books in Austin, Texas, includes a mix of books and artwork exploring liberation themes from many perspectives. Photograph by author, 2017.

While interning with Resistencia, Rosas developed a stronger sense of her own voice. "My biggest issue at the time was I didn't feel like I was a very strong writer." Salinas disagreed. "He thought that was just ridiculous. . . . 'You've been brainwashed by that institution,'" he told her. "'Of course you can write.'" To prove it, Salinas gave Rosas writing assignments as part of her internship duties. The assignments started as small projects, like drafting a newsletter or translating a report, but they were collaborative and iterative. "I would write it. He would rewrite it. I would write it again." For Rosas, this back-and-forth exchange "was really validating." Salinas, an internationally renowned poet, guided her through the writing process, taught her new skills, and gave her the opportunity to see herself succeed.

Another advantage of working at Resistencia is that it brought Rosas into close repetitive contact with grassroots organizations. In addition to several Latino/a collectives who use the bookstore as a meeting space, "We have a socialist group that meets here. We have an autonomous anarchist group that meets here. We have a Saturday Group . . . [of] folks from the community who represent a vast array of different organizations and networks and businesses that meet here." Listening to their conversations, Rosas realized academia did not have a monopoly on knowledge. "What was humbling was to think that not all these conversations have to exist in some kind of ivory tower. That all kinds of people are having really sophisticated conversations . . . tackling both small problems and large problems in ways that sometimes are much more imaginative than by being forced into certain parameters [dictated by] the institution."

After receiving her doctorate in 2012, Rosas began her career as a public intellectual, teaching students about the role of race, class, gender, and sexuality in U.S. history and culture. She assumed this position within a few years of also accepting the request to become one of Resistencia's official caretakers following Salinas's death. In this capacity, Rosas brings local high school students of color into the space to talk about activist literature, as well as to let "them know that there's a safe space that they can always come to." These two roles make Rosas a public figure in two different settings: the privileged space of the ivory tower and the Chicano/a movement space where she now plays the mentoring role Salinas once performed for her. With a foot in both worlds, Rosas advances change on both sides. She helps nontraditional students navigate majoritarian spaces without cramming themselves into an oppressor's mold. She also teaches students of privilege how to identify, acknowledge, and appreciate histories of oppression and the need for reform.

Conversations like this one at Resistencia do not only speak to the transformative power of everyday experiences in counterhegemonic spaces. They also highlight the entanglements linking mainstream and alternative spaces together. Financial support from a public institution paid for Rosas to spend time in a nonnormative environment. In this counterspace, through repetitive returns and humble tasks, Rosas developed a more empowered sense of her potential. As a movement-oriented bookstore, Resistencia is a clearinghouse for intellectual and cultural concepts fueling Chicano/a organizing. The business provides a meeting place where activists debate politics, both formally and informally, and plan interventions. Resistencia is also a place of empowerment where Indigenous, Latino/a, and Chicano/a communities come together to educate, heal, and support one another.

Despite these dynamics, counterspaces like Resistencia are systematically understudied in the social movement literature. My goal in this chapter is to establish the conceptual framework I will develop in greater detail throughout this book for understanding the significance of movement-oriented spaces like Resistencia. This includes explaining key concepts related to contentious politics, constructive activism, unruly geographies, and everyday experiences, which I discuss in turn.

In what follows, I start by selectively referencing the social movement literature to help readers understand how examples like Resistencia fit into the broader landscape of contentious politics. Social movement scholars have traditionally focused on collective movements to change formal political institutions. But in recent decades, new generations of scholars are establishing a beyond-the-state turn by exploring nonstate spaces of state-centered organizing, as well as by exploring beyond-the-state targets of collective campaigns. These "contentious politics" scholars, as they call themselves, are reformulating the field by keeping a focus on state-directed action while simultaneously adding analyses of nonstate spaces targeting nonstate systems of social authority.

Next, contentious politics includes "constructive activism," which is a common but understudied social movement repertoire. Like circulating petitions and holding rallies, activists construct durable infrastructure as a strategy for dissent. Although social movement scholars are often remarkable at analyzing institutional tactics, group relationships, and ideological content, they are often underprepared to analyze space and materiality. Happily, a wave of activist-oriented architectural historians who are less knowledgeable about political science but wonderful at studying contentious placemaking are now filling this gap. For instance, studies of "constructive feminism" are particularly adept at showcasing the role that built environments play in movements for change. Durable spaces where people can iteratively return are resources for rethinking subjectivity and constructing community, which does not happen overnight.

The durable spaces I describe in this book are best analyzed as "counterspaces." Counterspaces like Resistencia operate in parallel with a perceived mainstream without necessarily attacking it or wholly withdrawing from it. Additionally, the subset of counterspaces I analyze has the added distinction of being simultaneously oppositional and conforming. It would be fun to study squatted buildings, isolationist compounds, and other places on the edges of transgressive living. By comparison, rent-paying small business owners with retail licenses selling commodities may appear somewhat mundane. However, my analysis suggests that conforming enough to social systems to avoid eviction and increase accessibility helps create a stable base for awareness raising and alliance building.

These constructed counterspaces are politically significant at the "everyday" scale. Small and humble practices become meaningful through repetition. However, even scholars who embrace the everyday turn do not agree on whether and how counterspaces like Resistencia acquire significance. In this book, I approach counterspaces from the perspective of prefiguration, embodied performances, and the politics of the act. These theories frame counterspaces as places where people start doing things differently without waiting for institutional reform. Despite this lack of institutionalization, acting otherwise is valuable because it changes lives and exposes new potential. Additionally, like Rosas's dual career as an activist-entrepreneur and an ivory tower intellectual, the effects of doing things differently in counterspaces often manifest elsewhere through subsequent actions in other locations.

Cumulatively, I use this chapter to provide a context for understanding activist counter-placemaking as a social movement repertoire. I explain the advantages of constructing counterspaces proximate enough to the imagined mainstream to be comprehensible to a general audience even as activists use them to challenge the limits of normative thought. Additionally, even though iteratively returning to everyday spaces may not sound like a globe-shaking event, I confirm that durable counterspaces are useful venues for transforming political subjectivity and building dissenting communities.

Social Movement Theory Takes a Beyond-the-State Turn

Rosas's experience at Resistencia, which focused less on storming the gates of power and more on personal empowerment and community networking, is an example of contentious politics. In this section, I provide a brief overview of the theory of contentious politics to clarify the relevant goals, tactics, and spaces. Clarifying these details makes it easier to understand why many scholars believe self-directed activities in nonstate spaces can destabilize hegemonic social and cultural concepts with political effects.

Returning from my interviews at Resistencia and other print-based movement spaces, I investigated how social movement bookstores fit into the landscape of political activism. I agree with Rosas that Resistencia is a "movement-oriented" business and an important social movement space. But, in the 1970s when Salinas founded the venture, it is unlikely social scientists of the era would have agreed. One reason is that traditional social movement theory is state-centric. Standard definitions of "social movements" describe them as "organized groups of social actors that pursue collective political goals in society."[3] Politics in this traditional sense refers narrowly to institutionalized systems of rule, for instance feudal land ownership before the Industrial Revolution and the Westphalian nation-states in the centuries since.[4] Based on this definition, examples of social movements from the twentieth century include the civil rights movement, which demanded equal protection under the law, and the labor movement, which demanded government-enforced protections in the workplace. Activist repertoires within those movements targeted state policies directly through lawsuits and petition drives, as well as indirectly through public marches pressuring government officials to act.

Based on this state-centric definition, one reason earlier social scientists did not include places like Resistencia in the social movement canon involved categories of space. Resistencia is a commercial space with no official ties to political parties or government agencies, so its political significance—in the narrow, state-centric sense—was not readily apparent. However, for a new generation of scholars, political organizing extends beyond the public speeches of elected officials and beyond the legislative debates in city halls. Instead, for Michael Brown, "A great deal of activism occur[s] in places we do not necessarily think of as political (like bars or lifestyle magazine covers)."[5] Similarly, Leif Jerram's analysis of early twentieth-century European social movements highlights beyond-the-state trends. Movements for socialism and antifascism targeted state institutions, but people organized those movements using noninstitutional spaces like factories, docks, and working-class taverns.[6] In these "myriad nooks and crannies," people challenged "the very fundamentals of the way we think about the world."[7] By using spaces of labor and commerce for organizing, nonstate spaces and state-directed activism worked hand in hand.

Another reason earlier social scientists did not include places like Resistencia in the social movement canon involved the intended targets of activism. Much of Resistencia's contentious energy—like raising awareness of Chicano/a literature, aesthetics, and experiences—targets social and cultural concepts rather than government officials and state laws. Fortunately, a new generation of scholars now show that nongovernmental social and cultural institutions perform significant governing work. Schools socialize children, churches disseminate ideologies, hospitals administer biopower, and mass media shape public opinion. These social and cultural institutions regulate popular understandings of personhood, equity, and value. For Reuben Rose-Redwood, the governing effects of these beyond-the-state entities are deeply political and should not be dismissed "as somehow being of lesser importance than if the state itself were engaging in the very same activities."[8] State authorities codify aspects of social concepts in laws, but governments do not have a monopoly on inscribing concepts with meaning, nor do narrow legal definitions do justice to a concept's full weight.

A third reason earlier social scientists did not include places like Resistencia in the social movement canon involved questions of audience. Many of the activities occurring there—like mentoring nontraditional students—are self-directed activities benefiting participants rather than externally facing activities targeting large institutions. However, for a new generation of scholars, self-directed techniques like nurturance and empowerment are important organizing tools. When targeting beyond-the-state concepts like personhood and equity, political speeches and formal petitions play a role, especially if the state is complicit in oppression or a potential ally in reform, but beyond-the-state organizing involves other repertoires as well. Taking Bice Maiguashca's analysis of feminism as an example, "in terms of popular education, the aim is to empower women not only by raising their self-esteem and developing their social- and self-knowledge, but also by offering them the practical skills to make a living wage and to survive."[9] These repertoires are less about convincing state agents or social institutions to do things differently and more about allowing people to autonomously construct the changes they wish to see in themselves.

In response to evidence of beyond-the-state organizing on so many fronts, scholars began rethinking the state-centric focus of social movement theory. However, not everyone agreed on the need to broaden the scope of analysis. Some scholars preferred to redefine key concepts to better fit old frameworks with less ambiguity. Charles Tilly, for instance, argued in the late 2000s that politics necessarily meant government entities.[10] Tilly took this stance even as he acknowledged the need to disentangle the concepts of government and conflict. For one thing, Tilly challenged longstanding assumptions that state functioning is inherently conflictual. On the contrary, government agents spend a significant portion of their time overseeing administrative work that "involves little or no contention" as people "register for benefits, answer census takers, cash government checks, or show their passports to immigration officers without making significant claims on other people."[11] Tilly also challenged assumptions that conflict necessarily involves the state. "Most contention," such as "which football team we should support . . . [or] whether grandpa rightly divided his inheritance," occurs outside the realm of state institutions.[12]

Although these insights helpfully untangle government and conflict, Tilly did not then argue for a beyond-the-state turn in social movement theory. Instead, he offered a redefinition of contentious politics that included the subset of collective contestation targeting the subset of government practices relevant to adjudicating competing claims. Retaining this narrow, state-centric definition serves some purposes, but other social movement scholars nevertheless argue for a more comprehensive conceptual overhaul. The most significant aspect of this deeper overhaul involves broadening the definition of politics from its narrow focus on state institutions to also include more general connections linking individuals to the social milieu. These general connections include nongovernmental practices regulating collective life.

These beyond-the-state scholars coined the phrase "contentious politics" to capture the social and cultural aspects of collective organizing. The term "social movement" remains popular, and I use it throughout this book. But many scholars including me now read social movement theory through the contentious politics lens. For contentious politics scholars, this phrase refers to "concerted, counterhegemonic *social and political* action, in which differently positioned participants come together to challenge *dominant systems of authority,* in order to promote and enact alternative imaginaries."[13] This definition emphasizes both state institutions and beyond-the-state entities involved in social discipline. This broader definition validates contentious energy in nonstate spaces using nonstate-centric repertoires to challenge more-than-legal concepts embedded in beyond-the-state institutions. This conceptual reframing makes room to recognize and analyze the political significance of places like Resistencia as important movement-oriented hubs.

As an additional final point, state-centric social movements and beyond-the-state contentious politics are not mutually exclusive. As an example, the twentieth-century queer liberation movement involved both. States exerted normative discipline through sodomy laws, marriage contracts, and employment discrimination (for instance in the military). But other institutions were also complicit. Medical institutions classified homosexuality as a mental illness, religious leaders demonized queer intimacy from the pulpit, and vigilante thugs enforced homophobia on the streets. Given the distributed nature of oppression, mounting an effective movement for change involved state-centric repertoires, like lawsuits and protests, but the social movement work did not stop there. Activists also built queer-positive subcultures in commercial spaces, like gay bars and dance clubs. They challenged cultural attitudes, for instance by adding queer characters to television shows, which normalized nonbinary sexual identities. Activists also created self-directed spaces, like queer bathhouses and campgrounds, where people could explore and experience a range of queer intimacies. The state mattered, but it was not all that mattered, and the movement for change included many beyond-the-state spaces, tactics, and targets.

From these perspectives, places like Resistencia should be included in social movement theory. Instead of dismissing neighborhood businesses as supposedly apolitical commercial spaces, I highlight how people use movement-oriented bookstores and libraries to challenge, evade, and rethink the limits of normative political imaginations.

Constructive Activism Is a Repertoire for Durable Placemaking

Places like Resistencia are made, not found. Durable spaces enabling contentious politics exist because activists construct them. Activist placemaking involves material practices, as well as economic, symbolic, and regulatory techniques, that shape counterspaces and distinguish them from the surrounding environment. The resulting durable spaces are both practical achievements in their own right and tools for organizing new waves of change.

Making and maintaining durable spaces for organizing is a form of "constructive activism." Constructive activism is a term I've adapted from Daphne Spain's work on "constructive feminism," which highlights the material base of social organizing.[14] Ideas matter, but people are physical beings. The Underground Railroad required networks of safe houses. The temperance movement involved closing saloons and opening coffeehouses. The second wave women's movement likewise involved supportive infrastructure. As Spain explains, activists founded libraries documenting women's accomplishments, liberation schools teaching women new skills, health clinics evading male control over women's bodies, and domestic violence shelters protecting women from male aggression. These were political actions of evasion and empowerment. They were also physical actions involving brick-and-mortar buildings with literal street addresses where people could gather and organize.[15]

By coining the phrase constructive feminism, Spain put a name to a phenomenon other historians of feminist architecture likewise observed. Feminists in the late nineteenth and early twentieth centuries built women's clubhouses and dormitories to support women in educational and professional pursuits.[16] They built daycare centers and community dining halls to reduce domestic drudgery, professionalize domestic labor, and free women to pursue economic and political endeavors.[17] Feminists also developed new housing styles and renovated old ones to create safer living situations for women and children.[18] For Nancy Fraser, by engaging in these architectural strategies, "women of various classes and ethnicities constructed access routes to public political life, even despite their exclusion from the official public sphere."[19]

Although some scholars studying other contentious movements highlight similar constructive dynamics, from a social movement perspective, studies attending to materiality and the built environment remain the exception rather than the norm. To use the literature on the urban commons movement as an example, for Amanda Huron, scholars tend "to be concerned more with the commons in a formal theoretical sense and less in the material way the commons can be used to support everyday existence."[20] Despite this privileging of abstract concepts over material infrastructure, Davina Cooper highlights "the importance of *material* practices and spaces," and she claims, "it is in these differently forged ways of doing things that everyday concepts become both actualized and imagined otherwise."[21] Similarly, for Patrick Bresnihan and Michael Byrne, although the politically themed literature tends to overlook material dynamics, the process of commoning involves constructing "a set of material practices which generate alternative ways of producing, relating to, and 'governing' urban space."[22]

These invocations of activist architecture suggest constructive place-making is an important action repertoire that reworks the material infrastructure enabling social practice. However, the significance of progressive infrastructure, as well as the difficulties of mounting a resistance movement without it, is largely overlooked within the social movement canon. Social scientists have not always appreciated the spatial dimensions of social movements. As Deborah Martin and Byron Miller explain, social movement scholars are exceptional for their analyses of political processes, resource mobilization, protest repertoires, identity orientation, frame alignment, and brokering dynamics, but this rich canon is nevertheless stubbornly aspatial. "Where the 'spatial turn' has transformed many areas of social and economic scholarship, research on social movements and contentious politics has generally downplayed the spatial constitution and context of its central concepts."[23]

As an added challenge, when discussions about space do appear in the literature, social scientists privilege abstract concepts like scale, positionality, and mobility while saying relatively little about the concrete characteristics of material infrastructure.[24] Tilly's book *Contentious Performances* provides a paradigmatic example of this abstracted vision of space. Although Tilly devotes an entire chapter to "contention in space and time,"[25] space in his usage refers exclusively to institutional space. For Tilly, points on a map exist within national boundaries associated with specific governments. Because of this institutional cartography, where people are located in space affects whether political decision-making is democratic or authoritarian, whether state entities are strong or weak, and whether political rights include access to housing and medical care. These institutional structures with their different sets of opportunities and resources influence which types of action repertoires are likely to be effective within a specific institutional geography.

This state-centric analysis is enormously helpful in analyzing the geography of the formal political structures governing collective life, but from the perspective of activist architecture, it leaves questions of materiality and the built environment wholly unexplored. For Ulrich Oslender, this focus on institutional space rather than material space is ubiquitous across the social movement canon. In his survey of the field, "There was a deafening silence in the existing literature on social movements regarding the relevance of place in its theorizations."[26] This focus on abstract space produces many blind spots by not addressing, for instance, how physical characteristics, movement patterns, or sensory experiences influence political subjectivity or generate material resources for organizing.

Alongside these tendencies to prioritize institutional space over materiality and the built environment, another key challenge is that, when discussions about space do appear in the social movement canon, those discussions generally focus on provisional uses of other people's space while saying little about the durable infrastructure activists construct for themselves. I acknowledge there are good reasons to study provisional use. One reason is that activists who are prevented from voicing their concerns inside city halls often use public demonstrations to make themselves heard. Effective demonstrating requires an audience, which is why activists march in public streets and stage sit-ins in commercial venues where other people will see them. For Helga Leitner, Eric Sheppard, and Kristin Sciarto, in these campaigns, "Participants in contentious politics are enormously creative in cobbling together different spatial imaginaries and strategies on the fly."[27] Activists rent community centers for public meetings, they appropriate street corners for petition drives, and they occupy parks and bridges for rallies. These action repertoires in borrowed and seized spaces underscore the value of claiming space for externally directed action. Although I do not study provisional use in this book, I support scholars who do.

Another reason to study provisional use is that the limited range of alternatives reflects the structurally uneven distribution of spatial agency. By spatial agency, I mean the ability to make, use, or regulate space.[28] Everyone has spatial agency, but nonconformists usually enjoy less spatial privilege than their institutionally supported counterparts. Michel de Certeau's treatise on everyday life suggests people in positions of privilege have amplified spatial agency. Their economic, political, and social resources make it possible to reshape entire landscapes around their interests. Less privileged groups have fewer resources and less institutional support, but they still have spatial agency. It just manifests in more improvisational forms, such as appropriating public sidewalks and adapting underutilized buildings. This improvisational agency is enacted through (and often restricted to) the tactics of everyday life, including provisional uses of infrastructure designed to serve someone else.[29]

Because of these publicity needs and resource limitations, research on provisional use is a welcome and much-needed line of inquiry. However, without diminishing the value of provisional work, having less spatial privilege is not the same thing as having no spatial privilege. Also, provisional tactics and constructive strategies are not mutually exclusive. Provisional marches and rallies bring some benefits, constructed clinics and daycare centers serve other purposes, and activists need not limit themselves to one strategy or the other.

In this book, I respond to other scholars' tendencies to favor both abstract institutionalized space and provisionally appropriated space by shifting my focus to the complementary, constructive side of contentious politics. I do this by shining a spotlight on the durable spaces activists construct for themselves. By durable spaces, I mean physical spaces lasting at least a few years or perhaps a few decades as opposed to the minutes and hours typical of borrowed spaces. Durability is valuable for contentious organizing because it supports practices requiring longer time horizons. The literature on social movements is filled with accounts of great speeches, legendary battles, and sudden uprisings supposedly changing the course of history in an instant. But many social movement functions, like developing subjectivities, building alliances, and acquiring skills, do not occur overnight. Constructing durable, activist-controlled spaces where people iteratively provide emotional, intellectual, and practical support creates strategic venues for building trust, changing habits, and questioning norms. These long-term projects complement the more fleeting provisional interventions simultaneously occurring elsewhere.

Finally, I'd like to make two additional conceptual distinctions about "constructive activism" to help readers distinguish it from other theoretical concepts that may sound similar but are actually quite different. The first distinction involves the difference between placemaking for activism and placemaking for capitalism. Addressing this distinction is important because placemaking has become a catchphrase among urban designers and city planners who use placemaking to shape territories of profit. For Alesia Montgomery, placemaking in this urban design context is "a strategy for increasing commerce and rents in an area by crafting vibrant streetscapes."[30] These vibrant streetscapes selectively incorporate ethnic murals and artist studios, which resonate with lefty professionals' lifestyle preferences while excluding less marketable elements like soup kitchens and check-cashing facilities.[31] For David Madden, this symbolic inclusion of cosmopolitan diversity is a form of "publicity without democracy—a concept of the public that speaks of access, expression, inclusion, and creativity but which nonetheless is centered upon surveillance, order, and the bolstering of corporate capitalism."[32]

Because market-oriented placemaking is so profitable and so contested, this framework dominates placemaking discussions in much of the literature. However, these market-oriented projects are often diametrically opposed to the constructive dynamics I analyze in this book, which focuses on constructive placemaking for social movement purposes. Places are not just pieces of real estate or spaces for profit-making. For Michael Brown, places "can be thought of as unique geographical bundles of social and environmental relationships" where space and society become intertwined.[33] For Christian Norberg-Schulz, social and environmental relationships create an "existential" center "concretizing" modes of being in space.[34] Similarly, for Helga Leitner, Eric Sheppard, and Kristin Sciarto, places "have a distinct materiality . . . that is historically constructed" and that "regulates and mediates social relations and daily routines . . . and is thus imbued with power."[35] Given these tight functional relationships between space and society, just as geographers call for social movement theorists to attend to the reciprocal relationship between social movements and the places they inhabit,[36] I call for geographers, city planners, and architects to continue looking beyond market manipulations of placemaking for profit to also study constructive placemaking as a repertoire for dissent.

The second distinction I wish to make before proceeding involves differentiating between constructive activism and "new materialism." New materialism is an apt phrase summarizing a recent turn in the social sciences interpreting social dynamics through a tangible, posthumanist lens. This scholarship on "actor networks"[37] and "vibrant matter"[38] unsettles overly triumphant accounts of abstract cognition and human agency by emphasizing the concrete, deindividualized, more-than-human assemblages through which thought and action unfold.[39]

Although I appreciate this much-needed corrective to dematerialized social theory, I do not approach constructive activism from a new materialist angle. I agree that objects and assemblages matter. However, although ignoring materialism is problematic, I do not believe a fundamentalist approach to materialism is any better. In this respect, I side with critics who worry about new materialism scholarship that treats bottles, walls, and dirt as overenchanted entities, as though objects rather than people are responsible for history and oppression.[40] Even though I agree material and sensory characteristics are important, I also believe that social and administrative systems bring spaces to life. With these considerations in mind, the constructive activism framework keeps questions of politics, agency, and culpability center stage, even as I add questions of space and the built environment into the discussion.

Counterspaces Include Public-Facing Environments and Border-Crossing Elements

Places like Resistencia are a certain kind of constructed environment that I analyze using the lens of "counterspace." The term counterspace is one among many terms describing unruly geographies: "free spaces,"[41] "temporary autonomous zones,"[42] "concrete utopias,"[43] "urban commons,"[44] "lifestyle spaces,"[45] "cells,"[46] "circuits,"[47] "homeplaces,"[48] "offstage spaces,"[49] and "encounter zones."[50] These terms subcategorize unruly space based on how isolated it is, how long it lasts, and how equitable it is. Many terms are also group specific. For instance, there are *Black* homeplaces, *anarchist* temporary autonomous zones, *communist* cells, and *queer* circuits. Because of these nuances, I struggled to select an appropriate unifying term to describe the general phenomenon of constructive placemaking for activist purposes.

Although counterspace is not a perfect term, I use it as an umbrella term and organizing metonym throughout this book rather than coining a new phrase to add to the litany above. I chose it because counterspaces operate in parallel with normative spaces without necessarily attacking or supplanting them. I also chose it because counterspace resonates with a family of counter-X phrases that link space, people, institutions, and norms. In this section, I establish a foundation for the chapters that follow by defining the term counterspace and situating it in the context of other counter-X phrases. I also explain the somewhat unconventional perspectives I superimpose on the counterspace metonym, most notably by analyzing *public-facing* counterspaces that, like Resistencia, are not isolated environments and instead are *porous* environments that are functionally interconnected with mainstream politics, economics, and culture.

When thinking about the family of counter-X phrases, I prefer to begin with people. Nancy Fraser's analysis of "counterpublics" emphasizes the human dimension of alternative spaces by critiquing Habermasian theories of a purportedly unified public realm. For Fraser, these romanticized notions belie the gendered, raced, and classed assumptions encoded in supposedly universal norms. They also belie the inherent violence of forcing everyone into a common mold as though difference and differential privilege do not exist. As an alternative, Fraser uses the term "counterpublics" to highlight a diverse public realm where different social groups do not necessarily try to speak as one. Instead, counterpublics are "parallel discursive arenas where members of subordinated social groups invent and circulate counter discourses to formulate oppositional interpretations of their identities, interests, and needs."[51] Counterpublics divided by race, ethnicity, gender, sexuality, age, class, and other axes of difference produce multivoiced and sometimes exclusionary public worlds with "a variety of ways of accessing public life and a multiplicity of public arenas."[52]

Many counterpublics develop counterinstitutions. In a diverse and fractured social context, the dominant institutions regulating collective life often do not adequately respond to the needs of counterpublic communities. Underserved groups can develop individual solutions to the shared problems of neglect and oppression, but those groups can also build "counterinstitutions" to address their needs collectively. Examples of counterinstitutions include Black churches, grassroots free clinics, and anarchist funding agencies. These entities do not negate white churches, state hospitals, and capitalist banks, nor do counterpublics limit themselves to counterinstitutional services. Instead, counterinstitutions provide structured alternatives operating in parallel with hegemonic institutions that provide marginalized groups with options when needed.[53]

Counterpublics and counterinstitutions frequently encourage "counterconducts." In a society filled with diverse people and organizations, there is no one standard way of doing things. However, rejecting normativity is not the same as embracing individualism. Instead, counterpublics and counterinstitutions develop different blueprints for social interactions. This is why Michel Foucault defined "counterconduct" as "the pursuit of a different form of conduct: to be led differently, by other [women and] men, and towards other objectives than those proposed by the apparent and visible governmentality of society."[54] Counterconducts, including Foucault's examples of self-imposed asceticism and escapist mysticism, do not reject governing. Instead, they recode the social systems assigning meaning to beliefs, objects, and behaviors.[55]

Counterpublics, counterinstitutions, and counterconducts have a geography. Alternative norms and contentious practices do not unfold evenly in space. Instead, normative infrastructure supports one way of doing things, and counterinfrastructure supports other groups and other practices in other places. One word for this counterinfrastructure is "counterspace." Henri Lefebvre defines counterspace as "an initially utopian alternative to actually existing 'real' space," which people insert into the landscape "in opposition to the one embodied in the strategies of power."[56] Ed Soja similarly characterizes counterspaces as "spaces of resistance to the dominant order arising precisely from their subordinate, peripheral, or marginalized positioning."[57] In this spirit, and in combination with the family of counter-X phrases described above, I use the term counterspace throughout this book to indicate the spatial infrastructure activists construct for themselves to accommodate contentious political practices operating in parallel with established norms and pushing toward alternative futures.

Having defined "counterspace" and situated it within a family of counter-X phrases, I want to shift gears and zoom in on a subset of counterspaces that are explicitly public-facing. Counterspaces include a range of spaces, some of which are intentionally isolated and some of which are more accessible. This book focuses on public-facing spaces that exist on the porous end of the spectrum. This porosity amplifies opportunities to link mainstream and alternative spaces together. Rather than reductively over-emphasizing opposition, this approach challenges assumptions that "counter" means wholly Other, entirely separate, or fully antagonistic. Instead, public-facing counterspaces highlight the border-crossing dynamics where mainstream and alternative publics rework concepts from both sides.

In this endeavor, I am indebted to Davina Cooper's work on concrete utopias. Cooper acknowledges that some counterspaces, like intentional communities or survivalist compounds, are intentionally isolated environments "where people live out (or plan to live out) significant chunks of their life" separate from other groups.[58] However, not all counterspaces have this separatist intention. Some counterspaces, like feminist bathhouses and democratic free schools, "aren't totalizing lifelong places" and instead "are more akin to hotspots of innovative practice," which are "entered or engaged for discrete periods"[59] by people who spend most of their time elsewhere. These porous and proximate counterspaces are not hegemonically sealed. Instead, like Rosas's experience at Resistencia, people, money, and ideas pass back and forth between normative contexts, like UT Austin, and counterspaces, like the movement-oriented bookstore. Cooper does not see this permeability as a weakness. On the contrary, through brief but recurring visits to porous counterspaces over many years, these settings become "hugely fruitful places from which to *think* differently and imaginatively about concepts, particularly when such thinking is oriented to a socially transformative politics."[60]

This emphasis on porosity challenges commonplace assumptions that mainstream and alternative spaces have nothing in common. Instead, it highlights how people on both sides grab common elements, modify them, and release them in altered forms, which then invite new responses. Foucault uses the term "border-elements" to describe these dynamics where the struggle for counterconduct, as well as the counterspaces supporting it, is "not conducted in the form of absolute exteriority"[61] and instead involves a back-and-forth process of mutual adaptation. The system of authority "threatened by all these movements of counterconduct" co-opts the symbols of the opposition by "tak[ing] them up and adapt[ing] them for its own ends."[62] To use an example from the publishing industry, mainstream publishers losing market share to alternative presses incorporate Black bodies into romance novels and punk aesthetics into graphic novels to reclaim their market dominance. Counterpublics then do the same in reverse by appropriating print capitalism and retail environments, modifying them, and using them to advance Black and anarchist agendas. In this iterative dance, objects, symbols, and ideas get "continually re-utilized, re-implanted, and taken up again" by both sides.[63]

Highlighting porosity emphasizes mutual interdependence, which is often overlooked when studying opposition. However, I nevertheless acknowledge that my use of the word "counter" inherently puts me at risk of unintentionally reifying inside–outside divides. I agree with scholars who worry that words like "counter" imply a too sharply drawn duality between oppression and resistance.[64] These scholars also rightly note that "counter" is only intelligible relative to something else and that, linguistically, this other thing assumes the dominant position.[65] I share these concerns, which is why I avoid even more reductive, stigmatizing, and dismissive terms such as "deviant" or "underground." However, I disagree with scholars who attempt to avoid unwanted complications by adopting neutral terms like "micropublics,"[66] "diverse economies,"[67] and "variable governing."[68] Although neutral terms are wonderful in their implicit refusal to give dominant structures the upper hand, their neutrality comes at the cost of losing their political punch. Contentious placemaking is not only about plurality, nor is it about parallel processes operating on equitable footing. Instead, it is fundamentally about criticizing authority across unequal positions of power. "Counter" encapsulates this contentious spirit and the intention to deliver a political sting, which is why I use it throughout this book despite its risks and imperfections.

Everyday Practices Are Politically Salient

The final section of this chapter addresses questions of scale. Counterspaces operate at the scale of everyday life. Rosas's experiences at Resistencia, for instance, focused more on informal conversations and routine interactions than on explosive moments of political upheaval. This approach raises questions about whether and how everyday practices become politically relevant. Although there is some disagreement within the field, my assessment is that contentious practices—including small and humble ones—acquire significance in one of two ways. The first way involves repetition where humble practices performed many times become functionally, symbolically, and disciplinarily meaningful. The second way involves saving lives. Everyday counterspaces are significant when they provide lifelines to people in difficult circumstances who desperately need room to breathe and resources to begin living differently. I believe these lifesaving and life-altering dynamics are significant even when they bypass the privileged majority.

Social scientists have not always appreciated the significance of everyday life. For Michael Gardiner, "The everyday has traditionally been denigrated as trivial and inconsequential in Western thought at least since the Enlightenment, with its stress on the 'higher' functions of human reason untainted by the messy vagaries of the real world."[69] These Enlightenment-era philosophies favor elite culture, great man histories, and myths of universal truths. Although these frameworks are useful and informative, they are also partial. They bypass the vast majority of people, erase the infinite variety of human experiences, and reinforce unproblematized axes of privilege.

For scholars of contentious politics, this tendency to devalue everyday life generates troubling gaps in social movement theory. For Miriam Williams, "everyday banal forms of activism are often missed in favour of more dramatic, spectacular protest movements."[70] Mass riots leading to sudden revolutions or brutal repressions are splashy, world-publicized events, but they are also rare, built on years of behind-the-scenes maneuvering, and are only one of many mechanisms for reform. Because of these multipronged dynamics, "social change needs to be understood as more-than-resistance or reaction, but also as everyday practices and routines that make the city and provide viable alternatives to the mainstream ways of doing things."[71]

I agree with this call for social movement theory to take an everyday turn. However, just because some everyday practices are politically significant does not mean all everyday practices are equally important. One reason scholars who appreciate everyday practices may nevertheless dismiss the dynamics in spaces like Resistencia is that, although some everyday experiences are deeply institutionalized, most everyday practices in counterspaces are not. For Joe Painter, prosaic social interactions are central to the exercise of power. The grand moment of state officials signing legislation "has few immediate effects in itself. Rather, its effects are produced in practice through the myriad mundane actions of officials, clerks, police officers, inspectors, teachers, social workers, doctors and so on" who implement legislation in everyday settings.[72] These findings underscore the connection between prosaic experiences, political authority, and social discipline in situations where institutional frameworks govern in a distributed but nevertheless coordinated manner.[73]

By comparison, everyday practices in counterspaces are much less institutionalized. This lack of institutionalization leads some critics to dismiss everyday counterspaces as "trivial,"[74] "tenuous,"[75] "short-lived,"[76] and "politically insignificant . . . fads."[77] To clarify, not all movement-oriented businesses are disconnected in these ways. Some activist enterprises only last a few months, develop clique-like traits, or live off faded reputations. Those spaces are fun hangouts but not necessarily robust counterinstitutions. However, many movement-oriented businesses last several years or several decades, and many activist-entrepreneurs develop highly structured relationships with other organizations. Nevertheless, even taking these durable relationships into account, counterspaces are not institutionalized to the same degree as centralized, hierarchical, and standardized public schools, medical facilities, spiritual communities, and government offices, which suggests everyday practices in counterspaces may not achieve the same level of political influence in regulating collective life.

Although this concern about serial reproduction is valid, contrary to what critics may say, it is unclear why a lack of institutionalization should inherently disqualify everyday experiences from being politically significant. Sociologist Fran Tonkiss makes a parallel argument in her analysis of provisional urbanism. "It is easy to dismiss makeshift urban practices as merely 'temporary,' as if that in itself were a bad thing. However, it is not clear why anyone should be so ready to discount the near future."[78] Impermanent but politically engaged activist-entrepreneurs shape life right now, and chunks of time that are longer than a day but shorter than a decade can be influential. Returning to Tonkiss, "Three or five years is a short time in the life of a city, but quite a long time in the life of a child—or an asylum-seeker, for that matter."[79]

In a similar manner, for social groups living with and escaping from oppression, counterspaces are rare sites of self-actualization where people develop richer senses of their identities and live fuller versions of their politics. Even if these experiences are momentary and idiosyncratic, they can still have meaningful effects. The repetitive nature of these experiences in durable counterspaces amplifies these dynamics. Even if these spaces bypass the majority of the population, they have profound, life-altering impacts for the people opting in, who then go on to affect the lives of those around them.

Another reason scholars who appreciate everyday practices may nevertheless dismiss counterspaces like Resistencia is that opting out of normative systems and into parallel ones does not necessarily destabilize the systems left behind. Even when people use counterspaces to partially elude oppressive authorities, dominant structures of power usually function quite effectively despite their absence.[80] The nonautomatic link between counterpublics pursuing counterconducts in counterspaces and the comprehensive transformation of mainstream institutions is why, for Jonathan Davies, systemic change remains important. "Although change almost invariably originates in everyday life, strategies and struggles to transform *the system* remain indispensable."[81]

However, rather than dismissing counterspaces for not storming the gates of power, other scholars see focusing elsewhere as precisely what makes these places strong. There has been a shift in recent decades in both activist and scholarly circles from what Richard Day calls the "politics of demand" toward the "politics of the act."[82] As a protest repertoire, the politics of demand involves issuing cries for reform and demanding government officials change their ways. But demanding change can be ineffective. "The fundamental fantasy . . . is that the currently hegemonic formation will recognize the validity of the claim presented to it, and respond in a way that produces an event of emancipation. Most of the time, however, it does not; instead it defers, dissuades or provides a partial solution to one problem that exacerbates several others."[83] For Jonathan Davies, activists encountering system intransigence can easily become skeptical "that change will ever occur at the systemic scale" or that "organized resistance to governments and corporations" will ever produce meaningful results.[84]

When systems of authority refuse to change, instead of reissuing demands, many activists shift to the politics of the act. For Bresnihan and Byrne, the politics of the act is about "devising practical ways of escaping" a system refusing to be overturned.[85] Similarly for David Graeber, this repertoire is not "a grand gesture of defiance" and instead is about "acting as if one is already free."[86] The politics of the act is about doing things differently no matter that these actions are unsanctioned or that other people do not change. To use an example from the field of city planning, it's the difference between residents signing petitions asking municipal officials to improve public spaces and residents making improvements directly by building their own pocket parks or planting their own guerilla gardens.[87] The politics of the act does not ask permission. Instead, people find ways to live differently now, even if only in short bursts. Dominant systems of authority may continue unfazed, but these practical escapes are nevertheless important and consequential for the people choosing to participate. These escapes also generate material resources supporting structural change in the future.

A third reason scholars who appreciate everyday practices may nevertheless dismiss the contentious political energy in counterspaces like Resistencia involves distinguishing unruly spaces posing immediate threats from containment zones corralling irrelevant nuisances. For Foucauldian scholars writing about governmentality, total domination is both expensive and unnecessary. Once sufficient discipline is in place to stabilize a field of power, spending additional resources shoring up the margins is wasteful and yields diminishing returns. This ability to operate effectively without total authoritarianism explains why political leaders may establish a calculated band of tolerance where some types of nonconformity deemed unthreatening and irrelevant are given free reign. If that situation were to change, authorities could always take steps to rescind tolerance and squash resistance. In the meantime, calculated bands of tolerance conserve resources for other pursuits.[88]

For skeptics, these insights suggest that counterspaces operating parallel to mainstream institutions may owe their durability less to their political intransigence and more to their lack of political teeth. However, the literature on embodied performances suggests other reasons to value parallel spaces even if they do not pose an immediate threat to power. One argument evident in Judith Butler's work is that performing life otherwise has politically destabilizing effects. "Sometimes it is not a question of first having power and then being able to act; sometimes it is a question of acting, and in the acting, laying a claim to the power one requires."[89] This observation suggests that acting otherwise within counterspaces may be politically significant not because revolutionary potential already exists in those spaces but rather because it emerges from those spaces and then gets applied elsewhere. For Lilia Rosas with Resistencia, her experiences at the bookstore changed her future capacities as a professor. Resistencia "is the site where these conversations may start. It might not necessarily be the site where the conversations end."

Alongside theories of embodied performances, the literature on prefiguration likewise underscores the political value of living life differently, even when society does not (yet) change. For Chris Dixon, prefiguration involves "activist efforts to manifest and build, to the greatest extent possible, the world we would like to see through our means of fighting in this one."[90] For Davina Cooper, these aspirational spaces, however imperfect, "are oriented toward a better world."[91] By giving people practice living and relating differently, and by generating models for activists to emulate, prefigurative practices rework the limits of thinkability. From those perspectives, living differently now, even within calculated bands of tolerance, is a political accomplishment. Additionally, if new subjectivities, capacities, alliances, resources, and opportunities emerge through prefigurative actions, those resources then become building blocks for mounting more robust movements in the future, including ones that eventually pose a meaningful threat.

Having established the political value of contentious everyday spaces, the rest of this book explores the methods activists use to construct counterspaces. This includes counterspaces organized around retail, which is the subject of the next chapter.

CHAPTER 2

Creating Accessible and Autonomous Activist Enterprises

CARRIE BARNETT WAS THIRTEEN YEARS OLD IN 1973. "That was the year the [American] Psychiatric Association determined homosexuality wasn't a mental illness." It was also the year Barnett began grappling with her sexual identity. "I was a freshman in high school. I wrote a paper on homosexuality." Despite the medical establishment's recent change of heart, all the books she found at the library called it a mental illness. Barnett did not find anything affirming queer identities, nor did she find material confirming women—and not just men—might be queer. "But it didn't matter to me. I had all of these books. I wrote this paper. That was my way of going out and finding community and understanding that I wasn't the only person who felt that way."

Fifteen years later, Barnett cofounded People Like Us, the first joint gay and lesbian bookstore in Chicago, to help other people also know that they were not alone. The bookstore opened in 1988, the year after ACT UP—a direct-action AIDS-fighting coalition—was founded in New York. For Barnett, People Like Us and ACT UP were complementary tools within the same movement. "It was such a screaming-from-the-rooftops kind of act to have the bookstore. . . . I wish I could explain to you how just opening our doors was a bold political act. By simply being out, we were being political in a significant way. By being legitimate businesspeople. By being successful businesspeople. By advertising. . . . It was ridiculously radical."

The commodities sold at People Like Us supported queer liberation. The bookstore sold queer fiction, queer travel guides, and educational material about living with AIDS. This material helped people find each other, build communities, and reduce stigma. In addition to books, People Like Us sold Pride paraphernalia like rainbow bumper stickers, key chains, and "that Gran Fury poster 'Kissing Doesn't Kill.' We sold probably about five thousand of those." The bookstore supported activist fundraisers as well.

"We sold tickets to all the shows, and we would sell all the Pride buttons. Anybody who was raising money for something, we would sell [it], and then we would just keep the money in envelopes and give it to [the organizers]" when they came around to collect it.

Alongside selling queer-positive paraphernalia and raising money for advocacy groups, People Like Us was also a site for search and discovery. Young people "wandering down the street . . . would come into the store" not realizing it had queer themes. "They'd walk around for a while and look. And all of a sudden, it would come over them that, 'Oh my gosh, this is a gay bookstore!'" When in groups, accidental browsers often made public displays of disdain. "They would invariably say something completely rude and rush out the door. Except for one kid. He would be lingering with his eyes. And we'd be like, 'He's coming back.'" When those wide-eyed kids returned alone, away from their friends' prying eyes, the owners welcomed them and helped them explore.

In these discussions, books facilitated triangulation. For William H. Whyte, triangulation in public space occurs when something in the environment—such as a food vendor, art installation, or cultural event—generates an excuse for strangers to chat without having to introduce

The storefront canopy and window display at People Like Us in Chicago, Illinois, blends into the retail environment around it. Photograph by People Like Us, 1989; courtesy of Carrie Barnett.

themselves or disclose personal information.[1] At People Like Us, in an era where "people were afraid to ask questions" about queer sexuality, sales displays helped people warm up to each other and discuss topics they may otherwise avoid. "Because it was a commercial space, we could use that aspect of it to talk to people in a way that wasn't challenging." The gift-giving economy helped as well. "People would invariably say, 'I'm here for a friend.'" Barnett respected this need for anonymity and kept discussions in the third person for however long browsers preferred.

However, once people felt more comfortable, the yearning for community often came pouring out. For Barnett, "It was almost like being bartenders, the things that people would tell us. They would come in and say the craziest, most personal things to us." Customers spoke about sexual liaisons, family sagas, and medical travails. These conversations enhanced self-awareness while also creating the sense of togetherness that turned People Like Us "into something that was much bigger than a bookstore. It was a place of community. . . . It was our sacred trust."

As valuable as these experiences were, People Like Us was ultimately a business. It had to sell commodities to exist. "When we first started . . . we had this long conversation about whether our first priority should be to serve the community or to make a profit. And we talked around and around and around on that for, I don't know, months. And then we finally realized that, in order to serve the community, we had to make a profit. . . . We chose making a profit as our first goal because it enabled us to serve the community." This financial imperative explained why expensive art books were on the right. "We knew people moved to the right when they came in." It explained why pornography was in the back. "It was purely a commercial decision to put it back there." The magazines were "new every week, and we wanted people to walk all the way through the store." The pressure to boost sales also explained why key chains, buttons, and bumper stickers were stacked by the register. "There was a bigger margin on that stuff, so we made more money on junk than we did on books." By conceding to market dictates, the owners earned enough revenue to cover rent and wages, which then gave them control of a space advancing queer liberation through role modeling, community building, and fundraising.

Conversations like this one with Carrie Barnett illustrate the phenomenon of activist entrepreneurship. Analyzing the experiences of activist-entrepreneurs helps explain what people hope to gain by routing activism through retail. Understanding these motivations sheds light on the bigger and more important question of how capitalist consumerism inadvertently produces opportunities for contentious politics. Although shopping is often dismissed as a passive, frivolous activity, constructing counterspaces in the guise of storefronts creates low-stakes environments for search and discovery. These functions are especially useful in a society where people are socialized to shop for community and therefore primed to find camaraderie in activist storefronts. Selling things also generates revenue, which helps make counterspaces more durable and autonomous, assuming of course activists are willing to live with the compromises required to stay in business.

When talking about activists involved in retail, one word for this phenomenon is "activist entrepreneurship." As I explain in this chapter, activist entrepreneurship is not about finding ethical ways to do business. Instead, it's about finding affordable ways to do politics. Activist entrepreneurship is not the same as "corporate social responsibility," which emphasizes profits, or "diverse economies," which eschews capitalism. On the contrary, Barnett embraced capitalist practices because they helped the counterspace survive.

Additionally, activist enterprises like People Like Us are not standalone entities. Instead, they are hubs within larger social movement terrains. These terrains include a diverse range of contentious spaces. For Barnett, having control of a retail space did not negate the need for other movement spaces and other modes of organizing. Instead, inserting a business into the mix created additional, complementary resources accommodating tasks less easily managed elsewhere.

Despite these complementary dynamics, activist entrepreneurship is an understudied phenomenon. One reason it is understudied is because critical scholars tend to focus on retail as a site of exclusion. Concerns about security guards displacing panhandlers and harassing minorities underscore the political importance of critiquing exclusion. However, exclusion is only one part of the story. The full retail landscape also includes ethnic economies and subcultural businesses where vulnerable groups enjoy warmer welcomes. Even more importantly, retail comes with different terms of access compared to other types of social movement spaces, which are also exclusionary, just in different ways. Because of these relative differences, movement-oriented bookstores and infoshops accommodate complementary functions targeting people who feel unwelcome in other types of activist environments. Like the queer youth who stumbled into People Like Us by accident, radical booksellers construct low-barrier entry points where people not already assimilated into movements can connect and explore.

Another reason activist entrepreneurship is understudied is because running small businesses requires compromise. Compared to splashy images of squatters defying capitalism and protestors denouncing governments, the image of business owners paying rent, taxes, and license fees may seem anticlimactic. However, examples like People Like Us underscore the potential advantage of strategic deference. By complying enough with state and market dictates, activists can construct durable counterspaces where they call the shots. Instead of borrowing other people's spaces or relying on other people's patronage, retailing generates an independent source of income to pay for independent spaces where activists can make independent choices. Securing this independence comes at the price of capitulating enough to external market and government forces to stay in business, which involves compromise instead of outright resistance. But the benefit, when it works, is enhanced autonomy within a durable space under activist control.

A final reason activist entrepreneurship is understudied is because critical scholars tend to frame consumerism as a passive expression of class status instead of an active moment of political engagement. The transition from producer society to consumer society gave rise to the image of aspiring middle-class shoppers buying washing machines, entertainment systems, Levi's, and iPhones. These trends are important, but focusing exclusively on status symbols overlooks the changing role of retail as people find new ways to shop for community. In the era of "experience economies" and "third places," people frequent bookstores and coffee shops not merely for newspapers and cappuccinos but also—and often primarily—to feel a sense of connection. People shop for community, not by acquiring items to display elsewhere but by lingering in stores and interacting with customers and clerks. With the decline of workplaces as sites for political organizing, these trends create new opportunities to frame consumer space as potential places to build affinity around emerging political ideas.

This chapter explores these themes in four sections. First, I provide a definition of activist entrepreneurship and differentiate it from other economic trends. Next, I analyze the accessibility traits making storefronts valuable for search and discovery. Third, I explain the links between commodity sales and autonomous space. Finally, I consider the political opportunities arising from consumer demands for sociable shopping. Cumulatively, the accessibility, autonomy, and community aspects of retail generate macro-level opportunities for activists to route politics through businesses. These practices do not directly confront systems of authority, nor do they produce secret societies organized around hidden transcripts. Instead, the goal is to supplement other modes of organizing by creating durable, autonomous spaces with easy public exposure where newcomers can explore progressive ideas and connect with political communities.

Activist-Entrepreneurs Use Capitalism for Contentious Politics

Carrie Barnett's experience with People Like Us, where the business was less about capitalism and more about organizing, is an example of "activist entrepreneurship." In this section, I provide a clearer definition of what activist entrepreneurship is—and what it is not—to help readers distinguish this social movement repertoire from the background noise of other socially conscious economic activities.

I borrow the term "activist-entrepreneur" from Joshua Clark Davis who uses the phrase to describe activists who operated small businesses as social movement tools in the 1960s and 1970s. These activists from the New Left era "hoped to bring about political transformation . . . by operating small businesses *in direct collaboration with*, not instead of, collective social movements."[2] Using Black liberation bookstores as an example, these businesses were not merely about getting African American writers better industry representation. Activist booksellers also had ties with radical groups, provided meeting rooms for organizing, and disseminated commodities challenging white privilege.[3] Queer feminist booksellers did similar work by constructing dedicated quasi-public counterspaces organized around queer feminist canons.[4] In both instances, these public-facing spaces created beachheads to "draw people into these movements and mobilize them in the name of their causes."[5]

Although I focus on radical bookstores and infoshops, print-based venues are just one subtype of activist enterprise. Other examples of movement-oriented businesses from the 1960s and 1970s include gay bars and dance clubs, which provided entry points into queer culture, natural food co-ops, which rejected capitalist hierarchies and corporate agribusiness, and countercultural head shops, which nurtured subcultural rejections of mainstream social values. These venues were businesses, but they were also—and primarily—mechanisms for distributing radical ideas, modeling progressive alternatives, and creating counterpublic spaces.[6]

Black liberation bookstores and countercultural head shops are historical examples from the New Left wave, which rose and fell. However, the strategy of using businesses to advance movements has a longer history. As examples, this history includes communist bookstores in the 1930s[7] and temperance coffeehouses in the 1830s.[8] Similarly, in recent years, new waves of activist enterprises are emerging around intersectional anarchism, prison abolition, political asylum, and Latino/a and Indigenous peoples movements. This book focuses on these emerging waves.

To understand what activist entrepreneurship is, it helps to understand what it is not. Activist entrepreneurship is not the same as "corporate social responsibility." Corporate social responsibility is "the notion that companies should accompany the pursuit of profit with good citizenship,"[9] for instance by eschewing child labor or protecting the environment. Although the increased cost of ethical management undercuts short-term profitability, those costs come with long-term financial benefits, such as building social capital and protecting companies from tarnished reputations. This trade-off is about self-interest. "Driving this process is the belief that higher standards of corporate responsibility pay off for investors over the long term both through potential equity premia and through risk reduction."[10] From this perspective, adopting socially responsible practices is not about doing good for its own sake. Instead, it is about selectively adopting some ethical behaviors to pad the bottom line.[11]

For activist-entrepreneurs, it is a different story. The goal of using retail to advance politics is not the same as using ethics to maximize profits. Activist-entrepreneurs often strive to run ethical businesses, and those practices may yield financial benefits. But the ultimate goal is to advance the movement. To advance movements, activists sometimes make ethical decisions that risk financial losses, for instance when Left Bank in St. Louis refused to host events for "war criminals" like Henry Kissinger despite lost sales and despite the backlash of prank calls and gossip column critiques. Conversely, activists sometimes sacrifice ethics to advance other movement goals, for instance when Firestorm paid workers below minimum wage rather than allowing the counterspace to go bankrupt.[12] The deciding factor in examples like these is not whether ethics is profitable or whether cost cutting is ethical but whether the decision advances a larger political agenda.

Just like activist entrepreneurship is not the same as corporate social responsibility, activist entrepreneurship is also not the same as "diverse economies." Katherine Gibson and Julie Graham coined the phrase "diverse economies" to describe a research community dedicated to finding alternatives to capitalism.[13] For scholars using the diverse economies framework, this lens is a way to "recover and revalorize a multitude of noncapitalist practices and spaces that disrupt the assumption of a hegemonic capitalism."[14] Examples of not-fully-capitalist transactions include reciprocal babysitting agreements, fair trade coffee, and unpaid domestic labor, as well as sex trafficking, theft, and scrapping. By highlighting the ubiquity of noncapitalist techniques for organizing productive labor, Gibson and Graham demonstrate that there are always already-existing alternatives to capitalism, even within capitalist-dominated systems, and that these alternatives may or may not be ethical.

Some activist-entrepreneurs operate diverse economy businesses even without using this exact term. Firestorm, for example, states, "We believe in self-ownership, voluntary association and cooperativism, placing a high value on forms of organization that are organic and consensual."[15] This anarchist-inspired community space uses prefigurative business practices to model alternatives to capitalism. "Our organizational model avoids unnecessary and involuntary hierarchies, relying instead on team structures that maximize input from all our workers while giving everyone opportunities for creativity and entrepreneurship."[16]

Although venues like Firestorm fit the diverse economies paradigm, not all activists eschew capitalism. In many feminist-, queer-, and Black-oriented spaces, the goal is less about escaping capitalism and more about combating patriarchy, homophobia, and white privilege by getting more minorities into leadership positions, including business ownership. For instance, at Antigone, because women own the business, women call the shots. At Sister's Uptown, Black owners and Black authors dominate public debate. At Housing Works, profit maximization pays for the fight against AIDS. Similarly, for Carrie Barnett with People Like Us, selling commodities allows queer owners to construct a queer public space. For these activist-entrepreneurs, the point is to use retail for radical organizing. If adopting capitalist methods advances those goals, so be it.

These discussions about corporate social responsibility and diverse economies show that activist-entrepreneurs do not have a monopoly on ethics, nor are their practices ethical by every measure. What distinguishes activist enterprises from other businesses has less to do with ethics and more to do with the goal of advancing social causes. Activist venues support social movements through the commodities they sell, for instance at Resistencia where the literature and artwork support racial and ethnic liberation; through the business practices they model, for instance at Boneshaker where anarchists perform nonhierarchical decision-making; and by constructing counterpublic spaces, for instance at Wild Iris, which supports queer communities of color. This social movement repertoire of using retail as a means to facilitate organizing distinguishes activist enterprises from nonactivist businesses, including ones with socially responsible and noncapitalist elements.

Having distinguished activist entrepreneurship from the background noise of other economic practices, I want to say a quick word about the appropriateness (and potential discomfort) of the two words in the phrase activist-entrepreneur. The word "activism" in U.S. culture is deeply associated with state-directed tactics, which is why people involved in beyond-the-state projects, like education and nurturance, do not always describe their work using this label. Adrian (no last name given) with Left Bank in Seattle expressed this negative viewpoint. "Even though, yes, it's this anarchist bookstore . . . I don't see it as my form of direct action. It's still this capitalist bookstore . . . that's a place of refuge . . . but I'd never be so naive to say that this is my form of resistance." By contrast, Kristin Dooley with May Day expressed the opposite point of view. Her understanding of activism did not require her to "actually go out into the community and put on a program." It was more about inviting the community into the bookstore for education and self-actualization.

These opposing perspectives mark two ends of a spectrum where even people who agree that the point of a store is to advance a cause have different interpretations about the meaning of the word "activism." Without wishing to offend or pigeonhole anyone who prefers not to use this label, I nevertheless use the word "activist" throughout this book to refer both to people involved in state-centric campaigns, which sometimes occur in bookstores and libraries, and to people participating in beyond-the-state contentious politics, which often occur in bookstores or in libraries.

The second word, "entrepreneur," also has several possible meanings.

Although entrepreneurship is commonly used as a shorthand for small, independent businesses, sociologists define the key element of entrepreneurship as novelty. "The definition of entrepreneurship denotes the creation of some combination that did not previously exist."[17] Entrepreneurship can be economic, cultural, or political. Economic entrepreneurship is when people introduce new products, develop new manufacturing methods, open new markets, create new supply chains, or organize industries in new ways.[18] Cultural entrepreneurship is "the carrying out of a novel combination that results in something new and appreciated in the cultural sphere."[19] Similarly, political entrepreneurs "change the direction and flow of politics."[20]

Building on these definitions, not all entrepreneurial businesses are small, and not all small businesses are entrepreneurial. Instead, I use the term entrepreneurship with a generative sensibility in mind. Activist entrepreneurship is not about recreating mom-and-pop main streets with a progressive flair. Instead, it is about doing culturally and politically generative work by constructing new types of storefronts and developing innovative business practices as tools for promoting alternative ways of life. Additionally, from my perspective, the activist-entrepreneurs doing this work include not only the owners but also the managers, collective members, staffers, volunteers, board members, and other supporters who contribute labor to these spaces.

Retail Spaces Are Accessible Sites for Search and Discovery

The subset of activist-entrepreneurs described in this book route politics through retail, which raises the question, why retail? What do activists hope to gain by using stores for contentious organizing? As I explain in this section, one advantage of retail is its distinct pattern of accessibility. However, thinking about retail in terms of accessibility is not the norm. On the contrary, in the critical geography literature, retail landscapes are notorious as sites of unrelenting exclusion. Although I agree it is politically important to expose these exclusions, I also believe storefronts have inclusionary characteristics, especially when compared to other social movement spaces, which are likewise exclusionary, just along different lines. Because of this relative accessibility, activists in retail settings can connect with people who feel uncomfortable in other movement spaces, which creates supplemental inroads for organizing.

I make this argument even though the exclusionary traits of retail are extensive and significant. For one thing, retail environments are privately owned, market-oriented spaces. In these spaces, people experiencing homelessness are moved on, people of color are arrested, teenage skateboarders are unwelcome, and sidewalk vendors are banned.[21] For another thing, retail space is unevenly distributed. Chain stores like grocery stores, drug stores, and bookstores systematically underserve low-income communities.[22] Additionally, when it comes to gender, women are incorporated, but on inequitable terms reinforcing misogyny.[23] Minority groups likewise discriminate against each other, for instance when Arab Americans and Korean Americans operate gas stations in African American neighborhoods without liking their customers or helping them feel welcome.[24]

Alongside these examples from the literature, the activists I interviewed mentioned additional exclusions. One exclusionary dynamic is that social spaces like coffee shops have censoring effects. For John Wawrzaszek with the Chicago Publishers Resource Center, when nonnormative groups gather for readings and debates where "you might be talking about something sensitive that a customer might not want to hear . . . We're not allowed back because our subject matter was a little too difficult for whoever's there." Another exclusionary dynamic is that customers are not the only ones experiencing discrimination. Business owners face discrimination as well, for instance from homophobic landlords who refuse to rent to queer tenants or from intolerant neighbors who taunt anarchists and harass feminists. Additionally, retail space is only available to people with good credit scores who can pay consistent rent, which introduces class barriers.

These are just some of the many ways retail is exclusionary, which confirms it is not accessible for everyone. I revisit questions of exclusion throughout this book, including the management strategies activists use to mitigate exclusion, as well as the new lines of exclusion activist-entrepreneurs construct. But first, I want to establish another foundational argument by saying that, even though exclusion is real and important, it is not the whole story.

One missing piece of the story stems from scholars' tendencies to study privileged retail, such as suburban shopping centers and gentrifying commercial districts, while paying less attention to businesses serving underprivileged groups and providing those groups with much-needed counterpublic space. The literature on ethnic economies provides a notable exception. This literature highlights Black barber shops, Latino/a grocery stores, Islamic clothing stores, and Vietnamese strip malls where

owners do business in native tongues and sell culturally responsive products to customers who enjoy feeling a sense of community and identity in
those spaces.[25] Ethnic economies are not perfect. They are not free from
infighting, they do not welcome everyone, and they do not stop the exclusions occurring elsewhere. Despite these limitations, ethnic retail provides
counterpublic space for people who are unwelcomed and unsupported in
the commercial landscapes of white privilege. This literature also provides
a template for analyzing other types of counterpublic spaces—including
activist ones—where people who are queer, anarchist, feminist, and anticapitalist may find a warmer welcome than in conventional settings.

Another missing piece of the story is that retail is not unique for being exclusionary. Social movements involve all kinds of spaces like public streets,
private homes, political party offices, service institutions, religious buildings, and college campuses. Like retail, these other social movement spaces
are exclusionary, just along different lines. Understanding relative patterns
of exclusion is crucial to understanding how retail, despite its imperfections, is nevertheless accessible in unique ways when compared to other
movement spaces. Understanding these differential patterns sheds light on
how relative—rather than absolute—accessibility makes storefronts useful
for some movement tasks less easily accommodated elsewhere.

The accessibility characteristics of retail became especially clear when I
compared retail settings with other social movement sites. Public spaces
like streets and plazas are useful for activism because they are extremely
visible and open. Anyone can go there, and lots of people see what happens there, which makes public spaces prime locations for rallies.[26] However, despite these advantages, the high degree of exposure also makes
public space exclusionary. For people who are Black, transgender, undocumented, Muslim, or women, merely being visible in public risks assault, arrest, or deportation. Being visible in an act of defiance escalates
those risks, which is why joining protests in public spaces is a luxury many
people cannot afford.[27]

Alongside public space, private spaces like living rooms and kitchens
are important for organizing, but unlike public space, private space is not
visible and not accessible to most people. For Bice Maiguashca, social
movements do more than just transform people into revolutionary subjects ready to do "battle" in public streets; they also challenge oppression
through more humble practices like alternative education, knowledge pro-

duction, service provisioning, and progressive kinship.[28] These everyday practices often occur in private settings, like residential dormitories and housing cooperatives. In these private spaces removed from public censorship, people can let down their guard, which is useful for organizing.

However, whereas streets and plazas suffer from inadequate protection from public exposure, private spaces suffer from insufficient porosity. People can only participate if they literally buy into private communities or receive personal invitations from hosts. These boundaries can limit participation to narrow circles of like-minded friends, which excludes people whose life experiences may challenge group norms.[29] Turf-like feelings often persist even when owners explicitly invite more people to participate, which is why Ben (no last name given) with the Chicago Publishers Resource Center supported taking writing groups "out of the house" and into retail settings. In addition to reaching a broader audience, "not everyone feels comfortable going to somebody's basement." Boone (no last name given) with the Minnehaha Free Space described similar associations between housing and turf. At the Free Space, "the fact that nobody lived there . . . made it more accessible to people who weren't involved with the community. It doesn't feel like going to a punk house."

Alongside public and private spaces, civic spaces—such as political party offices, church meeting rooms, and college campuses—are useful for organizing, even as they come with other barriers to access. For instance, it can feel intimidating to walk into a Socialist Party office for the first time, especially for people who do not already self-identify as socialist. Similarly, although grassroots organizers often rent church basements and multipurpose rooms for meetings and events, some feminists do not appreciate the patriarchal overtones, and people who are Jewish or Black Baptist may feel distinctly out of place on white Christian turf.[30] College campuses are likewise both useful and restrictive. Political demonstrations often occur on college campuses, but other resources like meeting rooms and libraries are frequently reserved for members. John Wawrzaszek founded the Chicago Publishers Resource Center partly in response to those exclusions. "Although a university library can be a great resource, if you don't have a student ID, you don't have access."

For all these reasons, public, private, and civic spaces are useful for contentious politics, but no space includes everyone, and no space accommodates every function. Within this diverse social movement landscape, retail space is differently accessible than public, private, or civic spaces, and those differences generate distinct opportunities to welcome different social groups into contentious politics.

One reason commercial space can feel more accessible is because, accurately or otherwise, it often feels apolitical. Visiting a store has a different vibe than joining a protest or visiting a party office. Some people are comfortable making those choices, but for other people, the explicitly political setting can feel alien and terrifying. As a less threatening alternative, activist-entrepreneurs strategically use the depoliticized image of shopping to reduce feelings of trepidation and to construct casual-feeling environments for browsing political ideas. This casualness helps people warm up to contentious issues they may want to explore but are not (yet) ready to adopt, let alone defend.

The second-wave feminist movement provides an example of how this strategic depoliticization works. In this movement, feminist bookstores provided stepping-stones between staying in kitchens and marching in streets. For Carol Seajay, although some women joined marches, others feared public ridicule or felt tentative about the politics. However, because women were "socialized to shop," women's bookstores provided "a safer entryway into feminism. One could look at the books until she found the courage to ask the questions she needed to ask."[31]

These safer entryway functions persist today, and they occur across movement types. For Trudy Mills with Antigone, "We have this space that is very accessible to people." The business is in a prominent location. "It's just right here on the avenue" where people are already walking. Additionally, although the store is near the university campus and a high school, Antigone has the benefit of being "*just* a store. . . . You can just walk right in and walk right out." That freedom to enter and exit with no prior knowledge, no explanation, and no strings attached creates easy opportunities to investigate sensitive topics, like border rights and transgender experiences, without having to plan in advance, request permission to enter, or declare any political commitment.

Spaces like these are also free, at least to a significant degree. As George Orwell wrote in 1936, bookstores are "one of the few places where you can hang about for a long time without spending any money."[32] This open accessibility remains the norm. Unlike other commercial spaces like coffee shops and restaurants where purchases are required, retailers expect people to browse, and they know many browsers will not buy. This is why, for Lynn Mooney, one of the biggest advantages of Women & Children First is "you can come and spend time and you don't even have to buy a cup of coffee if you don't want." The shelves and displays create reasons to linger. As I describe in detail in subsequent chapters, this lingering then becomes an opportunity for organizing. Unlike conventional retailers, who use lingering amenities to put people in a buying mood,[33] activists use lingering amenities to expose people to progressive ideas and to engender radical consciousness.

Another reason retail feels accessible is because it minimizes self-limiting emotions, such as shame. For Carrie Barnett with People Like Us, bookstores and social service centers are part of the same queer liberation movement, but they target different groups and perform different functions. Young people on the cusp of sexual awareness may wander into a queer bookstore half-committed or by chance and encounter queer themes while there, but they are unlikely to amble into an institutionalized queer service center unless they have a prearranged appointment or an urgent need. The explicit labeling in institutional settings creates barriers as well, especially for people struggling with denial and fear.

Additionally, going to a bookstore feels different from going to a social service center. Focusing on services frames people as clients or patients needing assistance instead of hailing them as agents capable of organizing on their own behalf.[34] This difference in vibe is why organizers of a rape survivor support group asked Wild Iris if they could hold their meetings in the bookstore instead of using the rape crisis center next door. A rape crisis center is useful for one-on-one clinical assistance, but the bookstore had "a looser, more social feel," which helped people "feel more comfortable talking about their struggles" with other survivors.[35]

Cumulatively, these traits make retail space differently accessible than other public, private, civic, or institutional environments. Anyone can walk into a store without advanced planning. No invitation is necessary, and no previous knowledge is required. There are no membership rosters or upfront fees. The culture of browsing reduces stigma, and browsing comes with no obligation to buy. Additionally, as I explain in subsequent chapters, many owners take steps to design and manage movement-oriented businesses to help a wide range of people feel welcome.

Because retail space feels accessible in these ways, activists can use those businesses as low-barrier entry points into movement scenes. Storefronts do not accommodate every movement function, but they serve a few functions quite well. People who are curious about radical politics but not yet ready to commit can interact with seasoned activists in low-stakes ways. This juxtaposition of insiders and newcomers is one of the primary characteristics distinguishing movement-oriented stores from other activist hubs. Additionally, the strategically depoliticized, no-strings-attached stance encourages people to explore unsettling or risky ideas they may otherwise avoid, which creates a beachhead for search and discovery.

For all these reasons, retail space plays a complementary role within the social movement landscape. For James Schmidt with the Civic Media Center, creating and operating an activist enterprise "has not replaced or removed the need for traditional movement-building spaces such as churches, municipal and academic facilities, and people's homes. Rather, it has complemented the utility of such spaces and provided an alternative when one is needed, for practical or political reasons."[36] Adding retail into the mix expands flexibility and creates opportunities for growth. "The group that starts out meeting in its members' houses can move up to holding meetings and events at the Media Center, on its way to building the kind of mass interest that can fill a municipal hall or campus auditorium."[37] Additionally, because different constituencies prefer spending time in different types of spaces, "groups that regularly shift their activities from one space to another," for instance from churches to campuses to stores and back again, can use that mobility "to reach different segments of the population."[38]

These complementary dynamics support social movements by accommodating search and discovery, which is harder to achieve elsewhere. Like trying on clothes in a dressing room, people explore ideas and test unexpected finds. Sometimes browsers buy into the ideas and carry them home. Other times, they leave the politics in a metaphorical heap on the dressing room floor. Through these exploratory functions, retail space complements other social movement geographies and provides supplemental inroads into organizing.

Selling Commodities Enhances Durability and Autonomy

Alongside porous accessibility, another advantage of routing politics through retail is that the financial revenue from retail enhances durable autonomy. Virginia Woolf recognized the connections between space, income, and independence nearly a century ago. In her classic feminist text,

A Room of One's Own, Woolf emphasizes the importance of having independent spaces free from patriarchal interference, as well as independent incomes free from patrons' oversight.[39] Freedom to act without disciplinary constraint is likewise useful for anarchism,[40] Black power,[41] and queer liberation.[42] Having spaces and resources to explore without being interrupted and censored makes it easier to develop fledgling ideas into robust critiques. Selling things contributes to this autonomy, although maintaining adequate sales can be a constant struggle. Revenue does not always cover costs, and financial pressure often requires sacrificing at least some movement goals to make ends meet. Nevertheless, as I explain in this section, one primary goal of activist-entrepreneurship is to construct an independent revenue source to pay for autonomous space.

Activists claim space in many ways. According to David Graeber, one option is to occupy it, for instance by squatting in other people's buildings or camping in public parks. However, these illegally seized spaces are tenuous and "in constant danger of being taken away."[43] A second option is to accept patronage from wealthy supporters who, out of solidarity, pay activists' rent. However, patrons are fickle, and they can withdraw their support at any moment, leaving organizers scrambling.[44] A third option is to create "an entirely new funding base"[45] unencumbered by state evictions and patrons' whims. The downside is it takes considerable time and energy to establish new funding bases and to manage those resources. The benefit, when it works, is a more durable space where the terms of longevity are, to a greater degree, under activists' control.

Selling things is one way to create a new funding base. The rationale behind this strategy was especially apparent during my visit to Housing Works. Housing Works operates several thrift stores, including a second-hand bookstore, as fundraising engines. The proceeds cover rent, as well as social services for people experiencing homelessness and living with AIDS. For Nicholas Watson, the decision to get involved in retail felt politically necessary because activists were having trouble getting money from other sources. Their target social groups are "hard to fund through Medicare and other sources because they're politically unpopular" and because the services are experimental. Another problem is that the limited government funds that are available come with prohibitions against sex education and needle exchange, "the two things we really know work to stop the spread of AIDS." These complications explain why Housing Works decided to raise money itself, including by opening businesses.

When selling things to pay for space, there are many commodities to choose from. Activists sell food, coffee, and cocktails. They repair bicycles and teach art classes. They host concerts and use events to solicit donations and collect rental fees. Donation drives and crowdfunding campaigns are common as well. This revenue becomes the independent income needed to sustain independent spaces. The challenge is figuring out what kind of revenue generating model fits the social mission and is doable given the available skills, resources, and market constraints.

Most activist-entrepreneurs sell more than one thing to survive. Housing Works is the epitome of multitrack revenue generation. As Watson explains, "We're doing as many different businesses as we can in the one space." Selling books raises between $1,500 and $2,000 per day. Renting books by the foot for movie sets and office decor brings in a bit more. Selling coffee and pastries through the bookstore café generates additional revenue from people who enjoy spending time in literary settings. Housing Works also earns money by periodically closing the bookstore to customers and renting it for special events. People pay $4,000 to host a wedding, $6,000 to host a concert, and $15,000 for a day spent shooting a movie on-site.[46] These supplemental activities support the retail space, as well as the social services Housing Works provides.

Building an autonomous funding base does not mean other strategies for claiming space disappear. Squatting still plays a role. As an example, ABC No Rio has one of the largest zine libraries in the country. Activists built the library by collecting material when squatters were evicted from other locations, and they consolidated this material in a building that No Rio squatted in for roughly two decades before finally getting the deed.[47] Patronage still plays a role as well, especially in early years or times of struggle. As an example, Aurora Anaya-Cerda founded La Casa Azul using money from an Indiegogo crowdfunding campaign and a gift from an "angel investor."[48]

However, although squatting and patronage are always options, one primary reason activists get involved in retail is to transition toward more sustainable, self-directed models for constructing durable space. Activists make this effort because having independent funds and independent spaces facilitates independent decision-making. For Watson with Housing Works, "we have a measure of independence that a lot of nonprofits probably are jealous about." The bookstore's stock is donated, which reduces costs, and the revenue comes with no spending restrictions or deliverable requirements. The thrift store model is useful in recessions as well because, when private foundations and government funders are cutting back, thrift sales increase as more people shop for bargains.[49] For Watson, this independent income "is one of the big [reasons why] Housing Works has been able to be a leader" in the campaign to stop the spread of HIV in New York. The organization can do this self-directed, contentious work "because it's always had money that it raised itself."

Housing Works is fortunate in its ability to generate enough revenue to pay for space and have money left over for social programming. This venue is also unusual among activist retail in that it does not sell radical commodities, use a radical business structure, or create a radical public space. Instead, Housing Works advances its mission by selling mainstream commodities for maximum profits to pay for services in other locations. This setup is not the norm. For most activist-entrepreneurs, the content of the stock and the mode of selling it are supremely important because, in addition to generating revenue, activists use these commodities and practices to claim space, build community, and disseminate ideas. Pursuing these nonmonetary goals sometimes means accepting a reduced revenue stream. As Corey Farach with Bluestockings states, "it probably would be easier to pay rent if we had more mainstream stuff." Mainstream commodities sell faster and in higher volumes. However, for most activist-entrepreneurs, profit maximization is not the goal. Instead, the goal is to be capitalist enough to pay for space and then use commodities, business practices, and programming to build a durable counterpublic environment.

These more-than-economic aspirations get at the contradictions inherent in adapting capitalism for activist purposes. Retail generates revenue to pay for space, but as a social movement repertoire, this strategy often requires sacrificing (or at least softening) some movement goals in exchange for being able to claim space without relying solely on squatting or charity.

This need to attend to market constraints generates many challenges. One challenge is to balance consumer ability to pay with the goal of creating inclusive environments. For Kate Khatib with Red Emma's, "selling political books or making political books available is part of the political project. But it's also about providing space." In most cities, there simply "are not places you can go into if you do not have disposable income," which is why Red Emma's constructs "a space where people can feel like they're not being pressured by a traditional capitalist economic exchange system."[50] Nevertheless, consumerism remains a necessary consideration.

"Yes, of course we want people to [buy things]. We need that. If that doesn't happen, then we don't bring in the money we need to pay rent. And if we don't pay the rent then, unfortunately, we're gonna close. And that is a reality, and we [have] to find ways to balance that."[51]

Another challenge associated with capitalist-backed activism involves selecting which aspects of the business to keep radical, and which to not. Activist-entrepreneurs may choose to carry progressive commodities, model alternative business practices, or create radical public spaces, but it is not always financially possible to do all three. As an example, for Kristin Hogan, many second-wave feminist booksellers got their start using donated capital and volunteer labor in the 1970s, which made it possible to sell feminist-themed paraphernalia in women-oriented spaces using feminist-inspired cooperatives. However, these venues lived off special gifts, which could not last forever. Over time, many feminist bookstores became more general by selling mainstream titles alongside feminist ones. Going general in their commodities solidified women's hard-won positions as small business owners and kept feminist titles in print, but it came at the cost of diluting the political potency of those spaces.[52]

Activist-entrepreneurs often describe feeling uncomfortable grappling with these market pressures. For Katie Renz, there is a "weird contradiction" of "having to operate with one foot grudgingly stuck in the system while stretching to hand out tools to educate and inspire the overthrow of that system."[53] This inescapable embeddedness leaves some activists feeling uncomfortably complicit. The Long Haul Infoshop's website states, "We hate selling stuff, but we gotta pay our rent, (at least until someone gives us a house). So why don't you drop on by and buy our shit."[54] Similarly, at May Day, when I asked volunteers about their business structure, they immediately reframed the narrative. "We don't consider ourselves a business. We're more of a service." Even thinking about May Day as a business "drives us crazy."

These discomforts and contradictions are nevertheless the norm, not the exception. For Charles Weigl with AK Press, "We always have to make difficult choices under far-from-perfect conditions in a society organized around principles we despise."[55] However, just because a process is contradictory does not mean it does not work or is not worthwhile. On the contrary, activists' willingness to adjust themselves to retail despite discomfort speaks to the value activists place on having autonomous space.

Their willingness to sell things despite the contradictions underscores the utility of activist retail as a repertoire of dissent.

Experience Economies Transform Shoppers into People Seeking Community

Alongside accessibility and autonomy, another advantage of routing activism through storefronts is that it allows activists to tap into the changing social role of retail. As I explain in this last section, in consumer societies and experience economies, people are socialized to present themselves to retailers less as shoppers seeking commodities and more as people seeking communities. Although activists have always built counterpolitical networks through movement-oriented businesses, the growing trend of shopping for community means more people are primed to rethink political allegiances based on consumer experiences.

Historically, the shift from a manufacturing economy to a consumer economy brought many changes. One change involves the spaces used for political organizing, for instance the decline of workplace guilds and unions and their replacement with social movement spaces focused on lifestyles, values, and other identity traits. A related change involves the type of political identity enacted through consumerism, for instance the shift away from commodities as an expression of class status and the shift toward shopping as a performance of gender identity, countercultural convictions, and personal distinctiveness.[56] The emotional meaning of retail has changed as well, for instance with the rise of "retail therapy" where a person shops to "cheer one-self up through the purchase of self-treats"[57] or shops to spend time in a restorative environment where losing oneself in browsing has "attention restoration" effects.[58]

These changes are fueling another macroscale shift in consumerism, which is a shift characterized by the emerging "experience economy." For Joseph Pine and James Gilmore, the experience economy is a philosophy of merchandizing based on the notion that people nominally shopping for commodities are really in the market for pleasurable experiences. The experience economy is about "leveraging the experience of shopping,"[59] which occurs when "companies stage an experience" and "*engage* customers, connecting with them in a personal, memorable way."[60]

One subset of marketable experiences involves sensory stimulation.

These experience economy retailers make money by adding indulgent perks, for instance by serving champagne at Gucci, piping in mouthwatering aromas at Whole Foods, or painting colorful murals in gourmet eateries.[61] The mainstream bookselling industry taps into this market as well. For Laura Miller, booksellers use the "soft-sell atmosphere" of ambient lighting, soothing colors, comfy chairs, café snacks, public restrooms, and art exhibits "precisely to put customers in the mood to make a purchase."[62] These sensory indulgences attract consumers who want not only a commodity, which they could purchase more cheaply online, but also the pleasure of buying that commodity in a stimulating environment.

Having consumers who are socialized to approach storefronts as spaces for experiences, rather than just places to buy commodities, creates opportunities to leverage those expectations for political gain. For instance, when people shop online, they usually already know what product they want to buy. By contrast, consumers often choose brick-and-mortar locations when what they want is the sensation of discovery. According to Oren Teicher, CEO of the American Booksellers Association, "the discovery of books happens in physical shops."[63] Author and bookseller Emma Straub agrees. "When you walk through a bookstore . . . you see a cover that looks amazing, of a book you've never heard of by a person you've never heard of, and you pick it up, and you flip it over, and you read what it's about, and maybe you buy it. And that doesn't really happen online."[64] Many consumers value this experience, and they go to physical bookstores for the feeling of being surprised.

This consumer demand for the experience of surprise creates an opportunity for political organizing. Browsing in physical spaces is different from searching electronic databases where users are required to enter search terms in advance. Entering search terms only works when people already know what they are looking for, which limits open-ended exploration. In the words of one lesbian feminist, "I didn't know what to call myself, and I didn't know what name worked for me. . . . I'd look through all the books . . . [hoping] maybe to find something that sounded familiar . . . that resonated with my experience . . . trying to find a language for myself."[65] The limitations of keyword searches are even more pronounced for people who are not actively looking for progressive ideas but who may warm to them if they stumbled across them by accident. For people not already immersed in social movement lingo, it can be difficult to uncover that language online.

Activist-entrepreneurs overcome these limitations by displaying arrays of potential topics of interest for exploration and discovery. For collective members with Red Emma's, these arrays expose people to ideas they may not have thought to search for. "Even as the internet has made getting access to radical information easier, the physical presence of an infoshop can help pop 'filter bubbles,' exposing people to new ideas."[66] Similarly for Alan Chelak with PAT @ Giovanni's Room, "You don't know you want to read a book because you don't know it exists, but when you come into the store . . . we try to set it up so these are the first kinds of things we see." These strategies translate consumer demands for the experience of exploration into an opportunity not only to raise money by providing those experiences but also to raise awareness about progressive politics, especially among people who may not have intended to seek it out in advance.

Alongside the sensory experience of feeling surprised, a second subset of marketable experiences involves constructing feelings of social connectedness. Experience economy retailers target this subgroup by changing the way consumers interact both with sales staff and with fellow shoppers. Pine and Gilmore use the example of Barnes & Noble to illustrate this dynamic. In the 1990s, the CEO of this chain bookstore "realized that people visited bookstores for the same reason they go to the theater: for the social experience."[67]

One way to give consumers social experiences is through "third place" retailing, which emphasizes conviviality.[68] For Laura Miller, booksellers nurture convivial environments partly as a marketing ploy and partly in response to a deeply felt sentiment that "community service and community embeddedness has become an integral function" of brick-and-mortar retailing.[69] These strategies exploit nostalgia for "a 'lost world' of local communal structures and solidarity."[70] This nostalgia orients shoppers' behaviors even when it is more fiction than fact. Shopping then becomes less about buying commodities and more about experiencing social connections.

Having customers who present themselves as people seeking community creates opportunities for activists to build political alliances. By providing the convivial atmospheres consumers demand, activists can use conviviality to invite people to feel connected to radical politics. Building this sense of political community is one reason collective members with Red Emma's combined their bookstore with a coffee shop, event space, computer lab, restaurant, classroom, and bar. They wanted to give people a place where, in addition to finding radical information, "they could also come in and just find community . . . and have a one-on-one conversation with someone working behind the bar." These interactions facilitate frame alignment "because you can't hang around a bunch of anarchists for too long before you start to understand some of those politics, and hopefully get excited about them."[71]

Providing lingering amenities like armchairs and beverages expands the range of people likely to spend time in radical spaces. These tactics boost sales as well, but the bridge-building opportunities are equally important. For Sam Gould with Beyond Repair, "the ruse of, 'this is a marketplace, we sell these books,' is really a hook to bring people in." Bringing people in is likewise why Matt Dineen with Wooden Shoe wants to expand the bookstore to include snacks. Since "only certain people are attracted to books . . . if you have coffee and food, that draws people in. Like, 'Oh yeah, coffee. Awesome.' And then you can introduce people to radical ideas in a more sneaky way."

People bond during these face-to-face interactions. For Greg Newton with the Bureau of General Services, "to talk to someone by typing, or even Skyping . . . it's alienating. It doesn't feel completely real." By contrast, face-to-face interactions deepen the experience. "To be in the same physical space with someone and see their body language and facial expression and hear tone of voice . . . that's so important." These conversations become more than the tectonic interactions of people passing blithely by. Instead, they encourage people who are not familiar with radical ideas but who are socialized to perceive retail as a community space to evaluate movement-oriented businesses not merely for their commodity offerings and price competitiveness but also as potential sites of membership and belonging.

These community-building functions supplement search and discovery because, even when exploration happens online, it rarely stays there. For Alan Chelak with PAT @ Giovanni's Room, many young people explore sexuality on the internet. "Then you find out about this store, and you're like, 'Oh, there's a physical space I can go to, I don't have to be alone on my phone, or on the computer.' And so when you make that discovery, then you set out to the physical space." Community building happens through social media as well, but online interactions come with many challenges. The impersonal nature reduces empathy and encourages "flame wars."[72] Digital platforms are male-dominated.[73] They also exclude the millions of older, low-income, and minority residents who lack regular internet access.[74] By contrast, activist-entrepreneurs use physical places to circumvent some of these limitations, which creates opportunities to build political ties.

In conclusion, I revisit these themes of affinity and belonging in more detail in chapter 7. As a precursor, I used this section to first understand how consumer society socializes people to approach retail stores not merely as places to buy necessities but also as places to experience discovery and camaraderie. These consumer attitudes generate opportunities not only to boost sales but also to invite people to imagine themselves as potential members of the radical left. Studying activist entrepreneurship reveals what activists hope to gain by not only constructing contentious spaces but also by constructing them using market-based formats. Building on these themes, the next chapter explains the added value of organizing these businesses around print.

CHAPTER 3

Reinventing Activist Bookstores
in a Corporate Digital Age

NELL TAYLOR FOUNDED THE READ/WRITE LIBRARY in 2006 as an anarchist-inspired tool for advancing radical inclusion. The library contains a limited selection of trade books and corporate newspapers, but most of the collection comes from more humble sources. This humble material includes self-published poems, novels, pamphlets, and zines. It includes community plans, oral histories, and neighborhood newsletters. There are literary magazines from high school students and state prison inmates. There are also self-published cookbooks from settlement houses and parish churches.[1] For Taylor, "These are the kinds of documents that normally wouldn't survive" but that "matter for understanding the culture."

The Read/Write Library is a volunteer-run nonprofit operated by "underemployed" librarians who "got into library science because they wanted to make a difference," including by intervening in the politics of knowledge. "People in power have made a decision to exclude the things that we have here." Elites are socialized to believe their documents have value, which is why they routinely donate personal and professional records to institutions and why similar documents from marginalized groups are absent. For disadvantaged residents, "your story [and] your neighborhood's been left out of the discussion. It's been left out of the record. For reasons." Reasons of racism, classism, sexism, homophobia, and capitalism. The Read/Write Library disrupts "this self-reinforcing cycle" of libraries normalizing privilege by getting marginalized material "back in the record." This unfiltered inclusion gives people "a different angle on what Chicago is," and it encourages underrepresented groups to believe "maybe something that I have has value."

The library changed its name in 2011 to enhance the legitimacy of its documents and the communities they represent. It was originally called the Chicago Underground Library, but that name interfered with radical

The common area at the Read/Write Library in Chicago, Illinois, makes archival material accessible to readers without requiring special permission or handling. Photograph by Kristan Lieb, 2017; courtesy of the Read/Write Library.

inclusion. "Using the word 'underground' implied that the documents were 'Other' in some way. Although society did in fact Other them, the authors generally intended their documents to be seen and read, not marginalized." By contrast, the new name, Read/Write Library, asserts people's rights to participate in public discourse. "Instead of a library that's read only, like a public library, it's a library that's rewriteable. So you can come and add your story to the collection and change the shape of your neighborhood's history."

Another way volunteers foster inclusion involves programming that makes books and archives feel welcoming to nontraditional users. Volunteers organize "super-fun, really participatory, hands-on" events like "Loud Library" dance parties and jazz sessions. They built a book launch catapult to literally "shoot books down the street." They host science fair exhibits of unpublished work "to get people talking" through a playful format "that was slightly ridiculous." They also developed "a puppet show called 'Is death your friend?' And it was a skull puppet and an archivist sock puppet having a conversation about whether you should save things or whether you should throw them away and let them die." These events are "not the kind of thing" a public librarian "would ever be allowed to do in her day job."

These events help pay for space. The Read/Write Library was initially itinerant. "Because we didn't have any money, we were just thrown to the wind and at the whims of whoever would be cool with having a library in their space for any period of time." After six years and six borrowed homes, Taylor signed the library's first commercial lease for a converted storefront in 2011. Alongside periodic book sales, the library raises money by renting out its space for weddings, workshops, and concerts, as well as by collecting voluntary memberships from people who enjoy co-working in the space. Although acquiring commercial space was difficult, "when you do have a space, then the space can begin to help pay for itself."

Constructing durable space is important not only financially but also politically. "It's super, super important," Taylor explains, for social movement archives to have tangible documents and physical addresses. "A big part of it is credibility for the publications. There's really something about the authority and presence a library conveys for people." Credibility matters because people use documents to settle disputes. Compared to the random filing cabinets in people's basements or the online blogs of history nerds, which are easily dismissed as unreliable or irrelevant, physical libraries with material archives conform to social conventions of what reputable historic institutions are supposed to look like. Because the Read/Write Library conforms to those expectations, when conflicts arise surrounding real estate development or public policy making, vulnerable residents can go to elected officials and say, "No, that thing that you're doing is problematic in our neighborhood" because of this historical pattern, and then they "have this authoritative record" in a physical archive to back it up. This stamp of approval, certifying the documents and validating their messages, is "not the same kind of effect you would get if something was just digitized."

Conversations like this one at the Read/Write Library underscore the connections between space, print, and activism. As a social movement repertoire, activists construct counterspaces organized around print. Arranging documents in bookstores and archives confers legitimacy on alternative publications. It disrupts the silencing effects of state-regulated print capitalism by certifying unsanctioned writers and their nonnormative perspectives. This repertoire of combining place, text, and activism changes over time. Places like the Read/Write Library inherit techniques from the radical bookstores of the 1960s and 1970s, but instead of operating for-profit businesses selling books to pay for space, activist-entrepreneurs today are equally likely to construct nonprofit ventures selling space to pay for books. Despite this difference, the pattern of reading and writing as an act of resistance persists, and activists construct these spaces as labors of love.

With examples like the Read/Write Library in mind, this chapter explores two questions. The first question is, Why print? What do activists gain by constructing spaces organized around publications as opposed to bicycles, music, or coffee? To answer this question, the first half of this chapter summarizes the history of radical publishing and bookselling, which explains the legitimizing function of print objects in Western culture. Historically, print capitalism is a governing tool integrating people into shared functional units, including oppressive ones organized around race, class, and gender. In response, unauthorized authors circulate competing perspectives in book-like formats. Activist-entrepreneurs distribute this material through radical bookstores, reading rooms, and libraries, which then double as counterpublic spaces for gathering and organizing. As a social movement repertoire, these strategies take print—a privileged tool of political authority—and repurpose it to disseminate and validate political critique. Although scholars disagree about the relative influence of print-based action repertoires, this pattern repeats in nearly every major progressive social movement across the twentieth century, which suggests a widespread consensus that the repertoire has value.

After analyzing this history, my second question is, What do print-based repertoires look like today? I raise this question because many people assume books, bookstores, and libraries are antiquated. Answering this question requires explaining how print-based movement spaces remain viable in the era of corporate superstores and online retailing. Activist-entrepreneurs in the 1960s and 1970s favored the independent bookstore model, which worked financially until the 1990s when industry restructuring drove two-thirds of indies out of business. Indies are rebounding since 2009, but not because old business models are regaining viability. Instead, this partial resurgence is occurring because entrepreneurs are reformatting as events-oriented, nonprofit hybrids. Other trends like ethical consumerism help as well, but business restructuring—

alongside volunteerism and self-sacrifice—plays a larger role in construct-ing financially viable movement spaces.

Analyzing these constructive dynamics provides an important anti-dote to the usual narratives of decline. I agree that the rise of corporate conglomerates, digital media, and online bookselling has changed the industry and that independent bookstores are casualties of these trends. This decline makes it difficult for activists to continue using business mod-els from the past. However, focusing only on the postmortem of victims misses an equally important opportunity to study why some places sur-vive and thrive. By looking at stories of resilience and innovation, scholars and activists can potentially find the nuggets of a blueprint for emerging business models that make independent spaces viable, even in a corporate, digital age.

Print Capitalism Is a Tool of Oppression

The image of castaways finding solace and inspiration in libraries is one of my favorite cultural tropes. In Betty Smith's *A Tree Grows in Brooklyn,* Roald Dahl's *Matilda,* Shulem Deen's *All Who Go Do Not Return,* and Charlotte Brontë's *Jane Eyre,* repressed and misunderstood main char-acters take refuge in books and, through reading, find paths to brighter futures. The process is risky. These characters get mocked for their book-ishness, hit with flying books, and ostracized for reading unsanctioned material. These dangers reveal the disciplinary structure surrounding print objects. Only certain people are supposed to read, only certain topics are deemed acceptable, and conforming to these expectations stabilizes sys-tems of power.

For people like myself who loved and continue to love the romantic stories of readers using books to break free of restrictive life circumstances, it can feel uncomfortable to acknowledge the long historical association between print and oppression. As I explain in this section, writing has historically been a tool of governing and administration for city-states,[2] nation-states,[3] and empires.[4] Although the rise of print capitalism also had democratizing effects, it nevertheless facilitated new methods of rule.

Benedict Anderson's analysis of print capitalism provides a histori-cal perspective on the relationship between books and governing. Print capitalism is an apt phrase describing the commodification of writing and reading as opposed to older uses of texts as sacred objects or account led-gers. The rise of print capitalism is the rise of a system of authors, pub-lishers, and distributors who mass-produce comparatively inexpensive volumes written in vernacular languages for profit.[5] The invention of the printing press in the fifteenth century is an important part of the story because it reduced publishing costs, but the printing press had social consequences as well. One social consequence was that it stabilized lan-guage. While language changed quickly in the twelfth through sixteenth centuries, by the seventeenth century, the burgeoning mechanical repro-duction of standardized print slowed the rate of change, which made text available to readers several centuries after it was written.[6] Another social consequence was the integration of communities. People whose vernacu-lar languages previously kept them apart now had a written language in common, which "created unified fields of exchange and communication."[7] These new capacities to speak across both time and space "made it pos-sible for rapidly growing numbers of people to think about themselves, and to relate themselves to others, in profoundly new ways."[8]

This integrative potential is a powerful governing tool. Print capitalism enhanced rulers' capacities to organize people into economic, cultural, and political units. Although this capacity was not necessarily anticipated in advance, once it was realized, it was "consciously exploited in a Machia-vellian spirit."[9] In the sixteenth century, print capitalism was such a power-ful weapon in European religious wars that the king of France instituted a "ban on the printing of any books in his realm—on pain of death by hang-ing!"[10] In the eighteenth century, print commodities became a cornerstone of the British educational system, which, through the endless drilling of the managerial class, "work[ed] upon the population individually and continuously to make them into efficient parts of the [capitalist] produc-tive process."[11] Similarly, in the twentieth century, print technology was crucial to the communist movement in China where all soldiers carried copies of Mao's *Little Red Book* in their breast pockets that, when waved in the air during political rallies, "made the square resemble a field ablaze with butterflies."[12]

These political histories socialized people to associate print with au-thority. In a society where people are taught to defer to "the art and authority of writing,"[13] having an idea appear in print confers legitimacy, oftentimes even more legitimacy than the content of the writing itself.[14] Print com-modities written by experts in professionally bound volumes distributed by commercial presses "appear as something apart from life itself, a sepa-rate realm of instruction, representation, and truth."[15] Books and archives have a certifying effect. Certification in social movement theory involves "the validation of actors, their performances, and their claims by external authorities,"[16] including through cultural landscapes that normalize world-views. In Western culture, the authority associated with print objects pro-vides a stamp of certification on ideas privileged enough to get included in mass-produced volumes. These deferential attitudes also simultaneously stigmatize other modes of communication, such as working-class pam-phlets and indigenous oral histories, where non-book-like presentations implicitly discredit nonprivileged ideas.[17]

Because of the political power of print, a significant amount of energy goes into policing it to maintain the print-backed "division between the leaders and led."[18] One way authorities control print capitalism involves controlling who can read. In the antebellum era, "slaves were forbidden to read, and their owners could be punished for teaching them."[19] Women were often encouraged to be illiterate as well because "a woman who could read might threaten the social order . . . whether in private homes or in national politics."[20] When women were literate, informal gender codes po-liced access to information, for instance by giving men implicit permission to peruse newspapers with economic and political content while restrict-ing women to the emotional content of novels and poetry.[21]

Another way authorities control print capitalism involves controlling what people write. One disciplinary tool involves government legislation re-quiring publications to include author names. "This state-sanctioned form of literary identity *stripped* authors of their real individuality, subject as they now were to write within the established limits, at pain of censorship or prosecution."[22] Another disciplinary tool involves censorship laws prohibit-ing writing on unruly topics. Publishers in the 1910s and 1920s developed partial work-arounds to censorship laws by releasing provocative material in "limited edition" runs. Small print runs were more expensive than larger ones, which gave privileged readers access to material while keeping it away from others. "By virtue of their cost and high quality, such books, it was ar-gued, were not intended to corrupt those regarded as the most susceptible to their salacious influences (women and the working classes)."[23]

A third way authorities control print capitalism involves regulating distri-bution. A handful of examples illustrates this common trend. In the 1950s, booksellers with City Lights were arrested and charged with "willfully printing and selling lewd and indecent material" when they sold copies of Allen Ginsberg's *Howl* to young-looking undercover agents.[24] In the 1980s, Gay's the Word in London faced up to 100,000 pounds in potential financial losses when government officials arrested its booksellers, impounded their books, and threatened them with hefty fines for distributing queer material imported from Philadelphia.[25] Around the same time, the American Civil Liberties Union fought to get literature with queer themes into U.S. prisons. "Federal prison regulations allow prison administrators to ban sexually explicit materials from inmates," and many homophobic wardens assumed all "gay content" was inherently erotic.[26]

Throughout this history, different forms of print media came with different levels of social legitimacy. As Nicholas Thoburn explains, people are conditioned to associate different forms of print with specific types of information and levels of credibility.[27] Books are especially privileged because they often embody the authoritative speech of elites. Alongside books, other print objects include "book-like creations,"[28] such as newsletters, pamphlets, and zines. These less expensive and often self-published objects have a lower barrier to entry, which makes them a more democratic medium for political debate. Newspapers, pamphlets, and zines also serve different functions than books, for instance by communicating exploratory ideas quickly, cheaply, and in unmediated formats.[29] The downside, however, is that these publications on the fringes of print capitalism convey ideas with less authority than books.

The boundaries of legitimate publishing change over time. Paperbacks, for example, are now ubiquitous in the publishing industry. But until the 1950s, they "weren't considered real books by the book trade" and were instead dismissed as the dumping grounds for uncredentialed, sensationalist writers who might be entertaining but who were not taken seriously as public intellectuals.[30] Zines are undergoing a similar assimilation process today. After decades of being relegated to the subcultural fringe, the punk aesthetic of graphic novels is now a mainstay of corporate publishing. Additionally, many universities are now assembling zine libraries, and some college professors now include zines as required reading on course syllabi.[31] However, going mainstream is not the same as gaining political acceptance. Corporate publishers adopted paperback technology and zine aesthetics without necessarily adopting those genres' rebellious political content.[32] These stylistic changes diversify commodities without destabilizing print's regulatory effects.

Radical Publishing and Bookselling Are
Social Movement Repertoires

Most bookstores and libraries normalize the social, economic, and politial conventions reproduced through print capitalism. These venues collect publications and arrange them according to social regulations governing race, class, gender, sexuality, and violence.[33] However, the intense will to police print objects also speaks to their revolutionary potential. Radical booksellers and librarians sometimes describe feeling as though they are on the front lines of knowledge wars. For Nell Taylor with the Read/Write Library, radical librarians are "at the forefront of . . . making sure their users are free to read whatever they wanna read without fear of reprisal." For Carrie Barnett with People Like Us, "librarians are the most radical people you will ever meet because they will defend to the death the right of anyone to read any book they want." These sentiments reflect a belief that reading has political consequences and that censoring print is inherently unjust.

However, before waxing overly romantic, I want to acknowledge that scholars disagree about whether radical publishing is a significant social movement tool. On one side are people who celebrate its emancipatory potential. For feminist scholars, "Those in power have always known that subversive reading material can fuel a revolution."[34] For queer liberation scholars, "the [19]60s revolutions were built out of books."[35] For Black liberation activists, literary canons containing the "right information" are politically empowering because "people who don't know their history make excellent slaves, regardless of the type of slavery or time period."[36] For anarchist organizers, radical publishers provide "practical and intellectual tools to help people organize. Books aren't the only means of doing that, but they're an important part."[37]

However, other scholars feel that these statements are overblown. For critics, when it comes to fighting the revolution, "writing and publishing are in fact rather *ineffectual* political means."[38] One criticism is that radical publishing lacks authority. Manifesto writers have a lot of passion, but their claim to authority "is wholly fabricated" with "no basis in existent institutional power."[39] Another criticism is that other mediums—like theater, music, and film—may overshadow books and newspapers as tools for disseminating ideas.[40] A third criticism is that radical publications are fleeting. "With one or two notable exceptions publications and organizations in this sector have almost all been short-lived," the assumption being that ephemerality limits impact.[41] A final criticism is that subversive publishing is not institutionalized. Unlike authorized texts, which society drills into people through public schools, Sunday schools, and mass media, unauthorized texts circulate in a contingent, discontinuous manner with limited systemic effects.[42]

I agree that these are significant caveats and that radical publishing does not automatically change the world. However, the same can be said of any social movement repertoire. Petitions, lawsuits, and rallies often go nowhere,[43] but that does not stop people from doing them, nor do those tactics always fail. In a similar manner, although I agree that radical publishing is no silver bullet, I found no reason to suspect it fails with any greater frequency than other social movement tactics. Additionally, nearly every major social movement in the twentieth century involved print capitalism. This ubiquitously repeating pattern of unauthorized writers circulating contentious ideas in book-like formats suggests that activists believe this repertoire has merit.

Katie Renz's account of anarchist publishing provides an early example of this social movement repertoire. In this extended quote, Renz writes that anarchist publishing

> has roots in the French Revolution of 1848, during which Pierre-Joseph Proudhon, whose writings form a basis for anarchist doctrine, edited four radical newspapers, all subsequently destroyed by government censorship. Later in the 19th century, Peter Kropotkin, another anarchist heavyweight, founded a magazine called *Freedom*, along with Freedom Press, which continues to churn out radical works today. In the United States in the early 20th century, Emma Goldman started *Mother Earth*; Alexander Berkman had *The Blast*. Immigrant anarchist communities, trade unions, and writerly revolutionaries, in America and abroad, made pamphlets detailing manifestos and political visions a common currency.[44]

The pattern of using alternative publishing to build social movements repeats in the 1930s and 1940s class struggles. As an example, the cultural side of the Depression-era labor movement involved the proletarian literature of the Popular Front. This "proletarian avant-garde" had its own print genre, including "dozens of experimental magazines publishing proletarian stories, poems, and manifestos" that "marked the opening of a class war"[45] fought not only in factories but also on the pages of American culture. Similarly, from the 1920s until the 1950s, communist bookstores and reading rooms stocking Marx, Lenin, the *Daily Worker,* and the *Monthly Review* operated in every major American city. International political parties supported these sectarian reading rooms, which "were one of the most important public spaces for Marxism in the United States in the twentieth century."[46]

This pattern repeats again in the 1960s counterculture. The paperback revolution slashed production costs, "striking a blow on behalf of working class readers and all those of low-income—students, struggling writers, and artists—who could not afford higher-priced hardcover books."[47] The indymedia movement likewise critiqued government propaganda and postwar conformity. "In the four short years from 1965–1969, the subversive press grew from five small newspapers in five cities in the United States to more than 500 newspapers—with millions of readers—all over the world."[48] This burgeoning alternative press movement included newspapers, fanzines, posters, and comix addressing everything on the radical left, from the Black Panthers and Stonewall Riots to hippies, drugs, and sex in the streets.[49] New paperback bookstores like Kepler's and Peace Eye distributed this non-bourgeois literature. Those booksellers also constructed counterpublic spaces where nonconformists "could gather in peace without being harassed."[50]

The Black liberation movement embraced this print-based repertoire as well. "Between 1965 and 1979, the number of Black-themed bookstores in the United States skyrocketed from around a dozen to somewhere between seventy-five and one hundred."[51] Most of the owners were Black liberationists with direct ties to the Black Panther Party, Congress of African Peoples, Student Nonviolent Coordinating Committee, Communist Party, or the United Negro Improvement Association.[52] They used their bookstores to reclaim Black history from European perspectives. "An African proverb says, 'Until lions have their own historians, tales of the hunt shall always glorify the hunter.'"[53] As an alternative to white narratives, liberation bookstores consolidated a self-determined cultural and political canon. Liberation bookstores were also places to talk and organize. "With their devotion to radicalism and Black nationalism," Black-themed bookstores "represented a new generation of politically oriented public spaces available to African Americans."[54]

The feminist movement followed a similar pattern. The first wave of women-owned bookstores in the 1910s and 1920s were not necessarily radical in content, but they constructed new entry points into the male-dominated realms of urban space and public discourse.[55] By comparison, the second wave of feminist booksellers were explicitly political. Between 1968 and 1973, at the start of the Women in Print Movement, over five hundred progressive publications on gender and sexuality appeared nationwide.[56] "The women's liberation movement became a print movement out of necessity. In the late 1960s, little of what we needed to know was available in any written form. When we did get coverage in mainstream publications, our ideas were distorted and trivialized."[57] Feminist writers and publishers countered disempowerment by providing information on sexual harassment, job discrimination, and women's health.[58] Feminist booksellers supported the movement by distributing this material. "Starting in the early 1970s . . . women's bookstores started to open—at first in only a few major cities, and then throughout the country."[59] The movement included nine bookstores in 1973, sixty bookstores in 1978, and 135 bookstores in the early 1990s.[60] Feminist booksellers communicated through industry newsletters as well, where they coordinated letter-writing campaigns and promoted antiracist feminist ethics. "This advocacy work made feminist bookstores different from chain bookstores and other independents."[61]

This pattern of radical publishing and bookselling repeats again in the movement for queer liberation. Before the development of a comprehensive queer canon, only a handful of books touched on queer themes, and they were "stories of pain, shame, degradation, self-loathing, revulsion and, quite often, death. . . . This was the way our lives were described for us."[62] Queer writers challenged homophobic narratives by filling pages with coming-out stories, progressive psychology, and non-stigmatizing information about AIDS. Activist booksellers like Carrie Barnett with People Like Us disseminated this material. "People would say stuff to us like, 'Oh, your bookstore's really literary.'" This backhanded compliment reflects people's surprise that gay literature could be more than porn or smut and could instead look just as intellectual and legitimate as straight people's books. Alongside distributing and certifying queer-positive ideas, activist booksellers also constructed queer public space. For Lynn Mooney with Women & Children First, "This store on a Friday or Saturday night, it's a real gathering place." Bookstores were hot spots for the new "out" culture where people could ask questions and cultivate relationships at a time when "LGBTQ people weren't necessarily comfortable in every retail environment." For queer folks surrounded by a homophobic public, these books and spaces "were the politics of liberation incarnate."[63]

Activists used publications, reading rooms, and bookstores as social movement tools even though the process was difficult. One challenge was a shortage of cash. Feminists started Women & Children First even though women at the time could not access bank credit or open checking accounts without a father or husband cosigning. Another challenge was a shortage of books. It took time to build insurgent canons, which is why Giovanni's Room "opened in the 1970s with just a few dozen books,"[64] which the owners drove from New York to Philadelphia once a month in the back of a borrowed car.[65] A third challenge was negative public opinion. At People Like Us, "Our landlord wanted to have a clause in our lease that said we would only sell books that were in good taste." Even after striking that disciplinary clause, they were concerned they would get shut down by the police for obscenity simply because the commodities were queer. A final challenge was group infighting. At BookWoman, for example, half of the collective left during a dispute over whether men should be allowed to share the feminist space.[66]

As these examples show, the social movement pattern of unauthorized writers circulating contentious ideas in book-like forms was never easy. That so many people in so many movements did it anyway underscores the repertoire's importance. Radical publishing and bookselling integrate activist communities across time and space. They construct platforms for awareness raising, frame alignment, and movement coordination. Using print as a constructive tool is not the only option. Activist-entrepreneurs construct counterspace in other ways as well, for instance by selling coffee or repairing bicycles. However, the integrative and legitimizing functions of print add something extra to the mix, which many activists use to their advantage.

Industry Restructuring Led to the Decline of Independent Bookstores

That's the history, but what about emerging trends? Most of the communist, feminist, and Black liberation businesses that were part of these twentieth-century campaigns no longer exist. Some movement spaces buckled under political pressure, such as when McCarthy-era harassment crushed communist bookstores.[67] Others became victims of their own success, such as when feminist and African American authors gained more mainstream acceptance, which lessened the need for separatist spaces.[68]

Although the closure of activist counterspaces is significant to individual movements, the action repertoire of unauthorized writers circulating contentious ideas in book-like formats transcends specific movement scenes. According to social movement scholars, "Mass protest movements tend to come in 'bursts,' 'cycles,' or 'waves.'"[69] Repertoires, by contrast, are recurring tactics that activists use in many times and places. From these perspectives, the closure of Black, feminist, and communist bookstores is normal and expected, even as print-based repertoires live on. New movements emerge with evolving literary canons, and activists use this material to construct new variants of counterpublic spaces.

However, starting in the 1990s, many print-based movement spaces began closing for another reason: the financial model of independent bookselling was crumbling. Twentieth-century activist-entrepreneurs sold books to pay rent, which made it economically feasible to construct counterpublic spaces. If industry restructuring drives indies out of business, activists cannot continue using this business model, no matter how many new movement waves emerge.

The story of industry restructuring is a story of simultaneous growth and decline. In absolute numbers, the publishing industry dramatically expanded during the second half of the twentieth century. By 2000, it had become a quarter of the size of the agricultural industry.[70] The number of new titles published annually increased from 50,000 titles in 1980 to 200,000 titles in 1998 and 316,000 titles in 2010.[71] In 2017, the number of books sold in the United States was 687 million.[72]

This growth coincided with industry consolidation. For Ted Striphas, "The relatively small and genteel publishing houses of the early twentieth century seem quaint compared to the cutthroat multimedia conglomerates that now control 80 percent (and counting) of the book trade in the United States."[73] This consolidation was simultaneously about growth and decline. For John Thompson, mergers and acquisitions in the publishing industry led to a "polarization of the field,"[74] squeezing midsize publishers out of the market. The resulting landscape includes a few corporations dominating the market alongside many micropublishers—often one-man bands—with undercapitalized businesses overlooked by mainstream media and dependent on expensive third-party contractors for storage and distribution.[75]

These dual dynamics of consolidation and fragmentation in the publishing industry also occurred in the bookselling industry. After World War II, with production costs falling and consumer incomes rising, companies began selling books in mall-based stores like Walden's in the 1960s, in big-box stores like Borders in the 1980s, and through online retailing like Amazon.com in the early 2000s.[76] Using economies of scale, corporations could offer discounts that indies could not match. Other superstores, like Walmart and Costco, began selling books as well, often as loss leaders to attract shoppers who then purchased more lucrative items, like clothing and tires. Similarly, online retailer Amazon.com sold books at the cost price, forgoing a profit, both to promote e-reader sales, which were profitable, and to consolidate a customer base for its non-book products.[77]

These industry changes undercut independent booksellers who did not enjoy the same economies of scale and who did not have other commodities on offer. Until about 1980, industry growth lifted all boats, albeit in an uneven manner. Independent bookstores still grew in absolute numbers, although at a slower rate than corporate competitors. As a result, despite this growth, indies experienced a relative decrease in market share, which sank from 72 percent of trade book sales in 1958 to 40 percent in 1980.[78] Indie growth rates then leveled off in the 1980s, and, by the mid-1990s, the industry was shrinking in both absolute and relative terms. In absolute numbers, the estimated number of independent bookstores nationwide peaked at around 5,000 stores in the 1990s, then fell to 3,200 in 2004 and fell again to 1,650 in 2009.[79] In relative terms, indie market share dropped from 40 percent in 1980 to 23 percent in 2000, then fell again to 13 percent in 2006.[80]

With independent bookselling contracting so severely, many people felt indies were a thing of the past. In an era of corporate capitalism and online retailing, independent bookstores appeared "dead,"[81] "doomed,"[82] "endangered,"[83] and "terminally ill."[84] For Larry Robin with Robin's Bookstore, online bookselling "has cut into the traffic to such a point . . . that the business model of running a bookstore—probably the business model of all [brick-and-mortar] retail—is broke."[85] Catherine Bohne with Community Bookstore said, "I've gambled and staked everything I have, including every last asset [and] every ounce of my energy" on running an independent bookstore, but "it seems it isn't enough to make things work."[86] Similarly, for Karen Johnson with Marcus Books, being a bookseller is similar "to being a sharecropper—'You don't make enough on the sale of one book [to buy] another book.'"[87]

Activists using the independent bookstore model were likewise mired in these trends. In the 1990s and 2000s, two-thirds of Black-owned bookstores closed.[88] The number of feminist bookstores decreased by 90 percent.[89] Anarchist, anticapitalist, and queer liberation bookstores also closed, and the ones that stayed open struggled to survive. As an example illustrating this ubiquitous trend, BookWoman had "a severe cash crisis"[90] in 2004, which repeated again in 2007, leading to an emergency fundraising soiree to raise the $25,000 needed to keep the bookstore open.[91] Likewise, In Other Words "almost died" in 2008, and "the crisis made In Other Words' board of directors realize their old model wasn't going to cut it in this dire financial climate."[92] Similarly, Common Language began hosting its annual "Last Bookstore Standing" fundraiser and silent auction in 2010 to help with the "economic pain" and "financial woes" of independent retailing.[93]

The activist-entrepreneurs I interviewed in 2016 and 2017 echoed these sentiments. At Revolution NYC, "We cannot survive by selling books alone. . . . We're not even breaking even." At Burning Books, "We really work to stay open to keep doing this as long as we can . . . So many of these projects are open just for a short amount of time. Then they fizzle out." Experiences like these suggest that the decline of the New Left–era social movement bookstores may be more than the end of a movement wave. Instead, the data suggests that the decline may correspond with the end of an activist repertoire. This decline could conceivably mark the end of the financial opportunity for activists to use print capitalism and independent bookselling as tools for constructive placemaking.

Partial Revivals and Reinventions Are Emerging

Although independent bookselling was never easy, industry restructuring brought it to a game-changing precipice in the 1990s and 2000s. Independent retailers could not continue business as usual. Instead, surviving in this capitalist meat grinder meant getting creative, abandoning conventional business practices, and finding other ways to keep venues financially viable.

After reaching a nadir in 2009, the number of independent bookstores began to grow again with an estimated 22 percent increase between 2009 and 2015.[94] In light of these strong numbers, some commentators struck a triumphant tone. In 2010, the *New York Times* heralded "the surprising resurgence of indie bookselling."[95] In 2014, *Salon* declared, "Stop carving that gravestone. Brick-and-mortar bookstores aren't dead, yet. On the contrary, independently owned bookstores are growing in number."[96] Accounts like these celebrate the "real renaissance of spirit"[97] of indie bookstores that are "quietly resurging across the nation"[98] and "making a comeback,"[99] "like a phoenix from the ashes."[100]

Understanding the reasons for this partial revival requires a shift in focus. Scholars and industry analysts have spent significant energy conducting postmortems of the thousands of bookstores that did not survive. Although I agree that these postmortems are useful and necessary, it helps to look beyond the causes of death to also identify the causes of life. Some independent bookstores did not close, and new independents began opening. However, this partial resurgence is not a revival of the business models of yesteryear. On the contrary, it represents dynamic innovations in small business structures that, if continued, may breathe new life into independent spaces, including activist ones.

In the rest of this chapter, I explore the factors behind this resurgence. However, before getting overly excited, a few caveats are worth mentioning. One caveat is that the rebound may be temporary. As the Great Recession deepened in the late 2000s, big-box stores like Borders went bankrupt, and Barnes & Noble scaled back its operations, which led to the closure of hundreds of bookstores nationwide. These closures created a market vacuum for consumers and an unemployment glut for booksellers, which is why former chain store employees began opening independent businesses of their own. Although successful in the short term, it is unclear whether these indies will last indefinitely or whether new corporate conglomerates in the postrecession era will emerge and eclipse them yet again.

Another caveat is that the market vacuum following the partial decline of big-box stores is uneven. General independents stocking similar titles may get a boost, but activist bookstores carry different selections. Using Rainbow as an example, "At Borders, you could get a vanilla latte with your John Grisham," but "Rainbow leans more toward Noam Chomsky, with an 'I'd Rather Be Smashing Imperialism' bumper sticker on the side."[101] This difference in stock means radical booksellers are not necessarily in direct competition with corporate chains, which creates a comparative advantage but also limits their ability to profit from the spoils.

A third caveat involves potentially inaccurate measures of growth. When newspapers report a rise in the number of independent bookstores, what they are really measuring is a rise in the number of stores associated with the American Booksellers Association (ABA). The ABA is a national trade organization for independent bookstores, and its membership is rising. However, it is unclear whether this trend is exclusively because more independent bookstores are opening or whether it is also occurring because more booksellers are choosing to affiliate themselves with the ABA. In response to the near total collapse of indie bookselling in the 1990s and 2000s, ABA created new support programs and expanded old ones. These programs include the BookSense indie bookstore branding campaign,[102] the Winter Institute indie bookstore trade show,[103] and the ABA's national indie bookstore gift card program.[104] These enhanced services, combined with dire economic straits, may motivate a greater share of booksellers to join the trade association, which artificially inflates estimates of growth.

For all these reasons, although I appreciate the image of independent bookstores rising from the ashes, I take a somewhat tempered view. A revival of sorts is certainly underway, but interviews and archives suggest this revival is still partial and precarious. Independent bookselling remains difficult, especially for activists, and I don't want to minimize their struggles by suggesting otherwise. However, my intention in acknowledging these challenges is less about resigning to fatalism and more about underscoring the need to keep innovating so independent bookstores—activist or otherwise—can remain open.

Indie Bookstores Diversify and Take a Nonprofit Turn

Looking beyond numbers to instead analyze structures shows that the partial revival of independent bookstores is not a resurgence of old business models. Instead, the revival involves substantial industry innovations. These innovations help small print-based businesses coexist alongside superstores and online vendors by generating new and noncompeting revenue streams. Indies, like their competitors, now also sell non-book commodities. However, unlike their competitors, indie businesses also supplement their revenue by becoming nonprofits.

First, one of the biggest structural changes is that physical bookstores—

both indies and otherwise—aren't really about books anymore. I say this somewhat facetiously because of course bookstores still sell books and of course books remain central to the identity of these spaces. There has nevertheless been a fundamental change in the cultural role of brick-and-mortar retailing. For Robert Fader of Posman Books, "The public's opinion of what a bookstore should be has changed quite a bit."[105] Similarly, Andrew Laties urges indie booksellers to "create a new bookstore reality" that so thoroughly reinvents the mold that "perhaps your customers shouldn't even think of you as a bookstore."[106]

If physical bookstores in a digital age are no longer about books, what are they about? Bookstores—both chains and independents—have become less about commodities and more about experiences, emotions, and communities. People get married in bookstores and meet friends for coffee. "Bookstores have become sites of entertainment and sociability, espresso-scented 'third places' where you might pick up a date as well as the latest Stephen King."[107] They are places where people learn how to read and attend resume writing seminars. They host drum circles, wine clubs, support groups, tarot card readings, and live music. They are places to type on laptops in a literary ambiance while sipping tea in the passive company of strangers. They are also places to buy books, but most people go for other reasons.

For activist-entrepreneurs, tapping into these consumer trends means embracing a multitrack revenue stream. Expanding beyond books is less about abandoning print as the core focus and more about finding opportunities for cross-subsidies. Following the general trend in corporate bookselling, some activists supplement book sales with sidelines, which are more profitable. As an example, People Called Women raises half its revenue from mugs, T-shirts, coffee, and other objects sporting feminist slogans or produced by women artisans. Some activist-entrepreneurs sell food. For instance, Firestorm sells ready-made vegan items, which increases foot traffic and augments revenue without the labor intensity of a full-service kitchen.[108] Cross-subsidies also come from complementary businesses in adjacent spaces. For example, the owners of Common Language have supported their bookstore using income from their other business, the gay bar next door.[109]

In addition to sidelines, events are an even better way to diversify revenue. Sister's Uptown generates two-thirds of its income from events like Afro jazz sessions, African folk heritage storytelling, and women's guided meditation circles. Boneshaker hosts fundraising events "set up like a speed date" where participants describe recent reading experiences and a panel of "experts" matches them with progressive reads. Rainbow hosts "author appearances, study groups, poetry readings and mini-concerts to give people an in-store experience they can't get online."[110] Similarly, at the Read/Write Library, Nell Taylor started a Chicago-themed book club, which is their first program "intended to generate revenue, as well as be on mission."

This programming is useful because, at places like Charis, customers "don't want to buy [a book] at full price," but they "still want to browse," and "they are willing to pay for nonprofit programming all day long."[111] Books still matter, but in an online age, brick-and-mortar customers are buying the social experiences constructed around books rather than the books themselves. These social experiences are not available in places like Walmart or Costco, nor are they available online, which gives indies—as well as chains like Barnes & Noble—an edge.

Alongside events, a second, equally significant, structural change is that independent bookstores aren't really stores anymore. Again, I say this somewhat facetiously because of course businesses selling commodities and experiences are stores, and the overwhelming majority are still located in commercial storefronts. There has nevertheless been a fundamental change in the independent bookselling model, most notably through the rise of retail-nonprofit hybrids. These hybrids give independents a competitive edge unavailable to corporate competitors. Instead of running businesses with community functions on the side, many booksellers now run charitable organizations with retail on the side. This new industry model, which emerged in the 1980s and became widespread by the 2010s, helps indies coexist alongside chains like Barnes & Noble and online sellers like Amazon by supplementing revenue with grants and donations.

This macro-level change coincides with the rise of the nonprofit–industrial complex. The nonprofit–industrial complex is an apt phrase describing the tight relationship between corporations, charitable organizations, and social service provisioning. The Tax Reform Act of 1969 creates a mechanism for corporations to reduce their taxes by donating money to private foundations who then distribute it to smaller nonprofits, especially charities with 501(c)(3) tax status. For critics, this change is undemocratic because, instead of corporations paying taxes to governments who redistribute that money through democratic channels, corporations instead donate money with no public oversight to private organizations whose services align with their business objectives.[112] Despite this criticism, by the century's end, organizations involved in social services, community development, and political activism were rapidly reformatting as 501(c)(3)s to be eligible to receive this burgeoning funding.[113]

Small businesses reformatted as well, including independent bookstores. Kepler's is a particularly famous example. Kepler's was founded by a free speech pacifist in 1955 and then became a longstanding countercultural hub. However, after five successful decades, the bookstore began struggling financially. The situation became so dire that Kepler's closed in 2011. However, the closure provoked an outpouring of community support. Donations surged, and the bookstore reopened the following year using the hybrid model of a for-profit bookstore combined with a nonprofit children's literacy arm. "The reason [supporters] loved Kepler's so much [was] all its nonprofit work out in the community. It was an intellectual [and] cultural center. The only way to preserve that was to make that work nonprofit."[114]

Kepler's is a high-profile example of what has become an industry trend of combining bookstore-based events with nonprofit funding. Scores of independent bookstores are now either fully nonprofit or retail–nonprofit hybrids. This includes places like Daybreak in Minneapolis, Open Books in Chicago, Word Up in New York, Bookmarks in Winston-Salem, Readers Bookstore in San Francisco, and More than Words in Boston, just to name a few. The usual justification these kinds of venues use when requesting nonprofit status from the Internal Revenue Service is the cultural, educational, and literacy programming they provide. The primary financial advantage for booksellers is less about receiving tax breaks and more about becoming eligible to receive tax-deductible donations including foundation grants. These grants are not available to corporate competitors, and they help independent bookstores stay open.

Activist-entrepreneurs not only participate in the nonprofit turn, they also helped invent the model. Charis, a feminist bookstore founded in 1971, claims to be among the first independent bookstores to create a nonprofit arm. "Arguably that's the reason the store has been able to escape the fate of so many sister stores that have closed."[115] After two decades of running a successful business, Charis's finances got shaky in the mid-1990s. Around the same time, one of the co-owners was invited to join the advisory board for a queer youth services organization. "Serving on that board, I learned about nonprofits and realized that the programming work we were already doing at Charis was just such educational and social justice work."[116] Based on this insight, in 1996, Charis established a 501(c)(3) events arm, Charis Circle, to raise money for the nearly two hundred events the bookstore hosts each year, as well as to cover a portion of the bookstore's rent.[117]

Charis was not the first feminist bookstore to apply for nonprofit status. BookWoman applied in 1974, but "we were told we were too one-sided. We had books by, about, and for women," which the Internal Revenue Service said was exclusionary. "Where are the men?" Susan Post with Book-Woman felt this question was illogical. Churches have one denomination and are not expected to serve everyone equally. Regardless, in the mid-1970s, "it was unimaginable they would give nonprofit status to a place that men were not necessarily welcome. And we didn't have the money to fight that on appeal." By the early 1980s, however, things were beginning to change as other specialized bookstores began receiving nonprofit status. "So things change, but slowly." By the 2000s, however, the tide had turned, and it was much easier for booksellers—including activist ones—to register as 501(c)(3)s. As one small data point speaking to this change, about half (48 percent) of the venues included in my study operate either entirely as nonprofits or with support from nonprofit arms.

These trends represent less of a change in what activist-entrepreneurs do and more of a change in how they fund their spaces in a corporate and digital age. Activist booksellers always struggled to make a profit, they always relied heavily on donations and volunteer labor, and they always supported education and empowerment. However, the nonprofit–industrial complex created a new vocabulary formalizing these dynamics and augmented the revenue streams. Nonprofit venues retain the longstanding trinity of place, text, and activism, but they invert the business model of previous generations. Instead of selling books to pay for space where activists host social justice events, people sell events to pay for space organized around literature.

This nonprofit turn is undeniably helpful, but before getting overly excited about this new financial model, it is important to acknowledge that, for activists, nonprofit status is not risk-free. One reason it is not risk-free is because the charitable work activists are willing to undertake does not necessarily align with users' and funders' demands. The nonprofit–industrial complex is sometimes called the "shadow state" because it emerged concurrently with the dismantling of the welfare state and the off-loading of government services onto private providers.[118] Independent bookstores absorbed some of these services. For example, after the only public library in Sacramento's Oak Park neighborhood closed, the nonprofit book-store Underground Books became "a gathering place for neighborhood residents" working "to ensure that the students and the community had access to books."[119] Open Books in Chicago adopted a similar role by be-coming a "nonprofit social venture" offering programs that "cultivate the literacy skills of thousands of children and youth each year."[120] Nonprofit bookstores also absorb other social service tasks. For instance, The First Chapter in Leominster, Massachusetts, sells books while also "supporting individuals with developmental and/or intellectual disabilities with their vocational needs."[121]

Although some nonprofit booksellers are comfortable absorbing off-loaded services, these functions do not always align with activist goals. Boxcar volunteers, for instance, wanted to construct an anarchist space, not a social service center. "We are actively trying to convince people that we're not a social service agency. 'No, we do not have access to services for you. No, we do not have extra clothes here. No, we don't have these things.'" Collective members were sympathetic to people needing ser-vices, including the city's homeless population, and they tried to be polite to the scores of people requesting help. But they were not trained as social workers, they did not have an operating budget, and they felt disinclined to act as substitutes for a dismantled welfare state. To get out of this role, volunteers isolated themselves from service organizations. Even though they wanted to support those groups, opening the door even a little un-leashed a flood of demand that became so overwhelming that it crowded out other political goals.

This refusal to accept neoliberal off-loading does not mean activist en-terprises never provide those services. As an example, Housing Works partners with the social enterprise organization AHRC New York City to provide job training for adults with mental illnesses. But according to Nicholas Watson, Housing Works is careful to keep that element of the business contained. By design, the program is small and involves only a few people at a time, which helps Housing Works avoid becoming depen-dent on that alliance. Donor funding helps, but if it disappeared overnight, the overall business would still survive.

This concern about dependency gets at a second reason 501(c)(3) tax status is not risk-free, which is that living on donations makes recipients beholden to donors. Corporate-backed foundations provide the majority of funds surging through the nonprofit–industrial complex. These foundations write large checks, which is appealing, but they also use their financial strings to monitor, manage, control, redirect, and co-opt activism with decidedly anti-egalitarian effects.[122] Examples include revoking funding from activists supporting Palestine and rewarding activists who shift away from direct-action protests and toward more benign forms of organizing. This external discipline explains why many activist-entrepreneurs do not apply for grants and instead prefer to raise money through individual donations, crowdfunding campaigns, and membership drives. These donations arrive in smaller amounts, but the process feels more democratic for people who want to remain accountable to a broad social audience instead of hitching their wagon to one or two corporate-backed foundations.

A third reason 501(c)(3) tax status is not risk-free is because the Internal Revenue Service limits political organizing. For Alan Chelak with PAT @ Giovanni's Room, "As a 501c3 nonprofit organization . . . the store does not engage in any sort of political activism" that would "jeopardize our nonprofit status." The 1954 Johnson Amendment prohibits 501(c)(3) from participating in electoral politics, for instance by endorsing candidates and ballot measures. For scholars like Ruth Wilson Gilmore, these restrictions mean nonprofits operate "without political clout" since they are "forbidden by law to advocate for systemic change," and an organization can "suffer legal consequences if it strays along the way."[123] Fortunately, electoral politics is only one mode of activism, and contentious politics usually has a beyond-the-state focus. Constructing print-based movement spaces is about sparking debate, facilitating learning, providing nurturance, and supporting demonstrations. It is about embedding counterconducts into the rhythms of everyday life. It is rarely about elections.

Three additional caveats are worth mentioning, although they are less widespread than those already described. As one caveat, the IRS requires 501(c)(3)s to have a board of directors, which clashes with some activists' missions. This is why Firestorm became a nonprofit limited liability company instead of a 501(c)(3). For anarchist collective members who want workers and not board members to make decisions, the "ownership structure we require precludes us from applying for 501c3 nonprofit status."[124]

As a second caveat, nonprofits are structurally weak. This is why Leslie James Pickering made Burning Books a corporation, not a nonprofit. In the United States, nonprofits are subjected to government restrictions and disclosure requirements, while corporations are privileged entities with special rights and protections. For Pickering, "These corporate people commit crimes all the time and are never held accountable for it. If we're going to be attacked with indictments and accusations, then we're going to be set up with the same advantages that these other people have."

As a final caveat, nonprofit status is no silver bullet. Going nonprofit helps financially, but it does not save every struggling business. When Rainbow teetered on the edge of bankruptcy in 2014, collective members took steps to become a nonprofit,[125] but the bookstore still closed two years later. Likewise, Wild Iris created its nonprofit events arm in 2006, and the bookstore transitioned to full nonprofit status in 2014, but it still closed due to financial distress three years later.[126] Similarly, after Guide to Kulchur closed in 2016 for financial reasons, it reopened in 2017 as a 501(c)(3) only to close again two years later under allegations of financial mismanagement.[127]

For all these reasons, the nonprofit turn is imperfect. Despite these imperfections, the nonprofit turn combined with event-focused programming is a macro-level innovation breathing new life into independent bookselling. To the extent that these changes make it possible for independent bookstores to function in new guises, including by accessing revenue streams unavailable to corporate and online competitors, activists can continue using indie business models as constructive tools for radical placemaking.

Ethical Consumerism Has Mixed Results

Alongside the embrace of events and nonprofits, another useful trend involves the rise of ethical consumerism. Buy Local campaigns are a frequent talking point in indie bookselling circles. However, despite the popularity of ethical consumerism as a supposed bulwark against chain superstores and online retailers, my findings suggest ethical consumerism is only moderately helpful in sustaining activist counterspaces. As I explain in this section, the ethical consumerism movement is premised on individual consumers disregarding price signals each time they make a purchase. The trouble is, people often forget, or they prefer cheaper options. Buy Local movements are more effective when policymakers incorporate them into the structural landscape of real estate rather than leaving it to individual choice, but these structural reforms are rare. As a result, ethical consumerism appears less effective at sustaining movement enterprises than other industry changes like joining the nonprofit turn.

Ethical consumerism is a social movement tool. The premise is that shopping "is a way to create progressive social change" by "voting with your dollars."[128] This concept frames consumers as political actors who reward ethical companies by buying their products while punishing unethical ones by buying elsewhere. The term ethical consumerism emerged in the early 1990s from social movements devoted to fair trade and sustainability. It has since expanded to include other mantras, like "Buy Local, Buy Union, or Buy Black."[129]

The Buy Local mantra is especially popular among independent booksellers who see it as a way to help indies compete. For Katherine Solheim with Unabridged, "The party line is Buy Local right now. That's the thing that ABA has really come out behind in a very serious way in the last ten or fifteen years." Some activist booksellers support Buy Local campaigns for ideological reasons. At Rainbow, "Our slogan is 'Think globally, buy locally! You have nothing to lose but your chains!'"[130] Indie booksellers also publicize the economic benefits. Studies from across the country comparing independent stores with chain retailing found that, for every $100 spent at an independent business, between $47 and $68 stays in the city, whereas only $13 recirculates locally when buying from big box chain stores, and nearly nothing recirculates when buying online.[131]

The Buy Local movement also has political implications because it builds the local tax base. For Kris Kleindienst with Left Bank in St. Louis, "There's sales tax. There's property tax. There's payroll tax. There's a lot of pieces that are eliminated when . . . a majority of stuff is being brought in from Amazon[.com]." As a partial antidote, the ABA BookSense program promotes Buy Local movements by allowing customers to order books online, and those orders are then filled by whichever participating independent bookstore is geographically closest.[132] This program gives shoppers the convenience of online ordering without taking money out of the community. For Kleindienst, the alternative of allowing chain stores and online businesses to decimate local economies negatively affects "every single one of us and our quality of life" because "there are no dollars for healthcare, there are no dollars to fix streets, [and] there's nothing going into education." By contrast, Buy Local advocates promote it as an antidote to municipal decline and as a way to keep business districts vibrant.

In some cases, Buy Local movements lead to structural changes in urban development. An especially notable example involves the Keep Austin Weird campaign, which started in part when a real estate company recruited Borders to be the anchor tenant for a downtown development project, and Steve Bercu with BookPeople objected. Borders was set to be about four hundred feet from BookPeople and a block away from Waterloo, an independent record store. When looking into the real estate deal, Bercu discovered "the city's subsidizing this development by about two-and-a-half million dollars." Irritated by the subsidy, Bercu circulated an email that snowballed into thousands of people contacting the City Council to voice objections to the development. This public outcry led to an eighteen-month delay of the Borders project, which cost developers so much money they eventually pulled out. As part of this movement, Book-People and Waterloo gave away hundreds of thousands of free bumper stickers reading "Keep Austin Weird," a slogan coined by a local librarian that then became the mantra for a multipronged movement to stop subsidizing corporate development and to instead use municipal zoning to keep superstores out of downtown. In a rapidly growing and relatively affluent city like Austin, residents and city officials have the clout to endorse Buy Local policies. As a result, many Austin shoppers no longer have to remember to choose local options over chains. They simply go to them because local businesses are the only game in town.

Independent booksellers in other cities do not enjoy those structural protections. This absence does not mean ethical consumerism is irrelevant. On the contrary, at Sister's Uptown, customers come from "Philadelphia, Connecticut, Westchester, Queens, [and] Brooklyn, and they're like, 'Hey, we just googled "Black-owned store" or "woman owned business" and wanted to come and support [you].'" Likewise, at May Day, the activist community "will come to us when a new [social movement] book comes out ... [in] part because we're 15 percent off all the time, but [also because] they want us to be open." Similarly, at Women & Children First, "There are a lot of women out there ... who remember when there was a feminist bookstore in their town that maybe has long since closed," and these women order books from Women & Children First to keep the feminist space open. The owners encourage this consumer loyalty by including "handwritten notes in every package: 'Thank you for supporting our feminist bookstore.'"

Although ethically motivated purchasing helps, ethical consumerism alone does not appear to be significant enough or consistent enough to fully sustain print-based movement spaces. On the contrary, activist-entrepreneurs were equally likely to complain that ethical consumerism was declining and that those losses were undermining their businesses. For Kim Brinster with Oscar Wilde, "When I was coming out, it was drilled into us the importance of supporting gay restaurants, gay bars, [and] gay bookstores. But now gays take this all for granted."[133] For Janifer Wilson with Sister's Uptown, "When I started working in this arena there were at least 50 percent more Black bookstores than there are today. If you want more Black bookstores you need to support them. You can't walk in and say 'this is wonderful' and then go around the corner . . . [to] buy the book at a chain store."[134] Several booksellers also complained about customers who used their businesses like galleries, or places to explore diverse literature, but then purchased the books more cheaply online.[135] In situations like these, indies carry the overhead costs of physical space, but they lose the financial reward of the sale.

Another limiting factor is that many consumers—especially vulnerable customers—cannot afford to vote with their dollars. Elayna Trucker, a nonactivist but socially conscious bookseller in California, wrote an editorial describing the impossibility of buying locally on her wages. "Shopping local comes with a real price. . . . When a consumer chooses to Shop Local, she is knowingly spending more because she wants to support that business and keep it and its employees in her community, while helping to better that community through taxes."[136] Although ethical consumerism is often presented as a matter of choice, this choice is more accessible to wealthier buyers. For people with lower incomes, "There's not much wiggle room in there for voting with your wallet the way we ask our customers to. I'd love to purchase my furniture from a local carpenter, my meat and vegetables from a local farm, [and] my clothing from a locally owned boutique. I simply don't make enough money to do so."[137]

Because of the added costs, some activist-entrepreneurs see ethical consumerism as inconsistent with radical agendas. A movement strategy based on buying power can feel antithetical to the goal of subverting capitalism, consumerism, and class privilege. This is why, instead of encouraging ethical consumerism, Librería Donceles is "pay what you wish," which serves "kids whose parents can't drop twenty bucks on a really cool hardcover." It's why, instead of maximizing profits, Palabras Librería "takes the community to heart by dedicating a section of the store as a small library for local residents who can't afford [books]."[138] It's why, instead of asking people to vote with their dollars, Long Haul denounces "filthy commerce,"[139] and Left Bank in Seattle labels its cash register "a symbol of imperialism."[140] It's also why Bluestockings encourages customers who can't afford books to instead read them on site. For Corey Farach, "I cannot tell you how many times someone has picked up *Teaching to Transgress* [by bell hooks] and brought it to the counter. And then they learn that it is $36.95 because it's a Routledge textbook. And they're like, 'Well, I can't afford that.' And I'm like, 'Yeah, few people can. But you can still read it. Take it back to the café and read it. Just please don't get any coffee on it.' And that's fine."

Examples like these do not imply that buy local, buy queer, and buy Black movements are unethical or unhelpful. But they do point to a larger argument, which is that space and information should be available to people regardless of whether they can afford to pay extra. I agree activist-entrepreneurs benefit from ethical consumerism, especially when it gives them an edge over corporate competitors. However, instead of leaving the choice in the hands of individual consumers, ethical consumerism works best when its principles are embedded in urban development policies. Moreover, ethical consumerism favors people with privilege while leaving other equity-oriented goals unaddressed. For all these reasons, ethical consumerism helps, but activist enterprises cannot live on this movement alone.

Print-Based Counterspaces Are Labors of Love

Despite industry innovations, one thing that has not changed about print-based counterspaces—and arguably the factor that matters to activist-entrepreneurs most—is self-sacrifice. One euphemism for this phenomenon is "entrepreneurial volunteerism." Andrew Ross popularized this term in the late 2000s when precarity scholars showed that even privileged professionals were experiencing employment insecurity. In this context, knowledge workers often pursue unpaid and self-made labor aligned with their passions rather than accepting equally precarious but far less satisfying survival work with corporations.[141]

This cultural expectation that people should work for passion rather than profit—and pay a steep price for the privilege—explains some of the energy funneling into print-based movement spaces. This is how Greg Newton became an activist bookseller. Newton was a disenchanted college lecturer facing degraded working conditions with negligible job security, so he quit academia and started a queer bookstore. Like the other bookstore volunteers, Newton works without pay. He lives off his partner's earnings, and the arrangement works for them because it creates an opportunity to build a queer-positive public space, which they both value.

The concept of entrepreneurial volunteerism inflects self-sacrifice with new meanings in a precarious age, but the practice is longstanding. A particularly lyrical example involves *The New Tide*, a 1930s proletarian magazine that was part of the Popular Front. In the words of one observer, "What awed me, in those early days . . . were the sacrifices of its founders. I would ask myself why three starving men were willing to give up their hard-earned money to make an obscure magazine live, denying themselves the simple necessities of food and shelter. They had surrounded the publication as though it were a little life about to die, or dying, or dead, and breathed life into it one after the other."[142] These political writers put their bodies on the line to keep radical voices going.

Self-sacrifice was likewise common among radical booksellers in the 1960s and 1970s. For Alan Chelak with PAT @ Giovanni's Room, "the two people who started up this location . . . they weren't even paying themselves in the beginning." Customers made sacrifices as well. "There's an entire generation of people that worked to make Giovanni's Room exist." When landlords refused to rent to a queer establishment, the new owner "borrowed money from community members" to buy the bookstore a place of its own.[143] Alongside cash, people donated sweat equity. "One hundred people volunteered to help with the initial renovations."[144] Three decades later, when the building needed structural repairs, "people in the community came together" yet again "and donated that money and put in the time to hold fundraisers."

Similar stories of volunteerism and self-sacrifice are ubiquitous in print-based movement spaces of all stripes. At Resistencia, the owner lived for several decades on speaking fees and social security checks instead of taking a salary from his bookstore.[145] At the Civic Media Center, a retired librarian "funded the first year of operations almost solely out of his own money."[146] At People Called Women, the bookstore survives because the owner puts personal money into it. "Like when relatives died and I got some money, it went into the bookstore."

About half (51 percent) of the venues included in this study operate primarily or exclusively using volunteer labor. In the era of chain superstores and online retailing, these indie businesses do not generate enough revenue to pay consistent wages. These spaces survive because the people running them work for free while living off second jobs, partners' incomes, personal inheritances, and social security checks. Activists do this work because they value the experience and because they want to construct resources for social change. For Susan Post with BookWoman, "I work all the time, and I don't even get paid in real money. It is a labor of love. It's my passion [and] my religion. It's a way to give back. It's a way to empower new generations." Similarly, for Gina Mercurio with People Called Women, running a bookstore will never make her rich, but it is emotionally satisfying. "You do what you have to do. To me, it's very important that there's public feminist space."

Not everyone has the option of working for free. At Red Emma's, when the venue first opened in 2004, "most of us could afford to pay rent and have a job on the side. It was rarely anybody's full-time job. And when it was, it was usually a college student living in a warehouse space paying a hundred bucks a month rent."[147] But activists could not work for no pay, or extremely low pay, indefinitely. Gentrification increased housing costs, and collective members' lifestyles became more expensive as they had kids and planned for retirement. Being able to work for free was a luxury they could no longer afford. To keep Red Emma's open, the collective began offering full-time employment with living wages and benefits, which keeps the space going.[148]

Additionally, some activists feel it is counterproductive to work for free because it contradicts their political mission. For instance, a central tenet of the feminist movement is that women should be paid for their work. This feminist principle is why Sandy Torkildson with A Room of One's Own "is careful to keep staffing at a level where people receive a living wage and health benefits."[149] Similarly, the push for living wages is a cornerstone for anticapitalist organizing. At Firestorm, "People think we're crazy to think we can pay our worker/owners a living wage."[150] Paying a living wage was not possible at first, but the goal is to get there in the end. "We think we can eventually do it."[151]

Even when wages are not politicized, activist-entrepreneurs can still feel resentful about working for free. Larry Lingle expressed this type of anger when he announced the closure of Oscar Wilde and then received pushback from the queer community. "It's not my obligation to keep suffering a loss so the oldest gay and lesbian bookstore can stay in business. I have given more than my share to the gay and lesbian community."[152] Lingle felt so irritated that he refused to have a going-out-of-business sale. "If people can't support us when we were in business, we're not going to let them get below-cost bargains from our misfortune."[153]

Despite the drawbacks of entrepreneurial volunteerism, without some self-sacrifice, print-based movement spaces often struggle to survive. For Matt Dineen with Wooden Shoe, "if we were depending on paying ourselves, we probably would have [closed]." Dineen compared Wooden Shoe with other anarchist collectives that had closed in recent years in response to market pressure. "They had at least some members that were being paid and depending on that space for their livelihood." By contrast, at Wooden Shoe, "being volunteers is the only way we've been able to sustain it for so long."

These patterns of self-sacrifice underscore the emotional significance of activist retailing. For activist-entrepreneurs, constructing movement-oriented spaces is neither a simple job nor a mere hobby. Instead, it is a way to feel alive. These spaces exist not because they outcompete Barnes & Noble and Amazon—often they do not—but rather because volunteers pour energy into them as "a life-giving, life-altering activity, creating positive change in individual lives."[154] This labor is about "inspiring and nourishing one's soul,"[155] "watching people's lives change,"[156] and getting to "write down your mind to have another person read your mind." Statements like these reflect a basic human need to represent oneself and have those representations seen and acknowledged. Retail sales, event programming, nonprofit formats, and ethical consumerism help, but to compete in a corporate digital age, volunteerism is often crucial to keeping spaces open.

New Waves of Print-Based Movement Spaces Are Emerging

Industry changes connected to experience economies, nonprofit funding, ethical consumerism, and entrepreneurial volunteerism explain the partial resurgence of brick-and-mortar retailing, and this partial resurgence generates opportunities for new social movements to construct the next generation of print-based counterspaces. According to Chris Dixon's analysis of the "radical movements of today," new anarchist movements, transnational and people of color movements, and antiauthoritarian genderqueer liberation movements are on the rise.[157] As I summarize in this final section, these movements are reviving print-based movement spaces as a repertoire for dissent.

First, new anarchist movements combine the longstanding anarchist rejection of states and hierarchies with ideas adapted from other movements such as pacifism, direct action, and global justice.[158] These new anarchist movements operate in part through infoshops. Infoshops are a cross between radical bookstores and movement archives organized in the spirit of independent spaces,[159] free spaces,[160] and temporary autonomous zones.[161] Anarchist infoshops often start with disgruntled youth selling subcultural zines and manifestos at record stores and performance venues. Zines come in several flavors. One flavor dates back to the fanzines of the 1970s punk scene, which evolved through the 1990s riot grrrl scene to eventually become a typology of self-published booklets made with scissors and glue sticks telling the personal stories of their creators' lives. Another flavor of zines are open-source booklets downloaded from the internet that include polemical guides to anarchist theory, as well as practical guides to radical organizing. These low-cost, self-directed publications are well-suited to anarchists' political agendas, and the infoshops distributing them provide anarchist public space.

Second, transnational and people of color movements are constructing print-based enterprises to facilitate contentious politics. Some Black liberation bookstores still exist, but today they operate within a broader spectrum including Latino/a, Chicano/a, and Indigenous peoples movements. They also incorporate other border-crossing campaigns, for instance movements supporting racialized political asylum and racialized transnational spirituality. Activists of color are creating new bookstores as tools in these campaigns. These bookstores are often nonprofits housed within cultural institutions and performance centers. They often combine book sales with library services making literature available to communities of color. Some venues also include writing programs and publishing equipment to help authors of color make themselves heard.

Third, activists involved in antiauthoritarian genderqueer movements are opening intersectional print-based movement spaces. Some second-wave feminist bookstores still exist, although they often survived by becoming less activist and more business-oriented.[162] Others moved in the opposite direction by joining the throng of emerging venues focused on interlocking axes of oppression. These intersectional venues combine feminism with movements against racism, classism, transphobia, Islamophobia, ageism, ableism, xenophobia, fascism, capitalism, white supremacy, imperialism, and environmental exploitation. Unlike business-oriented strategies that water down the politics, this intersectional approach retains an uncompromising political stance. It updates feminism while also tapping into emerging movement waves, which diversifies revenue and constructs a multipronged activist space.

These areas of growth demonstrate that it is still possible to construct print-based counterspaces as social movement tools. Radical bookstores, infoshops, and libraries are places to explore and congregate, which provides important entry points into organizing. Constructing these spaces has always been difficult, and industry restructuring introduces new hurdles. The rise of retail-nonprofit hybrids partially counters these trends, as does ethical consumerism and entrepreneurial volunteerism. Activist-entrepreneurs are often on the leading edge of these innovative trends, which are helping indie spaces rebound even in the age of chain stores and online retail. However, the challenge of constructing counterspaces expands beyond corporate competition. The challenge also includes claiming space in gentrifying cities, which is the subject of the next chapter.

CHAPTER 4

Claiming Spaces and Resources
in Gentrifying Cities

G REG NEWTON, LIKE MANY IN THE QUEER COMMUNITY, moved to New York to escape the stifling intolerance of Christian evangelicalism. "So many people come here specifically because it is a mecca for queers and has been for decades." The Stonewall Inn, located a few blocks away, is the celebrated birthplace of the 1969 queer liberation movement. Another nearby landmark is the former location of the Oscar Wilde Memorial Bookshop, the first explicitly queer bookstore in the country, which was founded two years before Stonewall in 1967.[1]

Oscar Wilde closed in 2009. Walking past the former storefront, Newton and his partner Donnie Jochum did a double take. "We said, 'When did Oscar Wilde close? I can't remember.'" Another renowned queer bookstore, A Different Light, had likewise closed a few years earlier. "And then we stopped and were like, 'Wait a minute. Is there no gay bookstore in this city? That's embarrassing.'"

Having come to New York to find queer cultural institutions, Newton was unprepared to live with "the shame" of losing them. In response, he and Jochum replaced the lost bookstores with a new queer community space. "It's important to have a space that is set aside for queers." Despite legal advances, many people in the queer community still routinely experience being marginalized for their sexuality or gender identities. Given this stigmatization, for Newton, "it is very important to me to have spaces that are for us. This is dedicated to us."

Newton and Jochum founded the Bureau of General Services—Queer Division in 2012 as a combined queer bookstore, community center, and gallery space. They gave it "an official sounding name" to create the illusion it was "this big, ominous organization" normalizing queer rights, experiences, and culture. Since existing institutions validate heteronormativity, Newton thought, "Well, let's make our own government agency, The Bureau of General Services—Queer Division." They put their logo on boxes and tote bags so it "looks like they're shipped out from headquarters, as if you have satellites all over the place." Newton considered branding the bags with global city names as well as a form of political satire. Because the shopping bags of "fashion brands will say 'Milan,' 'Paris,' [and] 'London' . . . we were joking about doing bags [that said] 'Bureau of General Services—Queer Division' with cities in places" where people "couldn't really do this. Like Riyadh. Moscow. Tehran. Kabul."

Newton's joke raises larger questions about the relationship between place and activism. Location was a major factor influencing Newton's decision to start an activist enterprise. From personal experience, he knew queer spaces could not survive just anywhere. "But the Bureau is convinced that NYC is big enough and queer enough to sustain an event space and bookstore specifically dedicated to serving the queer communities of NYC and the many queer visitors to our city."[2] New York is a major metropolis. It

Cast of Characters, an immersive exhibition by Liz Collins, was displayed at the Bureau of General Services bookstore from June 14 through September 16, 2018, in partnership with the Bureau and the LGBT Community Center in New York City. Photograph by Regan Wood Studio, 2018; courtesy of the Bureau of General Services.

has a critical mass of queer residents, tourists, and activists. The city is also a major publishing hub. These resources help the Bureau thrive.

But operating a business in New York is not easy. The high cost of urban real estate is the biggest obstacle. The Bureau started as a pop-up bookstore inside a lesbian-owned art gallery and then moved into another shared storefront. Both locations had street-facing entrances on bustling sidewalks. "And that was great. Except for the rent. The rent was, like, four thousand dollars a month." Those prices were untenable. The Bureau left its second location after only nine months. Three years later, Newton and Jochum were still paying six hundred dollars each month toward the backlog of debt accumulated during their brief stay.

An invitation to share space with the Lesbian, Gay, Bisexual, and Transgender Community Center in Greenwich Village saved the project. The location is not perfect. On the positive side, the LGBT Community Center is centrally located in a prominent lower Manhattan building, which is good for accessibility. But being inside a branded institution means that people who do not already self-identify as queer or who are not seeking queer services may never enter. The location also comes with limited visibility. "We're kind of tucked away up here." The Bureau is in a room along an obscure corridor on the second floor with no street presence and minimal wayfinding aids. This near invisibility reduces foot traffic, which makes programming crucial. "We do a ton of events because otherwise it's kind of slow."

What the location lacks in visibility, it makes up for in cost. The community center "give[s] us a very sweet deal in terms of rent," which stabilizes the finances. "I don't know how we would have continued if the center had not offered us this space. We do pay rent here, but it's pretty minimal." The bookstore does not earn a profit. Sales and donations cover rent and inventory, but Newton and the other staffers work for free because the business cannot afford to pay wages. Although not ideal, it "has steadied the ship," and the venture lives as a labor of love.

Conversations like this one at the Bureau of General Services highlight the complicated relationship between cities and activism. Cities provide resources, like diversity and critical mass, which is one reason they attract radical migrants. Scholars often frame urban migration as though it were a thing of the past—a nineteenth- and early-twentieth-century phenomenon that is technologically irrelevant and only persists in the form of gentrification. However, my findings do not support this conclusion. In print-based movement spaces, migration stories are ubiquitous. People come from rural areas, small towns, and suburbs to cities where there are more resources for alternative lifestyles. This convergence consolidates a critical mass of contentious thought and buying power, which creates opportunities to route activism through retail.

Despite these locational advantages, cities also contain roadblocks. Cost is the biggest barrier because urban real estate is expensive and movement enterprises have low yields. Historically, activist-entrepreneurs circumvented this barrier by operating in marginal locations, like down-and-out neighborhoods and out-of-the-way buildings, which had lower property costs and relaxed social norms. Marginal locations were not perfect. They were often inconvenient, uncomfortable, and invisible, and these characteristics reinforced stigma. Despite these imperfections, these locations were effective enough to sustain counterspaces, including activist bookstores.

The challenge today is that this imperfect window is closing. As part of the bohemian fringe, activist-entrepreneurs often inadvertently facilitate gentrification. This recolonization of the urban core by people with privilege crowds out lower-income groups, including radical booksellers and librarians. These trends are one of the most pressing barriers preventing activists from capitalizing on urban diversity and critical mass. Many commentators watching counterspaces buckle under gentrification conclude that rising property costs make activist entrepreneurship a thing of the past. The implication is that, in a gentrification era, the spatial opportunity to use cities for organizing is ending.

I agree that locational challenges are significant, but I disagree that gentrification marks the end of urban counterspaces. Although rents are certainly rising, those accounts do not tell the whole story. Despite gentrification, many print-based movement spaces are at no risk or low risk of displacement. This includes venues in rapidly gentrifying and already gentrified neighborhoods where, even as several counterspaces disappeared, others remained, and new ones emerged.

Activist-entrepreneurs use many strategies to solve the locational conundrum of wanting to access urban resources without paying prohibitive rents. Some activist-entrepreneurs accept their complicity in gentrification and find ways to turn it to their advantage. Others cope by periodically relocating in tandem with the moving gentrification line. A third set of activists find ways to stay despite gentrification, for instance by cutting wages, buying property, or taking shelter within cultural institutions. In other instances, activists create businesses even knowing they cannot stay forever because they accrue benefits along the way.

This hodgepodge of locational strategies confirms that there is no one right way to claim space in gentrifying cities. I agree that this lack of a structural fix means print-based movement spaces remain vulnerable, but vulnerable is not the same as impossible. On the contrary, activist-entrepreneurs like Newton with the Bureau of General Services find enough effective work-arounds to keep contentious energy churning.

Marginalized Groups Still Migrate to Cities

Urban migration stories are common in radical bookstores and infoshops. Scholars often overlook these experiences because they don't fit either the farm-to-city urbanization narratives of the past[3] or the back-to-the-city gentrification narratives of the present.[4] Additionally, people now use digital technology to find community, which some scholars believe reduces the need to congregate in shared urban spaces.[5]

All this is true, yet the life experiences of staffers, authors, and customers in print-based movement spaces paint a different picture. For many of these people, urban migration is a pivotal life event, especially for those living as unrecognized internal refugees. These internal refugees face social, political, and economic persecution in conservative small towns and suburbs, and they escape this hostility by converging in large liberal cities for protection and opportunity. Even without crossing national borders, these migrants trade one political world for another when moving to cities of refuge. From these perspectives, urban migration is not a thing of the past or the purview of the privileged. Instead, going urban is a rite of passage allowing people to live life otherwise.

This migration culture is shared among staffers, authors, and customers. Starting with staffers, Aaron King provides a case in point. King grew up in a small town of five hundred people, which was "a rural place without physical places to buy stuff" like anarchist books and indy newspapers. Moving to a larger college town, population five thousand, "was great for taking my first steps on a path towards meeting people that weren't like me." The college town was more diverse, but its small size meant local shopkeepers still "had to serve the middle of the road," which meant the town "didn't have much [radical] infrastructure." King constructed a make-shift radical hot spot by setting up a vending machine at the local library filled with zines instead of food. To stock the vending machine, he traveled to the Twin Cities of Minneapolis–St. Paul where he found specialty bookstores dedicated to anarchism, genderqueer liberation, anticapitalism, feminism, and Indigenous peoples movements. After graduating, King moved to Minneapolis where he volunteered at an anarchist bookstore, edited a radical micropress, and emulated other progressive activists. "Their being actively good people really sets the bar for me."

Stories like King's are common among radical booksellers and librarians. I heard variations at the Bureau of General Services where Greg Newton moved to New York to escape the homophobic American heartland. I heard it again at Microcosm where Joe Biel moved to Portland from the suburban Midwest to find acceptance as a neuro-atypical punk rocker selling "the 'How to Protest' manual alongside the 'How to Make Soap' manual."

The narrative recurs with Jesse DeBey, who was profiled in the British *Observer*. DeBey grew up in a small town in Kansas "where the word queer does not exist unless it's thrown at you from a truck window."[6] To escape this hostility, DeBey moved to Portland and began volunteering at In Other Words, a feminist bookstore and community center where she found a sense of belonging. "There are not just lots of big, shaven-headed, tattooed women here, but some of them are also holding hands."[7] Stories like DeBey's show that, although Portland's alternative hipsterism "might be mockable to some," cities accommodating difference are almost magical places for people whose identities and experiences are routinely denigrated elsewhere.[8]

These migrating booksellers stock progressive authors, many of whom are migrants themselves. For example, for Staceyann Chin, embracing queerness meant leaving her fiercely homophobic rural Jamaican homeland "where I could get killed for talking about the things I want to do with women" and traveling to New York where she discovered "the bookstores: A DIFFERENT LIGHT, OSCAR WILDE, THE REVOLUTIONARY BOOKSTORE, THE PEOPLE'S REPUBLIC OF ANTI-IMPERIALIST LITERATURE—the names on the signs draw me in."[9] The United States as a whole did not offer liberation. Instead, Chin found it in the radical bookstores of a major metropolis. Those spaces affirmed her nonnormative experiences and connected her with people embracing queerness in many empowering variations.

The story was similar for Chavisa Woods who reportedly "cut her teeth" at Left Bank in St. Louis. Co-owner Kris Kleindienst remembers when Woods, "as a teenager, would make pilgrimages" from rural Illinois to their bookstore to explore radical politics. According to Kleindienst, for a self-described "queer goth girl in the country," the urban bookstore offered Woods acceptance and hope. It was "a big deal . . . to be able to come to the store and be able to see those [queer feminist] stories on the shelves and to feel welcome and safe and be able to buy them." Woods still visits the bookstore, but now she comes as an award-winning public intellectual living in New York and writing about her experiences for a national audience.

Alongside workers and authors, customers also share this migration culture. As an example, in Minneapolis, I observed a young woman introducing herself to the clerks at Boneshaker by saying she had just arrived from a small Michigan town and wanted to make friends with other queer anarchists. The clerk behind the counter had likewise grown up in a small Michigan town, and she described Boneshaker as a common entry point for newcomers like themselves. This scene recurred at Bound Together in San Francisco and Lucy Parsons in Boston where again I met customers from rural areas who came to urban bookstores to find a sense of radical camaraderie.

Margot (no last name given) with Trumbullplex aptly summarized the rationale behind these convergences. "It's always nice to have a space full of reading material," like a zine library, because reading creates an excuse to linger. These spaces then function as portholes where travelers can plug into movement scenes. From her perspective, infoshops are "a really good place to just go, and drink a cup of coffee, and read something, and maybe make a connection with somebody. Like, if you need a place to stay, or you need resources or help of any kind and don't know where to start, you can at least find some kind of amalgamation of where the hippies and the freaks are."

One important caveat, however, is that urban locations matter more to some progressives than others. For instance, although urban density disproportionately benefits women,[10] few of the feminists I interviewed reported moving to cities for political reasons. On the contrary, as feminism gains mainstream acceptance, women have more opportunities to access supportive infrastructure in nonurban contexts, which reduces the pressure to cluster in cities. Similarly, although movements like Black Lives Matter have a solid urban base, the segregationist histories of isolating and warehousing communities of color in disinvested cities means that many African American and Latino/a interviewees did not describe cities as magical places of freedom. Even though urban neighborhoods provide cultural and institutional resources for communities of color, unless those interviewees also self-identified as nonnormative in some other way, for instance as queer or anarchist, their enthusiasm for cities was muted.

By contrast, rural- and suburban-to-urban migration stories were ubiquitous in venues devoted to intersectional movements, queer liberation, and new anarchism. One reason may be that these movements are largely white. Whereas white people in small towns and suburbs can choose to move to cities, many people of color already live there. However, the accident of birth matters in other ways as well. Although people generally (but not always) identify with the racial and ethnic characteristics of their parents, when it comes to politics and sexuality, people often look farther afield to build communities of their choosing. A third reason for these differences may be that intersectional, queer, and anarchist movements are less institutionalized, at least for now, which may explain why participants have a harder time finding critical mass in less dense areas.

Whatever the reason, for the people I met in intersectional, queer, and anarchist spaces, geography mattered a lot. Radical bookstores and libraries are crossroads for people with similar experiences, and these crossroads cluster in cities.

Cities Provide Resources for Contentious Politics

Rural- and suburban-to-urban migration stories can be narrated in many ways. Some narratives are personal accounts of traveling sojourners seeking community. Other narratives emphasize group-level bonding around shared experiences of discrimination. But in this section, I want to consider structural accounts explaining why cities are useful for contentious politics and why they are hot spots for constructive activism.

One benefit of moving to cities is that their diversity enhances opportunities for choice. For Don Mitchell, cities are places to escape the "isolation and homogeneity" of rural life to instead enjoy "a thick fabric of heterogeneity."[11] Doreen Massey suggests heterogeneity thrives in cities because large numbers of strangers are "thrown together" in shared spaces.[12] For Leonie Sandercock, this jumbling together constructs hot spots of "difference, otherness, multiplicity, heterogeneity, diversity and plurality" where people live "alongside others who are different," which creates opportunities for learning from them and "creating new worlds with them."[13] This exposure to difference expands the social imagination. Instead of simply accepting the dominant worldview they are born into, people can choose among many options, including ones breaking with the expectations of their upbringing.[14]

Another benefit of moving to cities is that anonymity provides freedom to explore. Small-town gossip mills leave little room to escape social discipline around, for instance, gender and sexuality.[15] But in cities where people can disappear into crowds, there is more opportunity for nonconformity. The predominantly transactional nature of urban social relationships enhances anonymity as well. To paraphrase Georg Simmel, unlike the social intimacy of small towns, most interactions in cities are mediated by markets. In this transactional environment, strangers "require less of us," which means a person's "being and conduct" need only suit her or him.[16] This mechanical release from social care is admittedly a point of vulnerability, since being freed from other people's discipline also means being cut off from their support. Despite these risks, urban anonymity is nevertheless liberating because it creates opportunities to explore and develop other ways of associating.

A third benefit of moving to cities involves critical mass. In small towns, minority experiences often look like individual quirks rather than collective traits. For example, since only a small percentage of people self-identify as transgender or anarchist, those people often feel isolated when living in low-density areas where few others share their perspectives. By contrast, in cities, the same proportion translates into larger absolute numbers, which makes it easier to recognize the collective nature of nonnormative experiences.[17] This critical mass has generative effects. For Byron Miller and Walter Nicholls, critical mass makes it possible to "create and sustain associations, media, socializing venues, religious organizations, and other social institutions," which help people "bond with one another and form collective identities."[18] This supportive infrastructure generates positive feedback loops. "As distinctive groups form, grow, and build cultures of solidarity, these cities may become known as places of refuge for others."[19]

This mix of urban resources supports contentious politics. For Miller and Nicholls, these generative cauldrons make cities useful as "incubators and condensers of political protest."[20] Diversity facilitates innovation, anonymity facilitates choice, and critical mass consolidates energy and enhances legitimacy. For these reasons, "coalitions and mobilizations often begin and coalesce" in cities, even as, importantly, "they do not necessarily stay there."[21] Cities are politically useful not only because they are places of refuge but also because their new social norms radiate outward. From a social movement perspective, the point is not to create just one progressive neighborhood—it is to use urban resources, including capacities to organize, to advance institutional change at national and global scales.

A few caveats are worth mentioning. First is that cities do not have a monopoly on activism. For instance, in the 1950s and 1960s, "The hinterlands of America seemed to promise the possibility of building a new, collaborative society."[22] Although useful for some purposes, building isolated retreats limits opportunities for visibility and networking. By contrast, cities are "supreme site[s] of encounters,"[23] including among diverse and potentially sympathetic activists. For example, although white anarchists and Black liberationists may not collaborate on a regular basis, they share the same cities and can offer mutual support during critical moments. This is why, during the white supremacist demonstrations following the 2016 presidential election, the anarchist black bloc in Charlottesville protected African American demonstrators from violent attacks. For Cornel West, "They saved our lives, actually. We would have been completely crushed."[24] Activists are not required to organize in cities, but proximity with other groups is an asset when they do.

Another caveat is that urban locations come with no guarantees of social liberation. For Justus Uitermark et al., "Cities not only breed contention; they also breed control."[25] As hubs of subversive energy, cities are "the frontline where states constantly create new governmental methods to protect and produce social and political order, including repression, surveillance, clientelism, corporatism, and participatory and citizenship initiatives."[26] Repressive efforts to block social movement energy are significant concerns, but they do not negate the potential for cities to stimulate social movements, nor do they negate the value of urban resources for organizing. Urban resources, like proximity, diversity, anonymity, and critical mass, facilitate contentious politics. These urban resources help explain why so many nonnormative groups cluster in cities.

Activist Enterprises Rely on Urban Critical Mass

These urban characteristics provide useful economic and political resources for activist-entrepreneurs. By analyzing how activists use urban locations, this section highlights the subset of resources most useful for activist retailing. Understanding these details sheds light on the locational opportunity structure supporting activist counterspaces. It also explains why activists are willing to make significant trade-offs and compromises to hold onto urban locations despite gentrification.

Starting with financial considerations, all businesses require a critical mass of customers, and activist businesses are no different. For John Logan and Harvey Molotch, "The concentration of a large number of similar people stimulates the development of agglomerations especially appropriate to their needs."[27] Using ethnic economies as an example, "the presence of many Mexican-Americans in one place provides the necessary base for a bodega, which then attracts still more Mexican-American residents, who then provide the still larger base needed to support a Spanish-language movie theater."[28]

The same agglomeration dynamics supporting ethnic retail also support other specialty businesses, including activist ones. This economic need for critical mass explains why Antigone opened in "one of the more progressive parts of town" next to other "hippie" businesses, like the Food Conspiracy Co-Op. It explains why Eso Won operates alongside Black barbershops, Afrocentric boutiques, and Southern-style restaurants catering to African American consumers.[29] Anarchist venues cluster as well. For Stephanie Waller with Boxcar, "The same people are going to all those [anarchist] spaces anyway, the same people that are going to buy things."

By clustering together, these venues attract consumer attention, which consolidates foot traffic and boosts sales. Colocating sometimes involves sharing buildings as well. For instance, Boneshaker has "a friendly marriage of sorts" with 2D Cloud Publishing and the Women's Prison Book Project, which share Boneshaker's space. As other examples, the Bureau of General Services shares space with the LGBT Community Center, the Madison Infoshop shares space with Rainbow Bookstore, and the Steinem Sister's Library shares space with the feminist bookstore People

Called Women. Similarly, the Long Haul Infoshop shares space with the East Bay Prisoner Support Group, the publisher Slingshot Collective, and the bicycle advocacy group Cycles of Change.

One benefit of sharing space is affordability. With more groups paying rent, the price per group decreases. These economic factors are especially important for low-budget projects, like lending libraries and books-to-prisoners programs, that can rarely afford a space at any price. Another benefit involves the generative effects of Jane Jacobs–style "intricate cross-use."[30] Different products and different price points appeal to different consumers, and bringing those groups into shared spaces helps all the venues survive.

From one perspective, these economic dynamics are not noteworthy. All businesses need to be close to a large enough consumer base to support them. However, alongside economic considerations, clustering also has political implications. As one example, clustering is a way to claim turf. Retail businesses are public-facing entities, and their signage and window displays stamp identity onto space. For Katherine Solheim, Unabridged contributes to the identity of Boystown, "a very queer area of the city." For Aaron King, Boneshaker and the collectively run vegan café around the corner are "just part of the queer radical space in this neighborhood." Similarly, for Lilia Rosas with Resistencia, sharing space with other Latino/a justice organizations is a way to be "close to each other" and to connect "not only through our books, but through the land."

From a social movement perspective, this clustering is about more than economics. It is also about constructing political protection. Mutual protection is why Stephanie Waller wanted Boxcar to relocate to more "friendly territory" alongside other anarchists, instead of "getting beaten down from all sides" when surrounded only by capitalists. Constructing protection is likewise why Leslie James Pickering located Burning Books in an area where "we have roots and connections," which helped the bookstore "defend itself against things like the FBI investigation that we dealt with."

This last comment about government agencies gets at a more literal way that sharing space provides political cover, and the Long Haul Infoshop provides a case in point. Federal agents raided the infoshop in 2008. During the raid, officials seized files and computers belonging to the infoshop and to the micropublisher sharing its space. After the raid, with support from the American Civil Liberties Union and the Electronic Frontier

Foundation, the infoshop successfully won their $100,000 lawsuit against federal agents. They won because, under the federal Privacy Protection Act, Long Haul qualified for special protections afforded to publishers against government search and seizure.[31] Although the infoshop and not the micropublisher was the subject of the raid, sharing space meant sharing protections. Activists may not have considered this protective element in advance, but now that courts have upheld it, colocating with publishers—even fringe micropublishers—can become strategic.

Urban environments provide political cover in other ways as well. In small-town locations, business owners cannot afford to alienate customers, which is why Brian Donoghue with Inquiring Minds said he "broke one of the cardinal rules of doing business in a small town" when his business took a political stand.[32] Although Inquiring Minds is not an activist enterprise, Donoghue used his window displays to criticize the 2016 Trump campaign. In an editorial describing the backlash, Donoghue explained the financial risks.[33] Since his business depends on patronage from a large cross section of the small population, alienating even a subset of customers could spell financial ruin. In cases like these, if pickets are strong enough or boycotts last long enough, small businesses go under.

By contrast, the diversity and anonymity in large cities provide more leeway for assertive political action. Like Inquiring Minds, Fantom Comics is not an activist enterprise even though its staffers also used the business to oppose the Trump campaign. Staffer Jake Shapiro was aware of the financial risks. "We know anytime we take a stance we're going to make ourselves a target."[34] But Shapiro and his coworkers felt the risks were manageable because of their urban location. Washington, D.C., "is one of the most progressive cities in the country,"[35] which meant staffers could speak out without alienating too many customers. The anonymity of urban tourism helped as well. Offended out-of-towners would soon leave, and their replacements would have no memory of the bookstore's previous political stance.

Urban anonymity is also politically useful in more everyday contexts. For Richard Sennett, people in diverse cities "can develop multiple images of their identities, knowing that who they are shifts, depending upon whom they are with."[36] Anonymity allows people to capitalize on this shape-shifting potential without recrimination. As an example, Boone with the Minnehaha Free Space wears several hats. As a college student, he is bisexual but "closeted to most of my social group," while at the Free Space, there is "a queer community that I was a part of for the first time." Boone felt comfortable exploring queer sexuality in the Free Space because in a large, diverse metropolis, the anarchist circuit and the college circuit did not overlap. This segmented anonymity allowed Boone to disclose sensitive information, which created a foundation for organizing.

As a caveat, cities do not have a monopoly on activist businesses. For example, liberal college towns with large proportions of lefty intellectuals and above-average incomes can often support some progressive enterprises. However, the narrow demographics constrain the range of politics that are possible. For instance, feminist-themed venues may find a sufficient following, but other venues, like anticapitalist or Latino/a liberation venues, may not.

Despite this caveat, the proximity, diversity, anonymity, and critical mass in cities are useful resources both for social movements and for activist enterprises. Agglomeration provides a revenue stream, and the urban context provides political cover. This combination of resources is why Dan Folley with Bound Together felt San Francisco could sustain movement bookstores, but "we'd have a lot more trouble if we were in Iowa." Similarly, Katherine Solheim with Unabridged said someone had suggested that "all of the hipsters [should] go out and show the folks in the heartland that there are all sorts of different ways to be in the world. . . . But I don't see that existing outside of a large city." In Chicago, things felt different. "I feel very lucky to be in a very progressive metropolitan hub. . . . If I want to go out and canvas in southern Illinois, I can, and then come home knowing there isn't going to be a burning cross on my lawn. We have this wonderful base to work from."

These protections and opportunities help explain why urban migration remains so important. The farm-to-factory migration may have ended, but going urban still provides political refuge, and social movements remain a predominantly urban phenomenon.

But Cities Also Thwart Activism

The trouble is, although cities are rich in resources, they also pose barriers to entry. One obstacle is property costs. As Patrick Bresnihan and Michael Byrne aptly surmise, for people who want to claim space for non-market-oriented activities, finding a way to pay rent is "the principle challenge with regard to accessing urban space."[37]

Affordability problems have several causes, but the most significant factor is the "bid-rent curve."[38] To create a counterspace, "a major point of pressure lies in the fact that [space] must be wrenched from the capitalist landscape of cities."[39] When bidding for space in competitive markets, activist-entrepreneurs compete against other retailers for choice locations. This competitive environment increases prices for locations with high revenue-generating potential. Since higher-profit ventures can absorb higher overheads, they routinely outbid their less lucrative rivals.

On top of these market dynamics, public policies exacerbate affordability problems. Most U.S. cities have too few policies promoting class mixing or accommodating low-income groups. Instead, policymakers facilitate capitalist investment at the expense of social inclusion. Policies like fiscal zoning,[40] market-driven placemaking,[41] state-led gentrification,[42] and infrastructure financialization[43] encourage luxury housing, high-end retail, and pay-to-use infrastructure. These same policies discourage low-yielding but socially valuable land uses, like thrift stores and public housing.

Because of these dynamics, socially valuable but economically marginal businesses struggle to find affordable spaces in cities. Urban areas contain resources for organizing, but activists can only leverage these resources if they can pay for space in the costly urban core. Tactical organizing, such as squatting in abandoned buildings, distributing pamphlets on borrowed sidewalks, and holding meetings in rented church basements, is a partial work-around. But these repertoires lack the durability and autonomy to support longer-term overlay functions. In the rest of this chapter, I explain how activist-entrepreneurs get around these financial barriers, including in contexts of gentrification. None of the work-arounds are perfect, but they help activists claim space effectively enough to continue organizing.

Marginal Locations Are Imperfect but Affordable

In decades past, activists used marginal locations to circumvent the high costs of urban real estate. As I explain in this section, marginal locations are not perfect. One problem is reduced visibility and the potential for stigma. Another problem is the potential conflict between activists and other low-income groups. Despite these challenges, for much of the twentieth century, marginal locations provided an effective work-around allowing activists to tap into urban resources like diversity and critical mass at a price they could afford.

When thinking about marginality, one technique for reducing real estate costs involves locating in disinvested neighborhoods. Racial redlining,[44] neighborhood filtering,[45] and parasitic urbanism[46] create harsh landscapes with hyperinvestment in some places funded by disinvestment elsewhere. Without diminishing the injustice of these real estate practices, the reduced property costs in disinvested areas make them more affordable for non-normative groups. Of the venues I studied, just under half (44 percent) opened before 1990, which is to say before gentrification became a seemingly ubiquitous trend. All of those venues either opened in disinvested neighborhoods or spent significant time there. I'll give a few examples to illustrate this general trend. Giovanni's Room opened in 1973 in "'a battle zone' . . . but the rent was $85 a month."[47] Charis opened in 1974 in a neighborhood "full of gun shops, pawn shops, liquor stores, and seedy bars."[48] Similarly, after Modern Times opened in the Castro, it relocated in 1980 to the Mission with its carved-up Victorians, low-income Latino/a residents, and cheaper rent.[49]

Alongside disinvested neighborhoods, a related cost-reduction strategy involves operating in suboptimal parts of buildings. Retail space located on obscure side streets or lacking street frontage is less lucrative, which, in a competitive market, reduces the price. These economic considerations explain why Lucy Parsons opened in 1969 "in a small one-room basement shop,"[50] why Internationalist opened in 1981 in the rented room above a bar,[51] and why Bolerium opened in 1983 in the third-floor loft space above "sweat shops" and "sewing factories."[52] As another example, Revolution in Cambridge has had several locations since 1979, not all of which I could identify, but by the early 1990s it was operating in the underground basement of a parking garage. Revolution in Berkeley likewise spent several decades in a subterranean location underneath a parking garage.[53]

Although these locations are not ideal, activists are often willing to climb stairs, cram into dark rooms, and venture off beaten paths to claim durable space if the alternative is having no space at all. As Charles D'Adamo with the Alternative Press Center stated, "If we're activists who want space, we have to be able to afford the space." For D'Adamo, affording space means moving into formerly abandoned buildings, preferably those that can be "renovated DIY." These buildings are often in areas that are predominantly

Black or that border a lower-income neighborhood. They are usually "a little out of the way," without easy access to public transit, and disconnected from other commercial strips. For activists, the marginality of disinvested neighborhoods and out-of-the-way parts of buildings is precisely what makes them affordable.

Alongside the financial practicalities, locating in fringe spaces raises questions about the potentially liberating character of disinvested spaces. I raise this issue because, for some scholars, the "cracks and fissures,"[54] "loose spaces,"[55] and "drosscapes"[56] neglected by capital and government are exactly where "the possibilities for creative intervention and for all manner of innovative urban experimentations reside."[57] Low-income communities of color are the primary residents in these spaces, and they are less likely to romanticize disinvestment. Additionally, in the context of targeted policing and the carceral state, Black and brown bodies in marginalized spaces are hardly given free reign.[58] Nevertheless, for white nonconformists, marginal neighborhoods often look like affordable places to elude economic and social discipline while constructing alternative communities.

Histories of radical bookselling suggest there may be some merit to this liminal framing. As an example, the Poetry Bookshop in London in the 1910s and 1920s operated in the "drab and dirty grayness" of Devonshire Street.[59] The location was economically necessary because the owners could not afford a more prominent storefront. However, the drab grayness came with a silver lining. The bookstore "existed not only generically, but also quite literally, on the cultural and commercial margins of London. It was not a place that a casual book buyer was likely to come across."[60] Since bourgeois elites were unlikely to stumble in by chance, owners and customers felt more comfortable defying social conventions knowing there was little risk of social reprisal.

Similarly, some activist booksellers today associate the spatial fringes with a positive sense of transgression. For Liz Mason with Quimby's, being on a side street three blocks from a nearby commercial corridor establishes a satisfying psychic distance from the imagined mainstream. "We're just far away enough . . . that you kinda have to seek it out. Which I sort of like. Maybe [its] not the best for our pocketbook. But [it] feels symbolic to me. Like we're just accessible enough, but if we're doing our job right, we've expanded their mind."

These examples illustrate the relationship between social and spatial evasion. However, activists' ability to put a positive spin on a difficult situation does not mean they inherently prefer marginal locations. On the contrary, disinvested neighborhoods and obscure buildings come with significant trade-offs. One trade-off is limited visibility. For Sam Gould with Beyond Repair, if a venue is off the beaten path, "you would have to choose to go there. . . . You may not even notice [it.] You're just going to drive by." However, having a location people find by accident does not necessarily boost sales since general browsers often do not buy specialty products. What does increase, however, is the likelihood of chance encounters, which exposes people to progressive ideas without having to seek them out.

Another trade-off involves stigma. The ability to be seen in public without shame is inherently political, and operating in obscure, broken-down spaces can inadvertently reinforce feelings of inferiority and deficiency. As an example, participants in the second wave women's movement felt run-down spaces that looked like "'sleazy,' 'dingy,' 'ratty' 'holes'" created "an atmosphere that said, 'we aren't worth it.'"[61] By contrast, countering stigma is a key objective in many social movements, which is why Giovanni's Room set up shop in a street-level storefront with large plate-glass windows on the corner of a bustling commercial thoroughfare. Unlike the closeted culture of back rooms and covered windows, "we were trying to be out."[62] The bookstore's prominent location and transparent architecture reinforced the store's political message. "No back alleys. No embarrassment. No shame."[63]

Prominent locations symbolize legitimacy in anarchist circles as well. For Matt Dineen with Wooden Shoe, it felt like "this beautiful coup" for the anarchist collective to have withstood gentrification. "You're walking down [South Street]. There's all these commercial shops. And we're two blocks down from a Starbucks and a Whole Foods. And you saw our sign. It says 'Anarchist' right on the sign. There's something kinda beautiful about that."

Although the symbolism of prominent locations confers legitimacy on nonnormative groups, access to these spaces comes at a financial cost that many groups cannot afford. These challenges underscore another important takeaway, which is that activists' ability to make use of marginal locations does not imply that disinvestment is good for social justice. On the contrary, the lack of central and visible yet still affordable options is yet more evidence that society is unjust and does not accommodate everyone.

Another important point is that activist-entrepreneurs share marginal space with other low-income groups, but the shared need for cheap space does not automatically make people allies. The relationship activist-entrepreneurs have with their neighbors varies widely. Some relationships are symbiotic, for instance when a queer community grew up around Women & Children First. Other relationships are "tectonic,"[64] meaning social groups glide past each other without much meaningful contact.[65] As an example, Boneshaker is part of a queer anarchist circuit in a neighborhood that is also home to a burgeoning Somali and East African community. From Aaron King's perspective, although Boneshaker has "signage up [saying] we welcome everyone," the two groups rarely interact because immigrants "have their own safe spaces and don't need to be brought in or assimilated into Boneshaker's."

Racial divides are often a factor explaining tectonic relationships. For instance, at Revolution in Cleveland, although white communist booksellers tried to build alliances with their low-income African American neighbors, their Trotsky-ite tomes received a lukewarm reception. Instead, residents preferred the local Black-owned bookstore, which carried practical and culturally accessible information like "a book by Magic Johnson on how young people can avoid contracting AIDS."[66]

Some relationships go beyond indifference to become hostile, which occurs even when race is not a factor. For example, when BookWoman changed locations in the 1980s, their white working-class neighbors were unhappy about sharing the block with white lesbian newcomers.[67] Similarly, People Called Women in Toledo changed locations partly because the owner felt the antiauthoritarian record store next door was disruptive to the feminist mission. The record store "would have these punk bands that would play really loud, and we were trying to have a poetry reading." Both groups needed cheap rent, and both groups had progressive inclinations, but that did not make them allies.

To summarize, activist-entrepreneurs in the twentieth century routinely made use of marginalized locations where property costs were lower. Marginal locations involved trade-offs. Activists rarely preferred those locations over more prominent spaces, and tensions sometimes existed between activists and their low-income neighbors. Despite these caveats, historically, the overwhelming majority of movement-oriented bookstores opening before 1990 got their start in these disinvested, out-of-the-way urban environments.

Gentrification Is Reducing the Supply of Marginal Locations

Making use of marginal locations was never perfect, but until the 1990s, it provided a consistent, reliable work-around giving activists a toehold in expensive cities. Since the 1990s, however, this spatial opportunity structure is closing, or at least shrinking to a considerable degree. Cities are being remade at higher price points, and maintaining durability requires grappling with those changes.

An extreme but nevertheless widespread form of neighborhood change is gentrification. Urban neighborhoods previously subjected to decades of disinvestment are being rebuilt as mixed-use lifestyle enclaves for well-to-do buyers. These developments cater to affluent new arrivals who enjoy a sense of urban vibrancy and local distinctiveness. Real estate speculators build these elite-oriented districts over the marginalized neighborhoods where activist-entrepreneurs formerly found their footing.[68] The concern is that the arrival of well-to-do groups leaves no space for more vulnerable users, including the unacknowledged internal refugees using cities for social liberation.

Gentrification affects businesses as well as residents. From some perspectives, commercial revitalization is a welcome change bringing much-needed and long-absent commercial services and tax dollars. But these benefits come at the cost of soaring commercial rents. Rising rents displace small, local-owned businesses with ties to the community. As one Harlem resident aptly surmised, unlike mom-and-pop shops that pitch in with neighborhood events, "all these little boutiques and chains open, but they don't give anything to the community. . . . If you go in there and ask them to contribute, it's a problem."[69]

Activist enterprises are not exempt from rising rents. On the contrary, the increasing cost of commercial real estate is one of the most significant challenges facing print-based movement spaces today. Economic displacement is a ubiquitous theme in transcripts and archives. For brevity's sake, I'll reference just a few typical examples illustrating this general trend. In Other Words has been priced out twice, once in the late 1980s and again in 2006, because "the portion of Portland that was radical is being gentrified."[70] Wild Iris relocated in 2013 after its rent increased 50 percent.[71] Revolution NYC was priced out of Union Square in 1995, then priced out of Chelsea in 2015. The Independent Publishing Resource Center was likewise making plans to relocate in 2017 because a new public transit line was under construction and, as a result, "our current lease here is going up 300 percent."

Many activist enterprises do not survive displacement. One challenge is logistical. For Lilia Rosas with Resistencia, it is "a massive thing to move a bookstore . . . especially for grassroots." Heavy books make the process labor-intensive, and activists "don't have a moving fund." Relocating disrupts the customer base as well. The business moves, but customers may not follow, and the new locations are often even less central and less visible than the ones left behind.

These complications explain why People Like Us closed shortly after changing locations. Carrie Barnett said, "I didn't have the wherewithal to figure out how to overcome the difficulties that moved caused." It was a similar story at Modern Times. The bookstore was displaced in 2011 following a rent increase,[72] and it closed five years later. "Despite the small staff's best efforts, the store could not sustain itself following its move."[73] Wild Iris had a similar fate. The bookstore relocated in 2013 to reduce rental costs, but the new location farther off the beaten path also undercut sales, which is why the bookstore closed five years later.[74]

Another factor explaining why displacement often leads to closure is the limited availability of affordable alternatives. As an example, the Minnehaha Free Space lost its location in 2016. "The building was sold from one landlord to the next . . . and the new landlord immediately raised rent 50 percent. So it became pretty untenable to stay." Collective members wanted to reopen in a new location, but rents were rising citywide. "It's been hard to find [a new space] at a low enough price to be tenable." The scarcity of alternatives explains why, in 2017, activists had chunks of the zine library stored in bedroom closets waiting for the day a new location was found.

Activist-entrepreneurs often oppose gentrification. For instance, in 2010, volunteers with Bound Together opposed the passage of gentrification-promoting "sit-lie" laws that prohibited sitting on sidewalks or sleeping in public spaces.[75] Similarly, in 2012, owner-workers with Firestorm denounced plans to establish a Business Improvement District to pay for private security, street cleaning, and beautification.[76] In both instances, activist-entrepreneurs worried about the economic consequences of upscaling public space. They also worried these policies promoted social exclusion by discriminating against "stoned or just lazy locals"[77] who do not fit the image of affluent, hipster yuppies. Despite voicing opposition, both pieces of legislation passed, which transcripts and archives suggest is the norm.

Activist-entrepreneurs sometimes go a step farther by using public demonstrations to condemn displacement. These protest strategies work best when public officials are directly involved as landlords rather than incidentally involved as mediators. For instance, Revolution in Berkeley, which rents a government-owned storefront, was able to pressure its government landlord to make capital improvements while simultaneously reducing rents for existing tenants. The bookstore also got a new location out of the bargain, which moved it up from the basement to the ground floor.[78] Similarly, after collective members with ABC No Rio resisted eviction for two decades, city officials finally gave No Rio the deed, as well as money to demolish the old building and construct a more gentrification-friendly replacement.[79]

Those hard-won victories wrested from unsupportive hands are significant, but they are also the exception rather than the norm. More often, opposition to gentrification goes unheeded. Activists protest anyway. For instance, Marc Lasky with Lucy Parsons protested gentrification in Boston's Central Square in the late 1990s even knowing that the battle was lost, and evictions would proceed. "I'm confident we're going to lose, but we might as well be a pain in the ass on the way down."[80]

Alongside the economics of gentrification, displacement is politically symbolic since it affects social groups already living with long histories of erasure. For Lilia Rosas with Resistencia, land dispossession is a colonial process that has never stopped. Chicanos, Latinos, and Native Americans "continue to be displaced," and gentrification is just the next chapter in the dispossession story. This long history of dispossession makes it even more important "to hold onto sites and places and businesses and homes that represent a historic reminder of who was here" before colonization and gentrification land grabs. "It's important to actually have a physical space where people can actually understand that you exist, and you've always been here."

The politics of erasure affect queer communities as well. For Sarah Schulman, queer urban subcultures in disinvested neighborhoods in the New Left era were hedonistic, rebellious spaces rejecting many aspects of mainstream privilege. But in their gentrified form, rebellious energy gets repackaged into benign images of mainstream, monogamous, child-raising professionals conforming to middle-class norms in basically every way.[81]

Activist-entrepreneurs notice these trends, which is why John Mitzel with Calamus salvages print material like Colt Studio gay erotica photos from trash bins when residents move out. "For many years there was the issue of 'gay visibility.' . . . Well, of course, a community will be invisible if it has no document stream."[82] Mitzel cannot stop gentrification, but he does what he can to stop the re-erasure of nonconformist culture.

Alongside displacement and erasure, activist-entrepreneurs often become targets of gentrification-related revanchism. For Neil Smith, urban revanchism refers to wealthier residents in gentrifying areas who blame marginalized groups when property values level off after redevelopment is complete. Elites then reinvigorate real estate appreciation by driving low-income groups out of public spaces.[83] The above-mentioned "sit-lie" law is an example of a revanchist policy. Stephanie Waller with Boxcar provided another example highlighting the emotional strain of living alongside revanchist neighbors. "Our biggest issue is probably people sleeping here at night. That is the ultimate thing that has this whole town pissed off at us." From Waller's perspective, because of "a huge crackdown" sweeping people experiencing homelessness from downtown public spaces, those people had nowhere to go except to freely accessible private spaces, like Boxcar. This convergence of homelessness angered Boxcar's neighbors. Collective members who were already struggling to pay rising rents now also contended with irate neighbors complaining to their landlord, calling the police, "or coming over and screaming at the volunteer that's on shift." These incessant, aggressive confrontations became so overwhelming that, in 2017, the exhausted collective members gave up and closed the store. "We are done trying to fight to stay [downtown.] . . . I can't even do it anymore. We're definitely [running] on fumes."

Accounts like these of economic displacement, political erasure, and emotional strain confirm that gentrification is a significant factor affecting print-based movement spaces. The marginal locations where activists formerly resided are being rebuilt, and activist enterprises are on the losing side. With similar trends affecting artists,[84] musicians,[85] squatters,[86] and the urban commons movement,[87] many scholars now suspect a macroscale change is underway. For Bresnihan and Byrne, this "great enclosure" of urban property explains the "impossibility of accessing space for any form of activity which does not generate profit as their chief motivation."[88] The worry is, if these patterns continue, the spatial opportunities for urban activism will close for good.

Activist Enterprises Are Complicit in Gentrification

Although activist-entrepreneurs are victims of gentrification, their position is complicated because they are also complicit. Activists do not intend to promote displacement, but their presence nevertheless stimulates redevelopment. The story then gets even more complicated because some activist-entrepreneurs find ways to use gentrification to their advantage. This reciprocal entanglement does not mean activists support gentrification. Instead, it reflects an intransigent reality and the necessity of finding practical solutions.

Gentrification involves co-optation. It involves cultural co-optation, for instance when ethnic festivals and immigrant symbols get incorporated into neighborhood branding.[89] It involves labor co-optation, for instance when real estate developers cash in on the sweat equity of grassroots artists and do-it-yourself homeowners.[90] Activism gets co-opted as well. For Alesia Montgomery, "If capital and the state cannot crush a movement, they institute a new publicity regime that . . . converts elements of its culture of resistance into cultural and social capital to enhance place capital."[91] In these co-optation processes, the histories, locations, and symbols of radical resistance get incorporated into sanitized narratives of cultural edginess and place-based distinctiveness, which helps sell neighborhoods.

These trends put activist-entrepreneurs in a difficult position. Being pulled into other people's real estate ventures does not mean activists are the masterminds or architects of neighborhood change, but this lack of intentionality does not negate the effects. Print-based movement spaces fit the profile of "early" gentrifiers who inadvertently get the process started.[92] For Brian Godfrey, artists, activists, single women, college students, queers, counterculturalists, and anticapitalists move into marginalized neighborhoods partly for their affordability and partly because urban resources allow them to live differently. This "bohemian influx" then "constitute[s] the unintentional 'shock troops' for gentrification" who, without intending it, "encourage the beginnings of housing speculation."[93] Real estate speculation often displaces other residents and businesses more quickly than the new bohemian arrivals. For Damaris Rose, "those groups of people who may be developing alternative forms of reproduction of social life are in many cases displacing poorer residents with far fewer options."[94] However, artists and counterculturalists often get priced out eventually when more affluent consumers arrive on the scene.[95]

Because bookstores and event spaces fit so neatly into contemporary place-branding campaigns, they fuel gentrification regardless of owners' intentions. For Andrew Laties, "Indie bookstores are an engine for community economic development. . . . We know, in advance, that any time a new bookstore is added to ANY neighborhood, real estate values all around that store will rise."[96] Boone with Minnehaha echoes these sentiments. "We definitely recognize the huge potential for a place that hosts art events and concerts to be the first step in gentrification. The poor artists move in, and it becomes cool."

Given this market potential, real estate developers often recruit edgy indie booksellers—including activist ones—into the neighborhoods they want to redevelop. In Chicago, for instance, Lynn Mooney describes how the original owners of Women & Children First "were recruited" in 1989 into a disinvested neighborhood "by a group of businesspeople who had a vision for what this neighborhood could be." The queer feminist bookstore was among the first new retailers to open after several decades of white flight. "We were a very early stakeholder in this neighborhood" at a time when the area "was not gentrified. There were not all kinds of cute funky boutiques. It was very sleepy. [There were] a lot of empty storefronts." The bookstore helped stimulate a local commercial revival, first as a queer-oriented retail district, then as an emerging gentrification hot spot.

After becoming aware of how neighborhood change was encouraging gentrification, the new owners of Women & Children First took steps to limit speculative investment. Slowing gentrification is one reason Mooney joined the local Chamber of Commerce. As a board member, Mooney has more authority to advocate in favor of restrictive zoning laws, for instance by limiting building height, restricting commercial signage, and encouraging adaptive reuse. In theory, existing ordinances keep redevelopment "very strictly restrained," but real estate developers routinely request variances. Joining the board put Mooney in a position to learn about and argue against those requests, which helps preserve an ecosystem favoring small businesses.

Although some activist-entrepreneurs like Mooney get involved in institutional governing, most do not. This limited participation is partly because many activists oppose those systems for political reasons and partly because many activists are skeptical that formal participation makes much difference. On the contrary, a more common refrain was, if activist bookstores were complicit in gentrification regardless of intention, and if fighting gentrification usually failed, then perhaps activist-entrepreneurs should simply exploit their own complicity and turn it to their advantage. Not everyone agreed with this approach, and even those who did were not saying gentrification was good. Instead, this attitude was more like swimming laterally in a riptide that activists did not enter on purpose and could not successfully resist but nonetheless wanted to survive.

Activist-entrepreneurs participate in gentrification in many ways with mixed results. One participation technique involves using gentrification to incubate radical businesses. Incubation is why Red Emma's relocated to a neighborhood on the cusp of redevelopment in 2013. According to Charles D'Adamo, who observed the process from his position with the Alternative Press Center, the people who owned the building "were sitting on it," hoping to flip it when the market turned. Getting reputable tenants in long-vacant structures stimulates market demand, which is why the owners offered Red Emma's "X amount of years where their rent was low." The building had problems, but the collective "was in a [social] network that included people who were activists who had renovation skills" and could make grassroots repairs. Despite knowing that the rent would eventually rise to market rate, it was still a win-win because it gave Red Emma's time to grow the business. By the time the rent increased in 2018, the collective was strong enough to upgrade to a more prominent location with a street level bar and a larger event space.[97]

The Read/Write Library had a similar story. Nell Taylor started the library in a filing cabinet stashed in the basement of a coffeeshop. As the collection grew, she moved it to another shared storefront, then a shared artist space, then a theater lobby inside a church. After six nomadic years, Taylor signed the library's first commercial lease for a gutted, subdivided, sparsely converted theater in a gentrifying Puerto Rican neighborhood on Chicago's West Side. She got the place cheap because the owner, "a history nerd" and "former punk," was also the vice president of a development company, and he needed a reputable, long-term tenant, like a library, to strengthen his refinance proposal to the bank. Although clearly part of the gentrification wave, the commercial lease gave the library stability and credibility. The project then grew so quickly that, five years later, Taylor began looking for an even larger space to house the library's mushrooming collection and numerous events.

Alongside incubation, another way activist-entrepreneurs exploit their complicity is by using their "shock troop" role to document the gentrification process. Documenting communities being erased is one reason why Taylor with the Read/Write Library agreed to be the pilot tenant for a redevelopment initiative spearheaded by the City of Chicago. In 2015, city officials commissioned architects to create a prototype for converting shipping containers into kiosks for pop-up businesses. The city then took the prototype and "plunked down on a lot that had been vacant and owned by the city for years" in a predominantly low-income community of color experiencing displacement and gentrification. Activist librarians approached the project as an opportunity to do "outreach to the communities that were never paid attention to." They used the kiosk to teach residents how to document local history—including histories of community organizing and evidence of broken promises—before that evidence disappeared under the foundations of new mega-projects. The hope was that, by preserving these documents, community activists could use them to advocate for more equitable development elsewhere.

A third way activist-entrepreneurs turn gentrification to their advantage is by participating in promotional campaigns. A few examples illustrate these general trends. In Chicago, Unabridged is a key attraction in the chamber of commerce's annual "Wine & Sweets Stroll." La Casa Azul was featured in the city-sponsored "Neighborhood x Neighborhood" campaign encouraging New York residents and tourists to visit Harlem.[98] Similarly, Giovanni's Room collaborated with the Philadelphia Convention & Visitors Bureau on a million-dollar campaign to promote queer tourism. Participating in these promotional campaigns stimulates redevelopment while also revitalizing business. "If we can get people from out of town to visit us, that really drives our sales."[99]

Participating in promotional campaigns has economic benefits, but those benefits are not perfect. For one thing, increased sales often do not fully offset rising rents. Another issue is that the political missions are easily lost in the mix. For example, although Bound Together was founded to advance a movement, tourists flock there because it is one of Haight Ashbury's "shops of freaky yore."[100] They visit Quimby's because it has "the feel of an edgy alternative destination that evokes Wicker Park's grittier days."[101] They like Revolution because it symbolizes "the mythology of the People's Republic of Berkeley."[102] They make pilgrimages to Internationalist because the store's founder, "Commie Bob," was murdered on the anniversary of Malcolm X's death, and the case remains unsolved.[103] Similarly, at Left Bank in Seattle, tourists enjoy the European-style architecture. "I feel like I'm in Harry Potter!" This interest boosts sales, but it also reflects a superficial appreciation for the romanticized grit of legendary activism rather than a genuine engagement with present-day politics.

Accounts like these complicate victim-based narratives by confirming that activist enterprises are complicit in gentrification. They are complicit both as inadvertent shock troops and as willing participants, albeit with progressive goals. Complicity is rarely a clear win for activists, but if gentrification cannot be avoided, then tapping into its revenue-generating potential can help their venues survive.

Negotiating Gentrification Involves Difficult Choices

Whether activist-entrepreneurs intend to participate in gentrification or simply get caught in its wake, these real estate dynamics affect where people claim durable space and on what terms. Analyzing how activists claim space is important because many scholars assume that gentrification marks the end of urban radical organizing. For skeptics, even if cities contain resources like anonymity and critical mass, these resources do little good if activists cannot afford to access them.

Although it is helpful and important to perform postmortems of counterspaces buckling under gentrification pressures, some venues do not close or even feel pressure to close, and new venues are opening. Alongside the mutual co-optation described above, these last two sections analyze the geography of resilient and emerging venues to explain why some activist enterprises are surviving—and even thriving—despite rising rents. As with previous locational strategies, emerging trends are imperfect and involve trade-offs. When balancing durability against cost, accessibility, visibility, and ethics, it is rare for activists to have everything they want. Nevertheless, these patterns show that urban redevelopment is changing—but not ending—the locational opportunity structure for activists to claim durable spaces in cities.

One strategic response to gentrification involves accepting durability in motion. Moving is expensive, but so is staying as rents rise. Serial movers relocate once or twice each decade following the gentrification line, which generates durability for a time, as well as consistency in business identity, despite periodic moves. Resistencia is one such serial mover. "We were ousted from our previous location—this is our fifth location—because of gentrification." BookWoman is also on its fifth location. "It's all because we've been chasing cheaper rent. . . . You go to a place and it's OK for a while. But if you stay in one place long enough, it's going to gentrify." Lucy Parsons has likewise moved five or six times due to rising rents, including once when the landlord evicted them to demolish the building and replace it with "a mainstream super mall."[104] The story is the same at Eso Won, which has relocated five or six times, "each time seeking a foothold in a Black community that itself has been shifting."[105] These moves—often to new locations just a few blocks away—keep counterinstitutions locally embedded enough and financially stable enough to keep operating even as their exact locations follow the gentrification line.

When selecting new locations, some activists try to avoid at-risk areas, although this approach is controversial. For instance, when the Minnehaha Free Space needed a new location, collective members avoided looking in African American neighborhoods. Communities of color are prime targets for gentrification, and collective members did not want to repeat their previous role as the white anarchists who moved in and helped break up the neighborhood. For Boone with Minnehaha, "That's a mistake that we made the first time around [by] not being more mindful of the fact that we're a part of making a place a hipper neighborhood." However, despite the laudable ethical intention of subverting white colonization, this approach raises other ethical concerns because avoiding communities of color also means withholding resources and replicating segregation. Another challenge is that white neighborhoods are more expensive. As a work-around, collective members considered foregoing a storefront and moving into a shared house instead. However, the cost savings would come with the trade-off of reduced accessibility, and collective members like Boone felt conflicted about whether the trade-off was worthwhile.

As an alternative to serial relocation or domestic locations, another response to rising costs is relocating to the suburbs. However, there is considerable disagreement among activist-entrepreneurs about whether and under which circumstances this approach is effective. BookWoman in Austin is one venue that made the suburban move. Austin is one of the fastest growing cities in the United States, and the demand for space outstrips supply. With real estate prices skyrocketing, Susan Post moved BookWoman out of the central city in 2008. The move brought cheaper rent, but it also undermined visibility and reduced sales. The new location was only four miles away, but the suburban context created a psychic barrier. "It was like, 'Oh my god, we're in the frozen north. We're feminist pioneers . . . so far away from the center.' . . . People living in South Austin, they hardly come anymore."

For a well-established feminist business like BookWoman, moving away from the critical mass can be financially viable. Because feminism has gone somewhat mainstream, feminist merchandise appeals to a wider consumer base, which reduces the need for a large urban draw. Additionally, second-wave feminist enterprises are often run by women nearing retirement age, which means suburban locations are often sufficient to carry those venues through their remaining years.

But it's a different story for fringe, scrappy upstarts. People often ask Greg Newton with the Bureau of General Services if he would consider relocating to Brooklyn where property costs, while still high, are comparatively lower than in Manhattan. Newton says no. "It's going to be so hard to get people out there." The outlying location creates a cognitive barrier. "It's all psychological." Even though Brooklyn is accessible by subway, Newton felt it was too far off the queer community's mental map. If people are not regularly showing up for events, the store cannot serve its intended political functions.

Given these trade-offs, activist-entrepreneurs generally prefer to stay in central locations if possible, even if it means making cuts elsewhere. For example, at Bluestockings, when sales revenue dropped during the 2008 recession even as gentrification continued, the collective considered cutting costs by relocating to Brooklyn,[106] but then decided against it. As Corey Farach explained, having a street-facing storefront in a central location on the Lower East Side was too important. Instead of moving, the collective stopped paying wages and delayed capital investments. "We're just trying to spend as little as possible so the rest can just go to rent." Those cuts, plus an online crowdfunding campaign, helped the bookstore keep its space, and it was back in the black by 2017.

For anarchists, volunteer labor and charitable donations help people hold onto central spaces, but other groups are often worried about the ethical implications. For instance, given the long history of devalued women's labor, many feminists felt working without pay was counterproductive. Combatting this history is one reason why many feminist entrepreneurs do not work for free and instead look for other ways to pay for space, including by tapping into gentrification markets. For Sandy Torkildson with A Room of One's Own, even though downtown redevelopment increased

commercial rents, it also increased foot traffic and attracted affluent customers. The trade-off, however, is that tapping this market required compromise. "We felt we had to expand to be a more general bookstore. . . .
You have to have a big enough draw to make people want to spend an hour
browsing." Going general raises questions about how far activists are willing to stray from some aspects of their political mission to hold onto urban
spaces. A Room of One's Own still has a feminist mission. The employees
are paid, and general sales cross-subsidize the feminist stock. But going
general also means selling centrist and conservative authors, like a memoir written by Wisconsin's Republican governor, whom the booksellers
don't like. "Luckily his name starts with a W, so it's on the bottom shelf."

For some feminist booksellers, the compromise of going general is
justified because it keeps women-owned businesses financially viable.[107]
However, going general is not politically appealing for activists still in the
trenches. For Greg Newton with the Bureau of General Services, it's hard
to imagine a time when dedicated, safe, empowering public spaces supporting queer culture will no longer be needed. "Maybe someday we'll get
to a point where it's not an issue, but that seems like a millennium from
now." In the meantime, although the Bureau "is open to people who are
friends of queers and supportive . . . it's a space for queer people. And that's
explicit, that people know that." If locating in an obscure room inside an
institutional building is what it takes to have that central and undiluted
space, Newton is comfortable making that trade.

The takeaway from all this back-and-forth is that there is no perfect solution. Economics matter, but from a social movement perspective, locational choices also have political implications. Locating in the margins has
always involved trade-offs, and locational decision making in the gentrification age intensifies those trends. Activists still have choices. Old venues are adapting, and new ones are emerging. But no location is perfect,
and people have different opinions about which trade-offs are politically
justified.

New Locational Patterns Are Slowly Converging

Within this diverse landscape of improvisation and compromise, there are
some threads that may foreshadow a convergence yet to come. As I explain in this final section, four possibilities include the continued use of

marginal locations, the advantages of buying property, the tendency to join umbrella institutions, and the value of opening counterspaces even when displacement is likely.

The first trend—the continued use of marginal locations—simply acknowledges that a shrinking window of opportunity is not the same as an absent window. Even with gentrification, marginal locations still exist, and disinvestment has not ended. In New York, Bluestockings opened in 1999—well into the gentrification age—amid "skid rows" and "flophouses"[108] with a "brothel," a deli, and a pawn shop for neighbors.[109] The bookstore then operated for years in a building with inadequate plumbing. "As staffers would come and go in the middle of the day . . . one person would be like, 'Did the yoga studio [upstairs] flood today?' Answer would be, 'Yes.' And it's just a totally normal thing." I asked what happened when the building flooded. "We just had to run [and] get the books out of the way."

This pattern recurred in other cities. In Pittsburgh, The Big Idea opened in 2001 in an area where "a lot of people are pretty poor,"[110] and City of Asylum opened in 2016 in another still-disinvested neighborhood near downtown.[111] In New York, Revolution NYC relocated in 2015 to a disinvested section of Harlem where, for the first year, activists worked in a building without heating or air-conditioning. Similarly, in Buffalo, Burning Books opened in 2011 in a disinvested neighborhood where other retailers were warned against starting businesses on the block. "Don't do it. . . . You're in the middle of a war zone."[112] Venues like these are part of the bohemian fringe, and they opened in locations on the cusp of gentrification. These accounts nevertheless suggest that, even as gentrification advances quickly through some neighborhoods, it moves more slowly in other locations, and the margins have not entirely closed.

The second trend is that the most effective strategy in achieving place stability despite gentrification involves becoming property owners. Activist enterprises that own their spaces enjoy considerable stability despite the redevelopment occurring around them. For Paul Yamazaki, if City Lights hadn't bought the building in the 1990s, "given the real estate prices here [today] . . . it would be quite possible that we couldn't afford to be in this location." However, because City Lights owns the building, it can cover its property costs and have enough left over to replenish stock, pay wages, provide employment benefits, and earn a profit. This economic security enhances durability. It also enhances emotional well-being by releasing staffers from the "greater and greater anxiety about what the next lease would look like."

Among property-owning venues, City Lights's experience was the norm. In interviews and archives, activists who owned their locations expressed almost no anxiety whatsoever about economic displacement. Trudy Mills with Antigone said, "we are fortunate because we own our building, which is one of the difficulties that many bookstores face when an area becomes more popular." For Ed Hermance with Giovanni's Room, "Having paid off the mortgages is the only way the store has survived. . . . We could never afford the rent today."[113] For Charles D'Adamo with the Alternative Press Center, "owning the space was core to that [venue] being there for over twenty-five years." Owning property shields businesses from rising rents, which stabilizes them by reducing overhead. Ownership provides other benefits as well, which is why the owner of Quimby's bought the building as an investment. According to store manager Liz Mason, "one of the smartest things that you can do to run a small business is to buy the building . . . before a neighborhood [gentrifies]." That way, even if Quimby's never earns a cent of profit, the owner accrues equity for retirement.

Not everyone has the option of buying buildings. Women, minorities, and anarchist collectives have a harder time accessing conventional loans. Mortgages require down payments. Buying property requires long-term commitments. It requires accepting responsibility for building maintenance and capital improvements. It also requires owners who are willing to sell rather than hold out for higher post-gentrification prices. Regardless, for activist-entrepreneurs who can overcome those hurdles, buying buildings gives counterspaces significant stability despite gentrification.

Third, if buying the building is not an option, the next best strategy involves partnering with larger institutions. Whereas radical bookstores in the 1960s and 1970s occupied stand-alone storefronts, umbrella-style relationships are a growing trend today. As examples, City of Asylum is housed within Alphabet City,[114] Nuestra Palabra is located inside Talento Bilingüe de Houston,[115] Resistencia works under the auspice of Red Salmon Arts and is located in the PODER Mariposa Complex, and the Bureau of General Services is located inside the LGBT Community Center. Some of these arrangements come with street-facing storefronts, but some do not. Regardless, the shift from renting freestanding storefronts to nesting within cultural institutions is breathing new life into print-based movement spaces by reducing rent.

However, sharing institutional space comes with trade-offs. The most significant trade-off is decreased visibility. Decreased visibility may seem counterintuitive because colocating increases the thematic visibility for the group as a whole. However, some institutional spaces are less heavily trafficked than commercial corridors. For Resistencia, moving into a shared complex slashed the rent and brought Latino/a justice organizations together, but the institutional complex attracts fewer customers than Resistencia's former commercial locations. "You're just not gonna get foot traffic in the same way that you would somewhere else."

Another challenge is that, when banding together, the visibility of individual businesses is easily lost in the mix. For the Bureau of General Services, moving into the LGBT Community Center reduced rent, and the umbrella institution attracts three hundred thousand visitors each year,[116] which is significantly more than the bookstore could attract on its own. However, in its out-of-the-way location in a second-floor corridor, anyone not explicitly looking for the bookstore is unlikely to find it by accident.

Fourth, as a final takeaway, even when activist-entrepreneurs who oppose gentrification know that their venues will inevitably contribute to gentrification, they may feel it is important to open those businesses anyway. This is why Noëlle Santos, an Afro Latina woman in the Bronx, spearheaded a crowdfunding campaign in 2017 to raise $100,000 to launch The Lit Bar, "a bookstore/wine bar/community center" with a "graffiti & chandelier theme."[117] Santos knew a venture like hers might contribute to gentrification. "That's a possibility—that's the harsh reality of it."[118] But she felt justified taking the risk. "I want my borough to progress, and I want to do as much as one person and one business can to offer access to literature to the people of the Bronx."[119] Despite the risk of becoming complicit, not opening the business was unlikely to stop gentrification. For Santos, by opening anyway, existing residents would get at least some benefits along the way.

As these examples show, claiming locations for activist enterprises is not easy. Many people work in spaces they love, but there are always trade-offs. Although the options in a gentrification age are not perfect, they nevertheless push back against suggestions that the era of urban counter-spaces has ended. On the contrary, activist enterprises remain open. They remain concentrated in cities. And their durability supports constructive activism, including through constructive overlays, which are the topics of the next four chapters.

· CHAPTER 5 ·

Designing Landscapes That
Shout, Entice, and Heal

JANIFER WILSON GREW UP IN GEORGIA in an environment where
she felt invisible. In books, films, museums, and educational curricu-
lum, "there was no depiction of folk who look like me. During the time
I grew up, being dark was not popular."[1] Things changed when Wilson
moved to New York. "Harlem was then the place to be. Folk were
proud—and dressed. It was wonderful."[2] For Wilson, Harlem's Black-
themed businesses were anchors for this Black cultural mecca, including
Black bookstores like Tree of Life Bookstore and Liberation Bookstore.
"The books were so relevant."[3] In those movement-oriented spaces, Wilson found the reflection she'd long been denied, which felt inspiring and
hopeful. "It gave me the strength and the fortitude to see us excel."[4]

These businesses closed over the years as owners retired or died. In response, Wilson decided to replace them with a Black-themed business of
her own. She believed self-knowledge enabled success, she saw books as
healing tools, and she saw bookstores as beacons of hope. But Wilson's
friends were skeptical. "You know what people said? They said, 'She's not
going to make it. 'Cause black folk don't read.'"[5] Coming face-to-face with
this internalized stereotype within her own community only intensified
Wilson's resolve. Her business would challenge stigma by showing people
concrete evidence of Black intellectual, cultural, and literary achievement.

Wilson founded Sister's Uptown Bookstore and Cultural Center in
Harlem in 2000 as an intergenerational, family-run business. When I visited in 2017, Sister's Uptown had a cheerful facade on Amsterdam Avenue
with a purple canopy and a bright red door. Inside, Wilson stood behind
the cash register. Her daughter and store manager Kori worked the floor.
Kori's teenage son sat at the deli counter, and a toddler played in the back
under the watchful eye of an elderly man relaxing in a well-worn armchair.

The name Sister's Uptown evokes kinship, community, and race, and these themes are reflected in the decor. The walls and shelves contain masks, baskets, textiles, drums, and carvings from Africa. According to Wilson's daughter Kori, Wilson carried several of these items back with her after her Ashanti naming ceremony in Ghana. They import the rest from Mali, Kenya, and several countries in west Africa. The bookstore displays work by local African American artists and artisans as well, including Black-themed beauty products and wall art celebrating dark complexions and natural hairstyles. Near the back of the store, I noticed a bookshelf with an Africa-shaped hole cut through it, like a cookie cutter imprint in the wood.

For Wilson, this visual celebration of African heritage provides a partial antidote to the erasure of Black culture in other public spaces. These visual techniques are especially apparent in the children's section. Unlike at other libraries and bookstores where stories about white children predominate, "I can take the children right here to the shelves and tell them, 'Look at this. It's all stories about us.'"[6] However, not every title is explicitly Black. Sister's Uptown stocks bestsellers like *Diary of a Wimpy Kid* and *Brain Quest,* but those books are shelved discretely and framed by another set of books displayed faceout. These books include works by Maya Angelou, picture books about liberation movements, and winners of the Coretta Scott King Book Award.

For store manager Kori Wilson, the books' cover art is significant. "Just the tangibility of the page and the vibrancy of the pictures, especially in children's books . . . is important." The images depict Black bodies in many contexts, from Misty Copeland in a ballet leotard to African children in traditional dress. Strips of paper taped to the shelves read, "Black is Beautiful," "Be Yourself!," "BLACK ACHIEVEMENT," "Imagine," and "Read!!" These display strategies do more than put books on shelves. They also encourage African American children not to give up on literacy or their dreams. Instead, these healing displays give kids in Harlem an empowered and scholarly reflection of who they are and who they might become.

Display strategies like these show how activist-entrepreneurs use aesthetics to put progressive ideas on display. Sister's Uptown uses objects, images, and ambient text to dramatize heritage and inspire success. Other print-based movement spaces use similar methods to visualize the hopes and dreams of anarchists, feminists, Latinos, queers, and revolutionaries of many stripes. Showcasing aspirational visions is partly about providing a

The books, images, and signs on the bookshelves in the children's section at Sister's Uptown Bookstore and Community Center in Harlem, New York, celebrate Black experiences and accomplishments. Photograph by author, 2017.

reflection for people whose identities are systematically ignored, distorted, or denied. It is also about overcoming the will to avoid unsettling experiences. Choices about color, furniture, props, and layouts are opportunities not only to make identities visible but to make them visible in ways that make it harder for naysayers to avoid or reject the ideas on display.

Black bookstores do not have a monopoly on Black authors. However, just as people associate objects with meanings, people use environmental cues to interpret those meanings. Nicholas Thoburn uses the term "mediological ecosystem"[7] to describe how people perceive ideas differently depending on the setting. For instance, for written work, readers interpret the meaning, validity, and significance of a sentence differently depending on whether it is printed in perfect-bound books sold by corporate publishers or whether it is scribbled on notebook paper and stapled into homemade zines.

In a similar manner, the tokenistic inclusion of a few "urban" hits in chain superstores does not mean those spaces do justice to the full range of Black experiences. For Marjorie Coeyman, "While many African-American readers love to walk into a Barnes & Noble superstore and see books by Black authors prominently on display, few would argue that the emergence of a handful of popular authors means that their needs are truly being met by mainstream booksellers."[8] James Fugate with Eso Won echoes these sentiments. Superstore chains stock a few bestsellers, "but if you want a book like *The Destruction of Black Civilization* . . . or *The Mis-Education of the Negro,* you may not find that book or it may be very hard to find. . . . That's going to lessen those books' impact."[9]

These comments suggest that Black voices embedded in white environments can simultaneously be present and overshadowed. This observation gets at the core discussion in this chapter, which is about how activists construct mediological ecosystems to influence how people interpret information on display. I agree that making marginalized perspectives visible in the public realm is an important political accomplishment. But beyond merely rendering perspectives visible, how can activists design their spaces to help them more effectively be heard?

Rendering marginalized groups visible is an important political technique for claiming legitimacy. As other scholars have shown, there is an overrepresentation of privileged groups in public spaces, including an overrepresentation of their identities and customs in urban cultural landscapes. By contrast, less privileged groups get erased or depicted only in negative lights. These inequitable regimes of publicity have political consequences, which explains why so many social movements try to diversify cultural landscapes by claiming places where marginalized groups can make themselves visible in new ways.[10]

Although scholars increasingly appreciate the power of visibility in the public realm, they say less about the difference between being visible and being seen and accepted. People are socialized to avoid information they feel is controversial or irrelevant. Because of these avoidance patterns, even if activists claim space by painting murals or holding rallies, other people can still avoid the information by choosing different travel paths, whitewashing over the content, or mentally screening those images from view. For these reasons, rendering visible is no guarantee that the intended audience will allow itself to see. Even for those who do absorb the information, visibility comes with no guarantee about how they will respond.

Activist-entrepreneurs know that many people habitually avoid progressive messages. In response, they told me about the techniques they use to get around avoidance behaviors, including the ways they construct their aesthetics. Talking about aesthetics does not imply that other considerations—like location, programming, and protest support—are less significant. However, visual vocabularies are especially important when making first impressions. When entering new environments for the first time, visual cues provide immediate information about the purpose of the space. These aesthetics communicate at a glance, and they set a tone for interactions that follow.

When analyzing visual vocabularies in print-based movement spaces, I identified two overlapping strategies. One strategy, which I expected to find and which I mention here mostly in passing, is using subcultural codes to claim turf by marking it as feminist, anarchist, Latino/a, Black, or queer. For Ross Haenfler, subcultures use aesthetic markers like clothing and mannerisms to "set participants apart from 'normal' society (and other subcultures)" and to "establish a particular subcultural identity."[11] Activist-entrepreneurs tap into these subcultural codes when designing storefronts, for instance by featuring queer material in lavender-painted rooms or placing anarchist texts on salvaged red-and-black shelves. Displays of foundational reads like Karl Marx's *Capital* and Paulo Freire's *Pedagogies of the Oppressed* do similar work. Even though these classics may only sell once or twice a year, their presence establishes a genealogical identity for the lesser-known new releases around them. These subcultural codes render marginalized groups visible, and activist-entrepreneurs incorporate them into movement-oriented counterspaces.

However, claiming turf is not the only visual strategy at work in activist businesses. The second and unexpected strategy, which is the focus of this chapter, is modulating stylistic codes with another set of visual repertoires that helps people see the messages on display. This second set of techniques is less about claiming turf and more about responding to the audience's will to avoid. I explore this second strategy in this chapter by looking at three subtechniques, which I classify as landscapes that shout, landscapes that entice, and landscapes that heal. These subtechniques are crosscutting categories, meaning there are feminist, anarchist, Black,

Latino/a, and queer spaces in each typology. These crosscutting dynamics indicate that shouting, enticing, or healing are not unique to specific movements. Instead, these are flexible techniques that activists leverage to advance many different causes.

Starting with landscapes that shout, in response to the will to avoid, some activists construct visual displays designed to be graphic, visceral, and overwhelming. The hope is that these extreme presentations will speak so powerfully that passersby will be unable to tune them out or forget what they see. This approach targets people who may initially be unaware or apathetic but who may be moved to protest if they knew more about global injustice. The goal is to create environments visualizing atrocities with such force that it shocks people out of complacency and motivates them to resist.

Next, although forceful landscapes serve some purposes, shouting can also feel alienating, which can intensify the will to avoid. To reduce aversion responses, some activists opt for gentler methods, for instance by presenting information in a framework that feels familiar and intriguing. Activists construct enticing landscapes to encourage people who may otherwise avoid uncomfortable topics to instead willingly explore alternative viewpoints. The hope is to construct spaces sparking curiosity and openness where people get hands-on experience responding to cultural difference with empathy and validation.

A third approach involves landscapes that heal. Unlike landscapes that shout or entice, which are oriented toward people who do not already self-identify with the movement, landscapes that heal are designed to speak inwardly to people experiencing social harm. Avoidance is still a factor because healing from trauma is not only about affirmation. It also involves grappling with hurt and shame, which are difficult emotions that people often wish to avoid. As an alternative, the hope is to construct nurturing environments where people can see their experiences, face their fears, and develop stronger internal compasses for navigating an oppressive world with dignity and purpose.

These findings confirm what scholars already know, which is that people use subcultural codes to claim space, for instance by marking turf as Latino/a, feminist, anarchist, Black, or queer. However, these examples also point to an unexpected finding, which is that activist-entrepreneurs overlay a second set of visual vocabularies on top of subcultural codes. As a form of constructive activism, these overlay vocabularies reflect activists' understandings of how people seek and avoid information and how to get around that will to avoid. This finding underscores the general importance of moving beyond simple, binary questions of whether group symbols are present or absent to also address the intended impact of visualization both in quasi-public retail spaces and in other cultural landscapes.

Cultural Landscapes Reflect the Will to Avoid

Spaces like Sister's Uptown are part of the cultural landscape of cities. For scholars like Paul Groth and Chris Wilson, cultural landscapes are the material patterns facilitating a way of life.[12] These patterns are dialectical in that "we shape our buildings, and then they shape us."[13] Because of this mutual co-construction, landscapes are not merely the residue of cultural activity. They are also structuring agents that "have helped to shape (and reproduce) social hierarchies."[14]

The limited representation of marginalized groups in public spaces both reflects their weaker structural position and reproduces their marginalized status. Lynn Staeheli, Don Mitchell, and Caroline Nagel use the phrase "regimes of publicity" to describe these hierarchical aesthetics. Regimes of publicity are the "prevailing system of laws, practices, and relations that condition the qualities of a public and the ways that it is situated with respect to other publics."[15] For example, when thinking about linguistic landscapes, the words embedded in street signs, commercial signage, and building inscriptions do more than provide functional assistance with wayfinding. They also connect people to systems of authority, which is why it is so common during regime changes to rename streets,[16] change building names,[17] and post multilingual signage.[18] These reinscriptions of ambient text destabilize old regimes and naturalize new ones.

Because elites disproportionately control the institutions, policies, and resources generating cultural landscapes, regimes of publicity overwhelmingly reflect and advance elite interests at the expense of less powerful groups.[19] However, despite inequities, cultural landscapes are disrupted and contested. Groth and Wilson use the term "contested landscapes" to highlight not only how cultural landscapes reproduce social hierarchies but also "how individuals and social movements have opposed those hierarchies."[20] Activists subvert normative publicity regimes by erecting statues of African Americans,[21] preserving evidence of Chinese heritage,[22] removing references to oppressive historical figures,[23] showcasing women in business districts,[24] organizing parades celebrating queer culture,[25] and using graffiti to visualize poverty.[26]

These contested landscapes are deeply political. Jacques Rancière defines political activity as "whatever shifts a body from the place assigned to it . . . makes visible what had no business being seen, and makes heard a discourse where once there was only place for noise."[27] Erecting statues, removing plaques, and staging parades generate these political effects. For Don Mitchell, these practices are about "the development—or often the radical claiming—of a *space for representation,* a place in which groups and individuals can make themselves *visible.*"[28] For Teresa Caldeira, they are about "expanding the openness of the democratic public sphere."[29] Similarly for Staeheli, Mitchell, and Nagel, these interventions "shed light on the qualities of democratic inclusion in a society."[30]

Although cultural landscape scholars are increasingly paying attention to the contested politics of visibility, they generally limit their analyses to questions of presence or absence. Ethnic murals, bilingual signage, and racialized statues either exist, or they do not exist. The assumption is that, when present, contentious elements construct "a new visibility and a new type of presence for the subaltern that disrupts a certain order of things that used to constitute the public."[31] Scholars acknowledge that there is not a one-to-one correspondence between presence and influence, most notably because subcultural symbols get co-opted for other purposes, including gentrification.[32] However, the general sense in the literature is that, if a vulnerable group can make a visible mark on the city, other people will see it and be affected by what they see.

I do not wish to detract from this line of inquiry because I agree that subversive interventions construct much-needed places of counteridentity formation and social protection. However, I want to expand this analysis by also attending to questions of audience, which I explore from an unconventional perspective. Other scholars evaluating audience ask bystanders what they think about their environment, and they analyze how state and market audience members respond to contentious interventions. These methods shed light on how projects are received, but they say nothing about how activists' understandings of audience behaviors influence their choices, for instance through design and aesthetics. Activists are not always correct in their assumptions of audience behavior, but their perceptions—accurate or otherwise—orient their choices and explain why they construct movement-oriented spaces that look the way they do.

When reading transcripts and archives to understand how ideas about audience influence visual vocabularies, two scholarly lenses proved especially useful. One lens involved the will to avoid. According to Gary Burnett, Michele Besant, and Elfreda A. Chatman, people are socialized to seek out some kinds of information while avoiding others deemed "too costly," too "difficult," or of "an unacceptable social type."[33] These group-specific patterns of seeking and avoiding information are "normative," meaning the patterns reflect group-specific understandings of what a person needs to know to live a certain kind of life, as well as what information is deemed irrelevant, irrational, or off-limits.[34] Because of this normativity, painting a mural or hosting a radical festival does not guarantee that other groups will allow themselves to see the information on display. Instead, people often take steps to avoid exposure rather than allowing themselves to become productively unsettled.

When it comes to avoidance in print-based movement spaces, there are reasons to believe that aesthetics have a bigger initial impact on newcomers exploring movement scenes than on people who already self-identify with the cause. Unlike other spaces where people spend time out of necessity—for instance when passing through a subway station or responding to a jury summons—people can choose whether to enter and linger in commercial spaces, including activist ones. As Jan Gehl has shown, for spaces occupied by choice, design characteristics are especially influential in determining use.[35] However, some groups are more affected than others. For dedicated activists, although design matters, their commitment to the politics means they are likely to spend time in movement-oriented spaces regardless of the aesthetics. By contrast, for people new to a movement, whether an environment feels shouting, enticing, or healing can have a big impact on who comes in, how long they stay, and how they interpret the information on display.

Alongside avoidance, a related scholarly lens is understanding how environments influence responses. Cameron Duff uses the phrase "affective atmosphere" to describe both "the emotional feel of place" and the "store of action-potential, the dispositions and agencies, potentially enactable in that place."[36] Injecting cultural difference into normative environments changes the action potential of those spaces, for instance by signaling to queer couples that they can kiss on public sidewalks or signaling to Latino/a families that they can picnic in public parks.[37] But action potential affects other groups as well. Onlookers are invited to respond in specific ways, for instance with indifference, empathy, or support. Activist-entrepreneurs are not unique in creating affective atmospheres. What sets them apart from conventional retailers is their political intent. This is not about creating themed environments to boost sales. Instead, it's about dra-matizing ideas to advance progressive imaginations.

With these themes of avoidance and response in mind, this chapter ex-plores the presentation techniques activist-entrepreneurs develop to help overcome avoidance behaviors and encourage a willingness to explore. However, several caveats are worth mentioning before proceeding. First, although this chapter uses examples of landscapes designed to shout, en-tice, or heal, these typologies are not mutually exclusive. An environment that feels shout-y to one person can simultaneously feel enticing and heal-ing to someone else. Similarly, these environments are not deterministic. People have different levels of proficiency when it comes to reading land-scapes. Visitors make their own choices about where to put their atten-tion. They also respond in different ways to the messages they decipher, even when activists provide directional cues.

As another caveat, the coherence of contentious landscapes should not be overstated. Social movements are often "notoriously ephemeral,"[38] and print-based movement spaces—while more durable than other activist repertoires—do not fully escape makeshift trends. Counterspaces some-times appear haptic by choice, for instance in anarchist spaces where de-constructive aesthetics symbolize "the ordinary surfaces of life . . . either being patched together or torn down."[39] More often, the makeshift feel of movement-oriented businesses reflects the economic constraints of running a space on a shoestring budget. Happily, it doesn't cost much to sell feminist artwork on consignment, commission local artists to paint African-themed murals, or omit procapitalist merchandise from order forms. Even when the decor is inexpensively made, a good-enough decor can be sufficient to visualize progressive themes.

As a final caveat, focusing on the design of space in a print-based venue, rather than the content of its books, does not imply that publications don't matter. Words and texts are crucial, especially to people passionate enough about print to construct libraries, bookstores, and publishing collectives. But even the most ardent supporters only read a fraction of the material. By contrast, paint colors, artwork, furniture, props, ambient text, and body language are like wide-open books. Some people are more literate than others when deciphering their messages, but the ambiance is there for all to see. This environmental communication is overt, intentional, and difficult to ignore.

These caveats are important, but they do not diminish the communicative work that environments perform. Reading is a useful tool, but words on pages speak louder when embedded in ecosystems amplifying their messages, and the affective characteristics of these environments influence how people interpret the messages on display.

Landscapes That Shout Provoke Dissenting Imaginations

One common goal embedded in the design of movement-oriented retail is provoking outrage to galvanize action. How people see the world affects whether they are likely to protest. Recognizing injustice is no guarantee people will revolt, especially when resources, opportunities, or allies are scarce. However, when oppression goes unnoticed, collective movements are especially unlikely. The trouble is, oppression often goes unnoticed. White privilege is often invisible, international conflicts occur out of sight, microaggressions fly below the radar, misogyny can be difficult to measure, and witnesses often intentionally look the other way.

Several activist-entrepreneurs identified ignorance as an impediment to their social movement goals. Whether the goal was to combat racism, sexism, capitalism, or imperialism, these activists felt that other people's lack of awareness got in the way. Some interviewees blamed misinformation campaigns. Reiko Redmonde with Revolution in Berkeley said, "there's a lot of brainwashing in this society, and we're all subject to it." Similarly, for Jay Scheide with Lucy Parsons, people overlook oppression because of "what their schools tell them [and] the way they're indoctrinated." Other activist-entrepreneurs blamed ignorance on apathy. For Craig Palmer with May Day, "the problem in America is most people don't care or don't want to know. . . . There's all this killing going on everyday. . . . And the United States is involved in all of it. And nobody seems to talk about it or care. Most Americans are just in denial, or totally distracted."

Given this perceived will to avoid, some activist-entrepreneurs are not satisfied to merely render oppression visible. Instead, some activists set themselves the larger goal of rendering oppression so viscerally visible that even brief encounters punch people in the gut, shatter plausible deniability, and burn lasting impressions into people's consciousness. All kinds of activists (including nonprogressive ones) use graphic images for provocation. This is why antiabortion activists put photos of fetuses on posters. It is why Arab Spring demonstrators carried the corpses of people killed by state violence through the streets. It's also why Jihadist videos incorporate footage of Westerners being beheaded. These graphic images do more than just render a cause visible. On the contrary, these visceral images are intended to provoke outrage and galvanize support.

Some activist-entrepreneurs use similar tactics when designing retail spaces by arranging their stores as crash courses in systemic oppression. Having books about oppression helps because books provide symbolic authority, historical detail, and theoretical richness. But not everyone is inclined to read dense prose about every axis of oppression. Additionally, words on pages are easy to ignore. For Corey Farach with Bluestockings, chain bookstores may carry a few challenging publications, "but it's your call to pick that book up." By contrast, an entire ecosystem viscerally dramatizing oppression is harder to overlook.

One way to construct such provocative spaces is to push the most contentious material to the front. An object being displayed in a prominent position signifies importance, whereas being present but only in the background has the opposite effect. In conventional commercial spaces, prominence is about profits. Chain bookstores charge publishers to display books faceup on tables and faceout on shelves, which means visibility goes to those who can pay. This visibility attracts attention, which is why, in chain stores, 5 percent of titles—usually the ones prominently displayed—generate 50 percent of the sales.[40] Similarly, in chain superstores where 20 percent of the books generate 80 percent of the sales, industry representatives describe most of the stock as "wallpaper" indulging illusions of consumer choice that shoppers enjoy but rarely enact.[41] Activist-entrepreneurs subvert these profit-oriented regimes by displaying titles advancing their political goals and by featuring books acting as signposts within movement terrains.

Visual prominence makes an impression. The first time Corey Farach visited Bluestockings, "I just walked in, and I saw all of this super subversive literature pushed out to the front. And I was like, 'What is this place?'" Books by Naomi Klein and Noam Chomsky were displayed in the window. The front tables had publications about the Zapatista movement alongside information about U.S. police killing Black youth. That "subversive literature" was "*right there,* not in the basement. . . . Before I discovered this place, I went to a few other stores, and I was finding some good stuff.

But it's always tucked away in the basement or in the back of the store. Some book that's daring to criticize capitalism" or talking about "women of color coming to some kind of radical consciousness . . . you just don't see those in the window."

In many movement-oriented bookstores, activist-entrepreneurs not only move the provocative material from behind the scenes to center stage, they also display it faceout. Contentious publications often have accusatory titles like *Late Victorian Holocausts*,[42] *38 Nooses*,[43] and *A Little Matter of Genocide*.[44] These books have graphic cover art, including pictures of emaciated bodies on the verge of becoming corpses. These images depict the horrors of imperialism in stomach-curdling detail. Activists augment these jarring effects by filling entire walls from corner-to-corner and floor-to-ceiling with books displayed faceout. For Craig Palmer with May Day, "This stuff all hits you in the face and slaps you around. . . . We think it's important to face it out so people know about it."

By contrast, in most bookstores, if contentious books are present, people usually only see the spines, not the cover art. Even then, the spines are often hard to see because booksellers favor soft, ambient lighting for its atmospheric effect. Although soft lighting may put people in a buying mood, it does little to highlight global atrocity, which is why Raymond Lotta with Revolution NYC prefers to use bright spotlights instead. When it comes to oppression, "We want to make this very *visible* and dynamic so people see the books. You can see that it's very well lit." When books are displayed faceout under bright lights, people see those images and cannot so easily tune out their messages.

Alongside the visual prominence of provocative books and cover art, props are another way to augment the jarring effects of landscapes that shout. This is why Bound Together created "gruesome anti-war window displays of blown-apart mannequins and oil drums bleeding into the sand" to protest war in the Middle East.[45] It's why City Lights commissioned a street-facing mural depicting Zapatista activists, as well as a banner series denouncing xenophobic deportations, to publicize resistance and showcase oppression. It's also why Revolution NYC displayed a mock street sign warning pedestrians to beware of racist murdering cops for Black History Month and a poster of Trump dressed as Hitler surrounded by books on how silence contributes to genocide during the 2016 presidential election. For Raymond Lotta, these graphic depictions of "all of the horrors, the suffering, the poverty, [and] the wars . . . in the world [are] the backdrop for discussions about a yearning for a different future [and] a world crying out for revolution."

The intentionally utilitarian ambiance of many venues similarly underscores the brute force feel of oppression and resistance. As an example, Burning Books's bare-knuckled aesthetic of exposed brick walls and plain plywood shelves is less an homage to hipster culture and more about creating a "stripped down, bare bones, straight-to-the-point type of atmosphere." For Leslie James Pickering, this aesthetic is unpretentious and accessible. "It's not fancy at all. Just plain bookshelves on brick walls." The rawness of the decor and the directness of the politics reinforce each other. "If you walk in here and look at the books and stuff, you realize, 'Oh, [for] these people, there's no holds barred.' We're not pretending like anything is too radical for us."

Alongside books, images, and props, another important tool is ambient text. Activists use words for political purposes. For Charles Willet with the Civic Media Center, "Language is power because it categorizes reality.... We are in the process of creating our realities every day, and we create those realities with words."[46] Activist-entrepreneurs constructing landscapes that shout often fill their spaces with "text that hurts."[47] Guy Baeten uses this phrase to characterize words pointed enough to deliver a political sting. Using denuded words like "globalization" and "inequality," rather than accusatory words like "imperialism" and "exploitation," is problematic for Baeten because this sanitized language obscures and normalizes oppression.[48]

In a similar manner, activist-entrepreneurs make choices about how provocative to make their ambient text. For people constructing landscapes that shout, text that hurts sharpens the political critique. This is why, at City Lights, the U.S. History section is renamed "Stolen Continents," Politics becomes "Muckraking," and African American Studies becomes the "Radical Black Imagination." This explicit language is intended to pierce blissful ignorance in an unequivocal manner. For Paul Yamazaki, "We stand for a critical opposition, and that's how we highlight the books."

Alongside section names, activists use words on labels, stickers, and window displays with similarly provocative intentions. As an example, activists with Red Emma's paint signs on the windows reading "Navigating your whiteness," "FUCK TRUMP," and "RESIST! Racism. White supremacy. Sexism. Xenophobia. Fascism. Homophobia. Misogyny. Transphobia. Horizontal hostilities. Islamophobia."[49] Activists use this street-facing signage to disallow ignorance by injecting explicit language naming oppression and highlighting resistance into the public realm.

Alongside text that hurts, activist-entrepreneurs also leverage the power of their collections. Drawing on Kristin Hogan's concept of the feminist shelf, books collected together as part of a conversation create opportunities to define fields of knowledge, which influences how people interpret information.[50] In conventional bookstores, there are usually only a handful of feminist titles, and those titles get "grouped with the enemy" alongside fashion magazines and romance novels.[51] Although feminists may enjoy seeing their perspectives represented in chain stores, a handful of classics buried in an overwhelmingly heteronormative landscape does not mean that those spaces validate women's experiences or reflect the diversity of feminist thought. However, seeing a book as part of a feminist collection that is expansive enough to fill entire rooms and entire stores adds clarity, breadth, nuance, and legitimacy.[52]

The same concept applies in anarchist, anticapitalist, Black, Latino/a, and queer spaces. For Kristin Dooley, movement bookstores like May Day are not unique simply because they carry provocative, anticapitalist titles. "I can't think of any book here that wouldn't appear in a mainstream bookstore." The difference is that movement landscapes like May Day use the power of their collection to advance a social cause. Although radical books may be intermixed into the "wallpaper" at chain stores, that material is "not going to be [consolidated] in one place. And they're not going to exclude the opposite idea."

Excluding the opposite idea sharpens the provocative effect because, even if browsers try looking away and skimming past uncomfortable content, in landscapes that shout, there is simply nowhere else for them to look. These shouting environments are heavily filtered. The space is all anticapitalist with nothing telling the other side. It is all Black, all feminist, or all "in some respect queer." Filtering out competing perspectives and silencing background noise addresses the will to avoid by increasing the intensity of the countermessage. For Zoe Michael with Boneshaker, it feels "like somebody had taken a big bookstore and put it through a sieve and only the very best stuff came out. . . . So hopefully there's not as much noise, and you just get all the signal that you're looking for."

Filtering content not only sharpens key themes. It also frames preferred responses. This is why many activist bookstores skip the self-help section. For Reiko Redmonde, Revolution in Berkeley doesn't have a self-help section because "an actual revolution is what's needed." Gina Mercurio with People Called Women made similar comments. In response to violence against women, she said, "I can see where self-defense is a good thing. However . . . it's an individual solution. It's not a systemic change." Refusing the language of self-help keeps the spotlight off victim blaming and reactive coping to instead highlight the structures enabling ongoing oppression. For feminism, this includes rape culture. For other movements, it includes institutionalized segregation, white privilege, labor vulnerability, mass incarceration, and the social production of poverty. For Mercurio, this structural focus is "not to say that individual empowerment is bad or wrong. But it's not where I want to focus. I want to focus on systemic change."

Alongside objects, images, and words, activist-entrepreneurs constructing landscapes that shout use embodied performances to model a protest-oriented response to atrocity. For scholars writing about "performative theory,"[53] embodied performances reflect and reinforce social status. People are socialized to perform mannerisms conforming to their assigned rank in society. When women stoop while men stand tall, straight couples kiss publicly but queer couples do not, and African Americans step aside when white people approach, those embodied performances reinforce inequity. By contrast, when activists comport their bodies differently, they animate contentious landscapes in ways that assert the legitimacy of other social visions. These performances take progressive ideas off the page and dramatize their real-world applicability.

One way activist-entrepreneurs use embodied performances is by modeling assertive responses to injustice. In landscapes that shout, this includes performing the possibility of protest. For Paul Yamazaki, "A lot of my colleagues here at City Lights spend a significant amount of their time outside of the store doing political work." This includes its outspoken owner Lawrence Ferlinghetti who had been in Nicaragua during the Nicaraguan Revolution. As other examples, volunteers like Kristin Dooley and Craig Palmer with May Day organize and participate in several anti-war rallies each year. Tony Diaz with Nuestra Palabra is an avid protestor who "took to the streets to voice his opposition to some of the new policies of the Trump administration."[54] Similarly, Leslie James Pickering with Burning Books is locally infamous for having "been arrested two dozen times for acts of civil disobedience and convicted of a handful of misdemeanors."[55]

Although these protests occur outside the bookstores, they nevertheless become part of the folklore associated with them. Activist-entrepreneurs then use embodied performances inside print-based movement spaces to invite other people to protest with them. People visiting these spaces observe owners, staffers, and organizers making banners, buttons, fliers, and signs for upcoming demonstrations. At Women & Children First, staffers preparing for the 2017 Women's March hosted feminist craft circles where people knitted pink "pussyhats" and made protest signs.[56] At May Day, anti-war protestors routinely gather around the large central table to make posters and fliers for rallies. Browsers observing these preparations get curious and ask questions. For people who may not have considered participating in rallies or demonstrations in the past, these performances plant the idea and create an easy way to join.

Cumulatively, these books, images, props, words, and bodies come together to shape spaces that shout about oppression and shout about resistance. Banners, cover art, and window displays do more than just render global atrocity visible. Instead, these constructed environments render injustice so jarringly visible that, for people like Jay Scheide with Lucy Parsons, "the proverbial scales fell from my eyelids," and the need for resistance became clear. Although this may sound overly romantic, it was a common enough conversion story among the activists I interviewed to appear credible. Even if it does not work for everyone in every situation, the goal of shaking people to their core to get around the will to avoid nevertheless explains why some activist businesses look the way they do. The publications provide fine print, but people don't need to read the books to know what the space is about. Landscapes that shout vibrate with accusatory messages calling people to arms. These places go beyond using subcultural codes to claim turf. They also render atrocity so shockingly visible that, hopefully, the situation cannot be ignored, forgotten, or allowed to continue.

Landscapes That Entice Encourage People to Question Common Knowledge

Jarring landscapes serve a purpose, but they also have limitations. Although shouting can be attention-grabbing, being shouted at can feel reproachful and alienating, which can amplify the will to avoid. For instance, at May Day, some customers worried that they weren't "tattooed enough" to find acceptance.[57] They described "the awkwardness of having to walk through a meeting of pudgy Karl Marx juniors in order to look at books I will never actually buy."[58] Some customers stayed despite initial discomfort. "Since we're a mixed-race couple I thought there might be a section of books for us."[59] Other customers gave up and left. "I felt like I had just walked into a women's restroom with my dick out. I just left with my tail between my legs."[60]

These comments reflect the connection between discomfort and avoidance. People coming face-to-face with information that feels too difficult experience discomfort as an impulse to flee. Activists know that shouting spaces do not feel welcoming to everyone. For Craig Palmer with May Day, "The first impression we make is we scare a lot of people. We're hoping they start thinking. But a lot of people get scared, or look at us as crazy, and leave in a hurry."

Some activist-entrepreneurs see discomfort as inevitable. For Liz Mason with Quimby's, "some people are just not going to like being in here. . . . If they're a boring person, that's not my problem." If someone is scared of change and feels challenged by "things that are new, that is on them. That is not on us." For other activist-entrepreneurs, discomfort is not inevitable, but it is an acceptable price to pay if it shocks people out of complacency. For Kristin Dooley with May Day, "Watering it down is not something we're interested in." Craig Palmer agrees. "If you're just an average American, this ain't the place for you."

Without minimizing the validity of using provocative landscapes to make forceful wake-up calls, other activists have different ideas about how to tackle avoidance. This includes constructing landscapes that are less about shouting and more about enticing. For this subset of activists, comfort matters because alienation interferes with outreach and alliance building. People who feel so unsettled they cannot remain in a space or absorb information do not gain awareness or become allies. Instead, although they may remember feeling slapped around, they are unlikely to recall the content behind the aggression.

Therefore, alongside constructing landscapes that shout, another goal in print-based movement spaces is designing environments that entice browsers and normalize difference. These spaces invite people into friendly, familiar settings that work within their comfort zones to then stretch them in progressive directions. This enticement approach encourages people to willingly expose themselves to progressive worldviews, which gives them direct experience exploring difference in a nondefensive, nonaggressive manner. The hope is that this softer sell will build the movement by changing people's perspectives gradually in a manner they can tolerate.

Boneshaker is a prime example of a landscape designed to entice. Many of the volunteers who founded Boneshaker previously spent time in shouting spaces—like the anarchist bookstore Arise!—and they felt those environments were too hostile. For instance, Aaron King described Arise! as having "a weird lumpy garbage" aesthetic that, to him, signaled it was "a very niche place that expected you to have already done some learning, not a place where you could start learning." This comment resonates with David Graeber's observation that anarchist squats and performance venues often seem "designed to be somewhat off-putting for the uninitiated."[61] These stylistic codes can be a powerful technique for claiming turf, but group-specific claims also draw new lines of exclusion. For Zoe Michael, "You go in and be like, 'Whoa, there are cool people, but I'm terrified to be here.'"

To counteract feelings of trepidation and turf, Boneshaker's founders constructed an enticing environment they hoped would feel welcoming to people who did not already self-identify as radical. "We have the sky made up of flying books, and flying clouds, and flying lights. It looks like [a scene from] a whimsical children's book." There are no angry posters screaming from the walls. Instead, white paper globe lights cast a warm glow on the wooden shelves and periwinkle paint. "It feels like a warm, welcoming bookstore. . . . It just seems like a place you could bring your family. You could bring your parents that don't understand your radical politics. You could bring anybody, and they would be like, 'Oh, this is a neat book.'"

Volunteers at Wooden Shoe made a similar transition from a turf-like shouting environment to an accessible, enticing environment. The transition came when Wooden Shoe changed locations. For Matt Dineen, the goal in the new space was to "creat[e] a radical aesthetic that is also inviting," and color played an important role. "We actually had this meeting on the floor of the new space . . . and there was this lengthy discussion . . . about what color the walls were going to be." Instead of sticking with the conventional red-and-black anarchist palette, the collective decided to paint the walls purple and the shelves aquamarine. "It felt right to have more colorful walls to be attractive, to not alienate people walking by on South Street, [and] to actually try to inspire people to come in and be curious about the space."

Alongside color choices, activist-entrepreneurs constructing enticing landscapes use softer language to encourage people to explore. Text that hurts has its uses, but so does neutral language, which can ease defensiveness and encourage openness. This is why collective members with Red Emma's use the generic term "radical" instead of calling themselves anarchists. "As a space that's intended to welcome both people who have been in the struggle for decades and people just getting their feet wet for the first time, we felt that committing ourselves to a label and a specific ideological tradition was unnecessarily limiting."[62] The goal of using less contentious terms is to help newcomers feel at ease. "When people hear anarchist . . . it's a name that will scare people away."[63]

Importantly, bookstores using this soft sell approach carry all the same hard-hitting publications as venues that shout. However, they use generic headings, like Fiction and U.S. History. For Zoe Michael, "when you walk in and you see a U.S. History section like ours," which is filled with books about racism and imperialism, "you get a different understanding of how we see the world." The shelves implicitly embody radical perspectives, and the collection implicitly challenges taken-for-granted assumptions. But the hope is that, by labeling it U.S. History instead of Stolen Continents, the information feels less threatening. Neutral language comes with trade-offs because labels like Stolen Continents make the political critique explicit, but in exchange for the less explicit verbiage, activists hope to minimize the avoidance responses that prevent some people from browsing at all.

As another common feature of landscapes that entice, activist-entrepreneurs combine many different viewpoints. Mixing viewpoints invites people to envision themselves as sympathetic allies across axes of difference. Normalizing difference is why staffers at Women & Children First took the somewhat controversial step of dismantling their Women of Color section and instead integrating those titles into the general shelves. As Lynn Mooney recalls, this change made some customers unhappy. "There were customers who came in and said, 'You used to have a section on Hispanic and Latina women. Where is it?'" For underrepresented writers, having a clearly named section of their own enhances visibility. Although Mooney is sympathetic to this perspective, she worries about the ghettoizing effects of separatism. Placing authors of color in separate sections erases them from the general shelves, which can inadvertently signal that they are not legitimate members of the public realm. By contrast, mixing that material into one gigantic, extremely diverse display normalizes difference and makes it easier for white people to learn about minority perspectives without explicitly seeking them out.

Intermixing as a political statement occurs in fiction, history, and also spirituality. Feminist bookstores often have spirituality sections, and customers often ask owners to separate books by sect. However, owners like Sandy Torkildson with A Room of One's Own refuse. Spiritual communities, as well as their literature, are often deeply divided, and customers expect to see those divisions reproduced on the shelves. However, Torkildson has a different political goal. "People ask us to [separate the books], and we say no. If you're going to look for Christian books, you're going to come across a book on Islam. There's going to be other people there. So just get used to it."

The risk of mixing everything together is that minority voices, while present, may get lost in the crowd. This is where selective highlighting becomes especially useful. Instead of turning every book faceout, as is common in landscapes that shout, activists constructing enticing environments strategically highlight the subset of books that normalizes difference. This is why Torkildson with A Room of One's Own mixes feminist and queer-themed graphic novels into the general collection while turning those titles—and only those titles—faceout. "There's a lot of graphic novels, but the graphic novels that are feminist and gay oriented, if we just put them on the shelf with all the other graphic novels, people wouldn't find 'em very easily." Turning them faceout makes them easier to see. By both intermixing authors and selectively highlighting books written by authors with marginalized identities, those perspectives are rendered visible as part of the general public without the general public speaking over them and drowning them out.

Intermixing is also a way to build bridges among potential allies. At feminist bookstores, for instance, because the women's liberation movement has not always welcomed men, nonbinary people, or trans people: "There are still people out there who are intimidated by that and feel they won't be welcomed here."[64] Overcoming this reticence is why staffers with In Other Words use subject headings like "Men and Feminism"[65] and "Trans- and Inter-Sex."[66] These labels explicitly communicate that feminism is relevant to a range of social groups and that everyone has a potential role to play in the movement. Alliance building is likewise why In Other Words includes a section on "anti-porn and pro-porn,"[67] which signals that people can be Dworkin feminists opposing pornography or herotica feminists reclaiming pornography and still be part of the same feminist front. These discursive techniques construct environments encouraging people to nondefensively explore different perspectives, including ones that feel uncomfortable or that they may otherwise avoid.

Landscapes designed to entice also provide many entry points into political themes so that if one avenue feels inaccessible, other options are available. For instance, at City of Asylum in Pittsburgh or Common Language in Ann Arbor, people who do not feel inclined to read dry academic prose can browse travel, cooking, or science fiction and get at progressive themes from those angles instead. Duplicating entry points is likewise why Boneshaker sells fiction, poetry, and fantasy books alongside their nonfiction fare. "We have a lot of books that you would not necessarily expect in a radical bookstore" because volunteers believe "a well-told fictional story can [generate] as much or more change as reading facts or history." Diversifying entry points is why Birchbark shelves scholarly publications alongside general reading. "Depending on how much [browsers] want to get in depth with the subject matter, they can find something that's a little more leisurely or something more scholarly." It's likewise why Unabridged shelves books in more than one section. "The Ta-Nehisi Coates book, certainly we have it in African American Studies, but we also have it up front, and I think it might be somewhere else, too. You turn a corner and the book smacks you in the face." The point of constructing such multivoiced landscapes is to create many possible paths for exploration, which helps circumvent the will to avoid.

Lastly, booksellers play a different role in landscapes that entice than in landscapes that shout. In landscapes designed to entice, staffers spend less time proselytizing and more time feeling out people's comfort zones so they can recommend books nudging them in more progressive directions. This is why Carolyn Anderson with Birchbark does not "want to shame people or make them feel stupid or bad," and instead encourages people "to become curious about the history of where they live and realize that there are Native people who still live here." It's why Katherine Solheim with Unabridged tries to show people "something surprising that excites and challenges them, making them more aware of the big wide world they live in [by] pushing people to see beyond the narrow rural horizons of the Midwest towns they grew up in or are visiting from." These techniques do not force people to grapple with anything too shocking or too accusatory. Instead, the goal is to use a softer sell to expose people to perspectives that are just a little more progressive than where they are starting from, and then encourage them to build incrementally from there.

Landscapes that entice are not perfect at getting around avoidance. The political message is often implicit rather than explicit, and people can skip the information that feels too challenging by focusing on softer content instead. Nevertheless, the goal is to construct a warming-up space working gradually at a pace people can tolerate so that, through repeat exposures, they acquire an expanded sense of awareness, empathy, and appreciation for difference.

Landscapes That Heal Present Empowering Self-Portraits

The two previous examples of landscapes that shout and landscapes that entice are about constructing opportunities for people who are not already involved in movement scenes to see radical perspectives and show support. This focus on imagined outsiders does not mean people who already self-identify with the movement are irrelevant. But it does reflect the common assumption that more seasoned activists will enter, linger, engage, and organize in a variety of settings simply because they agree with the politics. By contrast, newcomers are more likely to consider the information conveyed through aesthetics when assessing whether to enter and linger in newly discovered spaces or whether to avoid them.

These externally facing strategies are useful, but sometimes the goal is not to speak "out" but instead to speak "in," for instance by constructing self-directed landscapes to heal and empower people who already self-identify with the counterspace. These self-directed spaces are open to people who are queer-friendly, anarchist-friendly, or who support communities of color, but the primary focus is on empowering "us" rather than trying to convince "them." Avoidance is still a factor because, although speaking inwardly can feel affirming, it can also feel uncomfortable because of internalized stigmas, unresolved traumas, and feelings of shame. Those are disconcerting emotions, and people often work hard to avoid them.[68] However, the hope is that, by facing their fears, people will be-come more confident and self-directed in their everyday lives, even when the larger world does not change.

Visual vocabularies play a role in constructing healing spaces, and the process often begins with activist-entrepreneurs using subcultural codes to change the way people see themselves reflected in their environments. For instance, the decor at Resistencia combines heritage objects—like Day of the Dead statues, Mexican pottery, South American textiles, and liberation photographs—with books and other symbols of Latino/a lit-eracy and education. One especially illustrative example involved a promi-nently displayed painting of a brown-skinned man in Aztec regalia deeply engrossed in a book. For Lilia Rosas, this painting uses stylistic codes to visualize identity but with an inspiring twist. "It's [the artist's] conceptuali-zation of how to broaden ideas about Aztec people. Not just as warriors, but as thinkers, readers, [and] educators." Displays like these celebrate cul-tural heritage while challenging reductive stereotypes by visualizing Lati-nos as public intellectuals.

Similarly, at the Shrine of the Black Madonna Bookstore, which closed in 2014, activist-entrepreneurs used cover art, cultural objects, and im-ported clothing to encourage African Americans to see themselves in more empowering lights. To challenge internalized stigmas about Black bodies, the children's section included "self-esteem building" picture books show-ing girls with naturally kinky hair and boys with unapologetically dark skin.[69] Instead of only showing images of protests, which keeps the theme of oppression center stage, the store's gallery displayed Kenyan carvings, Tanzanian animal skins, Senegalese textiles, Egyptian jewelry, and other artifacts from Ghana, Botswana, Burkina Faso, and Côte d'Ivoire. These objects celebrated identity without referencing inequity. Store owners also encouraged customers to try on traditional African clothing, not necessar-ily to buy the items but simply to observe themselves literally wrapped in ancestral garb.[70] The goal of environments like this one is to disrupt asso-ciations of Blackness with oppression, poverty, and failure and to instead promote associations of Blackness with an autonomous heritage and self-directed future.

In these spaces, the power of large collections amplifies the visibility of alternative cultures and diversifies the portrayal of what those cultures include. For Greg Newton with the Bureau of General Services, people entering the bookstore see entire walls and tables filled with literature and think, "Wow, all of this is in some respect queer." The Bureau uses some stylistic codes to claim turf. For instance, some cover art depicts homo-erotic men or butch women. But the visual scale of the collection pushes it beyond reductive stereotypes to add nuance, playfulness, and legitimacy. "It's not just a little section in Barnes & Noble that has maybe *Ruby Fruit Jungle* and *Giovanni's Room*. You know, two or three titles and 'there you go, your token acknowledgment.'" Instead, by including a few stylistic codes within a diverse collection, the bookstore claims queer turf and ren-ders queer culture visible in ways that destabilize reductive tropes.

Although landscapes that heal showcase a range of experiences, the activist-entrepreneurs constructing these spaces also omit the perspectives they deem hurtful and oppressive. At Giovanni's Room, Ed Hermance de-veloped a well-honed technique for showing reporters the importance of filtering. After leading reporters to his computer, he "punches in 'homo-sexuality' under Amazon Books. The second hit is *A Parent's Guide to Pre-venting Homosexuality*. He needn't mention that one would not find such a title in Giovanni's Room."[71] This filtering does not deny people's experi-ences with homophobia even as it allows people to explore stigmatized themes without accepting stigma as a valid perspective or allowing the fact of stigma to dominate the conversation.

Another important point is that spaces designed to heal use different shelving practices than other environments, especially when dealing with shame. People often come to movement bookstores looking for informa-tion they simultaneously want to know and want to avoid. Many activist-entrepreneurs are keenly aware of these contradictory emotions, and they take steps to arrange their spaces to ease the anxiety people feel when al-lowing themselves to see.

This sensitivity to internalized feelings of shame and the impulse to avoid it explains why, even in venues where activist-entrepreneurs intention-ally intermix some material, other sections remain separate. For example, Sandy Torkildson with A Room of One's Own intermixes graphic novels and spirituality titles, but she divides other books into many tiny sections with extremely clear labels. These named divisions are useful because, even if people feel comfortable discussing some feminist topics, such as women's accomplishments, other topics are more sensitive. "Some people may not be comfortable asking for a book about incest, or birth loss, or lesbian experiences, and so those areas are called out and labeled so people can find them without having to feel vulnerable exposing anything about themselves to others." Being able to find information without asking allows people to explore sensitive information without feeling like they are putting their vulnerabilities on display.

This sensitivity to vulnerability likewise explains why Women & Children First maintains a separate Queer Young Adult alcove near the rear of the store. In the adult sections up front, queer themes are intermixed with other progressive topics. But for Lynn Mooney, "Teenagers and preteens can be a little shy. [To] engage with an adult in a conversation" about sexuality, let alone nonnormative sexuality, "they might not be ready for that." Having a separate section with a clear label helps young people find information without having to say what they are searching for, and the alcove provides shelter from the stares of people passing by.

Other activist-entrepreneurs likewise combine clearly labeled microsections with furniture, like screens, tables, and chairs, to facilitate sensitive searches. This is why Susan Post with BookWoman keeps a chair and a low shelf near the Sexual Assault section. Customers can go there with a stack of books pulled from the nearby shelves, "and there's a little barrier, so there's a little more privacy" for people to flip through books on trauma-related subjects without feeling like anyone is looking over their shoulder. These explicit labels and sheltered alcoves target the will to avoid. It is not a perfect solution, but if people want to find information, and they don't want anyone to know what they are looking for, or they feel too shy or too vulnerable to discuss it, they can explore material without avoidance impulses getting so much in the way.

Other times, activists construct healing landscapes by using the opposite approach when dealing with shame. Instead of having a sheltered space, there is a front-and-center approach signaling that it is OK to talk about sensitive issues and that those issues are routine. For instance, many activist-entrepreneurs use images of bodies to do this normalizing work. In feminist and queer bookstores, the literal depiction of undressed bodies disrupts publicity regimes promoting stigma and shame. As examples, at People Called Women, the feminist decor includes mugs with artful paintings of women's nude bodies. At In Other Words, it includes a local artist's collection of ceramic vaginas.[72] At the Bureau of General Services, the shared bathroom down the hall sports a "mural of proudly pulsating penises."[73] At Giovanni's Room, the space includes collections of photos depicting intersex and transgender bodies.[74]

These depictions of nude bodies in the public realm are implicitly political. For Liz Spikol with Giovanni's Room, as a new volunteer, "I soon learned that ordering porn wasn't merely about salacious curiosity. There were so many people in different parts of the country who . . . couldn't break away" and move to queer-friendly cities. Instead, they lived in environments where their bodies and desires had no public reflection. "So they placed orders in whispers over the phone, grateful that someone in Philadelphia . . . could help them find a measure of who they were."[75] When bodies are stigmatized, making those bodies visible is an empowering political act.

Activist-entrepreneurs use their own embodied performances to counter stigma as well. This is why Carrie Barnett with People Like Us intentionally taught herself to say, flatly and directly, "'It's a gay and lesbian bookstore.' Just like that. With pride, and without any shame, or without any hesitation, or without giving the other person a chance to feel anything but OK about it." Countering stigma is likewise why Liz Spikol with Giovanni's Room practiced miming expressions of love. "I'd often be behind the cash register and spot someone looking in the window trying to summon the courage to come inside. If they did, and finally had the nerve to approach me at the cash register, I'd try to work my face into an expression that said, without words, You are loved."[76]

Activist-entrepreneurs challenge limiting stereotypes in other ways as well, for instance by visibly diverging from repressive norms. Janifer Wilson and her daughter Kori are successful African American businesswomen. The co-owner of Left Bank in St. Louis lives openly as a trans man. Resistencia's longtime owner is a Latino ex-convict who became an internationally renowned poet. These elements of activist-entrepreneurs' identities become part of the narrative of their spaces. People grappling with similar challenges know them by reputation, and they seek them out in their bookstores for inspiration and mentoring.[77]

For activist-entrepreneurs constructing healing spaces, the goal is to use images, words, furniture, and role modeling to create environments where "people don't have to struggle to see themselves."[78] For Beverly Haynes visiting Eso Won, "I can walk into a place like this and see books for me and by people like me. . . . This grounds me and molds me as a black woman."[79] For Tania Rivera visiting Resistencia, it is about getting "in touch with the spirit of the space and my indigenous background. . . .

It was coming at me like a flood. I finally got in touch with who I really was."[80] For Greg Newton with the Bureau of General Services, "So many of us, when we came out, or were discovering ourselves and our identities and beginning to identify as queer, the bookstores were where we learned about ourselves." Pointing to the shelves, Newton said with pride, "It belongs to us. This is our heritage."

These landscapes designed to heal are not about trying to convince outsiders of anything. Instead, they are about helping insiders see themselves in more nuanced, empowering lights. These depictions include positive themes, like cultural richness and political accomplishment. But claiming heritage can also be frightening. For Alan Chelak, visiting Giovanni's Room for the first time "was an important moment for me . . . because by walking into the store, I was accepting something about myself." For many people, the process of self-acceptance is exhilarating and terrifying in equal measure. Activist-entrepreneurs construct spaces that heal in the hope that, by grappling with those anxious moments instead of avoiding them, people will gain more control over their personal narratives and political futures.

Cumulatively, these concerns explain why print-based movement spaces look the way they do. Activist-entrepreneurs use decor, signage, layouts, and bodies to put ideas on display, which transforms vanilla-box showrooms into microscale cultural landscapes dramatizing progressive visions. However, because people are socialized to avoid difficult and stigmatized information, activists develop additional visual vocabularies to circumvent avoidance behaviors and encourage preferred responses. These visual vocabularies go beyond claiming turf to also construct environments where a greater range of people, including people who may otherwise avoid unsettling information, can see progressive ideas. These aesthetics set the tone for the conversations that follow, which is the subject of the next chapter.

CHAPTER 6

Governing Safe Spaces That Restructure Public Speech

K RIS KLEINDIENST STARTED WORKING at Left Bank Books in
St. Louis[1] in 1974 when she was twenty-one years old. She was an
English major, and she supported the bookstore's political vision. "We
didn't carry books by Watergate Criminals. That was the first wave of government stuff that we were opposed to." The bookstore was founded in
1969. As Kleindienst recalls, "Its focus in the beginning was a lot around
anti-war stuff and civil rights stuff. And they sort of backed into feminism."
Backing into feminism was a way to bring different social groups together
in a shared space. As a queer feminist, Kleindienst pushed for this diversity. "I . . . just started being more vocal," saying, "'You have to have Wom-
en's Studies.' Then I said, 'You have to have a gay section.' . . . So we had all
those things."

Kleindienst eventually became a co-owner herself, and she used this
position to build bridges and enhance inclusion. Buying the store gave her
control of a tool she could use for "unlearning the prejudice that we are
taught from birth." Unlearning prejudice requires reexamining assumptions about gender and sexuality, as well as race. Left Bank is located on
"the edge of two very different worlds," functioning like "a Mason-Dixon
line. North of us is basically almost all Black and a lot of poverty. And
south of us is much whiter and has a lot more money." To bridge this di-
vide, Kleindienst intentionally carries books for both audiences, and, as
much as possible, she hires staff from both communities so both groups
are represented.

Another way Kleindienst builds bridges is by using her management
role to construct respect and trust. "The ethos of the store is, we really
stress respect on every level." Cultivating this ethos is why Kleindienst
announces guidelines for courteous communication at the beginning of
store events and author readings, "so the conversations are, not guided,

The main floor of Left Bank Books in St. Louis, Missouri, is a light and airy space normalizing cultural difference. Photograph by Left Bank Books, 2015; courtesy of Left Bank Books.

but protected." These guidelines encourage safety and inclusion by stressing the importance of "not interrupting people and not attacking people" and making sure no one feels singled out for voicing minority views. These management decisions reflect a commitment to not taking safety for granted. Left Bank customers "have come to trust the store." Speaking across difference requires trust, and "every day you open your door, you have to re-earn that trust."

In addition to building bridges inside the store, Kleindienst uses her status as a small business owner to influence public debate. For example, when I interviewed her in 2017, Kleindienst was also getting "called on to talk about the Affordable Care Act quite a bit in the media," for instance by answering questions and writing editorials. "Since the mainstream conversation about this is that small business basically hates labor and wants no regulation and doesn't want to have to pay for anything, we're the group that says, 'Well, that's not actually true.'" As a small business owner, Kleindienst enjoys more clout than other activists when speaking in support of owner-provided health care and minimum wage reform, and she uses this status to inject progressive viewpoints into conservative debates.

Kleindienst also builds bridges by promoting children's literacy. According to Kleindienst, most children attending St. Louis Public Schools live in poverty, and they often "don't have any tradition of reading in the home." Because of these limitations, many students struggle with vocabulary deficits and knowledge gaps, which affects lifelong earnings. Print capitalism reinforces these barriers. "The way [children's authors] do their book tours is for the bookstores to set up school visits," which means authors "only go into school districts where people can send money to school with their kids." In this system, low-income students are excluded. As a bookseller, Kleindienst cannot solve racialized poverty. "So, we were thinking, 'What *can* we do with what we do?'" The answer was to create the Left Bank Books Foundation, which raises money for author visits in public schools where every student receives a free copy of the book with her or his name inscribed on the nameplate. In addition to being an anti-poverty project, these face-to-face encounters and personalized objects invite students to imagine themselves as readers, writers, librarians, and storytellers. "We get these thank you cards . . . [that] would make you cry, they're so sweet."

Conversations like this one with Left Bank in St. Louis reveal how activist-entrepreneurs construct frameworks for public expression. For activists like Kleindienst, stocking shelves, writing editorials, and supporting education are all part of one big movement to construct inclusive spaces where vulnerable groups are safe, represented, and empowered to participate. Management decisions around ordering, staffing, and fundraising diversify print capitalism by changing who is present as authors, readers, and decision-makers. These practices restructure public speech by bringing marginalized voices into the public realm and by giving vulnerable groups access to tools for public expression.

This example also illustrates that managerial practices are governing tools. Activists like Kleindienst do governing work inside counterspaces by ensuring that women, queer folk, and communities of color are represented and by establishing protocols for respectful interactions across difference. This governing influence also extends beyond the shop walls, for instance when activists change the relationship between print capitalism and low-income communities in incremental ways. These administrative dynamics influence the nature of social interactions, and they connect people with social networks usually kept apart.

For stigmatized groups who experience disempowerment and oppression in the public realm, constructing inclusive spaces is an important political strategy. Despite idealized notions of egalitarianism, public life is rife with denigration and exclusion. These exclusions are one reason why marginalized groups so often construct separatist spaces. However, although scholars increasingly appreciate the significance of autonomous space, this focus on separatism means scholars say relatively little about how autonomous spaces can function less like islands and more like bridges. Because hidden transcripts are largely opaque to outsiders, when well-intentioned people venture into separatist spaces, they often blunder and inadvertently cause harm. Conversely, because marginalized groups are excluded from the socialization processes that give privileged people symbolic mastery of institutional norms, those groups face added challenges when attempting to speak as public figures outside separatist spaces. From both perspectives, crossing borders safely and effectively involves some learning, which is the subject of this chapter.

One way activist-entrepreneurs support learning is by using their businesses less as separatist spaces and more as transitional zones. Emphasizing transitions through border-crossing does not negate the need for separatist spaces. Outside the shop walls, state and social institutions reinforce class privilege, racial hierarchy, and gender inequity. In response, activists construct alternative communities in private spaces organized around feminism, anarchism, and anticolonialism. However, alongside the development of hidden transcripts in isolated environments, activists also develop instructional guidelines for empowerment, education, and discipline in public-facing zones. The rationale is that, in order to gain symbolic mastery of another group's implicit norms, it helps to first have at least the minimal amount of social literacy allowing people to mingle without causing offense, which then establishes a beachhead for deeper exploration.

I analyze border crossing in this chapter using the lens of territorial governing. Even though most of the literature on territorial governing emphasizes defensiveness and exclusion, some scholars now suggest that spatial zoning not only constructs islands but also builds bridges between territories otherwise kept apart. As a form of constructive activism, activist-entrepreneurs construct physical spaces for mixing and learning. Additionally, by using store policies as bridging aids, activists play a governing role by regulating how this mixing occurs.

These governing practices are especially apparent in the techniques activists use to invert inequities in public expression. I analyze three such techniques in this chapter. One governing technique is constructing safe spaces that prevent denigrating behavior and encourage respectful inter-actions, as Kleindienst does when announcing communication guidelines for public events. Safe space policies claim turf because, although activist businesses are part of the public realm, private policies in commercial spaces establish alternative social scripts. Activist-entrepreneurs use safe space policies to provide instruction for the uninitiated, signal hospitality for the oppressed, and impose discipline on the noncompliant. These de-lineated rules also build bridges by helping people share movement spaces without reproducing oppression.

A second governing technique that inverts inequities in the public realm is restructuring public speech. Activist spaces organized around print have an advantage when it comes to mediating public speech because their commodities are, by definition, quintessential communication tools. However, people with privilege usually dominate public discourse, includ-ing in print. In this chapter, I present examples of activist-entrepreneurs who challenge hierarchies by using store policies to help marginalized groups speak more effectively, including through mainstream channels. Kleindienst's promotion of queer feminist voices, along with inner-city literacy programs, is an example of how activist-entrepreneurs expand op-portunities for public speech. By connecting nonnormative voices with public audiences, these practices subvert normative regimes by silencing the habitually vocal, empowering the habitually silenced, and construct-ing new entry points into the public realm.

A third governing technique that inverts inequities in the public realm is creating ownership structures that give more people a voice. Owner-ship status brings activists like Kleindienst into the public spotlight both as public commentators and as producers of public-facing spaces. Diver-sifying the population of business owners by getting more women, queer folk, and minorities into ownership positions is a useful first step. How-ever, in capitalist systems, staffers usually do not share owners' privileges. As a partial antidote, many activist-entrepreneurs replace capitalist busi-ness models with democratic alternatives, including collective ownership and consensus-based management. These administrative systems give more people access to ownership privileges, including the ability to de-cide which books to stock, which causes to support, and which editorials to publish.

These findings exemplify how activists use territorial zoning not only to claim turf, which they defend against oppression, but also to construct bridges between mainstream and alternative groups. These policies invite a range of people to participate in counterspaces while protecting vulnerable users from harm. As a governing process, these practices establish alternative protocols for public interactions. Additionally, these findings underscore the importance of moving beyond discussions of secret societies and hidden transcripts to also attend to the constructed countersystems of administration that encourage people to speak and spend time on other groups' turf.

A few caveats are worth mentioning before proceeding. One caveat is that constructing bubbles of progressive turf is an imperfect solution. For one thing, activists do not have total control over their spaces. Print-based counterspaces elude and confound external authority, but they do not fully escape it.[2] For another thing, activist policies are imperfect. Owners unroll progressive policies that are experimental, fall short, and sometimes go awry. The hope, however, is that iterative changes will ultimately lead to more effective alternatives.

Another caveat is that not all activist-entrepreneurs develop equally elaborate systems of countergovernance. Nor should they. Activists can use conventional operating procedures while being radical in other respects, for instance by selling contentious commodities or providing meeting spaces for organizing.[3]

Additionally, not everyone feels equally welcome in bridge-building zones. Some marginalized groups do not want to share space with their oppressors, and some people are unwilling to check their privilege at the door. Even among people who value shared spaces, these environments do not negate the need to also have intimate, separatist spaces of nurturance elsewhere.[4]

These caveats, while important, do not diminish the governing dynamics at work in activist spaces, nor do they prevent activists from reworking the conventions regulating public speech. By having durable control over private space in the public realm, activist-entrepreneurs can use their property rights not only to claim turf but also to facilitate and regulate social interactions. These constructed environments are not only places of escape. They are also countergovernance zones where people strive to construct more inclusionary societies where a greater range of voices can be heard.

Territoriality Constructs Both Islands and Bridges

One element of constructive activism is designing the rules and protocols that govern the counterspace. I analyze these governing dynamics using a territorial lens. Territoriality is the concept that control over space and control over people go hand in hand. In Robert Sack's classic definition, territoriality is "a spatial strategy to affect, influence, or control resources and people, by controlling area."[5] Other scholars expand this definition by emphasizing the concept of turf. For Deborah Cowen and Emily Gilbert, "territory is land or space that has had something done to it. Territory is land that has been identified and claimed by a person or people . . . against infringements by others who are perceived to not belong."[6] Claimed turf is not neutral. On the contrary, as Kevin Cox explains, territorial zones are inherently normative and exclusionary. "Territories are spaces which people defend by excluding some activities and by including those which will enhance more precisely what it is in the territory that they want to defend."[7] Territorial defenses assert authority over discretely defined spaces where social behavior is governed according to distinct interests, where social groups enjoy different levels of privilege, and where systems of governance differ from adjoining areas.

Although scholars usually explore territoriality at the national or regional scale,[8] there is a growing movement to also study territoriality at the microscale.[9] Urban geographers, for instance, explore territoriality at the scale of lots, blocks, and neighborhoods from both capitalist and activist perspectives.

Starting with the capitalist-themed literature, city officials use microscale zoning to establish secessionist zones for exploitation. For instance, in Export Processing Zones (EPZs) and Special Economic Zones (SEZs), small subsections of countries get cordoned off as exempt from national labor laws, environmental policies, ownership rules, and tax obligations.[10] Similarly, in Privately Owned Public Spaces (POPS) and Business Improvement Districts (BIDs), small sections of cities get cordoned off and overlaid with new rules, for instance rules prohibiting skateboarding, panhandling, or amplified sound.[11] Designations like these construct bubbles of space where the usual rules do not apply and where new rules favoring capitalism take priority.

Similarly, in the activist-themed literature, activists construct counterzones where some normative expectations are suspended. These spaces provide escapes not only from capitalism but also from patriarchy, hetero-normativity, and white privilege. Activist counterzones include Temporary Autonomous Zones (TAZs), which Hakim Bey describes as "a guerrilla operation which liberates an area" from state authority.[12] They include antiauthoritarian social centers, which Pierpaolo Mudu describes as places where people "renovate and refurbish privately or publicly owned empty properties and turn them into public spaces open to the general public."[13] They also include "urban commons" where, for Cesare di Felici-antonio, people "expelled" from public life "reappropriate urban space subject to speculation and use it to establish de-commodified social (and economic) relations."[14]

As these examples show, in both the capitalist- and activist-themed literature, territorial zones are bubbles of turf governed according to different rules. However, although these secessionist dynamics are important, they do not tell the whole story. An important missing piece of the story is border-crossing. Territoriality is as much about engagement as it is about exclusion. As a rare example speaking to this point, Aihwa Ong's innovative analysis of capitalist zoning technologies in China characterizes zones as both islands and bridges. The zones themselves are "mechanisms for creating or accommodating islands of distinct governing regimes," which operate in a detached manner, "like a country within a country."[15] The goal in constructing these islands, however, is "to intensify cross-border networks and economic integration," for instance by constructing a space where foreign capitalism and Chinese socialism interact.[16] These border-crossing themes recur in studies of the Maquiladora sister cities along the U.S.–Mexico border,[17] as well as in studies of the Western–Islamic interface in special zones in Dubai.[18] These zones are not only about constructing bubbles of space partially detached from national norms. They are also about constructing bridges connecting economic and political networks usually kept apart.

One of the most important elements of zone-style bridge-building is that the zone is detached from both sides' home turf. This detachment is both a protective measure against infringement and an enabling factor facilitating risky interactions. For Ong, because zones in China are both within China and cordoned off from China, the "economic and political experimentation" occurring there does "not threaten collective and national security" either for the host state, which remains authoritarian and socialist, or for foreign investors, who remain democratic and capitalist.[19] These zones are not wholly embedded in either camp and instead are "hinges"[20] linking different worlds. In some cases, these hinges become beachheads for eventual integration, for instance when zone interactions engender economic interdependence, cultural familiarity, and political alliances.[21] Other times, the hinge persists indefinitely as a meeting space between different camps.[22]

Like capitalist zones, activist zones also serve border-crossing functions. Those functions are understudied because scholars tend to focus on the defensive functions of separatist spaces. One notable exception, however, is Paul Chatterton and Jenny Pickerill's analysis of border-crossing tactics among activists who are "keen to translate their ideas into visions that would be connected and legible to people outside their immediate political community."[23] Activists need sheltered spaces to develop alternative ideas, and many activists then express their ideas through criticism and protest. However, alongside sheltering and protesting, another option is to make an "explicit attempt to turn activist identities outwards and engage with others in a less confrontational and aggressive manner."[24] One way to achieve this goal is to construct porous counterspaces that function as border-crossing hinges.

Not all counterspaces have this border-crossing intention. On the contrary, many counterspaces are intentionally secessionist. However, social movements are multipronged affairs, and different spaces serve different needs. Within this mix, activist enterprises are porous, public-facing spaces at arm's length both from officially designated public spaces and from the intimate privacy of intentional communities. This neither/nor position generates unique opportunities to shape counterspaces using island-and-bridge-style zoning, which constructs turf for border-crossing interactions.

Alongside border crossing, a second understudied piece of the microterritoriality story is counterinstitutionalization. My focus on counterinstitutionalization diverges from the scholarly literature, which emphasizes escapism. In the capitalist literature, zones purportedly liberate markets from state regulations. The activist literature likewise emphasizes escape,[25] openness,[26] and autonomy.[27] However, territorial islands are not only about escaping established systems of power. They are also about establishing alternative systems of rule. Whether in capitalist zones or activist ones, instead of constructing a free-for-all, zoning technologies prescribe new forms of coming together. In capitalist zones, international contract laws[28] and semi-sovereign zone authorities[29] specify exactly which rights and privileges are granted or suspended. Similarly, in many activist spaces, "activists adhere to a set of values which guide how they interact," which keeps the goals open-ended even as "the way in which [activists] pursue them are principled."[30] In both types of zones, the release from one governing system occurs because people actively construct substitutions.

These examples of re-embeddedness and reregulation suggest opportunities to use movement-oriented spaces to explore the currently understudied dynamics of counterinstitutionalized border-crossing at the microscale. Activist-entrepreneurs take many steps to facilitate managed intermixing. In the rest of this chapter, I offer three examples of how activist-entrepreneurs use store policies such as safe space guidelines, curation practices, and decision-making structures to guide and direct intergroup interactions. These examples shed light on how activist-entrepreneurs use territorial zoning not only to claim autonomous space but also to facilitate structured and disciplined interactions across social divides.

Safe Space Policies Regulate Social Interactions

One common governing strategy is regulating face-to-face interactions. As I explain in this section, aspiring toward oppression-free spaces is a nice idea, but not everyone agrees with this goal or knows how to achieve it. To overcome these limitations, some activists write policies defining what an oppression-free space should look like. These policies are not the hidden transcripts of niche communities, nor are newcomers expected to know or understand them in advance. Instead, these policies articulate the bare minimum of ethical decorum that people are expected to follow when spending time in movement-oriented zones. This minimum baseline then constructs an environment where sympathetic newcomers can familiarize themselves with the more intimate nuances of counterpublic cultures without causing offense.

Activist retail is filled with all sorts of people. There are staffers, writers, shoppers, organizers, friends, neighbors, and random people off the street. People come to browse books, attend events, or use computer stations. They work, eat, and socialize at tables and on couches. They solicit donations, ask directions, and use restrooms. Because these groups share the same space, they interact and overhear each other's conversations. However, these groups are not homogenous. People approach radical spaces from many different perspectives. They have different levels of familiarity with movement ideas, and they show different levels of support for progressive goals.

Champions of U.S. democracy like to imagine that the public realm is inclusive, but in reality, it is a routine site of social violence. For Don Mitchell, despite having some inclusionary characteristics, public spaces "have always also been spaces of exclusion."[31] Additionally, despite romantic invocations of strangers getting to know each other in shared spaces, commingling does not automatically lead to increased tolerance.[32] Instead, public space is an encounter zone where people interact across radically asymmetrical positions of power. Public streets, sidewalks, and parks are places where women get catcalled, immigrants get detained, African Americans get stopped and frisked, transgender people get assaulted, people experiencing homelessness get pushed along, and people with nonnormative bodies encounter disabling environments.[33]

When it comes to inclusivity, quasi-public spaces are often no better and sometimes considerably worse. As part of the neoliberal turn, private foundations and business improvement districts now control many formerly public spaces, and their managers often set stricter terms of use. As a related trend, many social activities formerly occurring in public streets and parks—like shopping, socializing, and exercising—now occur in private homes, malls, and gyms. Unlike in officially designated public spaces where government officials at least pay lip service to inclusion, the proprietors of quasi-public environments have no such legal obligations. On the contrary, classism, racism, and misogyny can be highly profitable, which is why private owners and administrators often go out of their way to make privileged customers feel welcome, including by removing anyone stereotyped as unsavory.[34]

Activist-entrepreneurs challenge these trends by governing their spaces according to different rules. Safe space policies are an example of counter territorial governing. Safe space policies are not about whether places are public or private. Instead, they are about how people conduct themselves when interacting with others on activists' turf. Activist-entrepreneurs use these policies to combat normalized aggression both among movement insiders and among newcomers who bumble, injure, or mock. As a territorial act, safe space regulations include defensive and exclusionary elements. The goal is to defend against oppressive behaviors and to provide resources for people to act otherwise.

The language of safe (and safer) space has become popular in recent decades. The movement originated with feminist critiques of sexual violence in activist spaces. These critiques draw attention to the demeaning and oppressive behavior occurring among activists fighting for justice. Oppression within movements is not new. The 1960s and 1970s feminist movement included racism, and the Black power movement included misogyny. These unjust norms within justice movements mean that spaces free from patriarchy or white privilege are not necessarily spaces where all women or all people of color are equally valued.

The safe space movement emerging today gives these older concerns a new conceptual framework for intelligibility and action. During the Occupy Movement, advocacy groups like the Coalition for Safer Spaces organized awareness-raising campaigns and provided sample policy language.[35] Many radical booksellers adopt this language verbatim. These policies include references to sexual violence, but the safe space concept now also incorporates a broader range of antiauthoritarian concerns. Additionally, the safe space movement is going mainstream. Policies now exist in a variety of contexts, not just in counterspaces but also on college campuses, in childcare centers, and in medical offices.[36]

One of the most important aspects of safe space policies is that they are not intended to be hidden. Safe space policies are not the hidden transcripts or inner protocols of secret societies. Instead, their purpose is to make baseline expectations extremely explicit and publicly known. Activists use them as socializing tools educating people on how to do less harm. In addition to protecting activists from in-group oppression, these policies are guidelines. They state how nonprogressives should behave in radical spaces, as well as how activists can curb holier-than-thou attitudes to protect newcomers from being "taunted for being 'square.'"[37]

The safe space movement has critics. For conservative pundits, safe space policies "limit . . . freedom of expression," "threaten 'innovation of thought,'" and "shut down debate."[38] Critics also describe safe space movements as "symptoms of a 'fragile,' 'entitled' and 'coddled' generation, unable to cope with the necessary brutality of the 'real world.'"[39]

However, for Marie Thompson, these criticisms grossly misrepresent the radical intention. Beneficiaries of safe spaces are not entitled or coddled, nor is the world required to be brutal. On the contrary, for Thompson, safe spaces are constructed by and for people experiencing lifetimes of unnecessary systemic oppression. The point is to defend against routinized forms of violence and make places where a greater variety of people can participate in public life with comfort and respect.[40]

Not all radical booksellers have these official policies. Ideology is one limiting factor. Safe space policies are especially common in anarchist and intersectional venues, and they are especially uncommon in nonintersectional Black, Latino/a, and queer spaces. Age is another limiting factor. Because safe space terminology is an emerging phenomenon, formal policies are less common in older venues and more common in enterprises opening or restructuring since the 2000s. Nevertheless, older venues like Left Bank in St. Louis often promote safe space behaviors even without using those exact terms.

A third limiting factor is ownership structure. Although safe space language is commensurate with feminist ethics of care, and although the movement got its start as a feminist critique, nonintersectional feminist venues rarely write official store policies around it. Ownership structure, rather than ideology, appears to account for this difference. Feminist venues tend to be sole- or partner-owned proprietorships. Unlike anarchist collectives, where official policies help coordinate large groups of volunteers, owners and co-owners can exercise authority without debating policies in advance. Again, these venues often support safe space principles even without written statements.

When it comes to governing, all these factors influence the degree of formality. Some venues write safe space policies as official documents that get printed, signed, and publicly posted. Other venues, like Left Bank in St. Louis, prefer implicit coaching and fluid role modeling. Across this spectrum, when it comes to implementation, activists use safe space policies for a variety of purposes. Three especially common goals are educating, welcoming, and disciplining. These three dynamics illustrate how safe space policies function as territorial governing tools both by claiming turf and by regulating social interactions.

Bluestockings in New York was an especially informative place to see all three functions at work. For Corey Farach, activists with Bluestockings construct a sheltered space where people can find respite in a hostile world. "I think there's a lot of decompression going on. If [people] are not coming to read the books, they're coming in to just chill out" in a protected environment. "People need a break from the way our society says it's OK to treat one another. . . . So they come in here for a different rule set."

Bluestockings uses explicit policy language to cultivate this relief-giving atmosphere. "We codify that by saying it's a safer space." Farach acknowledges that there are many definitions of safety. At Bluestockings, safer space "just means you can't come in here and use language that's going to either ignore people's experience or write them off or denigrate their experience."

The official safe space policy displayed on the counter and posted on-line includes language defining oppression, identifying vulnerabilities, and providing instruction on how to act otherwise. This document describes oppressive behavior "as any conduct that demeans, marginalizes, rejects, threatens or harms" vulnerable groups.[41] Vulnerable groups include people who experience discrimination "on the basis of ability, activist experience, age, cultural background, education, ethnicity, gender, immigration status, language, nationality, physical appearance, race, religion, self-expression, sexual orientation, species, status as a parent or other such factors."[42] The policy then provides a bullet point list explaining what respectful inter-actions should look like.

Respect peoples' opinions, beliefs, experiences and differing points of view.

Respect everyone's identity and background, including pronouns and names. Do not assume anyone's gender identity, sexual prefer-ence, survivor status, economic status, background, health, etc.

Respect everyone's physical and emotional boundaries. Check in before discussing topics that may be triggering (e.g. sexual abuse, physical violence or encounters with police), and use trigger warn-ing during presentations and events. Physical and/or verbal threats will not be tolerated at Bluestockings under any circumstances. Disruptive individuals may be asked to leave the space.

Be responsible for your own actions; be aware that your actions have an effect on others, despite what your intentions may be. Listen and change your behavior if someone tells you that you are making them uncomfortable.

Be aware of your prejudices and privileges and the space you take up at Bluestockings.[43]

For some activists, constructing safe spaces requires setting limits around public speech and perhaps even prohibiting entire topics of debate. For example, at In Other Words, the safer space policy states, "Cishetero-patriarchy exists, white supremacy exists, ableism exists, racism exists, co-lonialism never ended, capitalism is bad. This is not a space where we argue about the basics of the situation."[44] Similarly, although Revolution in Berke-ley does not have a formal safe space policy, informally, Reiko Redmonde felt that some perspectives were so hurtful that they should not be permitted as topics of debate. "[If] people come and promote slavery at our institutions, wouldn't we protest them? That shit is old. It's been proven wrong. And we don't want to revisit the whole question." These statements underscore the fact that denying, minimizing, or even just contemplating oppression is a further act of violence and that proprietors of privately owned spaces can prohibit this violence on their turf.[45] For Corey Farach with Bluestockings, "Everybody loves to say their free speech is being violated whenever they're criticized for anything. Of course, that doesn't work here."

Alongside policies codifying safe space conduct, activist-entrepreneurs use face-to-face interactions to raise awareness and model alternatives. For Kleindienst with Left Bank, "I use my gajillion years of therapy to urge people to make 'I' statements instead of 'you' statements" to create a space protected from fraught interactions. Modeling alternatives is likewise why Matt Dineen with Wooden Shoe performs respectful disagreement from behind the counter. "Sometimes people will come in, and they want to be really combative," for instance about Palestine or transgender justice. "But those are also important moments . . . to not just yell at people or tell them they're wrong or stupid, but to actually try to engage with them." The hope is that, by modeling respectful disagreement, activists can encourage similar respect in return.

In all these forms, safe space policies are governing tools. The distinction between "safe space" and "free space" makes this regulatory intention especially clear. Free spaces, like temporary autonomous zones, are supposed to liberate people from externally imposed social scripts.[46] Some print-based movement spaces fit this description. At Beyond Repair, for instance, the "transactional relationship" of capitalism "is totally thrown out the window," and, in its place, the owner cultivates a "kind of agendaless" space organized around the "vague notion of 'what do I have to offer?'" By constructing a playground for open-ended experimentation, venues like Beyond Repair embody the spirit of "anything goes."

Safe space, by contrast, is explicitly regulated. It comes with meticulously detailed rules defining acceptable and unacceptable behavior. The intent is not to release people from social constraints but rather to govern interactions according to precise behavioral codes. As a form of Foucaldian counterconduct, it's about "how not to be governed *like that*"[47] and how instead "to be led differently."[48]

Education is important, but awareness-raising and encouragement are not always sufficient to resolve policy violations and prevent their re-currence. In those moments, activists enforce policies using disciplinary measures. I asked Farach with Bluestockings to explain how this works. From his perspective, the process usually starts with "a volunteer or a cus-tomer coming up to me, and they're like, 'Yo, this person's saying some super fucked up shit to me in the café,'" for instance telling racist jokes or speaking against queer rights. When that happens, Farach's first step is to initiate a respectful dialogue. "So I take [the accused party] outside, ask them what's going on, [and] try to understand where they're coming from." Those conversations begin as an educational opportunity. "Usually it's somebody who does not have a lexicon for what we're attempting to do, or to undo, in this space. I have to kind of explain to them why what they're saying could be so offensive to someone else." Not everyone appre-ciates Farach's feedback. "People . . . either are really sorry, and they're like, 'Ok, I had no idea, I just want to learn.' Or they're totally obstinate, and they refuse to acknowledge that they said anything problematic." Whether or not people agree with the rebuke, if they do not agree to change their behavior, they get kicked out. I asked Farach how often these confronta-tions occur. "Probably every week."

Safe space discipline involves contradictions. For some activists, disci-pline and exclusion are uncomfortably associated with nationalism, tribal-ism, segregation, patriarchy, and neoliberalism. Enforcement is also an act of authority, which, for Stephanie Waller with Boxcar, "seems to go inher-ently against all of our belief systems." As members of an antiauthoritarian collective, many Boxcar volunteers feel uncomfortable telling people what they are allowed to say, how they are supposed to act, and when they need to leave. "It varied from shift to shift [and] person to person . . . how com-fortable people are enforcing these [rules]. Because, really, we don't want to enforce any of these things."

Exerting authority is also fraught when marginalized groups assert themselves over the habitually privileged. For Farach, "It definitely helps that I am who I am and that I project a super masculine figure into the world." During safe space confrontations, the patriarchal norms Farach opposes nevertheless give him advantages that many of his coworkers do not share. "When there is a sixteen- or seventeen-year-old woman behind the counter, people take her less seriously than they would take me if I ask them to step outside so I can talk to them."

For all these reasons, safe space enforcement sometimes fails. At Box-

car, for instance, volunteers constructed a large community space for anarchists, queer folk, and people of color. Because the space was open to the
public, volunteers did not initially mind when people experiencing drug
addiction and homelessness started sharing the space. But for Stephanie
Waller, things changed when some of those newcomers turned out to be
"shitty, misogynist, transphobic men" who drove the intended users away.
Waller and other collective members tried to reclaim their space by distributing copies of the safe space policy to everyone who entered. They
also took disciplinary steps, for instance "bouncing" people for the day.
"Like, you did this thing, you gotta leave today. You can come back tomor-
row, but you gotta leave today." Nothing worked. As an antiauthoritarian
venue dedicated to prison abolition, "we're not going to call the police on
them" to have them forcibly removed, "and they know that, and we've had
lots of issues surrounding being taken advantage of because of that."

Even under the best circumstances, safe space policies are aspirational
rather than guaranteed. This indeterminacy is why Zoe Michael with
Boneshaker "hate[s] the word safe space. No place is safe. You have to create safety within a dangerous world." Policy language at In Other Words
similarly acknowledges the impossibility of obtaining a utopian state.
"There's no such thing as a safe space. We exist in the real world, and we all
carry scars and have caused wounds. . . . This space will not be perfect."[49]

Fortunately, imperfection is not the same as failure. Striving toward
safety is significant even if aspirational dreams are never fully achieved.
This is why Firestorm frames its safe space policy as a living document.
"Our understanding of anti-oppression work is continuously evolving
and, as such, this text is subject to ongoing revision."[50] Similarly, at In
Other Words, the space "will not always be what we want it to be, but it
will be ours together, and we will work on it side by side."[51]

Because safe space policies are territorial acts, discipline and exclusion
cannot be avoided. However, despite this inevitability, another equally important point is that, for most activist-entrepreneurs, safe space policies
are primarily about welcoming people and helping them feel included.
Explicit policies provide support structures for well-intentioned but naive
newcomers who want to explore progressive ideas without causing offense. Safe space policies also let marginalized groups know they are valued. This is why Wooden Shoe includes gender-neutral bathrooms as part
of its safe space programming. For people "who are not on one side of
the mythical gender binary, that could be this really welcoming sign. Like,

'Oh, yes. This is the kind of space I want to be in. Absolutely.'" Welcoming people is likewise one of the reasons why Bluestockings publicly displays its safer space policy. "It's just to show people we take your experience seriously. If you want a place where you can decompress and expect to be respected, then you can do that here. It's a sign that says all of that."

To summarize so far, like other microzoning technologies, safe space policies construct a bubble of turf that exists within a larger territory but that is governed by different rules. These policies do not create free spaces where anything goes, nor are they the hidden transcripts of alternative societies. Instead, they are explicit codes of conduct claiming turf for some people, defending against infringements by others, and establishing protocols for intergroup interactions. Although exclusion cannot be avoided, the larger goal is to make activist retail less exclusionary by inviting people to participate in ways that reduce harm, which then generates opportunities for deeper interactions.

Curation Practices Restructure Public Speech

Safe space policies subvert hurtful regimes of public speech during face-to-face encounters. A related governing strategy is reworking social interactions in print. Encouraging people to join public debates through writing is a nice idea, but not everyone has the opportunity, skills, or confidence. Combatting those inequities is a primary objective in many print-based movement spaces. As I explain in this section, alongside the more commonly studied cry-and-demand approach of pressuring corporate publishers to keep radical titles in print,[52] activist-entrepreneurs also take direct action by curating their stock so that it silences the habitually privileged, empowers the habitually silenced, and constructs new inroads for public expression. These findings shed light on how spatial agency (and not just time, money, or connections) is an enabling resource for contentious politics. Retail spaces are part of the public realm, books are a form of public speech, and publishing is a way to participate in public life. By having control over quasi-public spaces, activists can use private property rights to construct zones of nonnormative expression and help marginalized authors become more effective when speaking to broader audiences.

To speak is a political act and a reflection of power. Despite Habermas's "bourgeois conception of the public sphere," which "stresses its claim to be open and accessible to all," this utopian fantasy "was not in fact realized."[53] As Nancy Fraser explains, many constraints prevent people from voicing opinions. Historically, people were excluded from public debate based on class, race, gender, and status as a property owner. These limits persist, and new barriers have emerged. One barrier is corporate media. Corporations are major players disseminating public speech, and "subordinated social groups usually lack equal access to the material means of equal participation."[54] For instance, corporate publishers favor authors with college degrees, professional credentials, the money to hire writing coaches and marketing consultants, and the savvy to work with developmental editors and literary agents. Another barrier is social conventions that frame some topics and modes of expression as irrational or unintelligible because of their associations with underprivileged groups. Speaking is also risky because people get sanctioned, formally and informally, for discussing anything sensitive or taboo.[55] Additionally, for Don Mitchell, although incoherent rambling receives free speech protections, whenever speech becomes persuasive—meaning there is "the possibility that her or his words might actually have an effect"—it gets tagged as a clear and present danger and shut down.[56]

For all these reasons, claiming a voice in the public realm is a contentious political act. Many activist-entrepreneurs use their commodities to subvert these inequitable public speaking regimes and to give marginalized groups a louder voice. For these activists, stocking shelves is no mere procedural task. Instead, it is a curatorial act restructuring public speech by withdrawing privileges from some authors and granting privileges to others.

When it comes to implementation, activists use countercuration for a variety of purposes. Three especially common goals are elevating the prominence of marginalized perspectives, encouraging underprivileged writers to develop their voices, and generating new entry points into public discourse. These three dynamics illustrate how activist-entrepreneurs use control over turf to subvert publicity regimes, including by constructing border-crossing tools helping radical writers gain access to capitalist modes of expression.

Beginning with the goal of making marginalized voices easier to hear, activist-entrepreneurs curate their stock to amplify progressive perspectives. One common amplification method is doing away with so-called fair and balanced reporting where the goal is to tell all sides of a story without judgment or bias.[57] Abandoning fair and balanced reporting is controversial. Many nonactivist but socially conscious booksellers, publishers, editors, reporters, and librarians believe that including as many perspectives as possible—including ultraconservative ones—is the democratic cornerstone protecting all minority viewpoints. This philosophy explains why Steve Bercu's inventory at BookPeople spans the full political spectrum. "I do want to have material for everybody. I don't want to have a place that only sells one viewpoint. I actually don't think that's healthy. . . . That, to me, is a very dangerous place to be in a democracy."

Although this interpretation of the First Amendment is the institutional default in U.S. culture, it almost never explains the curation in activist spaces where the goal is to advance progressive agendas. For Raphael Cohen-Almagor, "the fringe, alternative media . . . reject[s] all notions of objectivity and 'balanced reporting'" because critics believe these notions are both impossible to achieve and smokescreens that "mask, disguise, and legitimate the authority of society's powerful groups over weaker sections of the population."[58]

Many owners and staffers in print-based movement spaces echo these sentiments. For instance, Kris Kleindienst with Left Bank in St. Louis expressed sympathy for both the balanced reporting perspective and the corporate bias perspective. She spoke highly of progressive booksellers who protected freedom of expression even if it meant including conservative authors. "That's great, I understand that approach." However, that is not the system Kleindienst uses in her store. "Our approach is, we have so many shelf feet, and we're going to carry the books that we feel like we can be passionate about."

Deciding which books to carry is the process of deciding whose voices will be heard. It is difficult to hear people when louder voices talk over them. To illustrate this phenomenon, staffers with Loganberry (a nonactivist but socially conscious bookstore) celebrated Women's History Month in 2017 by turning their male-authored books spine-in for two weeks. Inverting those spines visualized the overrepresentation of male authors, and it put the spotlight on women's perspectives. "To give the floor and attention to women, you need to be able to hear them."[59] When it comes to speaking in public, men interrupt women, take more turns than women, and speak for longer than women.[60] For staffers at Loganberry, if the goal of speaking—including through writing—is to be heard, "if someone else is talking over them, that just doesn't happen."[61]

Media outlets posted stories about Loganberry's spine-in intervention, and many online readers responded with support, but some people used the occasion to mount a misogynistic backlash. For example, one critic wrote, "This dumb broad is why so many women-run businesses go belly up."[62] This derogatory comment disparages women for using businesses as a mode of public expression, even though men do this all the time. The explicitly gendered nature of the comment provides yet more evidence that speaking authority is unevenly distributed in the public realm.

As a nonactivist bookstore, Loganberry reversed male-authored books for only two weeks. By contrast, activist-entrepreneurs use similar strategies year-round. This is why, at In Other Words, 95 percent of the authors are women.[63] At Eso Won, the owner "carries works solely focused on African American interests and by African American authors."[64] Similarly, at May Day, the collective carries books critiquing capitalism from many perspectives but none speaking in its favor. In all these examples, the point is to construct a space where habitually privileged voices are muzzled so habitually silenced voices are heard.

Alongside moving away from so-called fair and balanced reporting, a second curatorial subtheme is encouraging more people to add their voices to the mix. For many groups, speaking in public is not an obvious option. At Resistencia, aspiring authors of color express anxiety that only people with college degrees are supposed to become authors, only white people get to be bookish, and only formal styles of expression are legitimate in print.[65] Since society conditions people to associate these traits with some groups and not others, internalized stigmas keep many potential authors silent.

Activist-entrepreneurs use a combination of curatorial practices and event programming to unsettle internalized stereotypes. One territorial tactic is moving public discourse out of privileged environments and into everyday settings. Just as Kleindienst with Left Bank brought books into low-income schools, other activist-entrepreneurs likewise challenge people to reimagine where writing belongs. For instance, Lilia Rosas with Resistencia uses programming to disrupt assumptions that writing happens elsewhere by people in spaces of privilege. As an example, the bookstore hosts grassroots writing groups like Mama Sana where Latina women write anthologies about decolonizing motherhood in low-income communities of color. For Rosas, this shift from the ivory tower to a low-income community of color is "one more way that we make sure that [ideas] are always accessible and democratic, not isolated in academic institutions, but organic to the very communities that are being . . . talked about."

Another way to disrupt regimes of public speech is to use curation to demystify the writing process so that nonnormative authors can more easily imagine themselves as writers. This commitment to transparency explains the otherwise idiosyncratic collection at places like Resistencia. Browsing the shelves, I noticed books on race and ethnicity, which I expected, but I also saw books on feminism, urbanism, anarchism, and ecology. At first, I thought this mix merely reflected intersectional sympathies, so I appreciated when Rosas explained further. "What's special about these books is that I either have had a conversation with the author . . . or people have literally, physically, brought their books *to me*." From those interactions, Rosas can tell visitors where the books came from and how they were produced. "There's a story. Not only this final product, but [a story] of labor that I think is important to demystify when it comes to books. They're not just these magical things."

Showing marginalized groups published work written by people like them on topics relevant to their communities encourages people not to take territorial borders for granted. Breaking down borders is why Paul Yamazaki with City Lights invites public school students to tour the bookstore's historic location, learn about activist publishing, and read poetry to classmates in the same room where Beat generation intellectuals held their famous salons. Bringing youth of color into the reading room is a literal invitation to share the space and imagine themselves as public intellectuals. The hope is that "once they start understanding that there's a lot of work that speaks directly to young people of color of various class and cultural backgrounds, the walls that may have once seemed high . . . become less high. And these young people can now see the library as another place that they can inhabit."

Back at Resistencia, Nancy Flores described how these practices affected her as an aspiring writer struggling to envision her future. "I realized that poetry didn't have to be academic or pretentious. It could be raw, relatable, and created by someone who looked like me."[66] The activist bookstore helped her find the courage to write even without knowing where her voice might fit. "For Latino and Latina poets who sometimes sprinkle Spanish or Spanglish in their work, or discuss identity, the border, or biculturalism, it's not always easy to fit neatly into a creative writing box."[67] Despite these challenges, Resistencia's poetry readings, writing groups, and curation practices gave Flores a vision of a public realm where her voice belonged.

Alongside selective curation and demystification, a third way activist-entrepreneurs use curation to restructure public speech is constructing new entry points into public discourse. Even when people choose to speak and write, they may not have opportunities to disseminate their work. One challenge is that print capitalism filters debate. Somewhat ironically, the consolidation of capitalist publishing grew the industry without necessarily diversifying its content. By the late 1990s, after decades of mergers and acquisitions, five international multimedia conglomerates controlled four-fifths of the U.S. publishing industry.[68] These mergers fueled industry growth, including a 500 percent increase in the number of new titles published annually between 1980 and 2010.[69] However, for John Thompson, "despite the enormous volume," this output "is not complemented by a diverse marketplace" because "a small fraction of titles . . . dominate the spaces of the visible."[70] The rise of chain superstores creates additional hurdles since a handful of corporate buyers decide which titles to sell nationwide.[71] These trends intensify industry pressure to find the next blockbuster hit, which favors known authors with broad audiences at the expense of new or fringe authors taking risks and pushing boundaries.[72]

Activist-entrepreneurs use control over space to subvert these exclusionary trends. Other scholars have already analyzed efforts to get marginalized authors better industry representation.[73] A complementary strategy, which I explore here, is taking direct steps to reformulate the supply chain by reducing barriers to entry.

One way to rework the supply chain is consignment. Consignment is when retailers handle sales on behalf of small producers like independent artisans and self-published authors. Quimby's is an especially informative example of how progressive retailers use consignment to expand speaking opportunities. As Liz Mason explains, "Our consignment form is right on our website, so people can print it out [and] send their zines." Authors do not need to coordinate in advance. If an author submits reading material retailing for twenty-five dollars or less that does not contain oppressive content, Quimby's will offer it for sale in exchange for a 40 percent share of the sales price. The result is an eclectic assortment of internationally sourced, progressive-friendly texts ranging from perfect bound books to doodle-style graphics held together with duct tape. "It's like Christmas every day. We don't know what we're gonna get."

The most significant challenge of selling on consignment is cost. At Quimby's, 85 percent of the stock is composed of self-published zines, chapbooks, comix, and other book-like items skirting the edges of capitalist discipline. These publications do not follow industry standards. They do not come with economies of scale. There are no barcodes, ISBN numbers, inventory tracking systems, or centralized distributors. Managing this nonstandard material is labor-intensive, which makes it expensive.

The benefit, however, is that consignment systems make space for boundary-pushing material that otherwise does not get a public airing. For Mason, this system "allows us to sell some of the things that you don't normally find at Amazon or at a regular book distributor." As examples, Quimby's sells material written by punks obsessed with whales, high schoolers critiquing advertising, and prisoners describing the criminalization of nonbinary genders. Instead of waiting for editors and publishers to grant permission to speak, these unconventional authors simply write about topics silenced elsewhere. Consignment then constructs a mechanism to disseminate these perspectives in the public realm.

Alongside making space for nonnormative voices, consignment facilitates border-crossing. Border-crossing happens for a couple of reasons. One reason is that staffers like Mason provide mentoring and technical support helping unconventional authors learn to navigate the publishing industry. "Inadvertently, my personal mission here—one of them—has been to help artists and creative types understand the business angle of how to get their stuff out into the world." Educating writers means saying things like, "Well, you know, you have to maybe put a title on the cover. You have to think about how much you are going to sell it for. . . . Do you want to think about paying yourself a wage? . . . Are you concerned with making a profit? . . . Do you want to fund your next project?" Gently encouraging people to think "in terms of—and this sounds like a gross word to say—the business angle" is a way to "raise the consciousness of how to disseminate your work in the world in a reasonable way" and "in a way that people who aren't artists can understand."

Places like Quimby's also provide incubation. During our conversation, Mason listed several authors who got their start "making something on their computer, or their kitchen table, or with the glue stick and scissors" and later signed contracts with corporate publishers or got reviews in major newspapers. "They started out as just these DIY publishers, consigners, creators, [and] artists doing these scrappy things. And to see them move their way up in the world is really fun." Not everyone wants corporate success. Plenty of authors write without any desire to become rich or famous. They "just keep doing it for the love of it." But for writers who do hope to break down barriers, Quimby's is a place to start.

To recap, curation is a governing tool. These operational procedures give usually silenced authors more opportunities to participate in the public realm. This inclusion does not happen because potential authors spontaneously imagine themselves as rights-bearing subjects with state-supported capacities for public speech. Instead, it happens because activist-entrepreneurs leverage their spaces, as well as their ability to control who speaks through their spaces, to challenge inequitable publicity regimes and to construct new opportunities for progressive nonnormative expression.

Horizontal Management Gives More People a Voice

Alongside safe space policies and curation practices, a third territorial governing strategy is democratizing systems of administration. Ownership confers legitimacy on public speech, which is one reason why diversity among business owners is politically significant. Having queer feminist activists in charge is a step in the right direction, as is having owners of color. However, because of worker–owner divides, the majority of people contributing energy to businesses do not share owner privileges. To challenge this inequity, some activist-entrepreneurs eschew hierarchical business models in favor of horizontal ownership and democratic decision-making. In addition to engendering equity in the workplace, these practices give more people the opportunity to express themselves publicly as small business spokespeople.

Historically, ownership and public speech go hand in hand. Property ownership was a prerequisite for voting until the mid-nineteenth century.[74] Although land ownership is technically no longer required, in my role as an urban researcher, I've attended countless meetings between residents and elected officials where residents say: I own my house, I own a business, I pay my taxes, and therefore my government ought to respect my perspective. Refrains like these are important reminders that, by social convention if not by law, ownership status remains a salient factor legitimizing political participation.[75]

Alongside owning property, owning businesses performs similar certification functions. Because business owners have long-term financial stakes in maintaining their customer base, merchants are disproportionately active in local politics.[76] Small business owners similarly act as "self-appointed public characters" in the Jane Jacobs sense of circulating information, safeguarding petitions, and monitoring public space.[77] Business owners also get recruited as spokespeople for the communities they supposedly represent, which is why reporters writing about Islam in the United States, for example, not only visit mosques and cultural centers but also interview the Muslim owners of ethnic bakeries and grocery stores, whom they then quote in the news.[78]

These trends illustrate some of the connections between ownership status and public speech. This opportunity (and also pressure) for owners to pick up microphones is somewhat ironic in a democracy because there is nothing democratic about capitalism. Despite being recruited to speak on behalf of others, small business owners are not elected mouthpieces, nor are they structurally accountable for what they say. Another challenge is that business owners occupy a distinct class position, which means their interests may clash with those of the workers and customers they supposedly represent. Despite these complications, business owners frequently volunteer or get recruited to do public speaking work.

For activist-entrepreneurs, public speaking can be a bridge-building tool. Unlike more intimate activist spaces, like collective houses, the public-facing nature of retail pushes activist-entrepreneurs to function as intermediaries translating between mainstream and alternative groups. Just as Kleindienst with Left Bank was recruited to provide a progressive take on the Affordable Care Act, people call on other activist-entrepreneurs to tell them what they think they should know about the group in question. Activist-entrepreneurs of many stripes provide these go-between services. This pressure to represent is why Carrie Barnett with People Like Us described herself as "a professional lesbian for years and years. It's sort of an odd profession, isn't it? . . . But if they ever needed any gay authority on anything, they would call us, and we'd be on the radio or the TV." This pressure to represent also explains why staffers at Birchbark "work with a lot of schools" and "work with teachers helping them fulfill academic standards in Native American literature." It's also why, when St. Louis city officials clashed with state representatives over whether the municipality could raise its minimum wage, Left Bank co-owners engaged the City of St. Louis by writing editorials saying that, for the change to be effective from a progressive perspective, "here are some ways that it could happen that would actually support the local businesses."

In all these cases, activist-entrepreneurship is not just about claiming turf for queer, Indigenous, or progressive counterpublics. It is also about constructing mechanisms for owners to engage in political debate. These public speaking opportunities are especially valuable given how frequently other activists—for instance people participating in street protests—get dismissed in the media as irrational, dangerous, and illegitimate.[79] By contrast, activists speaking as small business owners are assumed to have a valid point of view.

Having more business owners who are queer, feminist, radical, anarchist, anticapitalist, or of color diversifies these conversations. However, inequity remains a factor. Capitalist businesses are hierarchical. Owners have the option to invite employees to share their opinions, but they ultimately retain control over whether staffers get to speak, on what issues, and to which audiences.

This observation does not mean that hierarchical models are never useful. On the contrary, limiting internal debate can increase operational efficiency, which is financially advantageous. This is why, at City Lights, even though "having that dialogue within a group strengthens the idea . . . we don't go back and forth for a [long] while." Instead, one benefit of the management team is the ability to make decisions relatively quickly.

Although City Lights's approach is valid, other activist-entrepreneurs have different priorities, and they successfully incorporate direct democracy into their business structures. Direct democracy is about permitting and empowering everyone to participate in public life.[80] One way to implement direct democracy in business contexts is to use collective ownership. Of the venues I studied, about one-third (35 percent) were collectives. Because collective ownership distributes authority, it provides more people with opportunities to express themselves not only through microphones but also through their labor.

Collectively owned enterprises implement direct democracy in a couple different ways. One approach focuses on worker autonomy. This approach to direct democracy suggests that workers should be empowered to speak for themselves, for instance by making choices about how to spend their energy and what messages that sends into the world. For Adrian (no last name given) with Left Bank in Seattle, "In a collective, we're supposed to be making decisions together, but we're also empowering each other." As an example, when one volunteer wanted to create an Asian American section, collective members encouraged it. "You want to do something at the shop? Go ahead and do it." Assembling an Asian American section was a form of public speech because, alongside the already existing sections highlighting African American and Latino/a authors, this change made Asian American perspectives more visible in the public realm. As a worker-initiated action, this new section may not last forever. "If people don't like it, they can always change it back." In the meantime, the worker autonomy approach encourages people to do whatever work motivates them, and then see where it leads.

This worker autonomy approach builds on the legacies of 1960s and 1970s co-op culture. Henri Lefebvre uses the term "autogestion" to describe this New Left movement. According to translators, autogestion means "self-management or self-determination." The "ultimate goal of autogestion is 'the withering away of the state.'"[81] This co-op movement incorporated the antibureaucratic ideologies of Max Weber's iron cage, C. Wright Mills's cheerful robot, Herbert Marcuse's one-dimensional man, and Harry Braverman's degraded work. According to Joshua Clark Davis, activist-entrepreneurs inspired by these concepts decried the alienating and stultifying effects of capitalist hierarchy and profit maximization. As antidotes, they experimented with self-directed labor. "They believed that democratically structured small business enterprises could empower people to achieve real liberation."[82] By committing to principles like member voting and worker control over the labor process, activists hoped to "democratize and humanize workplace social relations."[83]

The goal of freeing people from hierarchies is a recurring theme in print-based movement spaces, especially older ones rooted in the New Left. For Kristin Dooley with May Day, "if I'm willing to do the work, the rest of us thank you for it, and allow you to do it in a way that you think is best." I asked Dooley for examples. "The worker who does our website, he gets to pretty much decide what happens. The worker who does our accounting, he gets to decide how to do it. I look for books, I get to decide how to do it. I do fliers, I generally get to decide how to do it." Emphasizing worker autonomy does not negate accountability. "If I do something wrong, I will get called on it. I will change it." However, when it comes to allocating responsibilities, the primary goal is for each worker to individually decide.

Alongside this worker autonomy approach, a second approach to direct democracy de-emphasizes individuals speaking for themselves and instead prioritizes consensus. Compared to autogestion, consensus-based governance is less about freeing people from oppressive bosses and more about increasing empathic collaboration among peers. This empathic approach is similar to what Miriam Williams observes within feminist traditions of mutuality and caretaking. "Care theory understands people as interdependent and as having responsibility for the wellbeing of others because of their mutual 'being-in-common.'"[84] This goal of being-in-common is why Red Emma's uses a different decision-making structure than Left Bank in Seattle or May Day in Minneapolis. Instead of asking individual workers to decide, at Red Emma's, "we move forward with a decision only when everybody is in agreement (or at least when no one disagrees so strongly that they'd leave the project if a decision was taken)."[85]

Activists using consensus-based systems develop administrative tools to facilitate the process. It is not enough to simply talk as a group and expect agreement to emerge. Instead, activists use policies to shape the field of engagement. Some policies govern group size, for instance by keeping the "group small enough to meet face to face with everyone's voice able to be heard."[86] Some policies promote equity, for instance by balancing ownership so "everyone has a more or less equal stake in the decisions being discussed."[87] Other policies govern assertiveness, for instance by "noting the people who we know don't always immediately voice their opinions, and asking them what they think about this stuff, and trying to make sure no one's lording over anyone else." These types of governing tools make consensus easier to achieve.

Even with supportive policies, empathic collaboration is not easy. Collective members at Boneshaker acknowledge that it can be an arduous process. "In the way that we run our store, we practice that radical, difficult communication where we are all committed to respecting each other and hearing each other out, even if that means things take longer [and] even if that means our ideas don't get pushed forward." This radical consensus building can feel tedious and time consuming. Getting sixty collective members to agree on a plan takes longer than letting one worker decide. Even for minor issues, it can lead to delays, like a two-month-long discussion over what color the collective's T-shirt should be, "or six months [of] very slow discussion about whether we should have a sweatshirt."

These challenges draw criticism from the worker autonomy camp. One criticism is that the delays associated with consensus building can lead to disempowering stalemates. This is why Kristin Dooley with May Day does not want to "meet and agree and discuss and discuss and discuss and discuss and discuss and discuss and discuss." She prefers feeling empowered to act for herself. Another criticism is that demanding consensus can have repressive effects, which is why, at May Day, "we don't demand that unity of purpose. We don't demand that we all believe the same thing. . . . We decided long ago that we would agree to disagree."

For these reasons, consensus-based methods are not ideal for living free from other people's expectations. But at places like Red Emma's and Boneshaker, the slow, deliberative process is worthwhile because it advances another political agenda. This goal is not to wither away the state or to turn workers into free agents. Instead, the goal is to construct alternative, equitable, but nonetheless regimented and disciplinary systems of governing based on empathy, mutuality, and solidarity. For Zoe Michael with Boneshaker, "as much as that [process] is punitive and frustrating, I wouldn't have it any other way."

As these examples illustrate, horizontal decision-making systems counterinstitutionalize the administrative aspects of territorial zones. In contrast to the usual zoning literature, which emphasizes the dedemocratizing effects of special assessment zones and privately owned public spaces, many activist-entrepreneurs use private control over public-facing environments to subvert inequitable speech. Administrative systems like these are counterterritorial governing tools. These place-based strategies construct bubbles of turf. This turf is claimed for some people and guarded against others. It is also a place where networks collide. Facilitating speech across social groups does not mean discipline and exclusion disappear. On the contrary, alongside bridge-building functions, activists also advance movements through social filtering, which is the topic of the next chapter.

CHAPTER 7

Nurturing Camaraderie in Filtered Third Places

A S A TEENAGER, Boone (no last name given) was a self-described "internet anarchist" listening to podcasts and following blogs. "My experience with radical politics had been reading about it [and] arguing about it in academic settings [and] with people on the internet." Later, in his twenties, Boone searched for a physical space where he could put his convictions into practice. "I was looking up 'radical bookstores in the Twin Cities,' or something like that, and I found out that they had this lending library at this place called the Minnehaha Free Space."

Setting out to visit the Free Space, Boone felt nervous, which surprised him. "It was funny, 'cause mentally I've done some political activism before." But going to a physical environment for face-to-face interactions still felt intimidating. "I was excited to meet some people I agreed with. But mentally, I was going over my interpretation of [Mikhail] Bakunin's work today." Boone worried whether he could keep up in a place where people might be "getting themselves riled up about their ideology ... [and] giving political speeches." What he found was more low-key. "I showed up, and they're like, 'We're teaching each other how to sew [and] how to fix holes in clothes today.'"

The Minnehaha Free Space was created in 2011 as an anarchist-inspired lending library and community center. According to Boone, "It was a space for pretty much anyone to plan whatever kinds of events they wanted to without having to pay the fees that community centers or coffee shops involve." The Free Space was located in a commercial storefront on Minnehaha Avenue. The collective paid rent by accepting donations, as well as by hosting concerts and dance party fundraisers, which supported a lending library, meeting room, communal kitchen, and childcare room.

Showing up at the Free Space marked a new chapter in Boone's journey through radical consciousness. He started cautiously by reading in the library and cooking with Food Not Bombs, which put him in the space without requiring much commitment or self-disclosure. As he acclimated,

Music and dance parties like this one celebrating the opening of the Minnehaha Free Space in Minneapolis, Minnesota, bring people together and help pay for space. Photograph by Eli Meyerhoff / Jecca Namakkal, 2011; courtesy of Eli Meyerhoff.

he began taking more risks. Boone was closeted to his college friends, but at the Free Space, he joined a queer support group to explore his bisexuality. Boone also deepened his anticapitalist lifestyle. "I wanted to find ways that I could withdraw my material support from some of the corporations that I spend lots of money on." When he raised the issue, someone else at the free space offered to teach him how to dumpster dive, "and now they and I go once a month."

Taking this radical journey with others, instead of reading online alone, diversified Boone's understanding of who and what belonged under the anarchist umbrella. When spending time in shared spaces, "you get exposed to the stuff people do that's not organized." While lingering in the common spaces, Boone met people teaching each other how to fix screen doors and bake vegan cookies. He overheard parents discussing radical child-rearing. He listened to Native Americans describing "being made into non-people for a long period of time." These unplanned interactions exposed Boone to new interpretations of anarchism—interpretations quite different from his own—which broadened his political imagination and, over time, expanded his affinity group.

This foundation of shared concepts and mutual trust then provided Boone with an instrumental support base during a tumultuous political moment. In the months surrounding the 2016 presidential election, Boone frequented the Free Space more regularly. "I was, like a lot of people, casting around for the most useful way to take any kind of direct political action." Listening to other people's conversations, Boone decided to shift from self-directed personal growth to state-directed political organizing by joining the Disrupt J20 protest of the presidential inauguration. "I was there to be part of the black bloc," which meant concealing his identity and standing shoulder-to-shoulder with others as a human shield protecting other demonstrators from police violence.

Boone had never participated in a black bloc before, and he was nervous about getting injured or arrested. "I'm in school. I really can't afford to miss extra days because I got imprisoned." He considered searching online for practical tips, but online searches through third-party internet providers are risky. If Boone was arrested, his search history could be used against him. Instead, Boone asked people at the Free Space for advice, and he scoured the lending library for zines on protest laws, demonstration techniques, protective gear, and aftercare. "It's got very basic stuff that I didn't necessarily want to have on my [digital profile]." Boone put those skills to work during the protest, and he returned feeling invigorated and empowered.

Conversations like this one about the Minnehaha Free Space reveal how casual interactions in filtered environments construct opportunities for affinity building and frame alignment. Ideological discussions play a role, but practical activities like sewing and cooking are equally significant for everyday bonding. These practical activities are low-stakes opportunities for strangers to interact and get to know each other. Additionally, because interactions occur in a filtered environment, people can be a bit more open than they are in other settings. In Boone's case, away from his college buddies and away from government oversight, he felt comfortable exploring ideas about sexuality and resistance that he otherwise avoided. Through informal hovering in a shared but sheltered space, Boone expanded his horizons, developed new skills, and connected with a support base for organizing.

These dynamics shed light on the difference between encounter zones and convergence spaces. For Helen Wilson, encounters are not neutral meetings among strangers. Instead, "encounters are historically coded as a meeting of opposites," and these meetings are "often marked by highly

unequal relations of power."[1] Encounters are generative because interactions across difference can be "exhilarating moments of wonder and
revelation" leading to "mutual understanding and new wisdom."[2] But the
opposite is also true. Because of power disparities, interactions across difference do not automatically lead to increased empathy. Instead, if the tone
is demeaning, exploitive, or violent, encounters spark "rage, incomprehen-
sion, and pain,"[3] which reproduces hierarchies and intensifies alienation.

Because activist retail is open to the public, it functions in part as an
encounter zone. All kinds of people pass through, which constructs opportunities for normative groups to cross paths with less privileged Others. Although these encounters can feel uncomfortable and antagonistic,
when countergoverning systems manage them effectively, they destabilize
taken-for-granted assumptions and enable alternative social scripts.

However, despite this potential, no one I interviewed described the
process as easy or painless, nor did anyone expect it to happen automatically in mainstream spaces, like public streets and chain superstores.
Instead, filtering plays an important role. Without minimizing the significance of intergroup encounters, activist businesses are also convergence
centers where people come together around similar themes. Anyone can
enter, but some people gravitate more strongly than others toward these
spaces and their progressive topics. Those subgroups are more likely to
informally linger and regularly return. Diversity is still a factor because,
even in filtered spaces, people approach radical ideas from many perspectives. This self-selected mutual hovering nevertheless constructs filtered
environments open to anyone but predominantly filled with people who,
in some way or other, self-identify with or are sympathetic to the social
and political ideas on display.

These convergence dynamics raise questions about how activists leverage social filtering as an alliance-building tool. Emphasizing social filtering, rather than universal inclusion, challenges scholarship on designing
cities for difference. I explore these issues in this chapter by combining
two perspectives. On the one hand, I analyze print-based movement
spaces as "third places"[4] for congenial interactions. On the other hand, I
use the lens of "offstage space"[5] to rethink the value of separatism in the
public realm. The usual assumption is that the best way to combat inequity
in the public realm is by constructing spaces where everyone is included.
I agree that inclusion is an important goal. However, it is risky for vulnerable groups to move into shared spaces before oppressive norms have

changed. As an example, because of race and gender oppression, "by definition, [shared] spaces became less 'safe' if shared with those who were not Black and female."[6]

Because of this vulnerability, third places where everyone is present are dangerous places to disclose and debate sensitive ideas. By contrast, social filtering in *offstage* third places, where disciplinary agents are absent, facilitates more open and democratic debate. Although filters that exclude vulnerable groups are inherently unjust, reverse filtering by congregating away from oppressive influences is an important social movement tool. For Patricia Hill Collins, these spaces "rely on exclusionary practices but their overall purpose aims for a more inclusionary, just society."[7]

Despite the potential benefits of reverse filtering, this phenomenon is understudied in the third place literature. One reason that reverse filtering is understudied is because scholars prioritize universal inclusion. Given the extent of race, class, and gender exclusion in U.S. cities, it is crucial to find new ways to break down barriers. However, power disparities linger, and commingling facilitates discipline. This discipline makes it difficult to build camaraderie around vulnerable identities when potential oppressors are present. By contrast, print-based movement spaces are not universal. They are open to the general public, but the social and political themes on display appeal more to some groups than others. This filtering is an asset, not a liability. Activists construct filtered spaces organized around vulnerable needs, which makes it easier to acknowledge experiences otherwise left unspoken. The hope is that, by airing shared experiences, strangers can build fellow feeling and construct alternative alliances.

Another reason reverse filtering is understudied is because third place scholars prioritize cheerful respite. For Ray Oldenburg, in a world of constant "aggression-provoking situations," third places provide "a blessed interlude" of friendly relaxation.[8] The yearning for cheerful respite in a stressful world is understandable. However, although maintaining a veneer of easy harmony by avoiding difficult issues can help strangers relax together, it is less useful for developing common frames of reference. Instead, exploring disagreement helps construct common ground. Because people approach progressive ideas from many perspectives, print-based movement spaces are not always relaxed and jovial. People approach these ideas from many angles. Instead of papering over those differences by limiting conversation to neutral topics, activists leverage feelings of affinity in filtered spaces to encourage communal learning, including through safe-enough contentious debate. Although grappling with difference can be uncomfortable, the hope is that, by engaging with difference rather than avoiding it, people can move toward the common understandings necessary to sustain collective organizing.

A third reason reverse filtering is understudied is because third place scholars explore generic caretaking without attending to specialized needs. Many people find everyday emotional support in third places. In activist enterprises, this support is not just about *supplementing* the support networks of home and work. It is also about *withdrawing* from the trauma of home, work, and other public spaces to find collective caretaking unavailable elsewhere. Unlike other venues that provide generic caretaking, filtered counterspaces provide specialized support responding to specific types of social violence. Additionally, although filtered caretaking is useful year-round, the protections afforded in filtered environments are especially significant—and significant in new ways—during moments of political upheaval. During those tense moments, when people withdraw from generic settings and converge in filtered spaces, specialized caretaking provides opportunities to coordinate political responses.

These findings show that offstage interactions in filtered third places facilitate affinity building, frame alignment, and collective caretaking in ways less possible in the fully exposed public realm. Social filtering in convergence zones generates opportunities for regular informal interactions among potentially empathic peers. The goal is to construct a durable counterspace that is porous enough to be diverse yet shielded enough to facilitate sensitive debate. These interactions, which build informal ties of familiarity and trust, then establish a support base for state-directed organizing. These findings also shed light on the democratic potential of allowing some types of shared spaces to remain filtered rather than pushing for every space in the city to be universally inclusive.

Offstage Third Places Are Socially Filtered Convergence Zones

I analyze social filtering using the lens of offstage space. Erving Goffman popularized the language of frontstage and backstage dynamics when describing how people behave differently in social contexts than when alone. For Goffman, people cultivate personas, which they present as a "performance . . . intentionally or unwittingly employed" when other people are around.[9] These public personas in the "front region" can be quite different from the thoughts and characteristics organizing behavior when no one is watching. In the privacy of "backstage" space, the mask can be dropped and "the performance is knowingly contradicted as a matter of course."[10]

Other scholars have expanded this stage metaphor by exploring the disciplinary power dynamics organizing onstage performances. For James C. Scott, during public encounters between subordinates and more powerful counterparts,[11] vulnerable groups often defer enough to oppressors' scripts to get through the encounter with minimal damage. Deference includes withholding portions of their thoughts, experiences, and identities "in favor of a 'performance' that is in keeping with the expectations of the powerholder."[12] By contrast, when out of the sight of authority figures, vulnerable groups have more options. In offstage spaces "beyond direct observation by powerholders,"[13] people can generate a "backstage discourse consisting of what cannot be spoken in the face of power,"[14] including critiques of hegemonic authority and hidden transcripts for other ways of being.[15]

Alongside these power dynamics, another important insight is that people can be offstage without being alone. A key characteristic of many offstage spaces is that they are simultaneously separate and shared. Offstage groups can be quite large. For Andrew Shryock, they can include "entire national communities, ethnoracial minorities, socioeconomic classes, religious movements, and global diasporas of almost any kind"[16] where groups live interspersed with others even as they live significant portions of their lives in polarized spaces. Additionally, because counterpublics include internal hierarchies, offstage spaces can always be further subdivided around new filters, each time adding additional degrees of polarization that allow more aspects of the public-facing mask to be temporarily discarded. These characteristics suggest that being onstage or offstage is less of an either/or proposition and more of a spectrum with many potential dimensions of selective transparency.

Collective separatism is a useful political tool. As an example, bell hooks coined the term "homeplace" to describe the collective offstage spaces of her youth. Hooks uses the term to refer to segregated African American neighborhoods "where we do not directly encounter white racist aggression."[17] Away from white oppressors, "black people could affirm one another and by doing so heal many of the wounds inflicted by racist domination."[18] Collective separatism was necessary for healing because

African Americans were not permitted to "learn to love or respect our-selves in the culture of white supremacy."[19] Collective separatism was also politically significant. In segregated homeplaces, "all black people could strive to be subjects, not objects," which is "a radically subversive political gesture" and which makes homeplaces "a crucial site for organizing [and] for forming political solidarity."[20] These dynamics do not justify the forced segregation of oppressed groups, but they do shed light on the value of constructing spaces where oppressors are absent.

Print-based movement spaces are likewise shared yet sheltered envi-ronments, and they deliver these political benefits third place–style. Ray Oldenburg, drawing heavily on Jane Jacobs, coined the phrase "third place" to describe environments away from home and work where people congregate for routine, cordial interactions among strangers. For Olden-burg, third places are shapeshifters. Instead of assuming a specific form, they are recognizable by their function. In these cheap or free environ-ments where people hang out as part of their daily round, "conversation is the main activity."[21] From Oldenburg's perspective, the relaxed atmo-sphere means people can "come as they are" without having to dress up or show off.[22] The noncommittal nature of conversations encourages in-teractions across difference.[23] Additionally, because these conversations occur in a setting that "serves virtually everybody,"[24] people interact across a wide spectrum of difference, which makes third places "ports of entry" and "sorting areas" where newcomers warm up to each other, get exposed to new ideas, and get plugged into "other forms of association."[25] For Old-enburg, these integrative dynamics are an invaluable community-building asset. "The first and most important function of third places is that of unit-ing the neighborhood."[26]

Bookstores and libraries fit this third place description almost per-fectly, and scholars frequently use them as quintessential places to study third place dynamics.[27] However, when it comes to *movement-oriented* ven-ues, many third place scholars disqualify them because of their social and political filters. For these scholars, third places can only occur on neutral ground.[28] They are supposed to be "judgment free spaces" containing "the full spectrum of local humanity," where "diversity is the most relevant characteristic."[29] These scholars also feel that the primary function of third places cannot be political because spaces can only serve everyone if they are politically inclusive.[30]

If scholars accept this definition, print-based movement spaces do not qualify as third places because they are filtered around contentious topics like race, gender, and anarchism, and also because they are not politically neutral. However, I do not believe this narrow definition of third places is either accurate or helpful. For one thing, no third place is neutral, universally inclusive, or apolitical. Oldenburg's own examples from history were notoriously exclusionary, for instance nineteenth-century working-class taverns,[31] which were fiercely segregated by race and nationality.[32] Oldenburg similarly notes that, historically, men had more third places, higher quality third places, and more access to third places than women.[33] Other scholars concerned about inequity likewise show that, despite inclusionary rhetoric, the reality is that race, gender, age, nationality, address, and income pose significant barriers to third place participation.[34]

Another reason third places are not universally inclusive is because they are usually organized around themes. Although third places can serve everyone, like the proverbial post office or general store, more often, they are convergence zones where people cross paths and connect with others who share their lifestyles and interests. For example, dog parks, hardware stores, and coffee shops are technically open to everyone, but only some people have pets, enjoy home improvement projects, or can afford leisurely cappuccinos. Because of these individual preferences, certain flavors of third places will always appeal more to some groups than others. These observations lead some critical third place scholars to concede that, in practice, third places are not universal and instead function as "connection points for socializing in and with a *niche* community."[35]

Then, for people opting in, participants develop internal hierarchies. For critical third place scholars, people frequenting these spaces organize themselves into "social clusters and cliques"[36] that "constantly introduce newer microhierarchies with which to elevate themselves" relative to others in the space.[37] Because of these dynamics, even when third places start as relatively neutral turf, through repeat interactions, participants "create an identity for themselves," including "a playful mood" that helps regulars feel connected with each other and that "reminds outsiders that they are not a part of the group."[38]

Scholars analyzing these dynamics usually conclude either with calls to abandon the third place concept as a utopian fantasy[39] or with calls to develop more inclusionary third place designs.[40] Although I agree the third place idea is more aspirational than actual, I do not support abandoning the concept because, in a society so heavily geared toward privatization,

I believe it is useful to have as much language as possible promoting informal public life. Then, if scholars are going to retain the concept, I agree that exclusionary dynamics are problematic, and I support the call to develop inclusionary retrofits.

However, without diminishing the push for equitable access, the literature on offstage spaces suggests that it is also valuable to have third places that exclude oppressive figures. As much as I enjoy Jane Jacobs's romantic image of strangers coexisting on "excellent sidewalk terms,"[41] the appearance of neutrality is not the same as genuine inclusion. As an example, communists and queers in the 1950s could pass a few idle minutes chatting with strangers on sidewalks, but only as long as they kept significant aspects of their identities and convictions concealed.[42] These cordial sidewalk meetings were not neutral. On the contrary, they were high-risk performances between powerful and vulnerable groups reproducing normative orders. For members of vulnerable groups to genuinely "come as they are" was to risk job losses, social ostracism, and vigilante violence. They could also be arrested, but gossipmongers could do considerable damage even without involving the state.

Patrick Joyce uses the term "omniopticon" to describe this distributed style of discipline. Instead of a panopticon with "the one viewing the many," omniopticons involve "the many viewing the many."[43] In situations like these, being visible to strangers—even ones without state authority—creates pressures to don Goffman-style masks. These dynamics suggest that, in repressive societies, places where everyone is likely to be present can be frightening and dangerous for people without privilege.

Because of these dangers, instead of only pulling vulnerable people into public places of exposure, evaluating third places through an offstage lens sheds a different light on how specialized—rather than universal—spaces encourage congeniality across difference. Arguing that social difference does not and perhaps cannot get leveled is not about making a virtue of exclusion. Instead, it is about attending to the ways collective separatism is useful—and perhaps necessary—when planning for cities of difference. For Robert Beauregard, "Transparency that hinders dissent is undemocratic in the same way that a lack of transparency thwarts justice and consolidates power."[44] If the goal is to build a movement large enough to mount resistance, sometimes that movement can only begin behind closed doors.

However, two important caveats should be kept in mind. The first caveat is that separatism serves many purposes, many of which are not progressive. Enclaving is a common tool of antidemocratic oppression. Feminists knew this when they infiltrated gender-segregated social clubs where men perpetuated patriarchy by making political and economic decisions behind closed doors. Fundamentalist religious sects likewise use spatial seclusion to evade national laws requiring universal education, prohibiting racial discrimination, and criminalizing domestic violence. Conservative separatism perpetuates conservative politics, including inequality.

Another caveat is that, even when separatism blocks some injustices, it sometimes simultaneously recreates others. This is why Bernice Johnson Reagon criticized the second-wave women's movement not for excluding men but for excluding Black women, poor women, transgender women, and any other women whose life circumstances were meaningfully different from white middle-class norms. These exclusions reproduced existing social hierarchies. Additionally, because these exclusions prevented feminists from developing robust responses to sexism across all axes of difference, they impeded the coalition building necessary to transform male-dominated institutions of power.[45]

These caveats are important, but tools have many uses, and my focus is on the *progressive* possibilities of offstage space. The point is to shed light on the potential utility of constructing filtered third places, at least as a temporary measure, while working to build more inclusive societies. Additionally, instead of seeing separatism as a disqualifying characteristic antithetical to third place functioning, it is important to recognize that filtering along some aspects of difference is inevitable. For vulnerable groups, filtering is not merely a practical reality—it is often the key factor making it possible for people to more truly come as they are, openly interact with strangers, and knit movements together.

Filtered Spaces Facilitate Affinity Building

One common characteristic of print-based movement spaces is that, even as they are open to everyone, Oldenburg's "full spectrum of local humanity"[46] does not opt in. In my assessment, this self-selectivity is not an obstacle to third place functioning. Instead, it is precisely what allows movement-oriented retail to become ports of entry knitting diverse groups together. As I explain in this section, neutrality does not come because everyone is present. Instead, filtering out normative discipline is what makes space feel neutral and level for nonnormative groups, which then facilitates friendly and open interactions among strangers.

Bookstores provide a case in point. Scholars often describe chain superstores as quintessential third places,[47] and the recent addition of Black, queer, and feminist titles in these spaces seemingly underscores their universal neutrality. The logic is that, if the book is present, the group is included. However, just because a book sits on the shelf does not mean it is safe to pick up. For instance, in Michigan where I live, at the time I was conducting research for this book, it remained legal for employers to fire workers on the basis of sexual orientation. These homophobic norms also expose people to harassment from sales staff and fellow customers in mainstream commercial settings. These damaging practices make it risky for people to browse queer titles at chain bookstores where Oldenburg's full spectrum of local humanity might see them. This is why, for a customer at Common Language, "You have a lot of [queer] youth who would be scared to death to set foot in a [general] bookstore, let alone purchase a book that has any sort of LGBT connotations."[48]

In an omniopticon world, fear of public exposure is often so ingrained that people police their thoughts even when no one is observing them. For Jay Scheide with Lucy Parsons, U.S. culture "makes you think that you're all alone . . . thinking the thoughts that should not be thought in respectable company. Like, 'Could there be democratic control of the economy?' 'Oh, you communist, you! What are you thinking!'" These self-rebukes illustrate that merely imagining having their thoughts exposed can ignite feelings of anxiety that keep people trapped in omniopticon performances, even inside their own minds.

By contrast, filtered spaces with explicit social identities and political convictions can help circumvent self-censorship. For Lilia Rosas with Resistencia, to be open with strangers, "you need to have a space where you always know you're safe." But some groups are simply not allowed to be safe in mainstream settings, no matter how neutral or level those spaces purport to be. "If you are a person of color, if you're a queer person, if you're a Black person, if you're a working person, if you are a woman . . . if you are a radical, if you're not part of the status quo, if you question basic ideas about the U.S., then you're not always welcome. And even just discussing these ideas [is unsafe], not to mention organizing around them."

Self-censorship impedes organizing because it makes it difficult to recognize when experiences are systemic instead of idiosyncratic. As long as people conceal contentious thoughts and defer to oppressors' scripts, nonnormative commonalities go unnoticed, and crossing paths has little progressive effect. However, people in offstage spaces can be more transparent and disclose information routinely withheld elsewhere. This disclosure creates opportunities for mutual recognition and affinity building. Affinity is when people recognize common experiences and feel a sense of camaraderie in those commonalities. Building affinity around shared but silenced struggles is a political endeavor because recognizing the systemic nature of oppression provides a base for collective organizing.

One way to get around omniopticon discipline is to connect with others through reading. For Walter Nicholls, "It is often the case that a person's sense of political community is more clearly shaped by her or his relations with others living on the other side of the world than those living next door."[49] Reading and writing connects people with absent others, which brings people together across space and time, even without their neighbors knowing about it. This is why proletarian activists reading mail-order "mushroom mags" during the Great Depression felt like they "knew each other through the mail," even if "not through meetings and coffee pots."[50] This is why New Left counterculturalists reading the *Whole Earth Catalog* "met in its pages," "peered across the social and intellectual fences," and found "the textual mirror of a physically dispersed tribe that felt itself linked by a shared invisible energy."[51] Similarly, for feminists and queer folk, groundbreaking books like Betty Friedan's *Feminine Mystique* and James Baldwin's *Giovanni's Room* showed readers they were not alone in their experiences of gender and sexuality. These books showed people that there were friends in the world, even if not right next door, "and what is a friend but someone who gets you?"[52]

Interacting with absent others can be a useful first step toward recognizing fellow feeling. Since readers learn about people's experiences without having to self-disclose in return, reading is a relatively low-risk way to recognize commonalities. But connecting through print is imperfect. I opened this chapter by describing Boone's experience at the Minnehaha Free Space. Before discovering Minnehaha, Boone read dead Russian theorists, and he felt connected to those absent anarchists, but they did not know Boone, they did not write about all aspects of their lives, and they were not present to participate in joint learning. Although connecting with absent others was useful, there were important reasons why Boone craved face-to-face interactions with people sharing his beliefs.

Fortunately, print objects and the places that collect them do more than just connect people with absent others. They also bring people together for real-time interactions in shared spaces. Joe Biel commented on these convergence dynamics when describing how Microcosm's annual national book tour brings strangers together. "We joke that it's a secret way to make people congregate in their own town." Even when activists live near each other, "in a lot of places, there's just not a social hub. Or there's just never a reason to get together." Book events create those catalytic moments. When authors held readings in coffee shops in Mobile, Alabama, or Reno, Nevada, "people came who had never met each other before. Even [though they] were from organizations that worked in the same fields, [they] had never been in the same room before."

Movement-oriented retail facilitates convergences year-round, sometimes even regardless of proprietors' intentions. When Biel founded Microcosm, he did not intend to create a physical meeting space. As someone on the autism spectrum, he preferred a mail-order business model over face-to-face interactions,[53] but Microcosm's readers had other ideas. "We kept having people come over. Just unannounced." These uninvited guests from the suburbs of California or the cities of Japan would show up at Microcosm's office and warehouse. At first, Biel thought they were looking for books, and he redirected them to the nearby independent bookstore stocking Microcosm's titles. But visitors pushed back. "Our fans got kind of upset. Because they were like, 'I wanna interact with you.' . . . It wasn't about the *books*. . . . They wanted to talk to *us*." These visitors converged at Microcosm because they felt a sense of camaraderie with absent others, and they wanted to intensify those bonds by connecting face-to-face with the radical public characters they'd gotten to know from a distance. Eventually, Biel relented. He created a storefront to accommodate (and contain) these impromptu visitors, which now functions as an informal meeting space for this globally dispersed community.

Even with filtering, people often feel nervous when visiting radical spaces for the first time. Unlike people who stumble into radical spaces by accident or approach them with indifference, many people who intentionally seek radical spaces are perhaps better described as sojourners seeking community. They come to print-based movement spaces looking for ports of entry, not knowing what kind of environment they will find and not knowing whether they will feel accepted. This is why, for Carrie Barnett with People Like Us, although books and blogs are great ways to let readers know "you're not the only one" who is queer, anarchist, anticapital-ist, or critical of white privilege, "that doesn't mean you know anybody" who shares those views. "And that doesn't mean that going to a place like Women & Children First or coming to a place like Gerber/Hart isn't scary and isn't empowering."

This is where reverse filtering becomes especially crucial. For Alan Chelak with PAT @ Giovanni's Room, since only some people opt into movement storefronts, they become "almost like a means of introduction [for] opening up that kind of conversation." People self-select into the space, as well as into specific shelving areas, where they see other people orbiting around similar interests. In that highly filtered context, people can be more forthcoming. "Your guard is dropped almost. You're more open to chatting with a stranger than you would be on the subway or at the grocery store." This ability to relax because of an assumed baseline of camaraderie around contentious themes facilitates friendly exchange. "You see people [who] didn't come in together, and they might have nothing in common, but they end up talking because they're both looking at the same section of books. . . . 'Oh, you're into the stuff I'm into? We have that in common.' And conversations happen."

Examples like these show that filtered convergence constructs oppor-tunities for more open communication in shared settings. Because only cer-tain people opt in, some aspects of the public-facing mask can be dropped. This increased transparency helps anticapitalists visiting Lucy Parsons see that "they're not the only [people] who think a certain way." It helps cus-tomers at Left Bank in St. Louis feel comfortable criticizing police for their violence against African Americans without feeling like they are "going to be attacked by saying that the police were in the wrong." In these contexts, instead of papering over contentious perspectives and letting them pass unspoken, people can share their thoughts and experiences, which creates potential to find fellow feeling.

Alongside shelf-based orbiting, which occurs throughout the day, special events create additional opportunities to heighten and intensify feelings of affinity. For instance, when Bluestockings hosted an event focusing on women of color coming to a radical political consciousness, "it felt like everyone in the space was so physically close and so emotionally close in that moment that an eighty-person family had formed for a couple hours." Similarly, when BookWoman hosted an immigration-themed event, "we had seventy-five people crammed in here. But no one felt crammed . . . because we're just all here as one entity." Successful events like these, with large audiences and energetic receptions, amplify feelings of being-in-common.

One reason why vulnerable groups value this sense of fellow feeling is because it is rare and often does not happen in generic third places. Activist-entrepreneurs said readings had a different vibe when they occurred in movement-oriented spaces versus mainstream superstores. At Black-themed bookstores like Eso Won, Black writers "come in and feel at home" in a place where "they can speak their mind, they know the owners, [and] there's a multicultural, diverse audience. Whereas when they go to a Barnes & Nobles, it's got to be a different feeling."[54] Similarly, for queer feminist zinesters at Bluestockings, "When those people are getting to read their work for a totally captivated audience" that is hungry to hear their perspectives, "it's the fact that they could not do that at Barnes & Noble that makes it so special."

The reason this congeniality is possible is because movement-oriented commercial spaces are simultaneously shared and sheltered. For people whose primary experiences in omniopticon settings are stigmatizing and punishing, offstage spaces at arm's length from naysayers generate "undreamed-of possibilities for connection with others."[55] For queer youths disowned by their families, PAT @ Giovanni's Room provides "the kind of home [they've] been denied,"[56] sometimes "for the first time."[57] For anticapitalists at May Day, the bookstore is "like a bar for activists" who need "someplace to go to vent and talk. . . . In the workplace, you can't talk about this stuff unless you want to get fired." Similarly, for African American women, Sister's Uptown is an environment where, "whatever I'm going through, I can come and find literature or have a conversation" with people who "understand yourself, your family, [and] your surroundings." For Susan Post with BookWoman, "It really is magic."

To summarize so far, these examples from print-based movement spaces touch on many third place themes. Activist enterprises are ports of entry into filtered environments where people interact away from home and work in an environment where conversation is the order of the day. But the reason self-disclosure works and is valued in retail counterspaces is because these spaces are not universal. Some social leveling occurs, for instance with class divides receding in queer bookstores and gender divides receding in anarchist infoshops. But other filters remain in place—

and need to remain in place—for the intended social dynamics to unfold. Conversations around sensitive themes require a space that is safe enough to drop some aspects of the public-facing mask, which then allows people to more genuinely come as they are, enrich their identities, and live fuller versions of their political ideas in the supportive company of strangers.

Exploring Difference Facilitates Frame Alignment

Many scholars describe third places as environments where difference and comfort coexist. From these perspectives, "Comfortable third places provide an inclusive environment giving users the opportunity to meet new people with new ideas."[58] They are places "to meet old friends and make new ones,"[59] including "people who know that they are not alike in some socio-demographic (or social identity) sense."[60] Interactions across difference occur because third places are "welcoming and comfortable"[61] and because "consideration for safety, comfort, enjoyment, and attractiveness is of central importance."[62]

However, despite these repeating references to comfortable connections across difference, other scholars and activists suggest that these two concepts might not actually fit together. For example, Iris Marion Young highlights the troubling associations between comfort and conformity. When comfort is defined as feeling at ease in like-minded company, achieving comfort "denies and represses social difference," which "validates and reinforces the fear and aversion some social groups exhibit towards others."[63] These repressive, exclusionary trends explain why alliance building is often an uncomfortable process. For Bernice Johnson Reagon, comfort is fine in private spaces, but movements require broad coalitions. "Coalition work . . . is some of the most dangerous work you can do. And you shouldn't look for comfort."[64]

Detaching comfort from coalition building does not mean that comfort has no role to play in contentious politics. Comfort is a priority in bell hooks's homeplaces, where nurturance in an oppressive society is a radical act. Interviews and archives likewise show that radical booksellers and librarians routinely prioritize comfort for people who are habitually discomforted in other public settings and that achieving comfort is a political feat. However, unlike other counterspaces on the more isolated end of the spectrum, movement-oriented storefronts are intentionally public-facing. This porosity means that, even though activist venues are convergence points, they are also encounter zones where people inevitably grapple with difference.

Grappling with difference is not always easy and not always comfortable. Nor should it be. Chantal Mouffe does not minimize the potential destructiveness of antagonistic rivalries even as she highlights the generative potential of creative tension. In a world full of internal contradictions, power hierarchies, and cultural difference, "the evasion of the political"—meaning the avoidance of conflicts and hostilities inherent in decision-making—"could jeopardize the hard-won conquests of the democratic revolution."[65] Mouffe uses the term "agonism" to refer to healthy disagreement and the process of channeling it in constructive, equity-promoting directions.[66] Grappling with difference agonistically is not about compromise or pacification, and it is certainly not about comfort. Instead, it is about harnessing tension to deepen debate and invent alternatives.

My goal in this section is to explore how activist-entrepreneurs agonistically grapple with difference in offstage third places. Although these spaces are filtered, they are not homogeneous. Filtering helps people warm up to each other and build common understandings around personhood, equity, and value. But because the people converging in activist storefronts approach progressive topics from many perspectives, the process can be riddled with disagreement. Instead of squelching conflict to preserve a harmonious facade, many activist-entrepreneurs embrace conflict as an opportunity for growth, and they attempt to steer it in productive directions so it does not tear the counterspace apart.

Despite filtered convergences in movement-oriented businesses, diversity is always a factor. For Alan Chelak with PAT @ Giovanni's Room, "LGBT . . . there are lots of different people under that umbrella." For Kori Wilson with Sister's Uptown, Black culture includes "people that have different cultural backgrounds or different opinions politically, or different socioeconomic status." Likewise, for Hajara Quinn with the Independent Publishing Resource Center, the indymedia movement is not a homogenous block. "We contain multitudes." There is often significant empathy around a baseline of shared experiences, but social difference and power disparities never disappear. Having experiences of racism, homophobia, and other oppressions in common does not guarantee people agree about what those experiences mean, nor do people necessarily feel that their shared experiences outweigh other factors keeping them apart.

For activist-entrepreneurs, one goal of grappling with difference is to use friendly interactions in shared spaces to build connections across demographic divides. This is why People Like Us started intermixing gay and lesbian fiction in the 1990s. As Carrie Barnett recalled, "We were the very first bookstore [where] our fiction was not separated into gay men and lesbians. It was just fiction. Doesn't that sound like nothing? It was *a huge deal*. People were aghast that we would do that. . . . They gave us an award [the Lambda Literary Award] for that." Building connections across difference is likewise why Barnett appreciates Gerber/Hart's mixed-age programming. "Intergenerational conversations begin because people of all ages come here. It's fascinating to see them spark organically. People who are twenty [are] having conversations with people who are seventy and sharing their lives and their experiences. That doesn't happen [elsewhere]."

A related goal is helping people to begin thinking about their similarities as more significant than their differences. This is why Women & Children First tries to be "like Switzerland" when bringing feminists together. For instance, in their children's programming, "Both lesbian and straight parents come . . . and they all get along. When you're dealing with kids— with diapers and tantrums—other things become more important than anyone's lifestyle."⁶⁷ Bringing kids to the same story times allows feminists to peer across the fences of sexual orientation and to feel affinity around common experiences of parenting.

These informal interactions facilitate cross-pollination across other differences as well. Boneshaker, for instance, is an intersectional environment where different strands of progressive activism collide. Some volunteers, like Zoe Michael, use the bookstore to build queer community while other volunteers, like Aaron King, are more interested in anticapitalism and self-publishing. These progressive yet diverse volunteers then "all get to know each other by being on shifts together," and they get to know each other's social groups by "hanging out [and] talking to each other" before and after events. These informal conversations expose people to new ideas even when they do not attend the same meetings. For Michael, instead of sticking only to queer literature and going "down these rabbit holes that I'm really comfortable with," she also rubs elbows with people talking about "really interesting books on labor," and vice versa. "So a lot of cross-community pollination happens that way."

Activist-entrepreneurs sometimes also use formal programming to integrate people into shared communities. The anarchist reading group at

Boxcar, for instance, creates a space where longtime activists and newbies can warm up to each other despite their different levels of familiarity with radical philosophies. For Stephanie Waller, these reading groups are an important port of entry. The anarchist scene is "a pretty tight-knit community. And it can be intimidating to first step your toe in if you don't really know anyone. . . . I think that reading group is a great space for that." Although the ideas and people are new, the familiar format helps people come together.

Structured study sessions are helpful, but playful interactions are often equally effective at getting people to explore challenging ideas. For Patrick White, "Let's face it . . . no one is going to say to each other, 'Hey, let's get together for the next ten years and promise that we'll grow together as spiritual beings.' It's too terrifying. So we say, 'Do you want to get together and read some books? Oh yeah, we'll read some books and it will be fun and interesting.'"[68] This strategic informality creates a less intimidating mechanism to then ease into serious discussions about social justice and spirituality. "You can't get people together to talk about literature in a serious way over time without touching on spiritual matters."[69] However, wrapping these conversations in a relaxed veneer is what allows them to occur in the first place.

Strategic informality also makes it easier for people to participate over long periods. For Gina Mercurio, People Called Women has hosted several politically themed reading groups over the years, and they last several months or maybe a year, but not much longer. By contrast, "The mystery book group, we've been doing [that] forever. . . . Because it's easy to read a mystery. [It just] takes a couple days." The ease of participation likewise explains the success of the bookstore's monthly "soup and salad night" where, potluck-style, people drop in for socialization. The bookstore hosts political meetings and film screenings as well, but the relaxed atmosphere of potlucks draws a more consistent crowd of regulars who keep coming back.

These recurring congenial interactions are precisely the type of social dynamics giving third places their strength, and they have many benefits for contentious politics. One benefit is the construction of informal networks for sorting people into political associations when needed or when opportunities arise. During soup and salad nights at People Called Women, "Invariably, topics would go to what's going on politically. And someone would [say,] 'Oh, I think I'll join NOW [the National Organization for Women],' or 'I'll work on Take Back the Night.' Things like that come out of socializing."

Another benefit is that people learn from each other not only during formal discussions but also through small talk when conversations go off script. Radical perspectives that may not surface during structured anarchist study sessions or formal queer book club meetings may surface quite naturally during the informal chatter before and after events. For Aaron King with Boneshaker, "As much as I learned from reading books here, I learned so much more by meeting people and hearing about their struggles and their lives . . . [and] all the ways that people live a day-to-day radical lifestyle."

These conversations are opportunities to learn not just what people have in common but also where they disagree. For Katherine Solheim with Unabridged, the book clubs she organizes include people who share a progressive mentality even as they "are coming to these books from very, very different places and understanding them in very different ways." Collectively exploring different perspectives then deepens understandings by bringing out "shades of literature that you would not get if you didn't have a community like this."

Exploring different perspectives through face-to-face interactions also intensifies the experience. For Kris Kleindienst with Left Bank in St. Louis, "Passively reading and actively saying are really two different functions." Similarly, for King with Boneshaker, the intensity of speaking instead of just reading increases "the chance for you to be changed by that reading," including by embracing new viewpoints after hearing other people's perspectives.

These back-and-forth dynamics do not guarantee that everyone agrees or gets along, nor is it clear how scholars should interpret disagreement when it occurs. Most of the third place literature is conflict-averse. With one exception, Oldenburg describes conflict and anything else that "interrupts conversation's lively flow" as "ruinous to a third place."[70] The one exception where Oldenburg embraces conflict is "a characteristic *im*politeness, which really communicates affection."[71] In these hazing-style interactions, "affectionate assaults on one another only lend spice to discussions."[72]

Although affectionate insults sometimes occur in movement-oriented storefronts, I am less interested in social bonding through hazing and more interested in jousting that occurs when environments feel safe enough for genuine disagreement. Kori Wilson with Sister's Uptown aptly described these dynamics. "When you mix family and business, sometimes you might have some conflict." Because many African Americans in Black-themed businesses feel at home to voice disagreement, conversations sometimes get "a little heated with different opinions.... That's what makes it so appealing. You can meet up with people that have different cultural backgrounds, or [a] difference in opinion politically, or [a] different socioeconomic status, and we still have that universal feeling of acceptance in the same space." Because the space is filtered around African American experiences, people can say things in ways they might not if the full spectrum of humanity were present. Then, when disputes end and amicable conversations resume, people have opportunities to repair rifts that emerged during the dispute.

The dynamics I've described so far sound harmonious, but grappling with difference can also feel unnerving, especially when the ties that bind are not readily apparent. This is one reason why Corey Farach with Blue-stockings described feeling somewhat uncomfortable the first time he visited the bookstore. "I was a super privileged dude. And I came in, and I saw a lot of literature that was obviously not written by people like me, or necessarily even for people like me." As an example, he pointed to a memoir about interracial transgender activism. "If you are not careful, you could read it and get super defensive and feel like it's calling you out in a way." But Farach felt it was important to forge ahead. "It was obvious that I had something to learn by reading these things."

Instead of tiptoeing around divisive issues, many activist-entrepreneurs confront them head-on by organizing events exploring contentious themes. One such event occurred at Left Bank in St. Louis after racialized police violence sparked civil unrest in Ferguson. For Kris Kleindienst, "Ferguson was really a huge trauma in our community. And it was also a huge opportunity to really break open this elephant in the living room." Rather than hosting separate reading groups—a Black Lives Matter group and a white guilt book club—Left Bank organized events combining both perspectives. Bringing these groups together in a shared, sheltered space helped people hear across the color line. "White people who might not actually get to hear it anywhere else get to hear Black people say things honestly" in the progressive bookstore. "That communication is very hard in St. Louis. There are just not very many spaces where it happens. But we have been a space where it happens."

Speaking across difference sometimes breaks down. Even with careful guidelines and social filtering, activist-entrepreneurs cannot always anticipate disagreements or channel them in constructive directions. A book event at Eso Won illustrates the challenges. The event brought African Americans together to discuss racial alienation in the aftermath of Hurricane Katrina. Erin Kaplan attended the event, and she felt "as ready to win as everyone else in the room," but she also worried that the evening might "dissolve into internal gripe sessions."[73] The breakdown Kaplan feared occurred during the question and answer session. "A bespectacled woman stepped up to the soapbox and chastised [the author]—not for his viewpoints on Katrina but for bringing up gays. . . . 'Gays,' she snapped. 'Who cares?' Immediately came groans, hoots of derision, a few murmurs of assent."[74] The conversation unraveled from there as people voiced disagreement with little commitment to mutual understanding. "And just like that, despite the abundance of energy . . . that had drawn people to Eso Won in the first place, another opportunity for unity was gone."[75]

Disagreements are problematic when they erode trust in offstage spaces and undermine capacities for collective action. But disagreements can also be less like a third rail and more like a controlled burn. When managed effectively, grappling with difference generates mutual insights and new alliances.

It was exactly this type of productive agonism that characterized Left Bank's multiracial discussion about police violence in Ferguson. As the conversation about racism and white privilege intensified, a "young white man raised his hand and said, 'Well, what can I do? What can I actually do?' And it was heartfelt, you know? And the young man next to him, who was Black, turned to him and said, 'You could start by talking to me.'" This response could be interpreted either as an invitation to collaborate or as an accusation of having already failed to engage his Black neighbor. "You could have heard a pin drop." But both men rose to the occasion and expressed their commitment to empathic understanding. "It was so amazing. And they introduced themselves to each other. And after the event was over, they kept talking, and they exchanged information."

Having these conversations on a regular basis has institutionalizing effects. For Corey Farach with Bluestockings, "The store is all held up by one large conversation that just keeps going." This continuity of conversation is partly a third place phenomenon where individual people cycle in and out while regulars socialize newcomers and set a friendly tone. An unacknowledged benefit of these iterative interactions is the opportunity to disagree without falling out. In book clubs or soup and salad nights, people disagree about minor things, like the quality of a paragraph or the quality of the olives, and then find their way back to points of consensus. Later, when the process repeats during political discussions, participants have a template for diverging and regrouping. This capacity to disagree enhances opportunities to navigate the fraught process of constructing common frames of reference.

Offstage Spaces Facilitate Collective Caretaking

Oldenburg describes informal public life as a third pillar of social support alongside home and work. Unlike the intimacy of private homes, public-facing third places accommodate more diversity, and they accommodate interactions without the domestic burden of hosting.[76] Similarly, unlike work settings, third places are leisurely environments that provide time for socializing, including across the class divides that separate people at work.[77] This third pillar is important, Oldenburg says, because "in the absence of an informal public life, people's expectations toward work and family life have escalated beyond the capacity of those institutions to meet them."[78]

Print-based movement spaces provide this third pillar, but not in a neutral way. Instead of merely supplementing the support people find at home and work, movement-oriented storefronts provide refuge from the oppressions people experience in those other spaces. For example, People Called Women is a place to escape the suffocating environments of heteronormative homes. As Gina Mercurio explains, the queer feminist bookstore is a meeting space for lesbians who grew up in the Midwest, moved to progressive cities, and fly back to visit their family during the holidays. "It happens this time of year a lot, actually, right before or right after that major Christian holiday. They come and say, 'Thank god you're still here, I just needed to get away from my family. I've been here for a week.'" As important as family reunions might be, in a heteronormative world, people need "an escape where they can breathe."

Alongside escape from home, counterspaces provide respite from hostilities at work. For instance, after the 2016 presidential election, Left Bank in St. Louis provided a space of progressive solace. For Kris Kleindienst, "So many folks are like, 'How do I go to work and talk to this Trump supporter who sits next to me? I feel sick to my stomach. I can't sleep at night.'" The radical bookstore was a refuge where people could express the anxiety they felt about encountering coworkers who celebrated a political development that threatened them so deeply.

These examples underscore the fact that third places are valuable not only because people need more support than they get at home and work but also because people need escapes from the harms they experience at home and work, as well as in other public and civic spaces. People sharing offstage space do not agree about everything, but they are united enough in denouncing patriarchy, homophobia, capitalism, imperialism, and white privilege that, during vulnerable moments, shared sympathy around common enemies outweighs the differences keeping them apart. These sympathies provide much-needed support and blunt the alienation people experience elsewhere.

As I explain in this final section, these places of refuge are places of collective caretaking. Collective caretaking through congenial interactions is a crucial third place function, but providing care around sensitive issues is sometimes only possible in offstage spaces. This caretaking is especially important during crisis moments. Whether it is an individual crisis, for instance following a date rape, or a collective crisis, for instance following a mass shooting, a crisis increases feelings of fear and needs for support. Because print-based movement spaces are simultaneously places of withdrawal and convergence, they facilitate this collective caretaking, especially during moments of upheaval.

All third places—not only activist ones—provide support during times of stress. Customers often spend time in commercial spaces because employees and customers offer listening ears and practical advice. Gestures of companionship and assistance with mundane tasks transform third places into "spaces of care in the city."[79] David Conradson uses this phrase to describe spaces prioritizing "everyday encounters between individuals who are attentive to each other's situation, who perhaps provide practical assistance, or who simply make time to listen to what the other has to say."[80] For Miriam Williams, this ethics of care extends beyond the formal caretaking of health clinics and social service centers. Instead, a place-based ethics of care is about embedding caretaking into routine environments by "structuring relationships in ways that enhance mutuality and well-being."[81]

Constructing spaces for collective caretaking contributes to social justice, but care and justice are not the same. From a feminist perspective,

Williams characterizes the practice of care as emotional, embodied, and particular, whereas justice is universal, rational, and external to the self.[82] Another difference is that justice is about acknowledging past wrongs and redistributing resources more equitably. Caretaking supplements those processes by also repairing damage and healing wounds.[83] These spaces of care serve therapeutic purposes.[84] They are sanctuaries where, for Gill Valentine, people find solace and "show interest in or support for the well-being of others."[85]

Although Oldenburg suggests that society as a whole benefits from informal caretaking, other scholars suggest that retail-based interactions are especially significant for people who have suffered a loss in their social support networks. This loss might involve a death or divorce at home or medical leave or retirement from work. These life events "motivate consumers to replace lost social resources by forming relationships with customers and employees in commercial 'third places.'"[86] The same logic applies to people whose friends and family reject them because of their radical politics or nonnormative identities. These dynamics explain why queer folk visiting the homophobic Midwest during the holidays or radical self-publishers migrating from rural towns to big cities might experience an intensified need for movement-oriented spaces where they can drop in and casually connect with people who understand their perspectives.

Alongside replacing lost social support, informal caretaking among strangers provides resources during crisis moments when the amount of support people need temporarily spikes. Trauma ignites feelings of grief, anger, and fear. The heightened need for caretaking during crisis moments can easily overwhelm existing networks at home and work, even for people who usually feel well-supported. Collective traumas also increase the anxiety people feel about spending time in unfiltered spaces where they risk encountering people who do not share their sense of outrage and who may instead condone injustice.

For these reasons, activity in print-based movement spaces surges during crises. Although counterspaces are useful in everyday contexts when they bubble along and provide everyday caretaking, intensive use comes in waves. For Andy Merrifield, "things have usually been gurgling within the bowels of society" for some time, but "when things explode, when they really erupt, when the proverbial shit does hit the fan, it's invariably by *surprise*."[87] This shock brings people together for mutual support, including by converging in counterpublic spaces. This is why, for Ayela Bennett, the

Shrine of the Black Madonna Bookstore became significantly more popular whenever society shifted from humdrum rhythms of everyday life to crisis moments of political turmoil. When "in a state of social upheaval . . . we need to have something firm that we can root ourselves in."[88]

Seeking social support in offstage spaces during tumultuous moments reflects a dual motion of retreat and convergence. For Nancy Fraser, "subaltern counterpublics in stratified societies" benefit from having places that "function as spaces of withdrawal and regroupment."[89] In my analysis of print-based movement spaces, the withdrawal motion is about taking refuge from a public realm that suddenly feels more fraught than usual. The regroupment motion is about connecting with similarly distressed people in sheltered environments where people affirm anxieties, provide nurturance, and facilitate healing. These dual dynamics underscore the importance of having filtered third places—and not just spaces where the full spectrum of humanity is present—where sympathetic strangers can support each other during tumultuous moments.

This dual motion of retreat and convergence explains the surge of interest in Black-themed bookstores like Eso Won in the aftermath of Hurricane Katrina. For Erin Kaplan, the hurricane "dealt us a huge psychic blow . . . pushing us a couple more degrees closer to an awful certainty that we are, and always have been, on our own in our own country."[90] Reeling with intensified feelings of alienation and vulnerability, African Americans converged in Black bookstores looking for answers to difficult questions. Filtered storefronts like Eso Won were already trusted Black public spaces, which made them logical places to gather. For Kaplan, these popular post-disaster get-togethers felt like "a welcome opportunity for all of us in this far-flung city to come together, compare notes and losses and, if we were lucky, coalesce around an issue or two."[91]

Archives provide glimpses into these dual dynamics of retreat and convergence, but observing these processes in real time provided additional information both on the significance of filtering during crisis moments and on the potential for caretaking to facilitate collective responses. Because of the timing of my research, I witnessed this type of catalytic moment in the hours, days, and months surrounding the contentious 2016 presidential election.

The election results ignited feelings of confusion and fear in many progressive communities. Lynn Mooney with Women & Children First described the threat from a queer feminist perspective. "We're in such jeopardy of losing ground in such fundamental ways on things that . . . a generation or two of women who have just come into adulthood have never known a world without." Mooney's eyes welled with tears as she spoke. "Gay marriage. Equal rights, in terms of benefits for the LGBTQ community. It could be disastrous."

This sense of heart-wrenching fear and angst resurfaced in every interview. Intersectional activists worried about white supremacy. Latino/a proprietors condemned xenophobic lawmaking. Anarchists denounced the fascist presidential regime. Anticapitalists recoiled at promises to manage the federal government like a corporation. Across the country, activist-entrepreneurs voicing these concerns joined mass protests and rallies. My question was, What happened in print-based movement spaces during the gap of time after election results were announced but before mass demonstrations unfolded?

One thing that happened was that people converged in movement-oriented businesses for companionship and validation among people likely to share their views. For instance, because People Called Women was a known and trusted space of feminist care, it became a spontaneous place to gather. For Gina Mercurio, "There have been several get-togethers. . . . Just for our sanity, it's important to have people" to connect with. "You can drop in this space and know there's going to be somebody there that is feeling what you're feeling." Quimby's performed a similar role for the countercultural community. For Liz Mason, "We are a place where people know they can come in, and people of their tribe were here."

This search to connect with specific types of strangers distinguishes offstage spaces from generic third places. The point was not only to talk informally with strangers but to also talk in places where certain types of strangers were unlikely to overhear. At Quimby's, people "knew they were safe to let their guard down." At People Called Women, unlike at work where "there are Trump supporters there, maybe even their boss," people could vent without recrimination. These filtered offstage spaces provided social support for processing and grieving not simply because likeminded people were present but also because opposition groups were absent.

Not all activist-entrepreneurs wanted to play this therapeutic role. For example, Adrian (no last name given) with Left Bank in Seattle found himself disengaging from collective caretaking. "People have a lot to get off their chest. [It's] something that they're ruminating over in their mind. It's political. And they come in thinking we're the perfect people to talk to about it. And I'm like, 'Sorry, I'm not going to be the person you can express all this to.'" Adrian tried not to be aloof. He enjoyed watching people make connections, and he enjoyed discussing certain topics. But because it felt emotionally overwhelming to provide endless support, "I don't see myself doing that with everyone."

However, among activist-entrepreneurs, experiences like Adrian's are the exception rather than the rule. Most activist-entrepreneurs went out of their way to provide solace for distressed strangers. Some even spent scarce resources facilitating the process. For Corey Farach with Bluestock-ings, caretaking involved opening early and staying open late. Customers were not necessarily buying anything, but people needed a haven in the storm. "We just opened the café up, and we spent money for the purpose of getting people coffee and bagels and stuff, so they could just come and chill out and talk to one another and just have breakfast on us. . . . Like, 'Let us be a place of sanctuary for you for the day. . . . Let us help you recharge.'"

It was a similar story at Unabridged where, in the days after the elec-tion, staffers prioritized caretaking over other business objectives. For Kath-erine Solheim, "It was a lot of very sad and distraught faces. . . . We just got a pizza and hashed things out with people." Hashing things out was about collective caretaking, not sales. "I won't say that we did terribly good busi-ness that day, but it didn't really matter. It was just kind of like, 'All right folks, come on in. . . . This is just what we're going to do here.' And it was a pretty amazing experience."

Other activist-entrepreneurs supplemented informal caretaking with structured programming. Through programmatic tweaks, these activists took the low-key rituals of social interaction already embedded in mystery book clubs and soup and salad nights, and they mobilized them to provide politically themed support. This is why Women & Children First turned its monthly open mic night into an open political forum, "just so people could talk through what was in their heads." It's also why Unabridged in-formally converted its largest reading group into "a Literature after Trump Book Club, just because nobody could deal with reading anything else."

Although movement-oriented enterprises have infrastructure for pub-lic engagement and collective caretaking ready to go, the surge in de-mand during crisis moments can overwhelm that infrastructure. For Corey Farach with Bluestockings, after the election, "there have been a lot of people that I've never seen in the space before who are walking in now [saying], 'I want to volunteer here. Tell me about this place. I want to help.'" Farach welcomed this enthusiasm, and he tried to plug people into the space, but the intensity of demand made it difficult. "It's actually been a little overwhelming, to be honest. There have been more people that want to help in the store than I have time to sit down and work with in order to translate their desire to help into something that would help the space. 'Cause it's just too much at once."

Activist-entrepreneurs also know that these surges are temporary. Given the wave pattern typical of social unrest, many activist-entrepreneurs worried less about plugging people into movement spaces in a permanent way and focused more on connecting people with progressive resources they could use even after routines returned to normal. This included giving parents age-appropriate books on feminism to share with their children. It included giving people a language they could use to critique fascism without alienating coworkers. The goal of providing people with takeaway resources is likewise why Women & Children First organized "The Conversation" as a series of public events where different activist groups made short presentations to raise awareness about their work and to let people know how to get involved.[92] For Lynn Mooney, these conversations were useful because "a lot of us haven't decided what our next actions will be." Similarly, at Left Bank in St. Louis, "Everyone was trying to find language and looking for resources . . . And we really just served that role." Discussions like these created ports of entry for newcomers—not for them to stay in print-based movement spaces indefinitely, but rather to sort themselves into functional associations for political organizing elsewhere.

These examples shed light on the dual motion of retreat and convergence in filtered third places. People converge in offstage spaces for collective caretaking, which provides platforms to construct common frames of reference. For many activist-entrepreneurs, the goal is to start conversations that do not conclude in their storefronts but instead empower people to continue debates in other times and places, including in the home and work environments people sometimes need refuge from. These discussions and alliances are then resources for externally directed public protest, which is the topic of the next chapter.

CHAPTER 8

Supporting Public Protests from the Wings

O N A SPRING DAY IN 2017, Adii (no last name given) rushed into Revolution Books in Berkeley with a backpack slung over his shoulder. Without a word, he located a discretely stored folding table in the corner of the store, set it up, and began writing. Adii is not affiliated with the bookstore, but he hangs around a lot. He is African American, college-aged, and says he has always been "activist inclined." As a child, he would ask his mother questions about society. "Why do I have to grow up and get a job and work for somebody, and why do we need to have money to have food?" Her answers left him unsatisfied. "She's like, 'That's just how the world works.'"

When Adii discovered the activist bookstore, he found other answers to his questions. Supporters of the Revolutionary Communist Party, a Maoist splinter group, opened several Revolution Books locations around the country in the 1970s. With their proselytizing staff and sectarian literature, these bookstores were mouthpieces for organizing. Although most of these venues had closed or were closing by the mid-2010s, the New York and Berkeley locations were going strong. Despite a lingering cult-like feel, these locations no longer have official party ties to communist groups. Instead, they are nonprofit, volunteer-run businesses specializing in literature on gender inequity, racialized incarceration, environmental degradation, immigrant exploitation, and imperialist violence. For staffers like Raymond Lotta in New York, this material is a call to arms. "What we're talking about is not just an abstract, fuzzy, 'wouldn't it be nice' kind of vision." Instead, these bookstores are an open call for "an actual revolution . . . to overthrow this system," construct "the new socialist republic," and "bring a whole new society and world into being."

Back in Berkeley, Adii made Revolution into something of a second home. It wasn't just being around books that made a difference. He'd been in bookstores before and found them uninspiring. "Your average bookstore, they have books about consumerism and entertainment. And they

This window display at Revolution Books in Berkeley, California, includes communist-inspired books alongside a large poster condemning police violence against people of color. Photograph by Revolution Books, 2018; courtesy of Revolution Books.

have fantasy novels and things to keep you occupied. But nothing to really get you active in the political landscape." But Revolution felt different and thought-provoking. "This is just a really cool place to learn about and become immersed in things that'll actually make a difference politically." Browsing the shelves, Adii learned about the Black Panther Party, Free Speech Movement, Revolutionary Communist Party, and other political movements founded within a few miles of his home. These stories of locally born activism felt empowering. "It really helps to be able to read a book and say, 'Hey, people actually did this. People made a difference. Maybe I could make a difference.'"

Reading about anarchist history inspired Adii to join the Refuse Fascism movement. Reiko Redmonde and other bookstore volunteers co-organized several demonstrations as part of that campaign. "A lot of the role of this store is to organize and create events where people can come together and discuss these things. Dig into what's happening, why it's hap-

pening, what can be done about it." Redmonde and other staffers part-
nered with grassroots organizers, academics, and authors to stage rallies
downtown and on the nearby college campus. Adii played the drums at
several rallies, and, at one protest, he played a starring role. "We had a skit
about putting Donald Trump on trial, and Adii played Donald Trump."

Redmonde and Adii laughed lightheartedly over the incongruity between Trump, a geriatric white supremacist, and his impersonator, a young
Black percussionist. But not all of their experiences have been playful.
National media outlets reporting on the so-called "Battle for Berkeley"
described violent street confrontations between black bloc anarchists and
alt-right agitators.[1] Redmonde felt Berkeley was being symbolically targeted by the alt-right because of its progressive legacies. "They want to
target Berkeley because they feel, 'If we can change the character of Berkeley, we can do it to the rest of the country.'"

A few weeks after our conversation, Revolution in Berkeley became
the target of white supremacist theatrics when several dozen alt-right agitators surrounded the bookstore, shouted insults, and harassed customers.[2] These groups repeated their attacks several times over the following
weeks. Protestors on both sides posted cell phone videos of the conflicts
on social media, which gave them national visibility.[3] Bookstore volunteers also reached out to activists and academics around the country asking people to "come into the store . . . mention RB [Revolution Books]
on social media . . . [and] email statements of support." I return to this
example later in this chapter. For now, it is enough to say that the radical
bookstore was no longer just an offstage space for exploration and caretaking. Instead, it was on the front lines of public protest.

Conversations like this one at Revolution in Berkeley illustrate the role
activist-entrepreneurs play in public demonstrations. In previous chapters,
I analyzed inwardly directed capacity building, a theme which recurs here
as Adii grows from a frustrated questioner into an informed activist. These
long-term empowerment projects build a social base for contentious
politics, and much of this work happens during the humdrum rhythms
of everyday life. However, many activist-entrepreneurs also support externally directed demonstrations. At Revolution in Berkeley, the bookstore
is a place to plan events, prepare costumes, and coordinate roles. Activists
store supplies at the bookstore and go there for breaks and to regroup after

rallies. This example also illustrates the risks involved when audiences respond by targeting progressive businesses with alt-right protests of their own.

Political organizing takes many forms, not all of which are physically unruly. One form of organizing, which is well documented in the social movement literature and which I mention primarily in passing, is civil society actions. People leave petitions at bookstores and libraries for customers and patrons to sign. Staffers collect donations for Planned Parenthood and the American Civil Liberties Union. They keep flyers and leaflets on their counters. They host voter registration drives and community meetings with elected officials. They also organize letter-writing campaigns to pressure government agencies to act. These civil society modes of organizing are common in print-based movement spaces. As low-cost, low-risk, institutionally sanctioned forms of political engagement, it is easy for people passing through to add their support.

However, civil society advocacy within institutionally sanctioned channels is not always effective. Petitions get dismissed, fundraising falls short, and requests for meetings go unanswered. Additionally, some activists prefer tactics that are more direct, disruptive, or visually dynamic, especially in the age of social media. These unruly, eye-catching tactics include public rallies, demonstrations, and marches, which are the focus of this chapter.

Public demonstrations include theatrical elements. Charles Tilly popularized the theater metaphor when comparing activists to troupes of street musicians following theatrical scripts in their "vigorously vital ways of making their voices heard."[4] Scholars building on the theatrical metaphor use it to emphasize the repetitive character of protest techniques where actors in different contexts use similar methods. For Charles Tilly, protest scripts include things like "presenting a petition, taking a hostage, or mounting a demonstration."[5] Activists unroll these repertoires in a variety of situations where, like actors performing adaptations of a play, they repeat the performance with only slight modifications.[6]

Although I appreciate this discussion of repetitive performances, and although I apply this logic when classifying print-based movement space as an action repertoire, in this chapter, I interpret the stage metaphor more literally by analyzing the spaces where activists prepare to perform progressive politics for a broad viewing audience. For Thomas Swerts, protestors use "public space as a theatrical stage to express claims to rights."[7]

Other scholars of performative theory analyze the performative aspects of civil disobedience,[8] alternative economies,[9] alternative citizenship,[10] and contentious visibility.[11] These studies generally focus on play-by-play accounts of the scene, including Judith Butler–style descriptions of bodies "showing up, standing, breathing, moving, [and] standing still" as part of "the expression of a public demand for more just economic, social and political conditions."[12]

Although play-by-play accounts are useful, this chapter focuses less on the content of performances and more on the logistical aspects of their production. This includes looking beyond the frontstage spaces where performances occur to also analyze backstage environments supporting the events. Analyzing backstage dynamics is about more than just looking beyond spectacles to also attend to the troughs between spikes of public protest. Instead, this chapter analyzes the interconnectedness of onstage demonstrations and offstage wings when spectacles unfold. Cycling between offstage and onstage—between internally directed capacity building and externally directed political agitation—is not about leaving the homeplace behind. On the contrary, in the trinity of strategies, tactics, and logistics, public action intensifies the need for counterspaces providing logistical support. Additionally, going public with a performance intensifies the need for activist-entrepreneurs to take precautionary steps shielding their spaces from potential recrimination.

I analyze these dynamics using the metaphor of a stage. Street theater protests occur in streets, parks, and plazas exposed to public view. During performances, movement-oriented businesses play supporting roles behind the scenes. Print-based movement spaces are planning spaces where organizers develop scripts, rehearse roles, and assemble props. They are greenrooms where protestors gather before events, take rest breaks, and regroup when performances end. Activist-entrepreneurs are also stage managers facilitating events and preserving boundaries between the public-facing performance and the backstage wings where actors' privacy is paramount.

Although the theater metaphor is useful, it is risky if misinterpreted. For one thing, terms like scripts, props, and rehearsals do not imply that demonstrations are merely pageantry while the substantive work of politics happens elsewhere. Instead, this language highlights the logistical aspects associated with staging compelling demonstrations. Similarly, the stage metaphor does not imply that space is a passive, neutral backdrop where actors are free to perform any scene they choose. On the contrary, people produce distinct onstage, offstage, and greenroom spaces because their unique characteristics facilitate different activities. In this chapter, I do not want my use of the stage metaphor to inadvertently reinforce these types of dismissiveness. Instead, my goal is to invite scholars to look behind the visual drama of street theater spectacles to also investigate the multisite mechanics of their construction.

To illustrate these logistical dynamics, in this chapter, I identify three common sets of support functions occurring in print-based movement spaces. One set of functions is the preparation. In the months and weeks before a demonstration occurs, people plan the event by deciding what to do and where to do it. They coordinate roles, decide how to respond to police pressure, and teach each other effective demonstration techniques. This preparation phase includes a prop shop component with activists making banners, buttons, flyers, and costumes. It also includes logistical tasks like advertising and transportation. Print-based movement spaces support these functions before events unfold.

A second set of functions I explore in this chapter is implementation. On the day of an event, counterspaces act as greenrooms. In theater lingo, greenrooms are communal waiting areas or lounges closer to the stage than private dressing rooms but still screened from public view. Protestors gather there in the hours before marches begin to review last-minute details and offer encouragement. As demonstrations unfold, activists circle back to counterspaces for restrooms, snacks, and equipment. Then, when events are over, protestors regroup in storefronts to debrief and recharge so they can march again another day.

After analyzing these planning and implementation functions, I shift gears by analyzing a third set of stage management functions occurring year-round. Public protests target state officials and opposition groups, and these targets then respond to activists' challenges. Some responses involve street skirmishes near demonstration sites, but people also sometimes respond by targeting the behind-the-scenes spaces providing protestors with logistical support. To use the theater metaphor, this is the equivalent of having angry audience members storm backstage to harass the actors and muck up the wings. Activist-entrepreneurs know the risks, and they take steps to deter unwanted intrusions, for instance by constructing anonymous environments. Anonymity is not something found or maintained by accident. Instead, it is a resource people construct, including by constructing spaces where organizing leaves no trace behind.

Not all activist-entrepreneurs participate in public protests. Some print-based movement spaces promote contentious politics through commodities, policies, and programming but not by offering direct protest support. Even when steady streams of activists pass through, and even when activist-entrepreneurs promote upcoming demonstrations, they may not necessarily offer logistical aid. There are many reasons why activists may not participate. Some activist-entrepreneurs prefer prefigurative approaches and eschew public demonstrations. Levels of involvement also fluctuate over time, for instance with changes in ownership or circumstance, especially in the aftermath of big events when activists know they are under surveillance. Additionally, the growing tendency for print-based movement spaces to register as nonprofits may influence participation since 501(c)(3) tax status comes with prohibitions against some types of organizing, although the full effects of this trend are not yet known.

Despite these variations, most activist-entrepreneurs provide significant logistical support for planning and participating in public demonstrations. For many activist-entrepreneurs, supporting protests is a primary reason why they constructed retail counterspaces in the first place. The goal is to maintain reliable, publicly accessible offstage spaces enabling social change, including by supporting demonstrations and marches.

Counterspaces Provide Logistical Support for Public Protests

Nancy Fraser has written about the dual character of counterpublic spaces. "On the one hand, they function as spaces of withdrawal and regroupment; on the other hand, they also function as bases and training grounds for agitational activities directed toward wider publics. It is precisely in the dialectic between these two functions that their emancipatory potential resides."[13] Print-based movement spaces embody these dual characteristics. They are simultaneously an offstage space for internally directed nurturance and a resource helping activists prepare for externally directed protests.

In this section, I provide a theoretical framework for understanding the many shifts involved when transitioning from offstage contentious politics to onstage public rallies. One shift is a change in repertoire from education

and nurturance to protests and marches. Another shift is a change in programming from inwardly directed affinity groups to externally directed
performances targeting government officials, media reporters, social op-
ponents, and general bystanders. A spatial shift also occurs from bringing people into the storefront to helping people be heard outside the
shop walls.

For many activists, these transitions are opportunities to make hidden
transcripts public. Geographer Ulrich Oslender describes this process as
"a strategic move to foreground local epistemologies as a political tool in
evolving [national] cultural politics."[14] As part of this strategic move, instead of following the usual bifurcated system where hidden transcripts
are used in homeplaces while deference to oppressors' scripts is shown in
public,[15] protests and marches dramatize hidden transcripts for external
consumption. Activists in queer, feminist, and anarchist bookstores—and
in other domestic and community spaces—nurture hidden transcripts
around kinship, gender, and labor, and they use their spaces to shelter alternative performances. But sheltering is a means to an end, not the end
itself. The intent is not to keep alternative scripts hidden but rather to nurture them until they are robust enough to withstand the risks of public
exposure. When the time comes, either because the scripts are ready or
because the political context provokes it, activist-entrepreneurs facilitate
the process of making these hidden transcripts public.

Going public is labor intensive. One of the key themes of this chapter is
analyzing the labor involved in constructing protest scenes. The transition
from offstage to onstage is less about crossing a thin dividing line and more
about going through a zone with spatial, temporal, and social thickness.
People do not simply go from speaking to peers to speaking into microphones. On the contrary, organizers construct opportunities for public exposure, and they manage that exposure to maximize success.

An important part of this thick transition from internally to externally
directed action is constructing mechanisms for public engagement. There
are no ready-made stages or roles. People have to decide where to go and
what to do when they get there. There are many options, but my interest is
less in the specific choice and more in activist-entrepreneurs' contribution
to the process by providing logistical space where protestors plan events,
train for them, and collect supporting resources.

Going public is also risky, which is why building solidarity and shared
frames of reference in advance is useful. Before and after protests, in the

relative safety of offstage environments, activists can discuss disagreements and anxieties. By contrast, when onstage, public displays of unity are a strategic part of the political spectacle helping activists speak strongly, confidently, and in one voice. For Robert Beauregard, "In public places, people want clear answers to questions, not speculation."[16] Similarly, marches and rallies are more effective when demonstrators have a plan and trust their peers to stick with the plan even when facing harassment.[17] These dynamics underscore the risks of public exposure. Dramatizing hidden transcripts in public encounter zones provokes open interaction between opposing groups with unequal power, which can lead to recrimination and violence.[18]

Fear of state repression encourages cautiousness and secrecy. For David Graeber, the perception of an increasingly intolerant state cracking down on public demonstrators engenders fear in movement scenes. This fear is sometimes palpable, not only during protests but also during their planning phases. Although Graeber speculates this fear may be overblown since activists do not get "arrested because of something they said, or were said to have said, in a meeting," he nevertheless recognizes that "activists are regularly arrested for being public spokespeople" for radical causes.[19] Concerns about detentions and arrests affect where and how people organize. When it comes to planning sessions, "Meetings themselves have become increasingly secretive. Those attending them have become more paranoid."[20]

The trouble is that minimizing exposure creates a paradox because public protests are collective endeavors. Retail politics is individual and intimate, but public rallies require strength in numbers. When planning rallies, activists simultaneously need to stay hidden and be found. For Thomas Swerts, "On the one hand, such spaces need to ensure a certain level of comfort, secludedness and invisibility in order to convince others that participation is safe. On the other hand, they need to be sufficiently visible, stable and recognizable as to allow other civic actors to respond."[21] Print-based movement spaces meet both needs. They are public spaces of search and discovery, but they are also filtered and sheltered spaces where trusted figures provide political cover. This infrastructure consolidates through everyday practices so that, when political sparks erupt, if a certain amount of trust is already established, grassroots groups can leverage counterspaces to plan demonstrations.

But what exactly happens in print-based movement spaces while an event is underway? This question is an important one because, in the social movement literature, homeplaces and counterspaces seemingly fall off

the map once protestors leave with their banners and signs for marches occurring elsewhere. As an example, in an insightful article on the spatiality
of contentious politics, Helga Leitner, Eric Sheppard, and Kristin Sciarto
share the story of a bus caravan reenacting the 1960s Freedom Rides by
collecting immigration activists from across the country and transporting
them to Washington, D.C., for large public rallies. This article looks behind the scenes by analyzing the days spent on the bus as an interstitial
safe space where, away from state observation, immigrants with different
backgrounds living in different cities shared personal stories, taught each
other protest songs, and coordinated responses to police intimidation.[22]

This example of logistical coordination in the provisional offstage space
of the bus looks beyond public protest to also analyze one of the behind-
the-scenes spaces involved in the protest's production. This reframing is
a useful first step, and I want to expand the analysis even further to include accounts of the places left behind. Narrating activist experiences en
route to Washington, D.C., says nothing about the people and places in the
cities the activists left when they boarded the buses. This framing implies
that there was no action there, either because those places were always irrelevant or because their usefulness ended the moment activists departed.

However, my findings suggest a more reciprocal dynamic. Counterspaces
are sometimes around the corner from demonstration sites or perhaps a
mere subway ride away. When protest sites are nearby, print-based movement spaces function as greenrooms. These spaces support the human side
of performances by attending to actors' bodily needs. Print-based movement spaces perform a similar role. Ideology alone is not enough to make
demonstrations successful. Protestors also have physical needs and emotional responses to the strain of street theater marches and rallies. Although
people can go home to eat, rest, and recharge when protests conclude, it
also helps to have a staging area closer to the action for shorter breaks while
events are still in progress. Similarly, even when protests occur several hundred miles away, people in the offstage spaces back home continue coordinating transportation, public relations, and legal aid.

Providing planning and logistical support is part of the labor-intensive
process of transitioning from offstage to on display, but activist labor does
not stop there. Staging successful theatrical performances also requires
managing the audience. Actors meet their admirers in the hallways outside theaters after performances end. Similar dynamics occur in radical

bookstores and infoshops where seasoned activists and newbies interact. However, not all audience members will like what they see, and critics sometimes harass actors offstage. Street theater performances are intended to provoke. However, making hidden transcripts public is not the same as making counterspaces public. Opposition groups infiltrating radical businesses violate the filtering and sheltering attributes supporting other modes of contentious politics, like vulnerable exploration and self-disclosure. To prevent these violations, activist-entrepreneurs take steps to disincentivize incursions. The subcultural aesthetics and safe space policies discussed in previous chapters usually offer sufficient protection during the troughs between spikes of public protest, but those protections fall short when a space is under siege. These shortcomings are especially apparent when intruders are state agents whose territorial authority supersede private ownership. Activist-entrepreneurs have limited capacity to shield people inside their spaces from agents they cannot legally exclude. Instead, activist-entrepreneurs can more effectively disincentivize infiltration by ensuring that, when under surveillance, there is nothing useful for government agents to find.

Importantly, activist librarians and booksellers are not alone in providing logistical support for public protests. To use the queer liberation movement as an example, other types of businesses like gay bars "provided much needed social interaction" and "inculcated a sense of community and belonging that formed a 'we', so necessary to social movement formation."[23] Private spaces like lesbian housing collectives were likewise "thoroughly infused with politics. Marches and protests were organized there. Debates flourished over political possibilities around kitchen tables and in bedrooms. Posters were painted on living-room floors."[24] Activists planned events in borrowed spaces as well, for instance in campgrounds and rented barns where organizers "walked the participants through all the necessary steps" for carrying out an event, "from planning the action to talking to the press afterwards."[25]

This distributed labor in no way diminishes the contributions of activist booksellers and librarians. Social movements are collective endeavors involving the convergence of many social circles. In what follows, I provide concrete examples illustrating how print-based venues contribute to these larger dynamics as people prepare for events, provide material support, and protect each other from recrimination and backlash.

Activist Storefronts Are Planning and Rehearsal Spaces

One of the most important goals motivating activists to get involved with retail is constructing durable spaces that other grassroots groups can use for organizing. Meeting rooms and planning sessions in activist bookstores are platforms for organizing. Social movements may look spontaneous, and many people participate extemporaneously, but contentious performances involve considerable coordination in advance. As I explain in this section, organizers have to decide where to go and how to protest. They teach newbies demonstration techniques. They assemble props and equipment. They also manage logistics like permitting, transportation, and advertising. Activist enterprises support this coordination.

Analyzing these dynamics sheds light on a division of labor where one group of activists does the constructive work of durable placemaking and other groups leverage it for planning and support. For Thomas Swerts, grassroots organizers often "rely on physical spaces that are partly regulated or owned by allied institutions . . . who temporarily bring safe spaces into being."[26] This division of labor reduces organizing expenses by eliminating the need for each group to construct an individual meeting space. My analysis also suggests that this division of labor helps protect durable infrastructure because, although the masterminds behind unruly marches and demonstrations risk arrest, the activists operating supportive spaces can claim to be mere hosts. This strategic distancing does not negate the significance of logistical support, but it does generate a partial shield protecting the counterspace from retaliation.

Constructing a counterspace that other groups can use for organizing is a primary reason why many activists begin selling books, food, and tchotchkes in the first place. For Zoe Michael at Boneshaker, the revenue from book sales supports "a meeting room that's attached to our bookstore that we own." Maintaining the meeting room is a big part of why Boneshaker exists. "I think that [meeting room] is one of the most important radical organizing tools that we have. Sometimes I think we sell books so that we can keep that meeting room alive." The meeting room doubles as an event space for book clubs and fundraising, but bookstore volunteers make it available free of charge to grassroots organizers who want to plan protests behind closed doors.

Boneshaker's meeting room is somewhat unique in that, despite its humble furnishings, it is a stand-alone, fully enclosed room on the ground floor.

Given the high price of urban real estate, this dedicated space is a luxury many activist enterprises cannot afford. Activist-entrepreneurs still construct planning spaces, however. They just have a more makeshift feel. Some activist-entrepreneurs set up tables and chairs in barely finished basements. At Guide to Kulchur, the large, windowless basement with exposed wires, milk crate furniture, and painted cinder block walls accommodated large groups having private discussions without disrupting the retail functions on the floor above. Loft space is another option. At Big Idea, "A loft-like second floor features a table and casual meeting space for lefties who need a roof under which to keep dry while they subvert the dominant paradigm."[27] Flexible reconfigurations are also common. At Charis, the bookshelves and display tables are on casters so activists can simply roll them aside and set up folding chairs to accommodate large groups.[28]

These techniques are not fancy, but they get the job done, and the result is a durable meeting space managed by activist booksellers and librarians for the benefit of other grassroots groups. In previous decades, these planning spaces often had sectarian associations, for instance with the Socialist Workers Party supporting Pathfinder Book Store, the Industrial Workers of the World supporting the Alternative Press Center, and the Revolutionary Communist Party supporting Revolution Books.[29] Sectarian affiliations are less common today. Instead, movement-oriented bookstores and libraries host a range of social justice groups organizing around socialism, civil rights, Palestine, digital privacy, unionization, immigration, education, world peace, prison abolition, animal rights, environmental protections, and police abolition. Even when counterspaces have a narrower focus, for instance on feminism or anarchism, activist-entrepreneurs invite a variety of progressive groups to share their meeting rooms.

Humble facilities and shared rooms make space available at prices grassroots organizers can afford. Affordability is important because many groups do not have resources to pay rental fees. Unlike other in-store events where programming is a primary revenue generator, radical booksellers usually make meeting rooms available to activist groups for free as a public service to the activist community. For Leslie James Pickering with Burning Books, having a place where "people can come and organize their own events" is a way to "support more grassroots, smaller organizations that don't have any infrastructure of their own." For Craig Palmer with May Day, a lot of small groups "don't have a space . . . [and] don't have a lot of money. So people meet down here. We might have a donation basket out.

But if you don't have any money, it's no big deal, as long as you're out there fighting the good fight." Similarly, for Matt Dineen with Wooden Shoe, it's important to have space available for free "as an act of solidarity with other groups in Philly that are doing similar work."

Alongside affordability, another benefit of meeting in counterspaces, as opposed to chain coffee shops or municipal libraries, is confidentiality. Organizers value confidentiality for many reasons. Some demonstrations are well publicized in advance, but others rely on the element of surprise. Some rallies comply with federal and local laws, but other direct-action campaigns are not entirely legal. Privacy is also highly valued in the era of online "doxing" where alt-right vigilantes use social media to publish the names, addresses, and phone numbers of progressives, who then become targets of intimidation and harassment. For all these reasons, groups like Antifa, Anonymous, and the Anarchist Black Cross prefer meeting in counterspaces like Monkeywrench where planning sessions are "done more off the record." Protecting anonymity is likewise why Boxcar intentionally fosters "a discrete meeting space for organizing," which means a space not under surveillance and managed by staffers who are trusted members of the community.

The role of activist-entrepreneurs in these dynamics is to construct affordable, trusted meeting spaces where groups can plan demonstrations and marches. As an example, for twenty-three years running, grassroots organizers in Toledo have met at the feminist bookstore People Called Women to plan Take Back the Night. Several hundred women participate in this march every year, and about fifteen women do the preparation work of applying for permits, securing public speakers, and managing public relations. Bookstore owner Gina Mercurio supports the cause, and she hosts planning sessions in a living room–like space that doubles as a feminist lending library inside her store. "We meet once a month starting in January [or] February. Then [in] March and April, we'll probably do weekly meetings. . . . That's one of the things that I'm most proud of at the bookstore, that we've done that work."

Take Back the Night is a somewhat unusual example because the bookstore owner is directly involved in planning the event. She can participate as a leader without exposing the bookstore to police harassment because the event is sympathetic and complies with public ordinances. But activist-entrepreneurs also host groups preparing for less docile spectacles. In those cases, the lack of affiliation with organizers shields planning spaces from direct culpability. Additionally, activist-entrepreneurs often host protestors who are preparing to join mass rallies in distant cities. Even when local activists are not directly planning those events, they still have a role to play in preparing people for the rally. Knowing how to protest is an acquired skill, and seasoned activists use meeting rooms in radical bookstores and infoshops to teach newbies how to perform this role.

Training sessions come in many flavors. Some sessions provide legal education, for instance when Red Emma's spent the week following the brutal police killing of a Black man in custody "hosting lessons on legal rights for those who might get arrested in protests."[30] Some sessions teach tricks of the trade, for instance when Minnehaha distributed zines explaining how to turn T-shirts into protective face masks, how to respond to tear gas and pepper spray, and how to do jail support work. Some sessions focus on the physiological aspects of demonstrating, which is why organizers meeting at the Madison Infoshop offered advice on how much water to carry to rallies and how to locate public toilets in unfamiliar cities. Other sessions focus on managing emotions, which is why Minnehaha distributed flyers explaining how to relieve anxiety using deep breathing techniques and how to provide emotional aftercare reducing stress and burnout.

Training sessions like these are important because, as Boone with Minnehaha aptly surmises, simply deciding to "storm the barricades" is usually not enough to make demonstrations successful. Instead, "It's just well thought out strategy to treat people like human beings." Training protestors how to manage their needs while performing their roles is empowering and can make demonstrations more successful.

Alongside hosting planning meetings and training sessions, activist enterprises also function as prop shops. Public spectacles communicate visually, not just verbally, which is why props, costumes, banners, buttons, and other symbolic elements are important. Print-based movement spaces stock these props. Giovanni's Room sells Pride paraphernalia like rainbow flags and body art. Bluestockings carries feminist buttons reading "Stop Victim Blaming" and "End Rape Culture."[31] Similarly, at Left Bank in St. Louis, "When you walk in our store, the Black Lives Matter yard signs that we sell are stacked against the front counter." Consumer demand for props on the eve of rallies is one reason why BookWoman saw an uptick in business before the 2017 Women's March. People wanted feminist books, but they also wanted the paraphernalia. "Where do you get a button? Where do you get a bumper sticker? Get 'em at BookWoman!"

When it comes to props for organizing, some counterspaces are veritable treasure troves. As an example, the Madison Infoshop has "a variety of resources for community activists such as banners, signs, costumes and props for street theater, a button maker, media contact lists, and literature for distribution."[32] Many print-based movement spaces also have special equipment for creating custom paraphernalia. For instance, the Independent Publishing Resource Center has screen printers and letter presses, which activists use to make posters for rallies. "So after the [2016 presidential] election, one of our screen printers made print runs of that screen print 'You Are Not Alone' and would bring those screen prints to protests and marches and would hand them out." Similarly, the Minnehaha Free Space "had a nice copier . . . so people would make their own" flyers and zines to distribute at rallies. "It's a cool way of spreading information." Activist businesses stockpile equipment as well, like pepper spray and other protective gear. At Boxcar, "people will drop stuff off here . . . and we can just pass that along to who needs it. I think that's been a huge asset."

Alongside training and props, transportation is another important logistical concern. Preparing for public spectacles includes helping demonstrators travel to and from protest sites, and activist-entrepreneurs often facilitate this process. As examples, Internationalist coordinated carpooling for activists traveling from Carrboro to Miami for anti–free trade rallies.[33] A Room of One's Own sold bus tickets for people traveling from Madison to Washington, D.C., to protest Republican presidential inaugurations.[34] The Civic Media Center organized fundraisers to cover the transportation expenses for activists traveling from Gainesville to Tallahassee for sit-ins at the state capitol during investigations into police violence against unarmed Black youth.[35] Similarly, protestors contacted People Called Women to find out how to get from Toledo to Washington, D.C., for the Women's March. "We have meetings, and we talk through all that stuff. . . . And people are calling the bookstore and saying, 'Are there buses, or is anything going on locally?'" Logistical coordination happens by word of mouth.

Alongside transportation, advertising is another important logistical task. Although organizers may prefer to keep some aspects of their plans confidential, marches and rallies are about strength in numbers. Activist-entrepreneurs encourage shows of support by using their spaces and resources to advertise upcoming events. In the digital era, a lot of this advertising happens online. For Alan Chelak with PAT @ Giovanni's Room, "if we were to retweet something about an event or another community gathering being held somewhere in the city," that's a way of "getting that information out there." Some radical entrepreneurs use their collections of books, props, and decor to embellish these notices and dramatize their themes. This is why Susan Post with BookWoman mounts flyers on cardstock, photographs them alongside her feminist paraphernalia, and posts the images on Facebook. "I try to do that as much as possible."

Although online advertising is useful, old-fashioned posters, pamphlets, and flyers remain important. For Charles D'Adamo with the Alternative Press Center, online notices help, but "how do you re-find it?" By contrast, putting "something in their hand to read" gives people something concrete to return to. Pamphlets and flyers are also more private because they give people information without leaving a digital trail. Confidentiality is one of the reasons why volunteers with Boxcar "let people flyer in our space. If people have free material associated with their protest [or] organization, we stock that here. We'll put it at the front desk so that people can easily grab that."

Cumulatively, these dynamics surrounding planning, training, equipment, transportation, and advertising illustrate the range of logistical support available for grassroots organizing in print-based movement spaces during the days, weeks, and months leading up to a march or rally. Radical booksellers and librarians are sometimes involved in leading preparations, and they often attend events to show support. But more often, the grassroots organizers using their spaces are not directly affiliated with the business. Instead, activist-entrepreneurs construct humble yet affordable and trusted spaces for organizing that other groups mobilize to plan events.

Activist Storefronts Are Greenrooms during Demonstrations

Another common way that print-based movement spaces support public protests is managing needs, emotions, and logistics on the days when demonstrations occur. Scholarly accounts tend to overlook these day-of dynamics. In the rush to study either frontstage spaces during protests or backstage spaces during everyday life, the role of backstage spaces during spikes of political upheaval remains understudied. This oversight is understandable since the shift from preparation to implementation is a geographic shift from the counterspace, which remains offstage, to the performance area where protests unfold. However, my findings show that, although these sites are geographically disconnected, they remain functionally linked.

These links became especially apparent when I shifted my focus away from play-by-play accounts of protest scenes to the multisite experiences of protestors. Activists perform roles during demonstrations, and, like other actors, it is easier for them to sustain these roles when their basic needs are met. As I explain in this section, before heading onstage, activists often appreciate feeling encouragement and solidarity among peers about to undergo a similar ordeal. During spectacles, activists benefit from opportunities for rest and nourishment. Then, as events wind down, protestors go through a recovery phase as adrenaline recedes and everyday rhythms resume.

Activist-entrepreneurs use their counterspaces to facilitate these dynamics. I use the analogy of a greenroom to describe these processes. Like greenrooms in the wings of a theater, movement-oriented businesses are waiting areas where actors congregate before taking their turn on stage. Like greenrooms, print-based movement spaces often provide food, toilets, and chairs where performers can rest between scenes. Then, after the curtain falls, they are places for performers to unwind and commiserate. In these offstage spaces, actors' needs—rather than their characters' personas—take priority.

In print-based movement spaces, in the hours when an event is dawning, demonstrators assemble to review last-minute details, offer encouragement, and warm up for their roles. The buzz at Women & Children First following the Trump inauguration illustrates these dynamics. The day after the inauguration, the feminist bookstore was "a de facto meet-up spot for volunteers for the Women's March."[36] Because the bookstore was a trusted space within the feminist community, it felt natural to many organizers to congregate there on that politically charged morning. In the early hours before the march began, people gathered "for coffee and doughnuts . . . before they all rode the L [train] to join in the downtown Women's March."[37] These warm-up functions of gathering, talking, and jointly entering the fray helped people transition from the rhythms of everyday life to the public-facing protest roles they were performing for the day.

These warm-up functions are common in print-based movement spaces. Similar dynamics occurred at Internationalist during the Great American Boycott when three hundred people gathered for a pre-protest rally outside the bookstore before marching together to join the thousand-person demonstration downtown.[38] The same thing happened at May Day when activists assembled at the bookstore for warm-up rallies denouncing Trump's foreign policy platform before marching as a group to the Minnesota Republican Party Headquarters to join an even larger demonstration.[39] People congregate in print-based movement spaces at the start of convivial marches as well, which is why the organizers of the Puerto Rican Christmas parade *Parranda Navideña* selected La Casa Azul as their starting point. At the bookstore, people could congregate in a space celebrating Latino/a heritage before joyfully marching through East Harlem.[40]

Next, once the protest or rally is underway, activist storefronts continue providing logistical support, for instance by offering respite and nourishment. The closer the venue is to the demonstration, the more intense these greenroom functions become. The buzz in A Room of One's Own during the 2017 Women's March provides a case in point. The bookstore is located near a major avenue connecting the state capitol with a large public university. Since feminist booksellers knew protestors would be marching along that street all day, they set up their space to provide snacks and bathroom breaks. Sandy Torkildson said, "We advertised for people to come in for a bathroom stop [and] free cookies. I made—homemade—a whole bunch of chocolate chip and oatmeal cookies, and we bought some coffee from a local coffee source so people could get warmed up, because it was a little chilly still back then."

This example from 2017 continues the long tradition of activists using movement storefronts as spaces of respite during demonstrations. As an example from history, Cody's Books provided medical sanctuary for protestors injured during the 1968 free speech and anti-war rallies in Berkeley. As Pat Cody recalls, "We had guys who had been medics in the Vietnam War volunteering to take care of people that had been injured in the march or in the teargassing. They asked if they could use our backroom to help people."[41] The owners agreed. In a film clip documenting the riots, an activist shouting into a bullhorn announces, "Take the injured to the back room of Cody's Bookstore. Anyone gets hurt, take them into Cody's Bookstore."[42]

Print-based movement spaces provide similar logistical support today. Some venues, like Left Bank in Seattle, become jacks-of-all-trades. "During extraordinary times like the WTO protests . . . our bookstore was at times transformed into a meeting place, an info shop, a storage facility, a medical clinic, a restaurant, and a sanctuary from the chaos on the streets."[43] Other venues, like People Like Us, do favors for activists frequenting their store, for instance by holding protestors' bail money during demonstrations. Activists would come in on their way to ACT UP rallies "and say, 'OK, here's my cash, so if I get arrested, you can come down and get me.' We'd be like, 'Yeah.'" Activist-entrepreneurs also bring refreshments and equipment to protestors, for instance when staffers with Left Bank in St. Louis set up tables distributing water bottles and protest signs to activists marching nearby.[44] These behind-the-scenes maneuverings do not appear in media-circulated photographs of protest-filled streets, but managing logistics is nevertheless an important part of staging a demonstration.

Activist-entrepreneurs provide respite not only to demonstrators but also to bystanders, both as a way to encourage spectator attendance and as a way to minimize collateral damage. Mass protests like the 2015 Black Lives Matter rebellion in Baltimore ostensibly targeted police officers and state officials. However, the scale of upheaval also affected vulnerable members of the African American community because school administrators closed public schools during the uprising. In a majority-Black city where 84 percent of students qualify for free meals,[45] school closures meant Black children would be going hungry. Red Emma's responded by not only providing training sessions and resting spaces for demonstrators but also "feeding the school children who wouldn't be getting a free lunch since the city locked them out of their school."[46]

Some activist-entrepreneurs get involved with stage management as well to support and protect protestors in the streets. Kris Kleindienst with Left Bank in St. Louis played this protective role. Kleindienst considered joining the march but then decided to hold back. She asked herself, "Where can I be the most effective? Do we need another warm body in the street today? Or should I do something else?" As a small business owner paying special taxes for private neighborhood security, Kleindienst could speak from a position of authority. "I, as a business owner, talked to the guy who runs the security organization of our neighborhood. . . . I said, 'Look, you need to really deal with this with a very light hand.' I said, '[Do] whatever you can do to keep the tanks off of our street." She also reminded security contractors of their obligation to protect local business interests, including the safety of their employees. "Some of my staff is going to be out there. And you just really need to back off.'"

To summarize so far, these support functions of gathering, nourishing, and protecting connect the geographies of offstage businesses with the onstage spaces where protests unfold. Next, as demonstrations wane and crowds disperse, activist-entrepreneurs perform additional functions by helping demonstrators regroup.

Regrouping takes many forms. One form is recuperation. Recovering from stress is a political act not only because it protects activists from burnout but also because it confers value on bodies under assault. For Audre Lorde, "Caring for myself is not self-indulgence, it is self-preservation, and that is an act of political warfare."[47] Evette Dionne echoes these sentiments. For marginalized and oppressed groups, practicing self-care is "a radical act because it goes against everything that we've been conditioned to believe."[48] Self-care is crucial during not only everyday moments but also public demonstrations because, as Judith Butler observes, during marches and rallies, "it is . . . the body that is on the line."[49]

Spikes in political upheaval intensify the need for recuperation, and activist-entrepreneurs use their businesses to provide it. This is why Bluestockings adjusted its operating hours in the early months of the Black Lives Matter movement. "We often kept the space open later than our closing time whenever there was more than two or three people that would come in and just needed a hot cup of coffee and to sit for thirty minutes after a demo had happened." Staying open later constructed "a safe place to decompress after a march."

Another aspect of recuperation is debriefing. Demonstrators regroup in trusted counterspaces after protests end to commiserate about their experiences and relay first-person accounts. Sharing stories is important because, as David Graeber explains, media portraits of public demonstrations frequently misrepresent events and disparage participants. "If police at a press conference level an accusation against activists, it can be reproduced immediately by TV reporters and treated at least provisionally as true; if activists at a press conference level accusations against police, it is unlikely to be reproduced at all, in the absence of eye-witness verification from one of the reporters themselves."[50] Given this biased and disparaging reporting, setting the record straight, even if only among empathic peers, is cathartic and empowering.

With a goal of providing logistical support for catharsis, activist-entrepreneurs with Internationalist hosted debriefing sessions after protestors returned from a twenty-thousand-person anti–free trade rally in Miami. "A dozen of them—gathered at Internationalist Books in Chapel Hill four days later—were determined to relate only what they'd done and seen first-hand. No need to exaggerate. Just the facts of what they were caught up in . . . were horrifying."[51] After having been "beaten and abused"[52] by police during the rally, demonstrators wanted to connect with peers and share their stories. "As much as they despise what happened to them, what really frightens the Chapel Hill bunch is how blithely the media either ignored the violence altogether or else blamed the demonstrators for daring to challenge authority."[53]

Alongside recuperating and debriefing, the post-rally recovery phase also involves managing financial costs. Demonstrators who are arrested can incur significant expenses defending themselves from state prosecution. These expenses are part of the production cost of showcasing radical politics, and some activist-entrepreneurs collect donations to help. This is why The Big Idea hosts fundraising brunches after major demonstrations. In 2017, it donated proceeds to the Red Warrior Fund to help Standing Rock demonstrators pay legal bills. It also donated money to a local legal fund defending Pittsburgh residents arrested while protesting the Trump inauguration in Washington, D.C. In addition to helping with financial recovery, these fundraisers build solidarity and emotional support. As one brunch-goer said, "If I can't be out there, then I should at least support people who can be."[54]

These dynamics highlight the functional relationship between offstage spaces providing logistical support and onstage spaces where protests unfold. Analyzing these connections sheds light on the multisite dynamics of protests, which highlights the distributed spatial division of labor sustaining public-facing events. Other scholars look at backstage spaces during quiet moments and frontstage spaces during rallies, but few scholars analyze their interdependencies while events are underway. Despite being geographically separate from demonstration sites, counterspaces provide greenroom functions and logistical support during an event's beginning, middle, and end, which makes them an integral part of staging a contentious show.

Offstage Spaces Become Frontstage Battlefields

Providing logistical support for public protests involves overlaying new functions on top of print-based movement spaces. Demonstrators go there to warm up for their roles before events begin. They return for rest breaks as protests unfold. They also regroup there when demonstrations end. This protest support work occurs alongside the awareness raising, bridge building, and frame alignment undertaken during quieter moments. Cumulatively, these activities dramatize progressive visions and, hopefully, push toward social change.

People respond to this progressive activism in many ways. Some people are curious, while others are dismissive. Some see personal lifelines while others see mortal threats. On the negative side, my analysis revealed two sets of actors who not only disagree with radical politics but also take steps to disrupt the contentious political work occurring in progressive counterspaces. This final section reviews these dynamics. I look first at alt-right activists who harass radical businesses. Then I look at government entities that infiltrate activist enterprises to thwart contentious organizing. Both types of intrusions violate the filtering and sheltering characteristics facilitating vulnerable exploration, affinity building, and protest planning. In response, I explain how activist-entrepreneurs attempt to limit these intrusions, most notably by shaping environments preserving anonymity despite potential surveillance.

I start with alt-right activists. Staging protests at symbolic sites is a common social movement technique,[55] including among alt-right activists who target places that symbolize the progressive themes they oppose. Movement-oriented bookstores were victims of these attacks in the past, and Kepler's is a particularly well-known example. Neo-Nazis firebombed Kepler's in 1968 for its communist sympathies, and the bookstore was attacked again in 1989 for carrying Salman Rushdie's *Satanic Verses*.[56]

Similar dynamics occur today when alt-right activists target booksellers who take progressive political stands. Even business owners who usually abstain from politics can become victims of these attacks. As an example, although Inquiring Minds in upstate New York is not an activist bookstore, owner Brian Donoghue created a window display denouncing the Trump campaign during the 2016 presidential election. The display included books comparing Trump to Hitler along with a banner reading "Make America Hate Again"[57] and posters emphasizing the dangers of staying silent. Soon, the bookstore was under siege. "The banner was up for three weeks before all hell broke loose. . . . We received several phone calls from people in the community warning us that the bookstore was going to be picketed. . . . The phone was ringing off the hook, mostly hangups mixed with a few nasty comments."[58]

This backlash was a response to a onetime political stand. Activist-entrepreneurs' businesses symbolize progressive politics year-round, which makes them ongoing targets of alt-right harassment. Bluestockings, for instance, was targeted in these symbolic ways during the 2017 white supremacy wave. On a late summer evening, "five 'alt-right'-affiliated individuals entered Bluestockings and began planting copies of Milo Yiannopoulos's book on our shelves and photographing it alongside our merchandise. When confronted about bringing a known white supremacist's book in[to] our store, they refused to stop."[59] After several rounds of taunting statements and verbal aggression, the white supremacists left, but staffers worried what the intruders might do with the staged photographs. "We anticipate that they intend to engage in further provocation on social media."[60]

Unlike at Bluestockings, where this one-off incursion was short-lived, other radical bookstores and infoshops experience recurring attacks. I opened this chapter by describing white supremacists who protested outside Revolution Books in Berkeley. On the evening of the first assault, a group of thirty to forty alt-right activists "charged into a hallway in front of the store and basically yelled threats and banged on our windows and made a lot of noise."[61] This scene recurred several times in the following months, with large groups heckling, harassing, and intimidating volunteers and customers. The bookstore received up to sixty threatening calls a day. Alt-right activists also posted a video online threatening future attacks in other radical spaces. "Wherever you hang out, wherever you spill Communist literature—we're coming to a fucking bookstore near you."[62]

Alongside alt-right attacks, which are not state sanctioned, activist-entrepreneurs also contend with government surveillance. Many activist-entrepreneurs are vocal critics of state policies, as well as the inequitable interests they serve, and grassroots groups use activist enterprises to organize protests and direct-action campaigns. State agents sometimes respond to these actions by infiltrating print-based movement spaces, which disrupts activists' work.

At several activist enterprises, especially those with anti-statist inclinations, activists experienced government surveillance firsthand. At Internationalist, "We had at least one undercover agent try to copy our computer files and volunteer lists as the Internationalist helped organize buses [taking] activists to Washington, D.C., for the World Bank protests in April 2000."[63] At Red Emma's, an ACLU investigation revealed that the bookstore was under FBI and police surveillance in 2005 and 2006 after hosting speakers who were critical of capital punishment and the war in Iraq.[64]

Similarly, at Burning Books, federal agents monitored the bookstore for several years in the early 2010s because of the owner's previous association with the Earth Liberation Front. "Agents watched Leslie Pickering's home and store, monitored his mail, and used grand jury subpoenas to gather information about him."[65] Some print-based movement spaces— for instance, those focused on race, gender, and sexuality—appeared less likely to become victims of surveillance, at least as long as their focus remained on self-directed empowerment rather than state-directed organizing. Nevertheless, in an era of intersectional organizing, no space was fully immune from potential surveillance.

The specter of government surveillance adds an aura of authentic radicalism that some people find appealing, but mostly, these intrusions undermine organizing. For Pickering, investigations like the one at Burning Books are "very public, especially locally. . . . Everybody knows when they come in here . . . 'Oh yeah, that's the [bookstore] that the FBI wanted to shut down.'" Investigations like these impede solidarity building and frame alignment. Being issued subpoenas and subjected to wiretaps encourages grassroots groups to stay away. Transcripts and archives revealed no instances where surveillance led to prosecutions. Instead, the sense among activists was that surveillance and wiretapping were intimidation tactics, not genuine efforts to protect public safety. For Mike McGuire with Red Emma's, "This is a clear indication that police were being used politically."[66]

Surveillance is unsettling, but government raids are even more disruptive. Raids are uncommon in print-based movement spaces, but when they occur, the effects can be destabilizing. As an example, anarchists with the Long Haul Infoshop lived through a government raid. The infoshop is designed to be "an open activist space,"[67] meaning anyone can use the lending library, computer room, and zine-making space without having to say who they are or what they're doing. Many low-income residents living nearby come for the free internet. Radical organizers concerned about animal rights, prisoners' rights, and needle exchange also use the public computers, which protect their anonymity online.

FBI agents and University of California police officers raided the infoshop in 2008. They seized computers and hard drives hoping to learn who used them to send threatening emails to animal researchers associated with the university. Raids like these destabilize activist enterprises not just because of lost equipment but also because the intrusion violates feelings of safety. "Perhaps the most intense result of the raid was psychological.

For a few weeks after the raid, there was an overall sense of tension, anxiety, and trauma. Having your home base invaded by police is ugly, scary, and brutal. It is hard to prepare for such a violation and it is hard to pick up the pieces afterward."[68] The infoshop successfully sued law enforcement agencies for violating federal privacy regulations during the raid,[69] and the group eventually recovered. But it was a long road back.

To sum up so far, alt-right activists and government agencies sometimes target counterspaces, which disrupts their capacity to support contentious politics. My next question is, How do activist-entrepreneurs resist these incursions?

Under normal circumstances, themed environments filter out harassers, and safe space policies keep menacing to a minimum. Additionally, when it comes to alt-right harassment, private property rights confer added protections both because people are socialized to defer to property owners and because staffers can call the police for help. Many venues prefer not to involve the police, even in extreme situations, but it is an option. By contrast, when state officials are the harassing agents, activist-entrepreneurs have decidedly less room to maneuver. Counterspaces are bubbles of turf embedded within larger territorial units, and business owners do not have the authority to ban government agents from monitoring their spaces.

Since some incursions cannot be resisted, activist-entrepreneurs look for other ways to disincentivize infiltration and minimize the damage. The most common and most effective tactic is constructing spaces where organizing leaves no trace behind. To use a spatial analogy, it is the difference between walking on soft sand, which leaves a trail of footsteps, and walking on granite, which preserves no evidence of impact. The people doing the walking do not change what they do or how they do it. Instead, it is the characteristics of the environment that reveal or conceal their activity. These dynamics are an important reminder that anonymity, which is a crucial resource for organizing, is not something people automatically possess. Instead, it is a resource that activists construct,[70] including through the environmental characteristics of the counterspaces they produce.

Responses to the Patriot Act illustrate how activists construct spaces for anonymity. The Patriot Act included a clause requiring libraries and bookstores to share records with federal agents of what people buy and read. This legislation prompted a wave of administrative retooling even in nonactivist spaces where socially conscious librarians and booksellers worried about people's ability to access information without government censorship. Instead of asking people to read differently, staffers took steps to change the reading environment to ensure there would be no records to share. Constructing anonymity is why, at A Room of One's Own, "When the Patriot Act went into effect, our store was even more careful to make sure that no record would be available to link a customer's name to any book we sell or purchase."[71] Volunteers with May Day echoed these sentiments. "If we don't keep records of what people buy, the FBI can't find out about it."

Alongside intentional non-record-keeping, print-based movement spaces construct anonymity by providing access to information in untraceable ways. Print is unique in this regard. For Sandy Torkildson with A Room of One's Own, "People can go into bookstores and browse, and they don't have to expose what they believe to anybody else." Browsing online is different. "The people in the computer world know exactly everything that I do. [They know] exactly what clothes I bought at L.L.Bean. They know I'm a size large, so now I'm getting all the ads for fat people clothes. They know. It's kinda creepy." Reading and buying online in the seclusion of one's bedroom may feel more private than browsing in person and buying from checkout counter clerks, but that privacy is an illusion. "If people want to find out stuff about you, a profile is pretty easy to compose by just looking at what you browse on the internet. Books are much more private."

Another way activist-entrepreneurs protect anonymity is by managing digital resources on readers' behalf. Many progressive bookstores and infoshops download open-source zines, print them, and sell them or give them away in their stores. These practices give browsers access to online resources in untraceable ways. These zines are technically available to anyone with internet access, but by downloading the material in the store, the business takes the hit of losing anonymity, and the broad reading audience remains unknown.

Similarly, activist-entrepreneurs construct anonymity through the way they manage public computers. Concerns about surveillance and exposure explain why the Long Haul Infoshop reconfigured its computing equipment after the FBI raid. Before the raid, there were no security protections on the computers, which made the data vulnerable to government search and seizure. After the raid, Long Haul volunteers considered encrypting their hard drives, but because encryption is not fail-safe, they decided to remove the hard drives instead. "The computers load an open-source operating system each time they are turned on. That way, all information disappears each time the computers are turned off."[72] Even if government agencies subpoena records of internet traffic, there is nothing stored locally to connect the content of that traffic with the identities of the users. Anonymity remains intact.

These dynamics highlight the risks associated with providing logistical support for organizing. The arm's length division of labor between the activist-entrepreneurs constructing durable meeting spaces and the grassroots groups organizing public protests confers some protections on counterspaces, but that division of labor is no guarantee against harassment and surveillance. Although activist-entrepreneurs often cannot prevent people from targeting their spaces, they can take steps to minimize the damage, most notably by constructing environments that function more like granite and less like sand. In their spaces, people can browse, talk, and plan without leaving a trail. Constructing environments that disincentivize incursions also protects other functions described in previous chapters, like exploration, education, alliance building, and caretaking. These sheltered, durable spaces then support contentious politics year-round between the spikes of public protest.

Evaluating Constructivism
in an Ephemeral World

O NE OF THE FINAL STOPS on my cross-country tour of activist bookstores was Librería Donceles, a secondhand, Spanish-language bookstore, or so I thought. "We're not really a bookstore," Maggie Cavallo told me. Surprised, I looked around. The industrial shelves were filled with books. There was a cash register on the counter. The walls were yellow, the rugs mismatched, and the books gently worn and artfully disheveled. Not a bookstore? I was confused. "It's like a work of art, like an installation performing as a bookstore." Cavallo pointed to the exposed brick walls and wooden joists. "You have this container, and then you pour the bookstore into it."

Librería Donceles was a traveling art installation in the guise of a bookstore. Artist Pablo Helguera debuted the work in New York in 2013. The twenty-five thousand books in the original collection came from donors in Mexico City, and every volume was written in Spanish.

After Librería Donceles's successful opening in the Kent Fine Art Gallery in Chelsea, Helguera packed and shipped the exhibit to Brooklyn, Phoenix, San Francisco, Seattle, Chicago, Indianapolis, and Boston. In each city, a host organization—in Boston's case, the Urbano Project, an educational arts nonprofit in the Jamaica Plain neighborhood—unpacks everything, sets up the exhibit, and runs it as a bookstore. "The books really are for sale. You can buy one book per visit. They are pay what you wish."

This art installation in the guise of a bookstore intervenes in political debates about cultural difference. Helguera explains his motives in videos accompanying the exhibit. "We're responding to what I think is a very important political moment regarding the debate on immigration in the U.S." This debate includes relationships to knowledge. "In that process of criminalizing immigration, there is a need to present the Other as someone uneducated, someone who has no knowledge and ultimately is only here

People browse the Spanish-language bookshelves at Librería Donceles, an installation project by artist Pablo Helguera, hosted by Urbano Project in Boston from January 13 to March 31, 2017. Photograph by Faizal Westcott, one of Urbano's Fellows, 2017; courtesy of Urbano Project.

to take advantage of the richness of another culture." For Helguera, the political marginalization of Latinos is reflected in and reinforced by the absence of Spanish-language literature in U.S. cities. "In New York City, where I live, there's two million Latinos, of which the majority are Spanish speaking. And yet there's a great scarcity of bookstores that carry books in Spanish."

Librería Donceles challenges this reductive, xenophobic erasure by putting Spanish writing and culture on display. The exhibit is a weighty portrait of a rich Latino/a heritage physically manifest in thousands of books. For Cavallo, this public display is explicitly political. "It is engaging in the politics of visibility. It is engaging in the politics of language and identity and ethnicity. Which are all very political." Alongside making Latino/a culture visible, Librería Donceles constructs space for organizing. In Boston, activists used the exhibit to call for more bilingual services in Jamaica Plain and to dramatize the ethnic overtones of local gentrification. The space and literature inspired bilingual "social movement story times," as well, where activists taught children ages four to seven about the history and practice of protest.

This Spanish-language art installation is an activist project organized around print, but it does not have a durable, autonomous space. As a traveling exhibit, Librería Donceles relies on borrowed spaces, and as an art installation, it is intentionally impermanent. After four years and numerous cities, Boston was Librería Donceles's final stop. Cavallo expressed mixed feelings about the upcoming closure. Constructing a cultural resource for the Latino/a community only to take it away again felt harsh, which is why "Everyone's like, 'Keep it open forever. Maybe you should open just a little bookstore in the corner.' We thought about that. We've totally considered it. . . . But that's really hard." Rents are rising in this gentrifying neighborhood, and the bookstore installation survives on foundation funding, not sales. "Ain't nobody keeping the lights on selling books, know what I mean?"

Cavallo is correct that indie bookselling is a difficult business, but difficult is not the same as impossible. Rosie Magaña lives in Phoenix. She visited Librería Donceles when it came to her city in 2014. According to newspaper interviews, that visit was "a lightbulb moment."[1] Phoenix, the United States' fifth largest city, is 30 percent Latino/a. And after visiting Librería Donceles, Magaña decided that the time was ripe to open a permanent Spanish-language bookstore dedicated to Latino/a history and culture.[2]

Magaña founded Palabras Librería the following year as a bilingual bookstore and community gathering space. She started with only five books and a call for donations. "There would be days that I would just walk up to the space, and I would see boxes of books that were donations and little by little, I started getting more books."[3] Within two years, Palabras had seven thousand titles.[4] By 2019, the collection had grown to twenty thousand, a third of which was donated.[5] Magaña's dream of transforming the traveling art exhibit into a durable community resource had come true.

Running a bilingual independent bookstore is not easy. For Magaña, "You have to contend with pretty horrible margins."[6] She runs Palabras with the help of a business partner, and she survives financially by working a second full-time job. Although her schedule is "kind of crazy,"[7] she is passionate about the project. "Palabras is much more than a bookstore. It is a safe and encouraging environment for inter-cultural community exchange."[8] The bookstore provides "a platform where people of color feel comfortable sharing their stories 'and know that their stories and experiences have value.'"[9] It hosts writing groups for "healing and liberation,"[10] community forums on current events, and art exhibits celebrating Latino/a culture. Librería Donceles may have been temporary, but the spin-off it inspired in Phoenix is a durable space that elevates the visibility of marginalized residents, promotes literacy among people of color, and constructs a platform for political debate.

Constructive Activists Are Both Tactical and Strategic

Examples like Librería Donceles and Palabras Librería raise questions about the relationship between space and time. Analyzing constructive activism illustrates how people ensnared in oppressive systems nevertheless find ways to construct autonomous spaces supporting contentious politics. This analysis pushes past the reductive assumption that marginalized groups are confined to the weak tactics of provisional use. Instead, it highlights the strategic spatial agency that everyone possesses. It also highlights how activists leverage durable spaces as tools for social organizing.

Michel de Certeau first made the distinction between short-term "tactics" and long-term "strategies" to show that people who are marginalized nevertheless find opportunities to temporarily turn the spaces and resources of powerful groups to their advantage. De Certeau uses colonial oppression as an example to highlight the power disparities between conquerors who reshape entire landscapes around their interests and subjugated groups whose spatial agency is denied. In contexts like these, marginalized groups unable to escape or overturn oppressive systems instead "play on and with a terrain imposed on it and organized by the law of a foreign power."[11] Despite structural disenfranchisement, oppressed groups improvise by using the oppressor's products to make "something quite different from what the conqueror had in mind."[12] Although this provisional repurposing is significant, it is also short-lived and quickly dissolves back into the status quo.

De Certeau's analysis of tactical resourcefulness had contradictory influences on urban scholarship. From one perspective, the concept of temporary evasion has become a cornerstone of studies celebrating tactical urbanism,[13] do-it-yourself urbanism,[14] and makeshift urbanism.[15] For the field of city planning, which historically used top-down methods to serve the needs of people in power, these bottom-up studies bring much-needed attention to the everyday work-arounds of underserved groups. Early scholars like Margaret Crawford approached these practices from a social justice perspective. For Crawford, everyday life is "the true realm of political contestation," and provisional interventions in everyday life "are producing new forms of urban citizenship."[16]

However, more recent work on provisional use sheds this earlier commitment to social justice and instead emphasizes place branding and economic growth. For Claire Colomb, in cities around the world, "temporary uses of space have been harnessed in recent economic and urban development policies," as well as "in the official city marketing discourse[s]."[17] As examples, pushcart vendors become Food Truck Fridays,[18] artist squats become tourist attractions,[19] and Pride parades become corporate advertising events.[20] Urban boosters use these co-opted tactics to sell real estate and attract global investment. In this context, short-term tactics are clearly not just for the marginalized. Instead, they are tools for constructing vibrant public spaces appealing to economic elites.[21]

Unfortunately, the mushrooming literature on romanticized and marketable tactical urbanism makes it easy to forget de Certeau's warning that short-term tactics are "an art of the weak."[22] Provisional tactics involve "poaching in countless ways on the property of others."[23] Unlike economic elites, who now have both a strategic base and an elite-friendly tactical overlay, marginalized groups working exclusively with makeshift methods are left without a planning base when, after a few hours or days, the status quo resumes. A group with resources to act strategically can capitalize on its labor by constructing a durable space to "stockpile its winnings, build up its own position, and plan raids."[24] These dynamics underscore the fact that, although everyone has spatial agency, provisional tactics have disadvantages, and durable placemaking remains crucial.

From my perspective, the rush among provisional urbanism scholars to discover the next trendy example of marketable improvisation risks obscuring how people in marginalized positions can, despite their disadvantages, act strategically and construct durable infrastructure. The tendency toward dualism—by writing as though people in weak positions are fully weak and fully tactical while people in strong positions are fully strong and fully strategic—contributes to this one-sided analysis. However, buried in de Certeau's book is a sentence suggesting a spectrum rather than a duality. Quoting from Karl von Clausewitz, de Certeau writes, "The weaker the forces at the disposition of the strategist, the more the strategist will be able to use deception," which for people in very weak positions is often the "only possibility" and the "last resort."[25] This description of a slide from one pole to the other implies a spectrum where, in between the polar

extremes of total control and total subjugation, most people are both partially privileged and partially marginalized.

Hypothetically, this mixed state suggests that tactics and strategies
could coexist within the same bodies and within the same projects. Crawford's work similarly suggests opportunities for people to work "both
from the bottom up (in terms of subject and sympathy) and from the top
down (utilizing sophisticated knowledge and techniques)."[26] However,
for Crawford, this both/and framework is achieved through partnerships
between top-down city governments and bottom-up local organizations.
By contrast, my analysis highlights both/and capacities adhering entirely
within activist groups as they provisionally use print capitalism to strategically construct autonomous spaces on their own behalf.

This potential for people to possess both/and characteristics, rather than
occupying either/or subject positions, has not received much scholarly
attention. On the contrary, juxtaposed against the mushrooming literature on the romanticized tactics of the weak and their co-optation by the
strong, we know very little about how marginalized groups also engage in
strategic placemaking. The historical scholarship on constructive activism
and constructive feminism provides evidence that oppressed groups act
strategically in the de Certeauian sense, but present-day dynamics remain
understudied, as do the ways that tactics and strategies may be mutually
reinforcing.

Despite this scholarly silence, projects like Librería Donceles and
Palabras Librería are tactical-strategic hybrids. Librería Donceles is on the
more tactical end of the spectrum because it lacks a place of its own. However, unlike in de Certeau's example of tactical reading where conquered
groups cobble together insurgent meanings from oppressors' books,[27]
Librería Donceles does not limit itself to "poaching" Eurocentric, English-
language literature. In contrast to the political dehumanization and cultural erasure in xenophobic discourses, Librería Donceles strategically
compiles an alternative, autonomous resource base reminding people of
the plentiful Spanish-language books written from Latino/a perspectives
in other countries.

Similarly, Palabras Librería combines tactics and strategies. Compared
to Librería Donceles, the durable spin-off is on the more strategic end of
the spectrum because, in addition to amassing its own cultural resources,
it also constructs an independent space enabling autonomy and organizing. Palabras Librería nevertheless includes tactical elements as well. It

does not escape capitalism, and it survives opportunistically on donated commodities and volunteer labor. Taken together, Librería Donceles and Palabras Librería reinforce the concept of a spectrum, rather than a dualism, linking strategies and tactics. These examples also highlight the coexisting, mutually reinforcing relationship between provisional and durable modes of organizing.

With so many other scholars focusing on provisional tactics, this book shines a spotlight on the other end of the spectrum: durable placemaking. Instead of presupposing that radical or marginalized groups are limited to the weak weapons of makeshift tactics, and instead of pigeonholing projects as either tactical or strategic, there is a need to understand the interlocking dynamics of hybrid projects iteratively building on each other. Constructing strategic infrastructure with limited resources is difficult, and there are many failings along the way. Regardless, activist-entrepreneurs find ways to build durable space and to leverage it as a beachhead for surveying society, developing alternatives, exercising authority, and planning raids.

Constructive Activists Are Successful Even When Businesses Close

Despite this strategic durability, an important question to address before closing this book is the inescapability of impermanence. No project, no matter how strategically executed, lasts forever. Constructed counterspaces are more durable than rallies and meetups, which is a productive step, but financial pressure nevertheless forces many venues to close, even when participants would rather keep them open. Of the venues I studied that were open when I began my research, Rainbow, Internationalist, Modern Times, Boxcar, Wild Iris, Calamus, Minnehaha, and several Revolution locations closed over the next two years. However, closing does not negate durability. On the contrary, these now-closed venues lasted an average of twenty-eight years. Additionally, new venues replaced them. City of Asylum, Violet Valley, Café con Libros, Black Feminist Library, Mahogany, Uncle Bobbie's, Nuestra Palabra, and many other venues opened in those same two years. These openings are encouraging. But the question of how to interpret impermanence remains unanswered.

On the pessimistic side, closure often feels like erasure. The storefronts turn over, the resources dissipate, and soon it may feel like they never existed. I push back against these loss-oriented narratives for several reasons.

One reason is that longevity is not the same as influence. Long lives are not inherently more meaningful than short ones, and short lives can be profoundly transformative. For many people, while in operation, movement-oriented businesses are lifelines facilitating counterconduct. Their energy also lives on in the lives they transform, and those imprints do not simply disappear. On the contrary, a related reason why I push back against loss-oriented narratives is that activist enterprises are not self-contained. When venues eventually close, people reconfigure their ideas, resources, and energy into new, durable counterspaces in other forms and locations.

Focusing on impact and reconfiguration challenges the assumption that closure is synonymous with failure. A common criticism leveled against activist bookstores is that they are idealistic, utopian fantasies incongruent with real-world demands. As a typical example, a publishing insider quoted in the LGBTQ magazine *The Advocate* said, "Some bookshops deserve to go under. . . . Stores that aren't doing well are those that insist on staying in 1974, where bookselling takes a back seat to activism. This is a different era, and these businesses need to operate like bookstores and not community centers."[28] The implicit assumption in statements like these is that staying open is the ultimate measure of success and that losing money by building communities or supporting politics means businesses will inherently fail.

In contrast to those perspectives, many activist-entrepreneurs value their social missions, and those missions provide alternative benchmarks for success. Economic considerations still matter. Prioritizing sales—at least enough to pay the rent—is a practical necessity. At Women & Children First, "We learned in a hurry that it's not enough to simply love books and have a powerful mission. The bottom line is that to survive you have to develop experience and acuity in business practice."[29] Similarly, although Beyond Repair is an anticapitalist project, venues like it "exist within a capitalist context and then therefore need to survive within that context." However, attending to cash flow does not imply that profitability or longevity should be the only—or even primary—measure of success. Prioritizing social missions at the expense of finances may mean accepting shorter lifespans. But lasting several years is still substantially different than lasting only a few hours, and not lasting indefinitely is not the same as being meaningless, transient, or politically insignificant.

Carol Seajay writes eloquently about the lasting impact of durable yet impermanent spaces from a feminist perspective. Scores of second-wave feminist bookstores opened and closed between the 1970s and the 1990s. "During the months and years the now-defunct stores were open, these hotbeds provided women with access to books, magazines, pamphlets, [and] ideas that weren't available anywhere else—and they changed women's lives."[30] In those decades, women learned "to feel entitled to books that reflected their experiences."[31] Mainstream publishers, librarians, and booksellers now routinely provide this material. "It was an enormous change that was achieved in just a few years."[32] Even though most of those second-wave venues are now closed, they were durable spaces for strategic organizing for a time, and their legacies persist in the cultural and economic transformations they engendered.

For Carrie Barnett, doing this radical work generates "the heady rush" of being on the front lines of something simultaneously precarious and transformative. Progressive businesses are contentious spaces where people explore ideas, build communities, and plan protests. For people caught in oppressive systems they cannot (yet) leave or change, movement-oriented retail constructs autonomous space for strategic organizing. Doing this work is "exhilarating, and it's scary, and it's exciting, and it's real." It's also temporary because, if things go well, "you're going to achieve your goal of assimilation. And it's not going to be as fun anymore."

When evaluating longevity, it helps to think about activist enterprises less like people with birthdays and deathdays and more like volumes in a collection. Because spin-offs rematerialize in new forms, closing is only the end of a chapter, not the end of the story. For Sam Gould with Beyond Repair, "There's not always a long shelf life for these things. That said, even when they break off, often they'll go and have these tendrils, and their networks will go and spawn these other things." As examples, the closure of Oscar Wilde prompted the opening of the Bureau of General Services. The closure of Arise! led to two new venues, Boneshaker and the Minnehaha Free Space. Internationalist spun off several punk houses and co-ops before it closed.[33] Black Planet was "eventually rebirthed as the current Red Emma's." And Red Emma's, which remains open, has already spun off a community events organization, free school, radical bookfair, and conference series on grassroots organizing.[34]

This capacity for reconfiguration is a strength. In these reconfigured forms, activists find newly durable ways to support contentious politics using books and retail as a means to an end, not an end unto itself. Although the movement-oriented businesses described in this book are intentionally more durable than many seized spaces, they nevertheless do not survive only by standing firm in a permanent, exhausting posture of defiance. Instead, activist-entrepreneurs strategically construct durable spaces for as long as they can, then dissolve them when external forces become overwhelming, hopefully to recongeal in adapted forms.

These print-based movement spaces are durably strategic even as they incorporate improvisational elements and even as they exist within continually evolving ecosystems. Closing is not failing, and it should not be stigmatized as such. For Susan Post with BookWoman, "It's not shameful for things to close or end. Because even when they do, they still help people imagine that they're possible." Individual stores fade from cityscapes. But these venues leave lasting, life-altering impressions. Their closures also encourage new generations of activists to find updated ways to get durable spaces back on the map as part of the infrastructure of dissent.

Constructive Activism Has an Unwritten Future

In conclusion, constructive activism is about making durable places supporting contentious politics. Some spaces are dystopian, others are optimistic, and many provide practical assistance for living differently now, even if only in intermittent bursts. Great counterspaces do all of the above. They connect with deep human needs, and they change the lives around them.

Counterspaces are constructed environments. Activists construct them materially through objects, aesthetics, and embodied performances, as well as experientially through governing protocols, event programming, and management decisions. Once constructed, other people encounter these spaces and use them for contentious politics. These cumulative dynamics consolidate a material base with social scripts that, yes, in order to exist, has to navigate commodity markets and real estate markets. But success is not measured by property values or quarterly returns. Instead, constructive activism succeeds when spaces are stable enough to showcase worldviews, govern interactions, nurture camaraderie, and support protests in an iterative, repeating way. These recurring, multipronged practices shape counterspaces and give them meaning.

Constructive activism is a tool that anyone can use but that many scholars undervalue. One reason for this is that constructivism gets mistakenly conflated with new materialism. Telling the story of activist entrepreneurship through actor networks and vibrant matter would emphasize the agency of books and the impacts of walls, as though objects rather than people make space and produce its effects. However, although materiality frames social action, constructivism is also about the governing work, management decisions, and cultural performances bringing objects to life. This broader interpretation of constructive placemaking applies not only to activist booksellers and librarians but also to anyone building homes, communities, or nation-states. Without a material infrastructure, aspirational imaginings are ephemeral dreams. But objects alone will not change the world. Instead, constructive placemaking is inherently a multipronged affair combining materialism with culture, economics, discourse, and agency.

Another reason why scholars undervalue constructive activism is that not everyone focuses on social movements. Cities are filled with many types of people who have many different convictions and are involved in many different projects. Only some people self-identify as activists, and only some people join intentional communities. However, counterspaces on the porous end of the spectrum are public affairs. Retail businesses are public-facing conjunctures where many social networks collide. A core group of people manage the day-to-day logistics, but a broad cross section of people passes through. This porosity brings spaces to political life. Activists construct conditions of possibility, which other people— including nonactivists—then use for discovery, autonomy, camaraderie, conflict, caretaking, planning, protection, and support. These practices co-construct the space and give it collective life.

A third reason why scholars undervalue constructive activism is that, in the absence of a language naming this phenomenon, the repertoire's repeating structure gets lost in anecdotes. Constructive activism is not about bookstores. Instead, it is about building all kinds of durable spaces supporting all kinds of contentious politics. My hope is that the framework of constructive activism helps scholars studying other phenomena identify similar strategies in different contexts. Some constructive activists build radical bookstores and libraries. Others construct housing collectives, performance venues, free schools, guerilla gardens, social centers, or commons spaces. Like radical bookstores and infoshops, these places are constructed environments combining material placemaking with administrative systems and enacted performances. These multidimensional aspects of placemaking make constructive activism a versatile tool that is available to everyone and applicable in a wide range of endeavors.

I wish other scholars well in their search to locate, analyze, and critique constructive activism in other times and places. Constructive activism is a shared concept, and additional contributions will only make it richer.

Notes

Introduction

1. Unless otherwise indicated, all quotes are taken from author interviews.
2. Oldenburg, *Great Good Place.*
3. Hogan, *Feminist Bookstore Movement,* 2.
4. Davis, *From Head Shops.*
5. Stanush, "Poet's Voice."
6. City of Asylum, "Creative Placemaking."
7. Willett, "Censorship in Libraries."
8. Red Emma's, "About."
9. Bresnihan and Byrne, "Escape into the City," 46.
10. Cooper, *Everyday Utopias,* 3.
11. Cooper, *Everyday Utopias*; Harvey, *Spaces of Hope*; Mitchell, *Right to the City,* 235.
12. AK Press does not maintain a storefront, but the radical press provides books to many of the print-based movement spaces included in this study.
13. Renz, "AK Press."
14. Lorde, "Master's Tools," 27.
15. Haenfler, *Subcultures*; Mitchell, *Right to the City*; Montgomery, "Reappearance of the Public"; Sorkin, *Variations on a Theme Park*; Zukin, "Whose Culture? Whose City?"
16. Blyth, *Great Transformations*; Hackworth, *Manufacturing Decline.*
17. Osborne, "Introduction," 1.
18. Streeter quoted in Singh, "Making Sense of Dark Times."
19. Thoburn, *Anti-Book,* 78–79.
20. Baeten "Western Utopianism/Dystopianism," 144.
21. Harvey, *Spaces of Hope,* 195.
22. Harvey, 195.
23. Brookes, "Explainer."
24. Enke, *Finding the Movement*; Hogan, *Feminist Bookstore Movement.*
25. Quan quoted in Hogan, *Feminist Bookstore Movement,* 46.
26. Edelman, "Social Movements."
27. McAdam, Tarrow, and Tilly, *Dynamics of Contention,* 4.

28. Özdemir and Eraydin, "Fragmentation in Urban Movements," 734.

29. Graeber, *Direct Action,* 243.

30. Hogan, *Feminist Bookstore Movement.*

31. Bernard, *Research Methods in Anthropology,* 189–91.

32. Bernard, 145.

33. Bernard, 210–12.

34. Kvale and Brinkmann, *Interviews,* 153–55.

35. Young, *Shoemaker and the Tea Party.*

36. Burawoy, "Introduction," 5.

37. Burawoy, "Reconstructing Social Theories," 8, emphasis in original.

38. Burawoy, "Reconstructing Social Theories"; Kvale and Brinkmann, *Interviews,* 201–3; MacLure, "Researching without Representation?"

1. Constructing Places for Contentious Politics

1. Flores, "New Chapter."

2. Gandara, "Latino Laureate."

3. Brown, "Working Political Geography," 285.

4. Brown.

5. Brown.

6. Jerram, *Streetlife.*

7. Jerram.

8. Rose-Redwood, "Governmentality, Geography," 471. See also Brown, "Working Political Geography"; Death, "Counter-conducts."

9. Maiguashca, "Looking beyond the Spectacle," 542.

10. Tilly, *Contentious Performances,* 5.

11. Tilly, 6.

12. Tilly, 5–6.

13. Leitner, Sheppard, and Sciarto, "Spatialities of Contentious Politics," 157, emphasis added.

14. Spain, *Constructive Feminism.*

15. Spain, 48.

16. Stratigakos, *Women's Berlin.*

17. Hayden, *Grand Domestic Revolution.*

18. Adams, *Architecture in the Family Way.*

19. Fraser, "Rethinking the Public Sphere," 61.

20. Huron, "Working with Strangers," 967.

21. Cooper, *Everyday Utopias,* 12, emphasis in original.

22. Bresnihan and Byrne, "Escape into the City," 37.

23. Martin and Miller, "Space and Contentious Politics," 143.

24. Leitner, Sheppard, and Sciarto, "Spatialities of Contentious Politics."

25. Tilly, *Contentious Performances,* 175–99.

26. Oslender, *Geographies of Social Movements*, 13.

27. Leitner, Sheppard, and Sciarto, "Spatialities of Contentious Politics," 158.

28. Montgomery, "Reappearance of the Public," 777.

29. De Certeau, *Practice of Everyday Life*. See also Caldeira, "Imprinting and Moving Around"; Cosgrove, *Social Formation and Symbolic Landscape*; Rojas, "Enacted Environment"; Wood, "Vietnamese American Place Making."

30. Montgomery, "Reappearance of the Public," 776–77.

31. Mayer, "First World Urban Activism"; Özdemir and Eraydin, "Fragmentation in Urban Movements."

32. Madden, "Revisiting the End of Public Space," 188, emphasis in original. See also Mayer, "First World Urban Activism"; Montgomery, "Reappearance of the Public"; Swyngedouw, "Antinomies of the Postpolitical City."

33. Brown, "Working Political Geography," 291.

34. Norberg-Schulz, "Phenomenon of Place," 279, 282.

35. Leitner, Sheppard, and Sciarto, "Spatialities of Contentious Politics," 161.

36. Brown, "Working Political Geography," 291. See also Oslender, *Geographies of Social Movements*, 16.

37. Latour, *Reassembling the Social*.

38. Bennett, *Vibrant Matter*.

39. See also Barry, *Material Politics*; Gibbs, "Bottles, Bores, and Boats"; Tolia-Kelly, "Geographies of Cultural Geography III"; Whatmore, *Hybrid Geographies*; Yaneva, "How Buildings 'Surprise.'"

40. Last, "Re-reading Worldliness."

41. Polletta, "Free Spaces in Collective Action."

42. Bey, *TAZ*.

43. Cooper, *Everyday Utopias*.

44. Huron, *Carving Out the Commons*.

45. Hanhardt, *Safe Space*.

46. Hurewitz, *Bohemian Los Angeles*.

47. Hurewitz.

48. hooks, *Yearning*.

49. Scott, "Domination, Acting, and Fantasy."

50. Pratt, *Imperial Eyes*.

51. Fraser, "Rethinking the Public Sphere," 67.

52. Fraser, 61. See also Mitchell, *Right to the City*, 34.

53. Bagchee, *Counter Institution*; Davis, *From Head Shops*; Oslender, *Geographies of Social Movements*, 30–31.

54. Foucault, *Security, Territory, Population*, 199.

55. Davidson, "In Praise of Counter-conduct"; Death, "Counter-conducts"; Foucault, *Security, Territory, Population*; Rosol, "On Resistance."

56. Lefebvre, *Production of Space*, 349, 382.

57. Soja, *Thirdspace*, 68.

58. Cooper, *Everyday Utopias*, 8.

59. Cooper, 8–9.

60. Cooper, 11, emphasis in original.

61. Foucault, *Security, Territory, Population*, 215.

62. Foucault, 215.

63. Foucault, 214–15.

64. Ferrell, "Anarchy, Geography, and Drift"; Foucault, *Security, Territory, Population*; Miller, *For Derrida*, 177–81; Painter, "Prosaic Geographies of Stateness"; Wortham, *Counter-institutions*, 1.

65. Haenfler, *Subcultures*, 8–9; St. Martin, Roelvink, and Gibson-Graham, "Economic Politics," 8.

66. Amin, "Ethnicity and the Multicultural City."

67. Gibson-Graham, "Diverse Economies."

68. Painter, "Prosaic Geographies of Stateness."

69. Gardiner, *Critiques of Everyday Life*, 531.

70. Williams, "Care-full Justice," 824.

71. Williams, "Care-full Justice," 824. See also Beveridge and Koch, "Urban Everyday Politics"; Chatterton and Pickerill, "Everyday Activism"; Rosol, "On Resistance."

72. Painter, "Prosaic Geographies of Stateness," 761.

73. Miller and Rose, *Governing the Present*; Mitchell, *Colonising Egypt*; Painter, "Prosaic Geographies of Stateness"; Rosol, "On Resistance."

74. Cooper, *Everyday Utopias*, 30.

75. Oslender, *Geographies of Social Movements*, 72.

76. Landry et al., *What a Way to Run*, 28.

77. Edelman, "Social Movements," 300.

78. Tonkiss, "Austerity Urbanism," 318.

79. Tonkiss, 320.

80. Baeten, "Western Utopianism/Dystopianism"; Cooper, *Everyday Utopias*, 30; Edelman, "Social Movements," 300; Nicholls, "Geographies of Social Movements," 80; Oslender, *Geographies of Social Movements*, 70–73.

81. Davies, "Just Do It Differently?," 497, emphasis added.

82. Day, "From Hegemony to Affinity," 733.

83. Day, 734.

84. Davies, "Just Do It Differently?," 497.

85. Bresnihan and Byrne, "Escape into the City," 36.

86. Graeber, *Direct Action*, 203. See also Beveridge and Koch, "Urban Everyday Politics," 10; Day, "From Hegemony to Affinity"; Duff, "Affective Right to the City"; Gilchrist and Ravenscroft, "Space Hijacking."

87. Kinder, *DIY Detroit*.

88. Foucault, *Security, Territory, Population*; Scott, *Seeing Like a State*.

89. Butler, *Notes toward a Performative Theory,* 57.

90. Dixon, *Another Politics,* 83.

91. Williams, "Care-full Justice," 824.

2. Creating Accessible and Autonomous Activist Enterprises

1. Whyte, *Social Life of Small,* 94.

2. Davis, *From Head Shops,* 16, emphasis in original.

3. Davis, "Black-Owned Bookstores."

4. Enke, *Finding the Movement;* Hogan, *Feminist Bookstore Movement;* Spain, *Constructive Feminism.*

5. Davis, *From Head Shops,* 21.

6. Davis, *From Head Shops;* Enke, *Finding the Movement.*

7. Davis, "Forgotten World of Communist"; Denning, *Cultural Front.*

8. Spain, *Constructive Feminism.*

9. Sadler, "Anti-corporate Campaigning," 852.

10. Clark and Hebb, "Why Should They Care?," 2015.

11. Sadler, "Anti-corporate Campaigning," 852. See also Lindgreen and Swaen, "Corporate Social Responsibility"; Smith, "Corporate Social Responsibility."

12. Chandler et al., "Sound-Bite Vandalism." See also Millard, "Room with a Viewpoint"; Postelle, "Caffiend Closes."

13. Gibson-Graham, "Diverse Economies."

14. Samers, "Myopia of 'Diverse Economies,'" 876. See also St. Martin, Roelvink, and Gibson-Graham, "Economic Politics for Our Times."

15. Chandler et al., "Sound-Bite Vandalism."

16. Chandler et al.

17. Carland et al., "Differentiating Entrepreneurs," 73.

18. Carland et al., 78. See also Gartner, "What Are We Talking About"; McMullen, Plummer, and Acs, "What Is an Entrepreneurial Opportunity?"

19. Swedberg, "Cultural Entrepreneur and the Creative Industries," 260. See also Klamer, "Cultural Entrepreneurship."

20. Schneider and Teske, "Toward a Theory," 737. See also Hogan and Feeney, "Crisis and Policy Change."

21. Bates and Fasenfest, "Enforcement Mechanisms Discouraging Black–American"; Duff, "On the Role of Affect"; Duneier, *Sidewalk;* Gabbidon, "Racial Profiling by Store Clerks"; Grazian, "Urban Nightlife, Social Capital"; Mitchell and Staeheli, "Clean and Safe?"

22. Dannefer et al., "Healthy Bodegas"; Diao, "Are Inner-City Neighborhoods Underserved?"; Freeman, *There Goes the 'Hood,* 61–67; Kirch, "College Towns and Car Trouble."

23. Grazian, "Urban Nightlife, Social Capital."

24. Chafets, *Devils Night*; Cheng and Espiritu, "Korean Businesses in Black"; Cho, "Korean Americans vs. African Americans."

25. Alexander, "Fading, Twisting, and Weaving"; Kinder, "Technologies of Translocality"; Lara, "Patterns and Forms."

26. Miller and Nicholls, "Social Movements in Urban Society"; Rafail, "Protest in the City"; Tilly, *Contentious Performances*; Uitermark, Nicholls, and Loopmans, "Cities and Social Movements."

27. Staeheli, "Citizenship and the Problem of Community"; Staeheli, Mitchell, and Nagel, "Making Publics"; Swerts, "Creating Space for Citizenship."

28. Maiguashca, "Looking beyond the Spectacle," 542.

29. McGirr, *Suburban Warriors*.

30. Enke, *Finding the Movement*, 228.

31. Seajay, "Books." For a similar account from the first-wave women's movement, see Brannon, "We Have Come to Stay."

32. Heyman, "Assessing the Health."

33. Miller, *Reluctant Capitalists*, 127.

34. Smith, "Introduction," 11.

35. Watkins, "Group Seeks Different Path."

36. Schmidt, "Infoshop Is Not the Revolution."

37. Schmidt.

38. Schmidt.

39. Woolf, *Room of One's Own*.

40. Bey, *TAZ*.

41. hooks, "Homeplace."

42. Hurewitz, *Bohemian Los Angeles*.

43. Graeber, *Direct Action*, 269.

44. Graeber, *Direct Action*; Smith, "Introduction."

45. Graeber, *Direct Action*, 271.

46. Kadet, "Bookstore Glut Proves Print."

47. ABC No Rio, "About"; Law, "ABC No Rio."

48. Booth, "Bookstore's Next Chapter."

49. Souccar, "Nonprofit Expansion."

50. Khatib, "Red Emma's Interview."

51. Khatib.

52. Hogan, *Feminist Bookstore Movement*, xviii.

53. Renz, "AK Press."

54. Long Haul, "Filthy Commerce."

55. Renz, "AK Press."

56. Brown, "Working Political Geography"; Day, "From Hegemony to Affinity"; Duff, "Affective Right to the City"; Gilchrist and Ravenscroft, "Space Hijacking"; Haenfler, *Subcultures*, 13; Hill, "Endangered Childhoods," 347.

57. Atalay and Meloy, "Retail Therapy," 638.

58. Laing and Royle, "Examining Chain Bookshops," 29–30.

59. Pine and Gilmore, *Experience Economy,* 68.

60. Pine and Gilmore, 5, emphasis in original.

61. Pine and Gilmore.

62. Miller, *Reluctant Capitalists,* 127. See also Pine and Gilmore, *Experience Economy.*

63. Jones, "Bookstore Trilogy Sprouts."

64. Crum, "There's a Reason Why." See also Coeyman, "Black Books"; Erickson, "Funeral for One"; Jones, "Bookstore Trilogy Sprouts."

65. Spain, *Constructive Feminism,* 108.

66. Red Emma's, "About."

67. Pine and Gilmore, *Experience Economy,* 68.

68. Oldenburg, *Great Good Place.*

69. Miller, "Shopping for Community," 387.

70. Miller, 386.

71. Khatib, "Red Emma's Interview."

72. Graeber, *Direct Action,* 326; Klinenberg, *Palaces for the People,* 42.

73. Graeber, *Direct Action,* 327.

74. Graeber, *Direct Action,* 326–27; Peterson, "Gap between Those Who."

3. Reinventing Activist Bookstores in a Corporate Digital Age

1. Levitt, "We Need the Read/Write Library."

2. Childe, "Urban Revolution."

3. Anderson, *Imagined Communities.*

4. Mitchell, *Colonising Egypt.*

5. Anderson, *Imagined Communities,* 37–38.

6. Anderson, 45.

7. Anderson, 44.

8. Anderson, 36.

9. Anderson, 45.

10. Anderson, 59.

11. Mitchell, *Colonising Egypt,* 75, 89.

12. Thoburn, *Anti-Book,* 129–30.

13. Mitchell, *Colonising Egypt,* 82.

14. Thoburn, *Anti-Book,* 64.

15. Mitchell, *Colonising Egypt,* 92.

16. McAdam et al. quoted in Martin and Miller, "Space and Contentious Politics," 151.

17. Thoburn, *Anti-Book,* 47–48.

18. Thoburn, 19.

19. Spain, *Constructive Feminism,* 89.

20. Spain, 89.

21. Price, *How to Do Things with Books.*

22. Thoburn, *Anti-Book,* 172, emphasis in original.

23. Osborne, "Counter-space in Charles Lahr's," 150.

24. Hubler, "City Lights Illuminates."

25. Hyde, "Government Hounds Unleashed?". See also Salisbury, "Gay Bookstore Battles British."

26. Woestendiek, "ACLU Protests Prison's Denial."

27. Thoburn, *Anti-Book.*

28. Thoburn, 79.

29. Thoburn, 91.

30. Emblidge, "City Lights Bookstore."

31. Dodge, "Collecting the Wretched Refuse"; Moynihan, "Zine Makers Grab."

32. Thoburn, *Anti-Book,* 79–80.

33. As an example, see Baumann, "LGBTQ publishing."

34. Spain, *Constructive Feminism,* 89.

35. Adams, "Built out of Books," 114.

36. Garza, "Otieno Nyangweso."

37. Renz, "AK Press."

38. Thoburn, *Anti-Book,* 18, emphasis in original.

39. Thoburn, 26.

40. Denning, *Cultural Front.*

41. Landry et al., *What a Way to Run,* 28.

42. Thoburn, *Anti-Book,* 85–88.

43. Tilly, *Regimes and Repertoires,* 177.

44. Renz, "AK Press."

45. Denning, *Cultural Front,* 200–201.

46. Davis, "Forgotten World of Communist."

47. Emblidge, "City Lights Bookstore," 31.

48. PM Press, "On the Ground."

49. Stewart, *On the Ground.*

50. Davis, *From Head Shops,* 7.

51. Davis, "Black-Owned Bookstores."

52. Davis, "Black-Owned Bookstores"; Fortier, "Civil Rights Worker Had"; Richmond, "Leonard Oscar Johnson."

53. Garza, "Otieno Nyangweso."

54. Davis, "Black-Owned Bookstores." See also McKinney, "Black-Owned Indie Bookstores"; Nishikawa, "Archive on Its Own," 176; Plummer, "Historicist."

55. Bishop, "Sunwise Turn"; Brannon, "We Have Come to Stay"; Hillard, "Lady Midwest."

56. Adams, "Built out of Books," 113.

57. Seajay, "Books."

58. Spain, *Constructive Feminism,* 89.

59. Communication Research Associates, "Overview."

60. Hogan, *Feminist Bookstore Movement*; Potter, "Other Amazon"; Spain, *Constructive Feminism.*

61. Hogan, *Feminist Bookstore Movement,* 63.

62. Brownworth, "Art of Reading."

63. Brownworth. See also Adams, "Built out of Books."

64. Panaritis, "Trailblazing Gay Bookstore Giovanni's Room." See also Shister, "Phila. Gay Bookstore Giovanni's Room."

65. Flynn, "Philadelphia Story"; Shister, "Phila. Gay Bookstore Giovanni's Room."

66. Hogan, *Feminist Bookstore Movement,* 29.

67. Davis, "Forgotten World of Communist."

68. Flaherty, "Women Try to Preserve"; Ho, "Diversity in Book Publishing."

69. Barker and Dale, "Protest Waves in Western Europe," 85. See also Tarrow, *Power in Movement.*

70. Stevenson, "Liveliest of Corpses."

71. Thompson, *Merchants of Culture,* 239.

72. Milliot, "Print Sales Up Again."

73. Striphas, *Late Age of Print,* 3.

74. Thompson, *Merchants of Culture,* 147.

75. Farmelant, "End of an Era"; Miller, *Reluctant Capitalists*; Rønning and Slaatta, "Marketers, Publishers, Editors"; Stevenson, "Liveliest of Corpses"; Striphas, *Late Age of Print*; Thompson, *Merchants of Culture.*

76. Miller, *Reluctant Capitalists*; Striphas, *Late Age of Print*; Thompson, *Merchants of Culture.*

77. Beckstead, *Paperback Dreams*; Coffman, "Building Earth's Largest Library"; Hoynes, "Building a Brand for Independent"; Miller, *Reluctant Capitalists*; Raff, "Superstores and the Evolution"; Rønning and Slaatta, "Marketers, Publishers, Editors"; Striphas, *Late Age of Print*; Thompson, *Merchants of Culture.*

78. Thompson, *Merchants of Culture,* 31.

79. Alter, "Plot Twist"; Charles, "Independent Bookstore Day Goes National"; Italie, "Independent Booksellers Continue"; Miller, *Reluctant Capitalists*; Thompson, *Merchants of Culture.*

80. Thompson, *Merchants of Culture,* 31.

81. Leonard, "Independent Bookstore Lives!"; Patchett, "Owning a Bookstore Means."

82. Kopytoff, "Indie Bookstore Resurgence"; O'Kelly, "Indie Bookstores Aren't Dead."

83. Arnold, "Making Books"; Banks, "Store That's More than Books"; Communication Research Associates, "Overview"; Dugdale, "Revolution Books."

84. Rosenwald, "Independent Bookstores Turn."

85. Carlin, "Robin's Bookstore Opens."

86. Popper, "Who's Buying the Bookstore?"

87. Rosen, "African-American Booksellers Look."

88. Rosen.

89. Hogan, *Feminist Bookstore Movement*; Spain, *Constructive Feminism*.

90. Salamon, "Local Poet Hits Homer."

91. McGarvey, "Best Bets."

92. Mirk, "Closing the Book."

93. Between the Lines, "Common Language Bookstore to Hold."

94. Italie, "Independent Booksellers Continue"; Pickett, "Community Sustained Indie Bookstores"; Sanderson, "Independent Bookstore Rises"; Stateside Staff, "Independent Bookstores Are on the Rise."

95. Laties, *Rebel Bookseller,* 32.

96. Leonard, "Independent Bookstore Lives!"

97. Blocker, "Local Booksellers Ponder New."

98. Clines, "Indie Bookstores Are Back."

99. Rosenwald, "Independent Bookstores Turn."

100. Robinson, "Abridged History of the Collective."

101. Erickson, "Funeral for One."

102. Clark, "BookSense.com"; Hoynes, "Building a Brand for Independent."

103. Filgate, "Rise of Independent Booksellers"; Scutts, "The Few, the Proud."

104. Cullen, "Book Sense"; Ukura, "Indie Bookstores Strive."

105. Rosen, "Where Up Is the New."

106. Laties, *Rebel Bookseller,* 62–63.

107. Griswold, "Reluctant Capitalists," 255.

108. Mountain Xpress, "Firestorm Semi-closes for Monthlong"; Sandford, "Firestorm Café to Close."

109. Carreras, "Staying Afloat."

110. Erickson, "Funeral for One."

111. Rosen, "Making Nonprofit Stores Pay Off."

112. Smith, "Introduction."

113. Smith.

114. Rosen, "Making Nonprofit Stores Pay Off." See also Altman, "Nonprofit Bookstore Grows in Pittsburgh"; Beckstead, *Paperback Dreams.*

115. Rosen, "Making Nonprofit Stores Pay Off."

116. Bryant, "Personal History of Charis."

117. Bryant, "Personal History of Charis." See also Figliolini, "Charis Books Announces Move"; Rosen, "Women's Bookstores."

118. Adams, *Markets of Sorrow*; Herbert, "Trapdoor of Community"; Wolch, *Shadow State.*

119. St. Hope, "About Underground Books."

120. Open Books, "About Us."

121. Button, "New Nonprofit Bookstore Employs."

122. Smith, "Introduction."

123. Gilmore, "In the Shadow of the State," 46.

124. Firestorm, "About Firestorm Café."

125. Siegel, "Rainbow Bookstore Faces."

126. Mallard, "Wild Iris Books Happy"; Stone, "Wild Iris Books Seeks."

127. Allard, "Detroit-Shoreway Bookstore Guide;" Allard, "Guide to Kulchur Bookstore Will Reopen;" Allard, "Guide to Kulchur Dissolving."

128. Johnston, "Citizen-Consumer Hybrid," 229. See also Clarke, "From Ethical Consumerism," 1873.

129. Hinrichs and Allen, "Selective Patronage and Social Justice," 229.

130. Reich, "History Supports Big Box."

131. Daily Sentinel, "Local Bookstores Continue to Rewrite"; Ivey, "Buying Local Gets Biggest"; Jelalian, "Staying Local May Save."

132. Clark, "BookSense.com."

133. Arnold, "Making Books."

134. Brown, "Taking a Read on Black."

135. Bentley, "Aisles Losing Browsers to Web"; Erickson, "Funeral for One"; Scutts, "The Few, the Proud."

136. Trucker, "Bookselling in the 21st Century."

137. Trucker.

138. Cervantes, "Don't Judge This Phoenix."

139. Long Haul, "Filthy Commerce."

140. Roberts, "Seattle, by the Book."

141. Ross, "New Geography of Work," 34. See also Armano and Murgia, "Precariousnesses of Young Knowledge"; Kalleberg, "Precarious Work, Insecure Workers"; Ross, *Nice Work if You Can.*

142. Denning, *Cultural Front,* 222.

143. Barned-Smith, "LGBT Bookstore in Peril."

144. Barned-Smith.

145. Gandara, "Latino Laureate."

146. Schmidt, "How to Maintain an Alternative."

147. Khatib, "Red Emma's Interview."

148. Abello, "Closing the Funding Gap."

149. Gross, "Longtime Patrons Wax Poetic."

150. Millard, "Room with a Viewpoint."

151. Millard.

152. Howell, "Oscar Doesn't Go."

153. Howell.

154. Adams, "Built out of Books," 132.

155. Quimby's, "FAQ."
156. Moore, "Southern Sensibility."
157. Dixon, *Another Politics*, xii.
158. Dixon, 41–45.
159. Bresnihan and Byrne, "Escape into the City."
160. Davis, "Black-Owned Bookstores"; Polletta, "Free Spaces in Collective"; Spain, *Constructive Feminism*.
161. Bey, *TAZ*.
162. Hogan, *Feminist Bookstore Movement*.

4. Claiming Spaces and Resources in Gentrifying Cities

1. Currier, "News"; Howell, "Oscar Doesn't Go."
2. Bureau of General Services, "FAQ."
3. Davis, "Urbanization of the Human."
4. Freeman, *There Goes the 'Hood*; Lees and Slater, *Gentrification*; Osman, *Invention of Brownstone Brooklyn*.
5. Wright, "From 'Third Place' to 'Third Space'"; McArthur and White, "Twitter Chats as Third Places."
6. Harris, "Portland, the US Capital."
7. Harris.
8. Harris.
9. Chin, *Other Side of Paradise*, 247, capitalization in original.
10. Rose, "Rethinking Gentrification"; Spain, "What Happened to Gender."
11. Mitchell, *Right to the City*, 18. See also Massey, *For Space*, 149–52; Valentine, "Living with Difference," 75; Young, *Justice and the Politics*, 238.
12. Massey, *For Space*, 149–52; Young, "City Life and Difference."
13. Sandercock, "Cosmopolitan Urbanism," 38.
14. Sennett, "New Capitalism, New Isolation"; Simmel, "Group Expansion and the Development"; Simmel, "Metropolis and Mental Life."
15. Wilson, *Sphinx in the City*.
16. Simmel, "Group Expansion and the Development," 269.
17. Miller and Nicholls, "Social Movements in Urban"; Uitermark et al., "Cities and Social Movements"; Young, "City Life and Difference," 346.
18. Miller and Nicholls, "Social Movements in Urban society," 459.
19. Miller and Nicholls, 459.
20. Miller and Nicholls, 465.
21. Miller and Nicholls, 463.
22. Turner, *From Counterculture to Cyberculture*, 74.
23. Merrifield, "Right to the City," 478. See also Wilson, "On Geography and Encounter."

24. Goodman, "Cornel West & Rev. Traci Blackmon."

25. Uitermark et al., "Cities and Social Movements," 2546.

26. Uitermark et al., 2546.

27. Logan and Molotch, *Urban Fortunes,* 108.

28. Logan and Molotch, *Urban Fortunes,* 108. See also Light and Gold, *Ethnic Economies.*

29. Mitchell, "Street Scenes."

30. Jacobs, *Death and Life of Great,* 101, 163.

31. Fakhoury and Zimmerman, "Radical Library/Publisher and Prison."

32. Donoghue, "Inquiring Minds Bookstore's Brian Donoghue."

33. Donoghue.

34. Nugent, "Comic Book Store Provides."

35. Nugent.

36. Sennett, "New Capitalism, New Isolation." See also Simmel, "Group Expansion and the Development."

37. Bresnihan and Byrne, "Escape into the City," 37.

38. Alonso, "Theory of the Urban."

39. Huron, "Working with Strangers," 696.

40. Orfield, "Metropolitics."

41. Montgomery, "Reappearance of the Public."

42. Shaw, "Gentrification."

43. Torrance, "Forging Glocal Governance?"

44. Rothstein, *Color of Law.*

45. Lowry, "Filtering and Housing Standards"; Smith, *New Urban Frontier,* 56.

46. Beauregard, *When America Became Suburban.*

47. Shister, "Phila. Gay Bookstore Giovanni's Room."

48. Bryant, "Personal History of Charis."

49. Stein, "Beatniks are Back in."

50. Herod and Bekken, "Early History of the Lucy."

51. Cox, "Fight for Revolution"; Hoppenjans, "Day Honors a Life"; Huler, "Leftist Bookstore Thrives Anew"; Trager, "Radical Reading S.F. Bookseller."

52. Trager, "Radical Reading S.F. Bookseller."

53. Scheer, "Berkeley Commercial Tenants Claim."

54. Swyngedouw and Kaika, "Making of 'Glocal' Urban."

55. Franck and Stevens, "Tying Down Loose Space."

56. Berger, *Drosscape.*

57. Swyngedouw and Kaika, "Making of 'Glocal' Urban," 7. See also Bey, *TAZ;* Holloway, *Crack Capitalism;* Osman, *Invention of Brownstone Brooklyn.*

58. Rothstein, *Color of Law;* Wacquant, *Punishing the Poor.*

59. Brinkman, "Place Known to the World," 127.

60. Brinkman, 118.

61. Enke, *Finding the Movement*, 226, 229.

62. Culhane, "Books' End."

63. O'Brien, "Pillar of Gay Pride."

64. Jackson and Butler, "Revisiting 'Social Tectonics.'"

65. Valentine, "Living with Difference."

66. Drexler, "Sharing the Black Side"; MacDonald, "Protest Downtown on Wednesday."

67. Hogan, *Feminist Bookstore Movement*, 79–80.

68. Brown-Saracino, *Gentrification Debates*; Godfrey, *Neighborhoods in Transition*; Lees and Slater, *Gentrification*; Osman, *Invention of Brownstone Brooklyn*; Rose, "Rethinking Gentrification"; Shaw, "Gentrification"; Smith, *New Urban Frontier*.

69. Freeman, *There Goes the 'Hood*, 69. See also Rankin and McLean, "Governing the Commercial Streets"; Zukin et al., "New Retail Capital."

70. Brinckman, "Rents Soar."

71. Clark, "Wild Iris Books Opens."

72. This quote came from the Modern Times Bookstore Collective website in 2016. The website was removed from the internet when the bookstore closed later that year.

73. McMurtie, "SF's Modern Times Bookstore."

74. Minta, "New Chapter."

75. Adams, "San Francisco Goes All."

76. Dixson, "BID Foes Gather for Alternative."

77. Adams, "San Francisco Goes All."

78. Khare, "Revolution Books to Renovate"; Lee, "Protesters Demand Rent Relief"; Shih, "City Council to Examine."

79. Graeber, *Direct Action*, 266–68; Moynihan, "ABC No Rio Gears,"; Moynihan, "For $1"; Moynihan, "Punk Institution Receives City."

80. Smith, "Elegy Written in a City."

81. Schulman, *Gentrification of the Mind*.

82. Harper, "Bias towards Books."

83. Smith, *New Urban Frontier*.

84. Luger, "But I'm Just an Artist."

85. Shaw, "Place of Alternative Culture."

86. Harvey, "Right to the City."

87. Bresnihan and Byrne, "Escape into the City."

88. Bresnihan and Byrne, 37.

89. Anderson and Sternberg, "'Non-white' Gentrification in Chicago's"; Leeman and Modan, "Commodified Language in Chinatown"; Montgomery, "Reappearance of the Public."

90. Mele, *Selling the Lower East Side*; Osman, *Invention of Brownstone Brooklyn*; Shaw, "Place of Alternative Culture"; Zukin, "Whose Culture? Whose City?"

91. Montgomery, "Reappearance of the Public," 781.

92. Rose, "Rethinking Gentrification"; Shaw, "Gentrification"; Smith, *New Urban Frontier.*

93. Godfrey, *Neighborhoods in Transition*, 177.

94. Rose, "Rethinking Gentrification," 66.

95. Luger, "But I'm Just an Artist!?"; Osman, *Invention of Brownstone Brooklyn*; Rich and Tsitsos, "Avoiding the 'SoHo effect'"; Shaw, "Gentrification" and "Place of Alternative Culture"; Slater, "Gentrification in Canada's Cities."

96. Laties, *Rebel Bookseller*, 24–25, emphasis in original. See also Mehta, "Look Closely and You"; Miller, *Reluctant Capitalists*; Miller, "Shopping for Community"; Sax, "What Barnes & Noble Doesn't."

97. Cassie, "Red Emma's Moving to Former"; McCauley, "Red Emma's Restaurant and Bookstore."

98. Vorgna et al., "Mayor Bloomberg and NYC." See also Pereira, "East Harlem in Spotlight."

99. Kirch, "Brotherly (and Sisterly) Love."

100. Higgins, "Forty Years After the Summer."

101. Duffer, "Quimby's Bookstore."

102. Cooper, "Lenin to Go."

103. Taurasi, "Legacy of an Activist."

104. McKim, "Critics of Facelift in Central Square."

105. Mitchell, "L.A. Black-focus Bookshop."

106. Zimmerman, "Aging Bluestockings Book Shop."

107. Brown, "Antigone Books at 40 Years"; Communication Research Associates, "Overview"; Flaherty, "Women Try to Preserve"; Hogan, *Feminist Bookstore Movement*; Liddle, "More than a Bookstore."

108. Fraser, "And the Bowery Beats."

109. S.D., "Exit, Stage Lower East Side."

110. Keppler, "What's the Big Idea?"

111. Machosky, "City of Asylum Works."

112. Sommer, "Horsefeathers Market and Residences."

113. Shister, "Phila. Gay Bookstore Giovanni's Room."

114. City of Asylum, "City of Asylum Bookstore @ Alphabet City."

115. Nawotka and Kirch, "Bookstores Get Political."

116. LGBT Community Center, "Center History."

117. Santos, "Meet the Owner."

118. Maunz, "Meet the Woman Bringing."

119. Maunz.

5. Designing Landscapes That Shout, Entice, and Heal

1. Wilson, "'Yah' Wilson Owner of Sisters."

2. Wilson.

3. Scott, "Harlem Book Treasures."

4. Wilson, "'Yah' Wilson Owner of Sisters."

5. Wilson.

6. Coeyman, "Black Books."

7. Thoburn, *Anti-Book*, 16.

8. Coeyman, "Black Books."

9. Sabathia, "Only the Community Can."

10. Mitchell, *Right to the City*; Mitchell, *Colonising Egypt*; Schein, *Landscape and Race in the United States*; Staeheli, Mitchell, and Nagel, "Making Publics."

11. Haenfler, *Subcultures*, 9.

12. Groth and Wilson, "Polyphony of Cultural Landscape," 2–5.

13. Winston Churchill quoted in Groth and Wilson, "Polyphony of Cultural Landscape," 15.

14. Groth and Wilson, "Polyphony of Cultural Landscape," 17.

15. Staeheli, Mitchell, and Nagel, "Making Publics," 640–41. See also Mitchell, *Colonising Egypt* on machineries of representation.

16. Alderman, "Naming Streets for Martin Luther King Jr."; Karimi, "Street Fights."

17. Brasher, Alderman, and Inwood, "Applying Critical Race and Memory"; Karimi, "Street Fights."

18. Byrne, "When Green Is White"; Leeman and Modan, "Commodified Language in Chinatown."

19. De Certeau, *Practice of Everyday Life*; Lewis, "Monument and the Bungalow."

20. Groth and Wilson, "Polyphony of Cultural Landscape," 17.

21. Leib, "Witting Autobiography of Richmond."

22. Hoskins, "Poetic Landscapes of Exclusion."

23. Brasher, Alderman, and Inwood, "Applying Critical Race and Memory."

24. Stratigakos, *Women's Berlin*.

25. Brown, "Working Political Geography though Social."

26. Caldeira, "Imprinting and Moving Around."

27. Quoted in Swyngedouw, "Antinomies of the Postpolitical," 607.

28. Mitchell, *Right to the City*, 32–33, emphasis in original.

29. Caldeira, "Imprinting and Moving Around," 385.

30. Staeheli, Mitchell, and Nagel, "Making Publics," 635.

31. Caldeira, "Imprinting and Moving Around," 413.

32. Caldeira, "Imprinting and Moving Around"; McLean, "Regulating and Resisting Queer."

33. Burnett, Besant, and Chatman, "Small Worlds," 538.

34. Burnett, Besant, and Chatman, "Small Worlds," 538.

35. Gehl, *Life between Buildings*.

36. Duff, "On the Role of Affect," 881–82.

37. Brown, "Working Political Geography though Social"; Byrne, "When Green Is White."

38. Edelman, "Social Movements," 310.

39. Graeber, *Direct Action*, 278–79.

40. Laties, *Rebel Bookseller*; Miller, *Reluctant Capitalists*; Thompson, *Merchants of Culture*.

41. Miller, *Reluctant Capitalists*, 78.

42. Davis, *Late Victorian Holocausts*.

43. Berg, *38 Nooses*.

44. Churchill, *Little Matter of Genocide*.

45. MacQueen, "War in the Gulf."

46. Willett, "Alternative Libraries and Infoshops."

47. Baeten, "Western Utopianism/Dystopianism," 148.

48. Baeten, "Western Utopianism/Dystopianism," 148. See also MacLure, "Researching without Representation?"; Rose-Redwood, "Governmentality, Geography, and the Geo-coded."

49. These signs are visible in photographs Red Emma's posted to its twitter account in 2016 and 2017.

50. Hogan, *Feminist Bookstore Movement*.

51. Cauley, "End of an Era?" 18.

52. Hogan, *Feminist Bookstore Movement*.

53. Butler, *Notes toward a Performative*. See also Bourdieu, *Logic of Practice*; Duff, "Affective Right to the City."

54. Nawotka and Kirch, "Bookstores Get Political."

55. Nixon, "Signed, Sealed, Delivered."

56. Bosman, "Bookstores Stoke Trump Resistance"; Prasad, "It Takes Generations."

57. Emme B. in May Day, "Comments."

58. Kevin M. in May Day, "Comments."

59. Emme B. in May Day, "Comments."

60. Zachary S. in May Day, "Comments."

61. Graeber, *Direct Action*, 259.

62. Red Emma's, "About."

63. Sessa, "New Page for Book."

64. Cauley, "End of an Era?"

65. Baker, "Homestead Heroine."

66. Willamette Week, "Best of Portland."

67. Willamette Week, "Best of Portland."

68. Herman, *Trauma and Recovery*; Kolk, *Body Keeps the Score.*

69. Spratling, "Drawing on Experience Local."

70. Enlow, "Shrine of Black Madonna"; Spratling, "Detroit's Shrine of the Black."

71. Culhane, "Books' End."

72. Owen, "Tracking Down the Portland."

73. Teeman and Fallon, "Want to Feel Gay."

74. Spikol, "Room with a Crew."

75. Spikol.

76. Spikol.

77. Flores, "New Chapter Unfolds for Resistencia"; Liscano, "Years in Prison Helped."

78. Hamilton, "Casa de Resistencia Bookstore."

79. Jennings, "L.A.'s Black History."

80. Flores, "New Chapter Unfolds for Resistencia."

6. Governing Safe Spaces That Restructure Public Speech

1. Left Bank Books in St. Louis is not affiliated with Left Bank Books in Seattle, which is an anarchist collective founded in 1973 that is also included in this study.

2. Bey, *TAZ*; Cooper, *Everyday Utopias*, 3–4.

3. Davis, *From Head Shops to Whole Foods*, 4.

4. See chapters 7 and 8.

5. Sack, *Human Territoriality*, 1.

6. Cowen and Gilbert, "Politics of War," 16.

7. Cox, *Political Geography*, 2–3.

8. Brenner, "Urban Governance and the Production"; Taylor, "State as Container."

9. Herbert, "Trapdoor of Community"; Painter, "Prosaic Geographies of Stateness."

10. Easterling, *Extrastatecraft*; Jauch, "Export Processing Zones"; Ong, "Chinese Axis"; Parthasarathy, "India's Silicon Valley."

11. Németh, "Defining a Public"; Rafail "Protest in the City"; Schaller and Modan, "Contesting Public Space and Citizenship."

12. Quoted in White, "Social Anarchism, Lifestyle Anarchism," 118.

13. Mudu, "Resisting and Challenging Neoliberalism," 917.

14. Feliciantonio, "Spaces of the Expelled," 710.

15. Ong, "Chinese Axis," 75–76.

16. Ong, 75–76.

17. Easterling, *Extrastatecraft.*

18. Davis, "Sand, Fear, and Money."

19. Ong, "Chinese Axis," 85–86.

20. Ong, 79.

21. Ong, 91.

22. Easterling, *Extrastatecraft.*

23. Chatterton and Pickerill, "Everyday Activism and Transitions," 482.

24. Chatterton and Pickerill, 480.

25. Bresnihan and Byrne, "Escape into the City"; Ince, "In the Shell of the Old."

26. Ferrell, "Anarchy, Geography and Drift"; Swyngedouw, "Zero-Ground of Politics."

27. Bey, *TAZ*; Luger, "But I'm Just an Artist!?"; Pickerill and Chatterton, "Notes towards Autonomous Geographies."

28. Torrance, "Forging Glocal Governance?"

29. Easterling, *Extrastatecraft.*

30. Maiguashca, "Looking Beyond the Spectacle," 544–45. See also Bresnihan and Byrne, "Escape into the City," 47; Thompson, "Discomfort of Safety."

31. Mitchell, *Right to the City*, 132.

32. Sennett, *Uses of Disorder*; Uitermark, Nicholls, and Loopmans, "Cities and Social Movements"; Valentine, "Living with Difference."

33. Freeman, "Great, Good, and Divided"; Grazian, "Urban Nightlife, Social Capital"; Herbert and Grobelski, "Dis/order and the Regulation"; Valentine, "Living with Difference."

34. Ferrell, "Anarchy, Geography and Drift"; Mitchell and Staeheli, "Clean and Safe?"; Oldenburg, *Great Good Place.*

35. Coalition for Safer Spaces, "What Are, and Why"; English, "Security Is No Accident."

36. Thompson, "Discomfort of Safety."

37. Farthing, "Evolution."

38. Thompson, "Discomfort of Safety."

39. Thompson.

40. Thompson.

41. Bluestockings, "Safer Space Policy."

42. Bluestockings.

43. Bluestockings.

44. In Other Words, "Safer Space Policy."

45. Peterson, "Living with Difference in Hyper-diverse."

46. Bey, *TAZ.*

47. Quoted in Death, "Counter-conducts," 240, emphasis in original.

48. Foucault, *Security, Territory, Population*, 199.

49. In Other Words, "Safer Space Policy."

50. Firestorm, "Anti-oppression Statement."

51. In Other Words, "Safer Space Policy."

52. Hogan, *Feminist Bookstore Movement*.

53. Fraser, "Rethinking the Public Sphere," 63.

54. Fraser, 64–65.

55. Thoburn, *Anti-Book*; Thompson, *Merchants of Culture*.

56. Mitchell, *Right to the City*, 60–61.

57. Cohen-Almagor, "Limits of Objective Reporting"; D'Alessio and Allen, "Media Bias in Presidential."

58. Cohen-Almagor, "Limits of Objective Reporting," 139.

59. Melchoir, "Ohio Bookstore Flips Male-Authored."

60. Fraser, "Rethinking the Public Sphere," 64.

61. Melchoir, "Ohio Bookstore Flips Male-Authored."

62. Kean, "Women's History Month Promotion."

63. Kawaguchi, "Feminist Feast and Famine."

64. Sabathia, "Only the Community Can Save."

65. Flores, "CantoMundo Poets Boost Literary Scene."

66. Flores.

67. Flores, "CantoMundo Poets Boost Literary Scene." See also Hamilton, "Casa de Resistencia Bookstore Serves."

68. Striphas, *Late Age of Print*, 3. See also Farmelant, "End of an Era"; Thompson, *Merchants of Culture*.

69. Thompson, *Merchants of Culture*, 239.

70. Thompson, 400–401.

71. Murray, "Black Bookstores"; Thompson, *Merchants of Culture*.

72. Laties, *Rebel Bookseller*; Miller, *Reluctant Capitalists*; Rønning and Slaatta, "Marketers, Publishers, Editors"; Thompson, *Merchants of Culture*.

73. Ho, "Diversity in Book Publishing"; Jay, "Is Lesbian Literature Going"; Naughton, "In Loving Color."

74. Einhorn, *Property Rules*; Fraser, "Rethinking the Public Sphere."

75. Shryock, Abraham, and Howell, "Terror Decade in Arab Detroit," 11.

76. Nicolaides, *My Blue Heaven*, 51.

77. Jacobs, *Death and Life of Great*, 68.

78. Shryock, "Other Conscious/Self-Aware."

79. Graeber, *Direct Action*, 439, 444–45.

80. Dixon, *Another Politics*, 85.

81. Waterman, "Critique of Everyday Life," 568.

82. Davis, *From Head Shops to Whole Foods*, 15. See also 10–11.

83. Davis, *From Head Shops to Whole Foods*, 21.

84. Williams, "Care-full Justice in the City," 828. See also Dixon, *Another Politics*, 85–95; Turner, *From Counterculture to Cyberculture*, 118, 121.

85. Red Emma's, "About."

86. Red Emma's.

87. Red Emma's.

7. Nurturing Camaraderie in Filtered Third Places

1. Wilson, "On Geography and Encounter," 452–43.

2. Wilson, 452, 457.

3. Wilson, 452, 457.

4. Oldenburg, *Great Good Place.*

5. Goffman, *Presentation of Self in Everyday*; Scott, *Domination and the Arts.*

6. Collins quoted in Thompson, "Discomfort of Safety."

7. Collins quoted in Thompson, "Discomfort of Safety."

8. Oldenburg, *Great Good Place,* 48, 55.

9. Goffman, *Presentation of Self in Everyday,* 22.

10. Goffman, 111–12.

11. Scott, *Weapons of the Weak,* 284.

12. Scott, 287.

13. Scott, *Domination and the Arts,* 4.

14. Scott, xii.

15. Scott, 25.

16. Shryock, "Other Conscious/Self-Aware," 3.

17. hooks, "Homeplace," 388.

18. hooks, 384.

19. hooks, 384.

20. hooks, 384, 388.

21. Oldenburg, *Great Good Place,* 26.

22. Oldenburg, 37.

23. Jacobs, *Death and Life of Great,* 62; Oldenburg, *Great Good Place,* 22.

24. Oldenburg, *Great Good Place,* xvii.

25. Oldenburg, xviii.

26. Oldenburg, *Great Good Place,* xvii. See also Jacobs, *Life and Death of Great,* 57, 130.

27. Laing and Royle, "Examining Chain Bookshops"; Lawson, "Libraries in the USA"; Montgomery and Miller, "Third Place"; Trager, "Reading in the Borderland."

28. Oldenburg, *Great Good Place,* 22–23.

29. Yuen and Johnson, "Leisure Spaces, Community, and Third," 295–98. See also McArthur and White, "Twitter Chats as Third Places"; Montgomery and Miller, "Third Place."

30. Wright, "From 'Third Place' to 'Third Space,'" 12–13.

31. Oldenburg, *Great Good Place,* 165–67.

32. Rios and Hoyt, *Chicago,* disc 2.

33. Oldenburg, *Great Good Place,* 230–33.

34. Freeman, "Great, Good, and Divided"; Grazian, "Urban Nightlife, Social Capital"; Yuen and Johnson, "Leisure Spaces, Community, and Third."

35. McArthur and White, "Twitter Chats as Third Places," 1, emphasis added. See also Yuen and Johnson, "Leisure Spaces, Community, and Third."

36. Grazian, "Urban Nightlife, Social Capital," 915.

37. Grazian, 915.

38. McArthur and White, "Twitter Chats as Third Places," 1, 3.

39. Grazian, "Urban Nightlife, Social Capital."

40. Yuen and Johnson, "Leisure Spaces, Community, and Third."

41. Jacobs, *Life and Death of Great,* 62.

42. Hurewitz, *Bohemian Los Angeles.*

43. Joyce, *Rule of Freedom,* 16.

44. Beauregard, *Planning Matter,* 87.

45. Reagon, "Coalition Politics."

46. Yuen and Johnson, "Leisure Spaces, Community, and Third," 295–98. See also McArthur and White, "Twitter Chats as Third Places"; Montgomery and Miller, "Third Place."

47. Laing and Royle, "Examining Chain Bookshops"; Montgomery and Miller, "Third Place"; Trager, "Reading in the Borderland."

48. Carreras, "Staying Afloat."

49. Nicholls, "Geographies of Social Movements," 80.

50. Denning, *Cultural Front,* 211.

51. Turner, *From Counterculture to Cyberculture,* 72, 73, 147.

52. Borrelli, "More than a Bookstore."

53. Biel, *Good Trouble.*

54. Ho, "Diversity in Book Publishing."

55. Adams, "Built out of Books," 122.

56. Spikol, "Room with a Crew."

57. Barned-Smith, "LGBT Bookstore in Peril."

58. Montgomery and Miller, "Third Place," 232.

59. Mehta and Bosson, "Third Places and the Social," 780.

60. Szreter and Woolcock quoted in Yuen and Johnson, "Leisure Spaces, Community, and Third," 300.

61. Mehta and Bosson, "Third Places and the Social," 780.

62. Yuen and Johnson "Leisure Spaces, Community, and Third," 299.

63. Young, "City Life and Difference," 337, 343. See also Roestone Collective, "Safe Space," 1353–54.

64. Reagon, "Coalition Politics," 346.

65. Mouffe, *Return of the Political,* 2.

66. Mouffe, 4–6.

67. Pick, "Outward Mobility."

68. Abood, "Talk amongst Yourselves."

69. Abood.

70. Oldenburg, *Great Good Place,* 30.

71. Oldenburg, 53, emphasis in original.

72. Oldenburg, 53.

73. Kaplan, "Tripping over the Soapbox."

74. Kaplan.

75. Kaplan.

76. Oldenburg, *Great Good Place,* 8, 12, 22–23.

77. Oldenburg, 12–13, 23–26.

78. Oldenburg, 9.

79. Conradson, "Spaces of Care." See also Oldenburg, *Great Good Place,* xxvi, 10; Rosenbaum et al., "Cup of Coffee with a Dash."

80. Conradson, "Spaces of Care," 508.

81. Williams, "Care-full Justice in the City," 825.

82. Williams, 821.

83. Williams, 824.

84. Conradson, "Spaces of Care," 507.

85. Valentine, "Living with Difference," 87. See also Lawson, "Instead of Radical Geography."

86. Rosenbaum et al., "Cup of Coffee with a Dash," 43.

87. Merrifield, "Right to the City," 279, emphasis in original.

88. Bates-Rudd, "Inspired to Write."

89. Fraser, "Rethinking the Public Sphere," 68.

90. Kaplan, "Tripping over the Soapbox."

91. Kaplan, "Tripping over the Soapbox."

92. Gossett, "Political Opposition Finds a Home"; Levitt, "Women & Children First"; Morgan, "Join Us for the First."

8. Supporting Public Protests from the Wings

1. French, "Battle of Berkeley."

2. Piette, "Right-Wing Protesters Attack Revolution"; Revolution Newspaper, "Four Fascist Attacks on Revolution."

3. Boog, "Revolution Books Weathers Harassment"; Dinkelspiel, "Right-Wing Activists Target Berkeley's"; Melendez, "Revolution Books in Berkeley."

4. Tilly, *Contentious Performances,* xiii–xiv.

5. Tilly, *Regimes and Repertoires,* 35. See also McAdam, Tarrow, and Tilly, *Dynamics of Contention,* 38; Tilly, *Contentious Performances,* xvi, 14.

6. McAdam, Tarrow, and Tilly, *Dynamics of Contention,* 38; Tilly, *Contentious Performances,* xvi; Tilly, *Regimes and Repertoires,* 35.

7. Swerts, "Creating Space for Citizenship," 379–80.

8. Graeber, *Direct Action,* 402, 408; Luger, "But I'm Just an Artist!?"

9. Gibson-Graham, "Diverse Economies"; St. Martin, Roelvink, and Gibson-Graham, "Economic Politics for Our Times."

10. Swerts, "Creating Space for Citizenship," 383.

11. Brown, "Working Political Geography though Social"; Duff, "Affective Right to the City," 520.

12. Butler referenced in Duff, "Affective Right to the City," 517, 520.

13. Fraser, "Rethinking the Public Sphere," 68.

14. Oslender, *Geographies of Social Movements,* 75.

15. Scott, *Weapons of the Weak.*

16. Beauregard, *Planning Matter,* 86.

17. Graeber, *Direct Action,* 402; Leitner, Sheppard, and Sciarto, "Spatialities of Contentious Politics," 167–68.

18. Bayat, *Life as Politics*; Scott, *Weapons of the Weak.*

19. Graeber, *Direct Action,* 10.

20. Graeber, *Direct Action,* 10.

21. Swerts, "Creating Space for Citizenship," 384.

22. Leitner, Sheppard, and Sciarto, "Spatialities of Contentious Politics," 166–68.

23. Brown, "Working Political Geography through Social," 294.

24. Brown, 295.

25. Swerts, "Creating Space for Citizenship," 388–89.

26. Swerts, 388.

27. Potter, "Little Shop, Big Idea."

28. O'Briant, "Adaptation and Survival."

29. Author interviews; Charles, "RIP, CCCP."

30. Grier, "In Weary Baltimore, Welcome Mats."

31. Curkin, "At Bluestockings, a Manhattan."

32. Madison Infoshop, "Infoshop Library."

33. Geary, "Miami."

34. Madison Newspapers, "Turn Your Back Basics."

35. Schweers, "UF Dream Defenders Chapter."

36. Gossett, "Political Opposition Finds a Home."

37. Bosman, "Bookstores Stoke Trump Resistance."

38. Maguire and Collin, "Boycott Makes Dent in Triangle."

39. Fight Back Staff, "Minnesota Protests on 1-Year Anniversary."

40. Lee, "Making Music Outdoors."

41. Beckstead, *Paperback Dreams.*

42. Beckstead.

43. Left Bank Books, "Left Bank Books."

44. Riverfront Times Staff, "Police Teargas Protesters."

45. Grier, "In Weary Baltimore, Welcome."

46. Red Emma's, "Few News Stories about."

47. Kisner, "Politics of Conspicuous Displays."

48. Kisner.

49. Butler, *Notes toward a Performative,* 18.

50. Graeber, *Direct Action,* 445.

51. Geary, "Miami."

52. Pearson, "Cold Case and a Hotbed."

53. Geary, "Miami."

54. Datner, "Brunch and Big Ideas."

55. Leitner, Sheppard, and Sciarto, "Spatialities of Contentious Politics," 161–62.

56. Beckstead, *Paperback Dreams.*

57. Donoghue, "Inquiring Minds Bookstore's Brian."

58. Donoghue.

59. Bluestockings, "Dear Bluestockings Community."

60. Bluestockings.

61. Button, "Revolution Books Stands Up."

62. Boog, "Revolution Books Weathers Harassment."

63. Pearson, "Cold Case and a Hotbed."

64. Dechter, "Spying May Have Started."

65. Fairbanks, "Bookstore Owner Turns Tables."

66. Dechter, "Spying May Have Started."

67. Oakley, "UC Berkeley Police, FBI."

68. Palmer, "Long Haul Infoshop Regroups."

69. Fakhoury and Zimmerman, "Radical Library/Publisher and Prison Support."

70. Thoburn, *Anti-Book,* 181.

71. Torkildson, "City Council Should Repeal."

72. Palmer, "Long Haul Infoshop Regroups."

Conclusion

1. Trimble, "Why Palabras Bilingual Bookstore."

2. Trimble, "Palabras Librería/Bookstore in Phoenix"; Trimble, "Why Palabras Bilingual Bookstore."

3. Estes, "Phoenix's Palabras Bilingual Bookstore."

4. Trimble, "Palabras Librería/Bookstore in Phoenix."

5. Estes, "Phoenix's Palabras Bilingual Bookstore."

6. Estes.

7. Estes.

8. Palabras, "About Us."

9. Estes, "Phoenix's Palabras Bilingual Bookstore."

10. Palabras, "Events."

11. De Certeau, *Practice of Everyday Life,* 38.

12. De Certeau, xiii.

13. McFarlane, "City as a Machine"; Mould, "Tactical Urbanism."

14. Douglas, *Help-Yourself City*; Iveson, "Cities within the City"; Kinder, *DIY Detroit.*

15. Thieme, "Hustle Economy"; Tonkiss, "Austerity Urbanism and the Makeshift."

16. Crawford in Chase, Crawford, and Kaliski, *Everyday Urbanism,* 7, 24.

17. Colomb, "Pushing the Urban Frontier," 131.

18. Furuseth, Smith, and Mcdaniel, "Belonging in Charlotte."

19. Shaw, "Place of Alternative Culture."

20. Greenwald, "Bradley Manning Is Off Limits."

21. Brighenti, "Graffiti, Street Art"; Colomb, "Pushing the Urban Frontier"; Shaw, "Place of Alternative Culture"; Stevens, "German 'City Beach'"; Zukin, "Whose Culture? Whose City?"

22. De Certeau, *Practice of Everyday Life,* 37.

23. De Certeau, xii.

24. De Certeau, 37.

25. De Certeau, 37.

26. Crawford in in Chase, Crawford, and Kaliski, *Everyday Urbanism,* 15.

27. De Certeau, *Practice of Everyday Life,* xiii, xxi–xxiv.

28. Pela, "Different Fight."

29. Zellar, "ABA's New President."

30. Seajay, "Books."

31. Seajay.

32. Seajay.

33. Pearson, "Cold Case and a Hotbed."

34. Red Emma's, "About."

Bibliography

ABC No Rio. "About." ABC No Rio web page. Accessed 2016. http://www
.abcnorio.org/about/about.html.

Abello, Oscar P. "Closing the Funding Gap for Worker Cooperatives." *Next City,*
July 8, 2016. https://nextcity.org/daily/entry/
red-emmas-working-world-nyc-financial-cooperative.

Abood, Maureen. "Talk amongst Yourselves: How Book Groups Are Brewing Up
Community." *U.S. Catholic* 66, no. 11 (2001): 12–15.

Adams, Annmarie. *Architecture in the Family Way: Doctors, Houses, and Women,
1870–1900.* Montreal: McGill Queens University Press, 1996.

Adams, Guy. "San Francisco Goes All Prim and Proper." *Independent,* April 4,
2010.

Adams, Kate. "Built Out of Books: Lesbian Energy and Feminist Ideology in
Alternative Publishing." *Journal of Homosexuality* 34, nos. 3–4 (1998): 113–41.

Adams, Vincanne. *Markets of Sorrow, Labors of Faith: New Orleans in the Wake of
Katrina.* Durham, N.C.: Duke University Press, 2013.

Alderman, Derek H. "Naming Streets for Martin Luther King Jr.: No Easy Road."
In *Landscape and Race in the United States,* edited by Richard Schein, 213–36.
New York: Routledge, 2006.

Alexander, Bryant K. "Fading, Twisting, and Weaving: An Interpretive Ethnography of the Black Barbershop as Cultural Space." *Qualitative Inquiry* 9, no. 1
(2003): 105–28.

Allard, Sam. "Detroit-Shoreway Bookstore Guide to Kulchur to Close." *Scene,*
November 10, 2016. https://www.clevescene.com/scene-and-heard/
archives/2016/11/10/detroit-shoreway-bookstore-guide-to-kulchur-to-close.

Allard, Sam. "Guide to Kulchur Bookstore Will Reopen in New Location This
Month." *Scene,* June 14, 2017. https://www.clevescene.com/scene-and-heard/
archives/2017/06/14/
guide-to-kulchur-bookstore-will-reopen-in-new-location-this-month.

Allard, Sam. "Guide to Kulchur Dissolving, RA Washington Dismissed as
Executive Director." *Scene,* March 5, 2019. https://www.clevescene.com/
scene-and-heard/archives/2019/03/05/guide-to-kulchur-dissolving-ra
-washington-dismissed-as-executive-director.

Alonso, William. "Theory of the Urban Land Market." In *Land Use Planning*, edited by Hugo Priemus, Kenneth Button, and Peter Nijkamp, 24–57. Cheltenham, U.K.: Edward Elgar Publishers, 2007.

Alter, Alexandra. "The Plot Twist: E-book Sales Slip, and Print Is Far from Dead." *New York Times*, September 22, 2015. http://nyti.ms/1QXZyvn.

Altman, Louis. "A Nonprofit Bookstore Grows in Pittsburgh: Has Amazon Met Its Match in New Business Models?" *Nonprofit Quarterly*, January 13, 2017. https://nonprofitquarterly.org/2017/01/19/nonprofit-bookstore-grows -pittsburgh-amazon-met-match-new-business-models/.

Amin, Ash. "Ethnicity and the Multicultural City: Living with Diversity." *Environment and Planning A* 34 (2002): 959–80.

Anderson, Benedict. *Imagined Communities: Reflections on the Origins and Spread of Nationalism.* London: Verso, 2006.

Anderson, Matthew, and Carolina Sternberg. "'Non-white' Gentrification in Chicago's Bronzeville and Pilsen: Racial Economy and the Intraurban Contingency of Urban Redevelopment." *Urban Affairs Review* 49, no. 3 (2013): 435–67.

Armano, Emiliana, and Annalisa Murgia. "The Precariousnesses of Young Knowledge Workers: A Subject-Oriented Approach." In *Precariat: Labour, Work and Politics,* edited by Matthew Johnson, 102–17. New York: Routledge , 2015.

Arnold, Martin. "Making Books." *New York Times*, June 20, 2002. http://www .nytimes.com/2002/06/20/arts/making-books.html?mcubz=3.

Atalay, A. Selin, and Margaret G. Meloy. "Retail Therapy: A Strategic Effort to Improve Mood." *Psychology & Marketing* 28, no. 6 (2011): 638–59.

Baeten, Guy. "Western Utopianism/Dystopianism and the Political Mediocrity of Critical Urban Research." *Geografiska Annaler: Series B, Human Geography* 84, nos. 3–4 (2002): 143–52.

Bagchee, Nandini. *Counter Institution: Activist Estates of the Lower East Side.* New York: Fordham University Press, 2018.

Baker, Jeff. "Homestead Heroine: The Independent Widow in 'Jump-Off Creek' Resonates with Readers." *Oregonian*, September 5, 1999.

Banks, Sandy. "A Store That's More than Books." *Los Angeles Times*, October 9, 2007.

Barker, Colin, and Gareth Dale. "Protest Waves in Western Europe: A Critique of 'New Social Movement' Theory." *Critical Sociology* 24, nos. 1–2 (1998): 65–104.

Barned-Smith, St. John. "LGBT Bookstore in Peril: Giovanni's Room Needs 50G for Renovations." *McClatchy–Tribune Business News*, July 28, 2009.

Barry, Andrew. *Material Politics: Disputes along the Pipeline.* Malden, Mass.: John Wiley & Sons, 2013.

Bates, Tim, and David Fasenfest. "Enforcement Mechanisms Discouraging

Black–American Presence in Suburban Detroit." *International Journal of Urban and Regional Research* 29, no. 4 (2005): 960–71.

Bates-Rudd, Rhonda. "Inspired to Write—Religious, Inspirational Books Are Hot Market for Metro Detroit Readers and Authors Alike." *Detroit News,* June 28, 2000.

Baumann, Jason. "LGBTQ Publishing: File under Queer." *Publishers Weekly* 262, no. 21 (2015).

Bayat, Asef. *Life as Politics: How Ordinary People Change the Middle East.* Redwood City, Calif.: Stanford University Press, 2013.

Beauregard, Robert. *Planning Matter: Acting with Things.* Chicago: University of Chicago Press, 2015.

Beauregard, Robert. *When America Became Suburban.* Minneapolis: University of Minnesota Press, 2006.

Beckstead, Alex, dir. *Paperback Dreams.* DVD. San Francisco: 4SP Films, 2008.

Bennett, Jane. *Vibrant Matter: A Political Ecology of Things.* Durham, N.C.: Duke University Press, 2010.

Bentley, Rosalind. "Aisles Losing Browsers to Web." *Atlanta Journal-Constitution,* December 18, 2011.

Berg, Scott. *38 Nooses: Lincoln, Little Crow, and the Beginning of the Frontier's End.* New York: Pantheon, 2012.

Berger, Alan. *Drosscape: Wasting Land in Urban America.* Hudson, N.Y.: Princeton Architectural Press, 2007.

Bernard, H. Russell. *Research Methods in Anthropology: Qualitative and Quantitative Approaches.* 4th ed. Oxford: Altamira Press, 2006.

Between the Lines. "Common Language Bookstore to Hold Fundraiser to Help Keep Its Doors Open." *Between the Lines,* February 18, 2010.

Beveridge, Ross, and Philippe Koch. "Urban Everyday Politics: Politicising Practices and the Transformation of the Here and Now." *Environment and Planning D: Society and Space* 37, no. 1 (2019): 142–57.

Bey, Hakim. *TAZ: The Temporary Autonomous Zone, Ontological Anarchy, Poetic Terrorism.* New York: Autonomedia, 2003.

Biel, Joe. *Good Trouble: Building a Successful Life and Business with Asperger's.* Portland, Ore.: Microcosm Publishing, 2016.

Bishop, Ted. "The Sunwise Turn and the Social Space of the Bookshop." In *The Rise of the Modernist Bookshop: Books and the Commerce of Culture in the Twentieth Century,* edited by Huw Osborne, 65–88. Farnham, U.K.: Ashgate Publishing, 2015.

Blocker, Susan. "Local Booksellers Ponder New Stores Effect on Them." *Wisconsin State Journal,* March 1, 1992.

Bluestockings. "Dear Bluestockings Community." Bluestockings Bookstore Facebook page. Accessed August 13, 2017. https://www.facebook.com/bluestockingsnyc/posts/10155460966216259.

Bluestockings. "Safer Space Policy." Bluestockings Bookstore web page. Accessed 2016. http://bluestockings.com/about/safer-space/.

Blyth, Mark. *Great Transformations: Economic Ideas and Institutional Change in the Twentieth Century.* Cambridge: Cambridge University Press, 2002.

Boog, Jason. "Revolution Books Weathers Harassment Campaign by Alt Right Activists." *Publishers Weekly,* October 20, 2017. https://www.publishersweekly.com/pw/by-topic/industry-news/bookselling/article/75137-revolution-books-confronted-by-conservative-activists.html.

Booth, Laura. "Bookstore's Next Chapter: Latino Culture Shop La Casa Azul—6 Years in the Making—to Open in Spring." *New York Daily News,* April 2, 2012.

Borrelli, Christopher. "More than a Bookstore: Women & Children First Specializes in Feminist, Gay, Lesbian literature." *Chicago Tribune,* November 10, 2009.

Bosman, Julie. "Bookstores Stoke Trump Resistance with Action, Not Just Words." *New York Times,* February 15, 2017.

Bourdieu, Pierre. *The Logic of Practice.* Stanford, Calif.: Stanford University Press, 1990.

Brannon, Barbara. "'We Have Come to Stay': The Hampshire Bookshop and the Twentieth-Century 'Personal Bookshop.'" In *The Rise of the Modernist Bookshop: Books and the Commerce of Culture in the Twentieth Century,* edited by Huw Osborne, 15–30. Farnham, U.K.: Ashgate Publishing, 2015.

Brasher, Jordan P., Derek H. Alderman, and Joshua F. J. Inwood. "Applying Critical Race and Memory Studies to University Place Naming Controversies: Toward a Responsible Landscape Policy." *Papers in Applied Geography* 3, nos. 3–4 (2017): 292–307.

Brenner, Neil. "Urban Governance and the Production of New State Spaces in Western Europe, 1960–2000." *Review of International Political Economy* 11, no. 3 (2004): 447–88.

Bresnihan, Patrick, and Michael Byrne. "Escape into the City: Everyday Practices of Commoning and the Production of Urban Space in Dublin." *Antipode* 47, no. 1 (2015): 36–54.

Brighenti, Andrea M. "Graffiti, Street Art and the Divergent Synthesis of Place Valorisation in Contemporary Urbanism." In *Routledge Handbook of Graffiti and Street Art,* edited by Jeffery Ross, 158–67. Abington, U.K.: Routledge, 2016.

Brinkman, Bartholomew. "'A Place Known to the World as Devonshire Street': Modernism, Commercialism, and the Poetry Bookshop." In *The Rise of the Modernist Bookshop: Books and the Commerce of Culture in the Twentieth Century,* edited by Huw Osborne, 113–30. Farnham, U.K.: Ashgate Publishing, 2015.

Brinckman, Jonathan. "Rents Soar. Creatives Edged Out. Who Will Keep Portland Weird?" *The Oregonian,* March 16, 2007.

Brookes, Stephanie. "Explainer: What Is Retail Politics?" *The Conversation,* August 18, 2013. https://theconversation.com/explainer-what-is-retail -politics-16997.

Brontë, Charlotte. *Jane Eyre.* 1847. Reprint, New York: Penguin, 2006.

Brown, Ann. "Antigone Books at 40 Years: Radical Feminism Literature to Community Bookstore." *Arizona Daily Star,* October 13, 2013.

Brown, Michael. "Working Political Geography though Social Movement Theory: The Case of Gay and Lesbian Seattle." In *The SAGE Handbook of Political Geography,* edited by Kevin Cox, Murray Low, and Jenny Robinson, 285–304. London: Sage, 2008.

Brown, Monique. "Taking a Read on Black Bookstores: Insiders Reveal How These Enterprises Stack Up against Their White Counterparts." *Network Journal* 10, no. 2 (2002): 22.

Brown-Saracino, Japonica. *Gentrification Debates.* New York: Routledge, 2010.

Brownworth, Victoria A. "The Art of Reading: Do You Know Where Your Books Are?" *Lambda Rising Book Report* 2, no. 5 (1990): 12.

Bryant, Linda. "A Personal History of Charis." Charis Books and More web page. July 2009. http://www.charisbooksandmore.com/personal-history-charis -linda-bryant.

Burawoy, Michael. "Introduction." In *Ethnography Unbound: Power and Resistance in the Modern Metropolis,* edited by Michael Burawoy, 1–7. Berkeley: University of California Press, 1991.

Burawoy, Michael. "Reconstructing Social Theories." In *Ethnography Unbound: Power and Resistance in the Modern Metropolis,* edited by Michael Burawoy, 8–27. Berkeley: University of California Press, 1991.

Bureau of General Services. "FAQ." Bureau of General Services—Queer Division web page. 2017. http://bgsqd.com/faq/.

Burnett, Gary, Michele Besant, and Elfreda A. Chatman. "Small Worlds: Normative Behavior in Virtual Communities and Feminist Bookselling." *Journal of the Association for Information Science and Technology* 52, no. 7 (2001): 536–47.

Butler, Judith. *Notes toward a Performative Theory of Assembly.* Cambridge, Mass.: Harvard University Press, 2015.

Button, Liz. "New Nonprofit Bookstore Employs Workers with Disabilities." *American Booksellers Association,* May 9, 2017. https://www.bookweb.org/ news/new-nonprofit-bookstore-employs-workers-disabilities-36121.

Button, Liz. "Revolution Books Stands Up to the Alt-Right." *American Booksellers Association,* October 25, 2017. http://bookweb.org/news/revolution-books -stands-alt-right-102162.

Byrne, Jason. "When Green Is White: The Cultural Politics of Race, Nature and Social Exclusion in a Los Angeles Urban National Park." *Geoforum* 43, no. 3 (2012): 595–611.

Caldeira, Teresa. "Imprinting and Moving Around: New Visibilities and Configurations of Public Space in São Paulo." *Public Culture* 24, no. 2 (2012): 385–419.

Carland, James W., Frank Hoy, William R. Boulton, and Jo Ann C. Carland. "Differentiating Entrepreneurs from Small Business Owners: A Conceptualization." In *Entrepreneurship*, edited by Álvaro Cuervo, Domingo Ribeiro, and Salvador Roig, 73–81. Berlin: Springer, 2007.

Carlin, Romano. "Robin's Bookstore Opens a New Chapter." *McClatchy–Tribune Business News*, February 16, 2009.

Carreras, Jessica. "Staying Afloat." *Between the Lines*, August 13, 2009.

Cassie, Ron. "Red Emma's Moving to Former Spike & Charlie's Space in Mt. Vernon." *Baltimore Magazine*, June 1, 2018. https://www.baltimoremagazine .com/2018/6/1/radical-red-emmas-moving-to-mt-vernon.

Cauley, H. M. "End of an Era? Bookstore Fights to Stay Open." *Atlanta Journal-Constitution*. December 22, 2005.

Cervantes, Raquel. "Don't Judge This Phoenix Bilingual Bookstore by Just Its Cover." *ABC 15 Arizona*, December 9, 2016. http://www.abc15.com/news/ region-phoenix-metro/central-phoenix/dont-judge-this-phoenix-bilingual -bookstore-by-just-its-cover.

Chafets, Ze'ev. *Devils Night: And Other True Tales of Detroit*. New York: Random House, 1990.

Chandler, Emma, Evan Edwards, Scott Evans, Meg Hen, and Daniel Lee. "Sound-Bite Vandalism." *Mountain Xpress*, May 12, 2010.

Charles, Nick. "RIP, CCCP." *Plain Dealer*, September 7, 1991.

Charles, Ron. "Independent Bookstore Day Goes National May 2." *Washington Post*, April 30, 2015. https://www.washingtonpost.com/news/arts-and -entertainment/wp/2015/04/30/independent-bookstore-day-goes-national -may-2/?noredirect=on&utm_term=.622f3e55465e.

Chase, John L., Margaret Crawford, and John Kaliski (editors). *Everyday Urbanism*. Expanded ed. New York: Monacelli Press, 2008.

Chatterton, Paul, and Jenny Pickerill. "Everyday Activism and Transitions towards Post-capitalist Worlds." *Transactions of the Institute of British Geographers* 35, no. 4 (2010): 475–90.

Cheng, Lucie, and Yen Espiritu. "Korean Businesses in Black and Hispanic Neighborhoods: A Study of Intergroup Relations." *Sociological Perspectives* 32, no. 4 (1989): 521–34.

Childe, Gordon V. "The Urban Revolution." In *The City Reader*, 5th ed., edited by Richard T. LeGates and Frederic Stout, 31–39. New York: Routledge, 2011.

Chin, Staceyann. *The Other Side of Paradise: A Memoir*. New York: Scribner, 2009.

Cho, Sumi K. "Korean Americans vs. African Americans: Conflict and Construction." In *Reading Rodney King / Reading Urban Uprising*, edited by Robert Gooding Williams, 196–211. New York: Routledge, 1993.

Churchill, Ward. *A Little Matter of Genocide: Holocaust and Denial in the Americas 1492 to the Present.* San Francisco: City Lights, 2001.

City of Asylum. "City of Asylum Bookstore @ Alphabet City." City of Asylum web page. Accessed 2019. https://www.cityofasylumbooks.org/.

City of Asylum. "Creative Placemaking." City of Asylum web page. 2015. http://cityofasylum.org/creative-placemaking/.

Clark, Anthony. "Wild Iris Books Opens at New Location." *Gainesville Sun,* July 3, 2013.

Clark, Gordon L., and Tessa Hebb. "Why Should They Care? The Role of Institutional Investors in the Market for Corporate Global Responsibility." *Environment and Planning A* 37, no. 11 (2005): 2015–31.

Clark, Philip. "BookSense.com." *Lambda Book Report* 8, no. 3 (1999): 9–10.

Clarke, Nick. "From Ethical Consumerism to Political Consumption." *Geography Compass* 2, no. 6 (2008): 1870–84.

Clines, Francis X. "Indie Bookstores Are Back, with a Passion." *New York Times,* February 12, 2016. https://www.nytimes.com/2016/02/13/opinion/indie-bookstores-are-back-with-a-passion.html.

Coalition for Safer Spaces. "What Are, and Why Support, 'Safer' Spaces." Coalition for Safer Spaces web page. 2010. https://saferspacesnyc.wordpress.com/.

Coeyman, Marjorie. "Black Books: The Word on the Street." *Christian Science Monitor,* August 28, 2001.

Coffman, Steve. "Building Earth's Largest Library: Driving into the Future." *Searcher* 7, no. 3 (1999).

Cohen-Almagor, Raphael. "The Limits of Objective Reporting." *Journal of Language and Politics* 7, no. 1 (2008): 136–55.

Colomb, Claire. "Pushing the Urban Frontier: Temporary Uses of Space, City Marketing, and the Creative City Discourse in 2000s Berlin." *Journal of Urban Affairs* 34, no. 2 (2012): 131–52.

Communication Research Associates. "Overview: The 'Women in Print' Movement and its Status Today." *Media Report to Women* 31, no. 2 (2003): 5–10.

Conradson, David. "Spaces of Care in the City: The Place of a Community Drop-In Centre." *Social & Cultural Geography* 4, no. 4 (2003): 507–25.

Cooper, Ann. "Lenin to Go." *The New Republic* 206, no. 5 (1992): 15.

Cooper, Davina. *Everyday Utopias: The Conceptual Life of Promising Spaces.* Durham, N.C.: Duke University Press, 2013.

Cosgrove, Denis E. *Social Formation and Symbolic Landscape.* Madison: University of Wisconsin Press, 1998.

Cowen, Deborah, and Emily Gilbert. "The Politics of War, Citizenship, Territory." In *War, Citizenship, Territory,* edited by Deborah Cowen and Emily Gilbert, 1–30. London: Routledge, 2008.

Cox, Christopher. "Fight for Revolution—Bookstore Holds Its Ground in New Times." *Boston Herald,* August 27, 1998.

Cox, Kevin R. *Political Geography: Territory, State and Society.* Malden, Mass.: John Wiley, 2008.

Crum, Maddie. "There's a Reason Why Indie Bookstores Are Thriving." *Huffington Post,* January 5, 2017. https://www.huffingtonpost.com/entry/books-are-magic-emma-straub_us_586d6a00e4b0c56eb4b6ea7f.

Culhane, John. "Books' End." *City Paper,* May 15, 2014.

Cullen, Dan. "Book Sense: Independent Bookstores for Independent Minds." *Publishing Research Quarterly* 21, no. 2 (2005): 30–34.

Curkin, Charles. "At Bluestockings, a Manhattan Activist Center, Radical Is Sensible." *New York Times,* November 25, 2015.

Currier, Jameson. "News." *Lambda Book Report* 11, no. 6 (2003): 37–38.

Dahl, Roald. *Matilda.* 1990. Reprint, New York: Puffin Books, 2007.

Daily Sentinel. "Local Bookstores Continue to Rewrite the Book on How to Compete with Online Giants." March 4, 2017. http://www.gjsentinel.com.

D'Alessio, Dave, and Mike Allen. "Media Bias in Presidential Elections: A Meta-analysis." *Journal of Communication* 50, no. 4 (2000): 133–56.

Dannefer, Rachel, Donya A. Williams, Sabrina Baronberg, and Lynn Silver. "Healthy Bodegas: Increasing and Promoting Healthy Foods at Corner Stores in New York City." *American Journal of Public Health* 102, no. 10 (2012): e27–e31.

Datner, Max. "Brunch and Big Ideas: Bookstore Raises Funds for Arrested Protesters." *The Pitt News,* February 13, 2017. https://pittnews.com/article/116802/top-stories/brunch-big-ideas-bookstore-raises-funds-arrested-protesters/.

Davidson, Arnold. "In Praise of Counter-conduct." *History of the Human Sciences* 24, no. 4 (2011): 25–41.

Davies, Jonathan S. "Just Do It Differently? Everyday Making, Marxism and the Struggle against Neoliberalism." *Policy & Politics* 41, no. 4 (2013): 497–513.

Davis, Joshua C. "Black-Owned Bookstores: Anchors of the Black Power Movement." *African American Intellectual Historical Society,* January 28, 2017. http://www.aaihs.org/black-owned-bookstores-anchors-of-the-black-power-movement/.

Davis, Joshua C. "The Forgotten World of Communist Bookstores." *Jacobin.* August 11, 2017. https://www.jacobinmag.com/2017/08/communist-party-cpusa-bookstore-fbi.

Davis, Joshua C. *From Head Shops to Whole Foods: The Rise and Fall of Activist Entrepreneurs.* New York: Columbia University Press, 2017.

Davis, Kingsley. "The Urbanization of the Human Population." In *The City*

Reader, 5th ed., edited by Richard T. LeGates and Frederic Stout, 20–30. New York: Routledge, 2011.

Davis, Mike. *Late Victorian Holocausts: El Niño Famines and the Making of the Third World.* London: Verso, 2001.

Davis, Mike. "Sand, Fear, and Money in Dubai." In *Evil Paradises: Dreamworlds of Neoliberalism,* edited by Mike Davis and Daniel Bertrand Monk, 48–68. New York: The New Press, 2008.

Day, Richard J. F. "From Hegemony to Affinity: The Political Logic of the Newest Social Movements." *Cultural Studies* 18, no. 5 (2004): 716–48.

Death, Carl. "Counter-conducts: A Foucauldian Analytics of Protest." *Social Movement Studies* 9, no. 3 (2010): 235–51.

De Certeau, Michel. *The Practice of Everyday Life.* Berkeley: University of California Press, 2002.

Dechter, Gadi. "Spying May Have Started Earlier than Police Said." *Baltimore Sun,* October 1, 2008.

Deen, Shulem. *All Who Go Do Not Return: A Memoir.* Minneapolis: Graywolf Press, 2015.

Denning, Michael. *The Cultural Front: The Laboring of American Culture in the Twentieth Century.* London: Verso, 1998.

Diao, Mi. "Are Inner-City Neighborhoods Underserved? An Empirical Analysis of Food Markets in a U.S. Metropolitan Area." *Journal of Planning Education and Research* 35, no. 1 (2015): 19–34.

Dinkelspiel, Frances. "Right-Wing Activists Target Berkeley's Revolution Books Again." *Berkeleyside,* March 7, 2018. http://www.berkeleyside.com/2018/03/07/right-wing-activists-target-berkeleys-revolution-books.

Dixon, Chris. *Another Politics: Talking across Today's Transformative Movements.* Berkeley: University of California Press, 2014.

Dixson, Romando. "BID Foes Gather for Alternative Vision." *Asheville Citizen-Times,* July 27, 2012.

Dodge, Chris. "Collecting the Wretched Refuse: Lifting a Lamp to Zines, Military Newspapers, and Wisconsinalia." *Library Trends* 56, no. 3 (2008): 667–77.

Donoghue, Brian. "Inquiring Minds Bookstore's Brian Donoghue Reflects on the Consequences of Taking a Political Stand." *American Booksellers Association,* December 6, 2016. http://www.bookweb.org/news/inquiring-minds-bookstore%E2%80%99s-brian-donoghue-reflects-consequences-taking-political-stand-35143.

Douglas, Gordon. *The Help-Yourself City: Legitimacy and Inequality in DIY Urbanism.* Oxford: Oxford University Press, 2018.

Drexler, Michael. "Sharing the Black Side of Literature." *Plain Dealer,* April 26, 1992.

Duff, Cameron. "The Affective Right to the City." *Transactions of the Institute of British Geographers* 42, no. 4 (2017): 516–29.

Duff, Cameron. "On the Role of Affect and Practice in the Production of Place." *Environment and Planning D: Society and Space* 28, no. 5 (2010): 881.

Duffer, Robert. "Quimby's Bookstore." *Chicago Tribune,* December 12, 2009. http://www.chicagotribune.com/news/chi-books-quimbys-bookstore-story .html.

Dugdale, Emily. "Revolution Books: Berkeley's Radical Bookstore Relocating." *Berkeleyside,* June 29, 2015. https://www.berkeleyside.com/2015/06/29/ berkeleys-revolution-books-relocating-launching-fundraiser.

Duneier, Mitchell. *Sidewalk.* New York: Macmillan, 1999.

Easterling, Keller. *Extrastatecraft: The Power of Infrastructure Space.* London: Verso Books, 2014.

Edelman, Marc. "Social Movements: Changing Paradigms and Forms of Politics." *Annual Reviews of Anthropology* 1 (2002): 285–317.

Einhorn, Robin. *Property Rules: Political Economy in Chicago, 1833–1872.* Chicago: Chicago University Press, 2001.

English, Claire. "Security Is No Accident: Considering Safe(r) Spaces in the Transnational Migrant Solidarity Camps of Calais." In *Protest Camps in International Context: Spaces, Infrastructures and Media of Resistance,* edited by Gavin Brown, Anna Feigenbaum, Fabian Frenzel, and Patrick McCurdy, 353–70. Bristol, U.K.: Policy Press, 2017.

Enke, Anne. *Finding the Movement: Sexuality, Contested Space, and Feminist Activism.* Durham, N.C.: Duke University Press, 2007.

Enlow, Rose. "Shrine of Black Madonna Cultural Center Well of Knowledge." *Michigan Citizen,* November 5, 1998.

Emblidge, David. "City Lights Bookstore: A Finger in the Dike." *Publishing Research Quarterly* 21, no. 4 (2005): 30.

Erickson, Doug. "Funeral for One, Anniversary for the Other: A Tale of Two Bookstores." *Wisconsin State Journal,* July 29, 2011.

Estes, Christina. "Phoenix's Palabras Bilingual Bookstore Celebrates People of Color." *KJZZ,* April 24, 2019. https://kjzz.org/content/895476/phoenixs -palabras-bilingual-bookstore-celebrates-people-color.

Fairbanks, Phil. "Bookstore Owner Turns Tables, Questions Why He Was Target of FBI Probe." *Buffalo News,* March 17, 2016. http://buffalonews.com/2016/ 03/17/bookstore-owner-turns-tables-questions-why-he-was-target-of-fbi -probe/.

Fakhoury, Hanni, and Matt Zimmerman. "Radical Library/Publisher and Prison Support Group Settle Lawsuit with FBI and UC-Berkeley Police over Improper Raid." Electronic Frontier Foundation press release, April 11, 2012.

https://www.eff.org/press/releases/radical-librarypublisher-and-prison
-support-group-settle-lawsuit-fbi-and-uc-berkeley.

Farmelant, Randie. "End of an Era: Will the Feminist Bookstore Soon Be a Thing of the Past?" *Off Our Backs* 33, no. 5/6 (2003): 18–22.

Farthing, Jesse. "Evolution." *Mountain Xpress,* February 26, 2014.

Feliciantonio, Cesare D. "Spaces of the Expelled as Spaces of the Urban Commons? Analysing the Re-emergence of Squatting Initiatives in Rome." *International Journal of Urban and Regional Research* 41, no. 5 (2017): 708–25.

Ferrell, Jeff. "Anarchy, Geography and Drift." *Antipode* 44, no. 5 (2012): 1687–704.

Fight Back Staff. "Minnesota Protests on 1-year Anniversary of Trump's Inauguration." *Fight Back! News,* January 21, 2018. http://www.fightbacknews.org/es/node/6493.

Figliolini, Rico. "Charis Books Announces Move to Decatur." *Atlanta INtown Paper,* December 15, 2016. https://atlantaintownpaper.com/2016/12/charis
-books-announces-move-decatur/.

Filgate, Michele. "The Rise of Independent Booksellers in the Time of Amazon." *BuzzFeed,* February 26, 2015. https://www.buzzfeed.com/michelefilgate/the
-rise-of-the-independent-bookseller-in-the-time-of-amazon.

Firestorm. "About Firestorm Café." Firestorm web page. Accessed 2016. https://firestormcafe.com/about-firestorm-cafe/.

Firestorm. "Anti-oppression Statement." Firestorm web page. Accessed 2016. https://www.firestorm.coop/anti-oppression.html.

Flaherty, Julie. "Women Try to Preserve a Place of Their Own." *New York Times,* June 23, 2003. https://www.nytimes.com/2003/06/23/books/women-try-to
-preserve-a-place-of-their-own.html.

Flores, Nancy. "CantoMundo Poets Boost Literary Scene." *Austin American Statesman,* June 27, 2014.

Flores, Nancy. "A New Chapter Unfolds for Resistencia." *Austin American Statesman,* March 30, 2014.

Flynn, Elisabeth. "Philadelphia Story." *Lambda Book Report* 12, no. 1/2 (2003): 36.

Fortier, Bill. "Civil Rights Worker Had Eyes on Prize." *Telegram & Gazette,* February 4, 2000.

Foucault, Michel. *Security, Territory, Population.* Translated by G. Burchell. New York: Palgrave, 2007.

Franck, Karen A., and Quentin Stevens. "Tying Down Loose Space." In *Loose Space: Possibility and Diversity in Urban Life,* edited by Karen A. Franck and Quentin Stevens, 1–34. Abingdon, U.K.: Routledge, 2007.

Fraser, Lisa. "And the Bowery Beats On." *AM New York,* June 27, 2013.

Fraser, Nancy. "Rethinking the Public Sphere: A Contribution to the Critique of Actually Existing Democracy." *Social Text* 25/26 (1990): 56–80.

Freeman, James. "Great, Good, and Divided: The Politics of Public space in Rio de Janeiro." *Journal of Urban Affairs* 30, no. 5 (2008): 529–56.

Freeman, Lance. *There Goes the 'Hood: Views of Gentrification from the Ground Up.* Philadelphia: Temple University Press, 2006.

French, David. "The Battle of Berkeley." *National Review,* April 17, 2017. https://www.nationalreview.com/2017/04/berkeley-riot-leftist-mob-violence-undermines-rule-law/.

Furuseth, Owen, Heather Smith, and Paul Mcdaniel. "Belonging in Charlotte: Multiscalar Differences in Local Immigration Politics and Policies." *Geographical Review* 105, no. 1 (2015): 1–19.

Gabbidon, Shaun L. "Racial Profiling by Store Clerks and Security Personnel in Retail Establishments: An Exploration of 'Shopping while Black.'" *Journal of Contemporary Criminal Justice* 19, no. 3 (2003): 345–64.

Gandara, Ricardo. "Latino Laureate." *Austin American Statesman,* June 12, 1997.

Gardiner, Michael. *Critiques of Everyday Life: An Introduction.* New York: Routledge, 2002.

Gartner, William. "What Are We Talking about When We Talk about Entrepreneurship?" *Journal of Business Venturing* 5, no. 1 (1990): 15–28.

Garza, Mary Lou. "Otieno Nyangweso: From Nairobi to the Twin Cities." *Twin Cities Daily Planet,* October 28, 2012. http://www.tcdailyplanet.net/otieno-nyangweso-nairobi-twin-cities/.

Geary, Bob. "Miami: Don't Just Let It Go By." *Independent Weekly,* December 2, 2003.

Gehl, Jan. *Life between Buildings: Using Public Space.* Washington, D.C.: Island Press, 2011.

Gibbs, Leah. "Bottles, Bores, and Boats: Agency of Water Assemblages in Post/colonial Inland Australia." *Environment and Planning A* 45, no. 2 (2013): 467–84.

Gibson-Graham, Julie Katherine. "Diverse Economies: Performative Practices for other Worlds." *Progress in Human Geography* 32, no. 5 (2008): 613–32.

Gilchrist, Paul, and Neil Ravenscroft. "Space Hijacking and the Anarcho-politics of Leisure." *Leisure Studies* 32, no. 1 (2013): 49–68.

Gilmore, Ruth. "In the Shadow of the State." In *The Revolution Will Not Be Funded,* edited by INCITE!, 41–52. Durham, N.C.: Duke University Press, 2007.

Godfrey, Brian. *Neighborhoods in Transition: The Making of San Francisco's Ethnic and Nonconformist Communities.* Berkeley: University of California Press, 1988.

Goffman, Erving. *The Presentation of Self in Everyday Life.* New York: Anchor Books, 1959.

Goodman, Amy. "Cornel West & Rev. Traci Blackmon: Clergy in Charlottesville Were Trapped by Torch-Wielding Nazis." *Democracy Now,* August 14, 2017.

https://www.democracynow.org/2017/8/14/cornel_west_rev_toni
_blackmon_clergy.

Gossett, Stephen. "Political Opposition Finds a Home at New Women & Children First Series." *Chicagoist,* January 26, 2017. http://chicagoist.com/2017/01/26/women_children_first_conversation.php.

Graeber, David. *Direct Action: An Ethnography.* Chico, Calif.: AK Press, 2009.

Grazian, David. "Urban Nightlife, Social Capital, and the Public Life of Cities." *Sociological Forum* 24, no. 4 (2009): 908–17.

Greenwald, Glenn. "Bradley Manning Is Off Limits at SF Gay Pride Parade, but Corporate Sleaze Is Embraced." *Guardian,* April 27, 2013. https://www.theguardian.com/commentisfree/2013/apr/27/bradley-manning-sf-gay-pride.

Grier, Peter. "In Weary Baltimore, Welcome Mats Begin to Replace Riot Gear." *Christian Science Monitor,* April 29, 2015.

Griswold, Wendy. "*Reluctant Capitalists: Bookselling and the Culture of Consumption,* by Laura J. Miller." *Contemporary Sociology* 36, no. 3 (2007): 255–56.

Gross, Elizabeth. "Longtime Patrons Wax Poetic about Place." *Wisconsin State Journal,* April 11, 2005.

Groth, Paul, and Chris Wilson. "Polyphony of Cultural Landscape Study." In *Everyday America: Cultural Landscape Studies after J. B. Jackson,* edited by Chris Wilson and Paul Groth, 1–22. Berkeley: University of California Press, 2003.

Hackworth, Jason. *Manufacturing Decline: Race, Space, and Policy in the American Rust Belt.* New York: Columbia University Press, 2019.

Haenfler, Ross. *Subcultures: The Basics.* Abingdon, U.K.: Routledge, 2013.

Hamilton, Mae. "Casa de Resistencia Bookstore Serves as Refuge for UT Students." *Daily Texan,* June 25, 2016. http://www.dailytexanonline.com/2016/06/25/casa-de-resistencia-bookstore-serves-as-refuge-for-ut-students.

Hanhardt, Christina B. *Safe Space: Gay Neighborhood History and the Politics of Violence.* Durham, N.C.: Duke University Press, 2013.

Harper, Jonathan. "A Bias towards Books." *Lambda Book Report* 12, no. 3/4: 42.

Harris, Paul. "Portland, the US Capital of Alternative Cool, Takes TV Parody in Good Humour." *The Observer,* February 12, 2012.

Harvey, David. "Right to the City." *New Left Review* 53 (2008): 23–40.

Harvey, David. *Spaces of Hope.* Berkeley: University of California Press, 2000.

Hayden, Delores. *The Grand Domestic Revolution.* Cambridge, Mass.: MIT Press, 1982.

Herbert, Steve. "The Trapdoor of Community." *Annals of the Association of American Geographers* 95, no. 4 (2005): 850–65.

Herbert, Steve, and Tiffany Grobelski. "Dis/order and the Regulation of Urban Space." In *Cities and Social Change,* edited by Ronan Paddison and Eugene McCann, 115–29. London: Sage, 2014.

Herman, Judith L. *Trauma and Recovery: The Aftermath of Violence—From Domestic Abuse to Political Terror.* 1992. Reprint, Philadelphia: Basic Books, 2015.

Herod, James, and Jon Bekken. "An Early History of the Lucy Parsons Center." Lucy Parsons Center web page. Accessed 2016. http://lucyparsons.org/history.php.

Heyman, Stephen. "Assessing the Health of Independent Bookshops." *New York Times,* February 25, 2015. http://nyti.ms/1zeOSxp.

Higgins, Mike. "Forty Years after the Summer of Love Peaked in San Francisco, Mike Higgins Visits the City to Find Out If Anything Remains of the Hippie Dream." *The Independent,* June 16, 2007.

Hill, Jennifer A. "Endangered Childhoods: How Consumerism Is Impacting Child and Youth Identity." *Media, Culture & Society* 33, no. 3 (2011): 347–62.

Hillard, Celia. "Lady Midwest: Fanny Butcher—Books." In *The Rise of the Modernist Bookshop: Books and the Commerce of Culture in the Twentieth Century,* edited by Huw Osborne, 89–112. Farnham, U.K.: Ashgate Publishing, 2015.

Hinrichs, C. Clare, and Patricia Allen. "Selective Patronage and Social Justice: Local Food Consumer Campaigns in Historical Context." *Journal of Agricultural and Environmental Ethics* 21, no. 4 (2008): 329–52.

Ho, Jean. "Diversity in Book Publishing Isn't Just about Writers—Marketing Matters, Too." *Code Switch.* National Public Radio, August 9, 2016. https://www.npr.org/sections/codeswitch/2016/08/09/483875698/diversity-in-book-publishing-isnt-just-about-writers-marketing-matters-too.

Hogan, John, and Sharon Feeney. "Crisis and Policy Change: The Role of the Political Entrepreneur." *Risk, Hazards & Crisis in Public Policy* 3, no. 2 (2012): 1–24.

Hogan, Kristen. *The Feminist Bookstore Movement: Lesbian Antiracism and Feminist Accountability.* Durham, N.C.: Duke University Press, 2016.

Holloway, John. *Crack Capitalism.* London: Pluto Press, 2010.

hooks, bell. "Homeplace (a Site of Resistance)." In *Available Means,* edited by Joy Ritchie and Kate Ronald, 383–90. Pittsburgh, Penn.: University of Pittsburgh Press, 2001.

hooks, bell. *Yearning: Race, Gender, and Cultural Politics.* London: Turnaround, 1991.

Hoppenjans, Lisa. "Day Honors a Life Lived 'in Opposition.'" *News & Observer,* February 22, 2006.

Hoskins, Gareth. "Poetic Landscapes of Exclusion: Chinese Immigration at Angel Island, San Francisco." In *Landscape and Race in the United States,* edited by Richard Schein, 95–112. New York: Routledge, 2006.

Howell, Kevin. "The Oscar Doesn't Go to . . ." *Publishers Weekly* 250, no. 3 (2003): 25–27.

Hoynes, Michael F. "Building a Brand for Independent Survival." *Publishing Research Quarterly* 17, no. 1 (2001): 15–20.

Hubler, Shawn. "City Lights Illuminates the Past." *Los Angeles Times,* May 26, 2003.

Huler, Scott. "Leftist Bookstore Thrives Anew: Internationalist Finds that Location Is Key to Market." *News & Observer,* January 18, 1996.

Hurewitz, Daniel. *Bohemian Los Angeles: And the Making of Modern Politics.* Berkeley: University of California Press, 2008.

Huron, Amanda. *Carving Out the Commons: Tenant Organizing and Housing Cooperatives in Washington, D.C.* Minneapolis: University of Minnesota Press, 2018.

Huron, Amanda. "Working with Strangers in Saturated Space: Reclaiming and Maintaining the Urban Commons." *Antipode* 47, no. 4 (2015): 963–79.

Hyde, Sue. "Government Hounds Unleashed? London Bookstore Harassed, Shipments Seized." *Gay Community News* 12, no. 16 (1984): 1.

Ince, Anthony. "In the Shell of the Old: Anarchist Geographies of Territorialisation." *Antipode* 44, no. 5 (2012): 1645–66.

In Other Words. "Safer Space Policy." In Other Words web page. 2012. https://inotherwords.org/about-us/safer-space-policy/.

Italie, Hillel. "Independent Booksellers Continue to Add New Stores." *AP News,* May 26, 2015. https://apnews.com/43d578a30dc646169e531622981594ef.

Iveson, Kurt. "Cities within the City: Do-It-Yourself Urbanism and the Right to the City." *International Journal of Urban and Regional Research* 37, no. 3 (2013): 941–56.

Ivey, Mike. "Buying Local Gets Biggest Bang." *Madison Capital Times,* January 12, 2005.

Jackson, Emma, and Tim Butler. "Revisiting 'Social Tectonics': The Middle Classes and Social Mix in Gentrifying Neighbourhoods." *Urban Studies* 52, no. 13 (2015): 2349–65.

Jacobs, Jane. *The Death and Life of Great American Cities.* New York: Random House, 1961.

Jauch, Herbert. "Export Processing Zones and the Quest for Sustainable Development: A Southern African Perspective." *Environment and Urbanization* 14, no. 1 (2002): 101–13.

Jay, Karla. "Is Lesbian Literature Going Mainstream?" *Ms* 4, no 1 (1993): 70–73.

Jelalian, Matthew. "Staying Local May Save Independent Book Sellers." *Deseret News,* April 6, 2015. https://www.deseretnews.com/article/865625807/Staying-local-may-save-independent-book-sellers.html.

Jennings, Angel. "L.A.'s Black History: Eso Won Books." *Los Angeles Times,* February 25, 2016.

Jerram, Leif. *Streetlife: The Untold History of Europe's Twentieth Century.* Oxford: Oxford University Press, 2011.

Johnston, Josée. "The Citizen-Consumer Hybrid: Ideological Tensions and the Case of Whole Foods Market." *Theory and Society* 37, no. 3 (2008): 229–70.

Jones, Diana N. "Bookstore Trilogy Sprouts in Bloomfield." *Pittsburgh Post-Gazette,* November 11, 2013.

Joyce, Patrick. *The Rule of Freedom: Liberalism and the Modern City.* London: Verso, 2003.

Kadet, Anne. "A Book Store Glut Proves Print Isn't Dead—Just Used." *Wall Street Journal,* July 16, 2016.

Kalleberg, Arne. "Precarious Work, Insecure Workers: Employment Relations in Transition." *American Sociological Review* 74, no. 1 (2009): 1–22.

Kaplan, Erin A. "Tripping over the Soapbox: For Blacks, the Need to Sound Off Can Become the Obstacle to a Conversation." *Los Angeles Times,* March 1, 2006.

Karimi, Ali. "Street fights: The Commodification of Place Names in Post-Taliban Kabul City." *Annals of the American Association of Geographers* 106, no. 3 (2016): 738–53.

Kawaguchi, Karen. "Feminist Feast and Famine." *Publishers Weekly* 247, no. 30 (2000): 24–26.

Kean, Danuta. "Women's History Month Promotion Sees Bookshop 'Silence Men's Voices.'" *Guardian,* March 8, 2017. https://www.theguardian.com/books/2017/mar/08/womens-history-month-promotion-sees-bookshop-silence-mens-voices.

Keppler, Nick. "What's the Big Idea? Collective Binds Together for Bookstore." *Pittsburgh City Paper,* July 7, 2001.

Khare, Shagun. "Revolution Books to Renovate, Open New Store within Telegraph Channing Mall." *Daily Californian,* July 22, 2016.

Khatib, Kate. "Red Emma's Interview." Unpublished interview by Matt Dineen. August 6, 2013.

Kinder, Kimberley. *DIY Detroit: Making Do in a City without Services.* Minneapolis: University of Minnesota Press, 2016.

Kinder, Kimberley. "Technologies of Translocality: Vegetables, Meat and Dresses in Arab Muslim Detroit." *International Journal of Urban and Regional Research* 40, no. 5 (2016): 899–917.

Kirch, Claire. "Brotherly (and Sisterly) Love." *Publishers Weekly* 251, no. 4 (2004): 108–10.

Kirch, Claire. "College Towns and Car Trouble." *Publishers Weekly* 254, no. 22 (2007): 26.

Kisner, Jordan. "The Politics of Conspicuous Displays of Self-Care." *The New*

Yorker, March 14, 2017. https://www.newyorker.com/culture/culture-desk/the-politics-of-selfcare.

Klamer, Arjo. "Cultural Entrepreneurship." *The Review of Austrian Economics* 24, no. 2 (2011): 141–56.

Klinenberg, Eric. *Palaces for the People: How Social Infrastructure Can Help Fight Inequality, Polarization, and the Decline of Civic Life.* New York: Crown, 2018.

Kolk, Bassel van der. *The Body Keeps the Score: Brain, Mind, and Body in the Healing of Trauma.* New York: Random House, 2014.

Kopytoff, Verne. "The Indie Bookstore Resurgence." *Fortune,* September 20, 2013. http://fortune.com/2013/09/20/the-indie-bookstore-resurgence/.

Kvale, Steinar, and Svend Brinkmann. *Interviews: Learning the Craft of Qualitative Research Interviewing.* 2nd ed. Thousand Oaks, Calif.: Sage, 2009.

Laing, Audrey, and Jo Royle. "Examining Chain Bookshops in the Context of 'Third Place.'" *International Journal of Retail & Distribution Management* 41, no. 1 (2013): 27–44.

Landry, Charles, David Morley, Russell Southwood, and Patrick Wright. *What a Way to Run a Railroad: An Analysis of Radical Failure.* London: Comedia Publishing Group, 1985.

Lara, Jesus J. "Patterns and Forms of Latino Cultural Landscapes." *Journal of Urbanism* 5, nos. 2–3 (2012): 139–56.

Last, Angela. "Re-reading Worldliness: Hannah Arendt and the Question of Matter." *Environment and Planning D: Society and Space* 35, no. 1 (2017): 72–87.

Laties, Andrew. *Rebel Bookseller: How to Improvise Your Own Indie Store and Beat Back the Chains.* New York: Vox Pop, 2005.

Latour, Bruno. *Reassembling the Social: An Introduction to Actor-Network Theory.* Oxford: Oxford University Press, 2007.

Law, Victoria. "ABC No Rio: Twenty-Three Years of Art and Culture in a Four-Story Tenement." *Clamor* 24 (2004): 34.

Lawson, Karen. "Libraries in the USA as Traditional and Virtual 'Third Places.'" *New Library World* 105, no. 3/4 (2004): 125–30.

Lawson, Victoria. "Instead of Radical Geography, How about Caring Geography?" *Antipode* 41, no. 1 (2009): 210–13.

Lee, A. C. "Making Music Outdoors." *New York Times,* December 20, 2013.

Lee, Jean. "Protesters Demand Rent Relief for Tenants of Telegraph Channing Mall." *Daily Californian,* June 4, 2014.

Leeman, Jennifer, and Gabriella Modan. "Commodified Language in Chinatown." *Journal of Sociolinguistics* 13, no. 3 (2009): 332–62.

Lees, Loretta, and Tom Slater. *Gentrification.* New York: Routledge, 2008.

Lefebvre, Henri. *The Production of Space.* Translated by Donald Nicholson-Smith. Oxford: Blackwell, 1991.

Left Bank Books. "Left Bank Books." *Anarcho-Syndicalist Review* 29 (Summer 2000): 26.

Leib, Jonathan. "The Witting Autobiography of Richmond, Virginia: Arthur Ashe, the Civil War, and Monument Avenue's Racialized Landscape." In *Landscape and Race in the United States,* edited by Richard Schein, 187–212. New York: Routledge, 2006.

Leitner, Helga, Eric Sheppard, and Kristin Sciarto. "The Spatialities of Contentious Politics." *Transactions of the Institute of British Geographers* 33, no. 2 (2008): 157–72.

Leonard, Andrew. "The Independent Bookstore Lives! Why Amazon's Conquest Will Never Be Complete." *Salon,* April 4, 2014. https://www.salon .com/2014/04/04/the_independent_bookstore_lives_why_amazons _conquest_will_never_be_complete/.

Levitt, Aimee. "We Need the Read/Write Library Now More than Ever." *Chicago Reader,* January 11, 2017. https://www.chicagoreader.com/chicago/ read-write-library-nell-taylor-neighborhoods/Content?oid=25001117.

Levitt, Aimee. "Women & Children First Starts a Conversation about Art and Resisting the New Administration." *Chicago Reader,* January 25, 2017. https:// www.chicagoreader.com/chicago/women-and-children-first-conversation -sarah-hollenbeck/Content?oid=25251256.

Lewis, Peirce. "The Monument and the Bungalow." In *Everyday America: Cultural Landscape Studies after J. B. Jackson,* edited by Chris Wilson and Paul Groth, 85–129. Berkeley: University of California Press, 2003.

LGBT Community Center. "Center History." Lesbian, Gay, Bisexual, and Transgender Community Center web page. Accessed 2017. https://gaycenter.org/ about/history.

Liddle, Kathleen. "More Than a Bookstore: The Continuing Relevance of Feminist Bookstores for the Lesbian Community." *Journal of Lesbian Studies* 9, nos. 1–2 (2005): 145–59.

Light, Ivan, and Steven Gold. *Ethnic Economies.* Bingley, U.K.: Emerald Group Publishing, 2000.

Lindgreen, Adam, and Valérie Swaen. "Corporate Social Responsibility." *International Journal of Management Reviews* 12, no. 1 (2010): 1–7.

Liscano, Miguel. "Years in Prison Helped Outspoken Poet, Activist Find His Voice, Cause." *Austin American Statesman,* February 14, 2008.

Logan, John, and Harvey Molotch. *Urban Fortunes.* 20th anniversary ed. Berkeley: University of California Press, 2007.

Long Haul. "Filthy Commerce." Long Haul Infoshop web page. Accessed 2018. http://thelonghaul.org/filthy-lucre.

Lorde, Audre. "'The Master's Tools Will Never Dismantle the Master's House.'"

In *Feminist Postcolonial Theory: A Reader,* edited by Reina Lewis and Sara Mills, 25–27. New York: Routledge, 2003.

Lowry, Ira S. "Filtering and Housing Standards: A Conceptual Analysis." *Land Economics* 36, no. 4 (1960): 362–70.

Luger, Jason D. "But I'm Just an Artist!?: Intersections, Identity, Meaning, and Context." *Antipode* 49, no. 5 (2017): 1329–48.

MacDonald, Evan. "Protest Downtown on Wednesday Notably Smaller than One Tuesday." *Plain Dealer,* November 27, 2014.

Machosky, Michael. "City of Asylum Works on New Home." *Pittsburgh Tribune Review,* May 11, 2016.

MacLure, Maggie. "Researching without Representation? Language and Materiality in Post-qualitative Methodology." *International Journal of Qualitative Studies in Education* 26, no. 6 (2013): 658–67.

MacQueen, Ken. "War in the Gulf: Winter of Haight." *Ottawa Citizen,* January 29, 1991.

Madden, David. "Revisiting the End of Public Space: Assembling the Public in an Urban Park." *City & Community* 9, no. 2 (2010): 187–207.

Madison InfoShop. "Infoshop Library." Madison Infoshop web page. Accessed 2016. https://madinfoshop.wordpress.com/infoshop-library/.

Madison Newspapers. "Turn Your Back Basics." *Madison Capital Times,* January 4, 2005.

Maguire, Marti, and Kristin Collin. "Boycott Makes Dent in Triangle." *Knight Ridder Tribune Business News,* May 2, 2006.

Maiguashca, Bice. "Looking Beyond the Spectacle: Social Movement Theory, Feminist Anti-globalization Activism, and the Praxis of Principled Pragmatism." *Globalizations* 8, no. 4 (2011): 535–49.

Mallard, Aida. "Wild Iris Books Happy in New Location." *Gainesville Sun,* March 12, 2014.

Martin, Deborah G., and Byron Miller. "Space and Contentious Politics." *Mobilizations* 8, no. 2 (2003): 143–56.

Massey, Doreen. *For Space.* London: Sage: 2005.

Maunz, Shay. "Meet the Woman Bringing a Bookstore Back to the Bronx." *Glamour,* February 28, 2017. https://www.glamour.com/story/meet-the -woman-bringing-a-bookstore-back-to-the-bronx?mbid=social_twitter_ glamourmain.

May Day. "Comments / Links / Where the Lefty Folks Hang Out." May Day Books web page. Accessed 2017. http://maydaybookstore.org/index_files/ page0004.htm.

Mayer, Margit. "First World Urban Activism: Beyond Austerity Urbanism and Creative City Politics." *City* 17, no. 1 (2013): 5–19.

McAdam, Doug, Sidney Tarrow, and Charles Tilly. *Dynamics of Contention*. Cambridge: Cambridge University Press, 2001.

McArthur, John A., and Ashleigh F. White. "Twitter Chats as Third Places: Conceptualizing a Digital Gathering Site." *Social Media + Society* 2, no. 3 (2016): 1–9.

McCauley, Mary C. "Red Emma's Restaurant and Bookstore Is Moving to Mid-Town Belvedere." *Baltimore Sun,* June 1, 2018. http://www.baltimoresun.com/entertainment/dining/baltimore-diner-blog/bs-fe-red-emmas-moves-20180601-story.html.

McFarlane, Colin. "The City as a Machine for Learning." *Transactions of the Institute of British Geographers* 36, no. 3 (2011): 360–76.

McGarvey, Shannon. "Best Bets." *Austin American Statesman,* December 16, 2007.

McGirr, Lisa. *Suburban Warriors: The Origins of the New American Right*. Princeton. N.J.: Princeton University Press, 2002.

McKim, Jenifer. "Critics of Facelift in Central Square Point to Traditions." *Boston Globe,* June 29, 1997.

McKinney, Kelsey. "Black-Owned Indie Bookstores Look Forward to the Next Chapter." *Splinter News,* October 20, 2016. http://splinternews.com/black-owned-indie-bookstores-look-forward-to-the-next-c-1793863048.

McLean, Heather. "Regulating and Resisting Queer Creativity: Community-Engaged Arts Practice in the Neoliberal City." *Urban Studies* 55, no. 16 (2018): 3563–78.

McMullen, Jeffery, Lawrence A. Plummer, and Zoltan Acs. "What Is an Entrepreneurial Opportunity?" *Small Business Economics* 28, no. 4 (2007): 273–83.

McMurtie, John. "SF's Modern Times Bookstore to Close." *SF Gate,* October 12, 2016. http://www.sfgate.com/business/article/San-Francisco-s-Modern-Times-Bookstore-to-close-9962634.php?utm_source=fark&utm_medium=website&utm_content=lin.

Mehta, Vikas. "Look Closely and You Will See, Listen Carefully and You Will Hear: Urban Design and Social Interaction on Streets." *Journal of Urban Design* 14, no. 1 (2009): 29–64.

Mehta, Vikas, and Jennifer K. Bosson. "Third Places and the Social Life of Streets." *Environment and Behavior* 42, no. 6 (2010): 779–805.

Melchoir, Jillian K. "Ohio Bookstore Flips Male-Authored Books, Displaying Them Backwards." *Heat Street,* March 6, 2017. http://archive.fo/SkNHH.

Mele, Christopher. *Selling the Lower East Side: Culture, Real Estate, and Resistance in New York City*. Minneapolis: University of Minnesota Press, 2000.

Melendez, Lyanne. "Revolution Books in Berkeley Becomes Target for Right-Wing Group." *ABC 7 News,* March 8, 2018. http://abc7news.com/politics/revolution-books-in-berkeley-becomes-target-for-right-wing-groups/3191606/.

Merrifield, Andy. "The Right to the City and Beyond: Notes on a Lefebvrian Re-conceptualization." *City* 15, nos. 3–4 (2011): 473–81.

Millard, Hal L. "Room with a Viewpoint." *Mountain Xpress,* May 21, 2008.

Miller, Andy. *The Year of Reading Dangerously.* New York: Harper, 2014.

Miller, Byron, and Walter Nicholls. "Social Movements in Urban Society: The City as a Space of Politicization." *Urban Geography* 34, no. 4 (2013): 452–73.

Miller, Joseph. *For Derrida.* New York: Fordham University Press, 2009.

Miller, Laura J. *Reluctant Capitalists: Bookselling and the Culture of Consumption.* Chicago: University of Chicago Press, 2008.

Miller, Laura J. "Shopping for Community: The Transformation of the Bookstore into a Vital Community Institution." *Media, Culture & Society* 21, no. 3 (1999): 385–407.

Miller, Peter, and Nikolas Rose. *Governing the Present: Administering Economic, Social and Personal Life.* Cambridge: Polity Press, 2008.

Milliot, Jim. "Print Sales Up Again in 2017." *Publishers Weekly,* January 5, 2018. https://www.publishersweekly.com/pw/by-topic/industry-news/bookselling/article/75760-print-sales-up-again-in-2017.html.

Minta, Molly. "A New Chapter." *The Fine Print,* March 5, 2018. http://thefineprintmag.org/a-new-chapter/.

Mirk, Sarah. "Closing the Book." *Portland Mercury,* December 25, 2008.

Mitchell, Don. *The Right to the City: Social Justice and the Fight for Public Space.* New York: Guilford Press, 2003.

Mitchell, Don, and Lynn Staeheli. "Clean and Safe? Property Redevelopment, Public Space, and Homelessness in Downtown San Diego." In *The Politics of Public Space,* edited by Setha Low and Neil Smith, 143–75. New York: Francis and Taylor, 2006.

Mitchell, John L. "L.A. Black-Focus Bookshop May Close." *Los Angeles Times,* October 5, 2007.

Mitchell, John L. "Street Scenes: Leimert Park Pulsing with Culture." *Los Angeles Times,* July 21, 2008.

Mitchell, Timothy. *Colonising Egypt.* Berkeley: University of California Press, 1991.

Montgomery, Alesia. "Reappearance of the Public: Placemaking, Minoritiza-tion and Resistance in Detroit." *International Journal of Urban and Regional Research* 40, no. 4 (2016): 776–99.

Montgomery, Susan E., and Jonathan Miller. "The Third Place: The Library as Collaborative and Community Space in a Time of Fiscal Restraint." *College & Undergraduate Libraries* 18, nos. 2–3 (2011): 228–38.

Moore, Lisa. "Southern Sensibility." *Lambda Book Report* 13, no. 3 (2004): 44–45.

Morgan, Adam. "Join Us for the First 'Conversation' on Art and Resistance."

Chicago Review of Books, January 23, 2017. https://chireviewofbooks.com/2017/01/23/join-us-for-the-first-conversation-on-art-and-resistance/.

Mouffe, Chantal. *Return of the Political.* 1993. Reprint, London: Verso, 2005.

Mould, Oli. "Tactical Urbanism: The New Vernacular of the Creative City." *Geography Compass* 8, no. 8 (2014): 529–39.

Mountain Xpress. "Firestorm Semi-closes for Monthlong Makeover." *Mountain Xpress,* September 12, 2012.

Moynihan, Colin. "ABC No Rio Gears Up for a Razing and a Brand-New Home." *New York Times,* May 16, 2016.

Moynihan, Colin. "For $1, a Collective Mixing Art and Radical Politics Turns Itself into Its Own Landlord." *New York Times,* July 4, 2006.

Moynihan, Colin. "Punk Institution Receives City Money for New Building." *New York Times,* June 29, 2009.

Moynihan, Colin. "Zine Makers Grab Their MetroCards and Go to Work." *New York Times,* July 14, 2014.

Mudu, Pierpaolo. "Resisting and Challenging Neoliberalism: The Development of Italian Social Centers." *Antipode* 36, no. 5 (2004): 917–41.

Murray, Leslie Ann. "Black Bookstores." *Clamor Magazine,* Fall (2006): 18–19.

Naughton, Julie. "In Loving Color: Romance 2014." *Publishers Weekly* 261, no. 45 (2014).

Nawotka, Ed, and Claire Kirch. "Bookstores Get Political." *Publishers Weekly,* March 10, 2017. https://www.publishersweekly.com/pw/by-topic/industry-news/bookselling/article/73032-bookstores-get-political.html.

Németh, Jeremy. "Defining a Public: The Management of Privately Owned Public Space." *Urban Studies* 46, no. 11 (2009): 2463–90.

Nicholls, Walter. "The Geographies of Social Movements." *Geography Compass* 1, no. 3 (2007): 607–22.

Nicolaides, Becky M. *My Blue Heaven: Life and Politics in the Working-Class Suburbs of Los Angeles, 1920–1965.* Chicago: University of Chicago Press, 2002.

Nishikawa, Kinohi. "The Archive on Its Own: Black Politics, Independent Publishing, and the Negotiations." *Multi-Ethnic Literature of the United States* 40, no. 3 (2015): 176–201.

Nixon, Ron. "Signed, Sealed, Delivered—and Duly Logged." *International Herald Tribune,* July 5, 2013.

Norberg-Schulz, Christian. "The Phenomenon of Place." In *The Urban Design Reader,* 2nd ed., edited by Michael Larice and Elizabeth Macdonald, 272–84. New York: Routledge, 2013.

Nugent, Edie. "Comic Book Store Provides Safe Space for DC Inauguration Protesters." *Comics Culture: The Beat,* January 19, 2017. http://www.comicsbeat.com/comic-book-store-provides-safe-space-for-dc-inauguration-protesters/.

Oakley, Doug. "UC Berkeley Police, FBI Raid Activist Cooperative." *Oakland Tribune,* August 27, 2008.

O'Briant, Don. "Adaptation and Survival: Independent Feminist Bookstore Charis Thrives for 30 Years by Emphasizing Community and Caring." *Atlanta Journal-Constitution,* August 22, 2004.

O'Brien, Ellen. "Pillar of Gay Pride." *Philadelphia Inquirer,* October 7, 1998.

O'Kelly, Kevin. "Indie Bookstores Aren't Dead—They're Making a Comeback." *Huffington Post,* September 29, 2014. https://www.huffpost.com/entry/indie-bookstores-arent-de_b_5884584.

Oldenburg, Ray. *The Great Good Place: Cafés, Coffee Shops, Community Centers, Beauty Parlors, General Stores, Bars, Hangouts, and How They Get You Through the Day.* New York: Marlow & Co, 1989.

Ong, Aihwa. "The Chinese Axis: Zoning Technologies and Variegated Sovereignty." *Journal of East Asian Studies* 4 (2004): 69–96.

Open Books. "About Us." Open Books web page. Accessed 2018. https://www.idealist.org/en/nonprofit/6e74961183ad4d00a4aa80794ca9e075-open-books-chicago.

Orfield, Myron. "Metropolitics." In *The City Reader,* 5th ed., edited by Richard T. LeGates and Frederic Stout, 296–314. New York: Routledge, 2011.

Osborne, Huw. "Counter-space in Charles Lahr's Progressive Bookshop." In *The Rise of the Modernist Bookshop: Books and the Commerce of Culture in the Twentieth Century,* edited by Huw Osborne, 131–62. Farnham, U.K.: Ashgate Publishing, 2015.

Osborne, Huw. "Introduction: Openings." In *The Rise of the Modernist Bookshop: Books and the Commerce of Culture in the Twentieth Century,* edited by Huw Osborne, 1–14. Farnham, U.K.: Ashgate Publishing, 2015.

Oslender, Ulrich. *The Geographies of Social Movements: Afro-Columbian Mobilization and the Aquatic Space.* Durham, N.C.: Duke University Press, 2016.

Osman, Suleiman. *The Invention of Brownstone Brooklyn: Gentrification and the Search for Authenticity in Postwar New York.* Oxford: Oxford University Press, 2011.

Owen, Rob. "Tracking Down the Portland, Ore., Sites Used in the TV Comedy Show." *Ledger,* January 11, 2015.

Özdemir, Esin, and Ayda Eraydin. "Fragmentation in Urban Movements: The Role of Urban Planning Processes." *International Journal of Urban and Regional Research* 41, no. 5 (2017): 727–48.

Painter, Joe. "Prosaic Geographies of Stateness." *Political Geography* 25, no. 7 (2006): 752–74.

Palabras. "About Us." Palabras Bilingual Bookstore web page. Accessed 2019. https://www.palabrasbookstore.com/about-us.html.

Palabras. "Events." Palabras Bilingual Bookstore web page. Accessed 2019. https://www.palabrasbookstore.com/events.html.

Palmer, Jesse. "Long Haul Infoshop Regroups after Police Raid." *Earth First!* 29, no. 1 (2008): 3.

Panaritis, Maria. "Trailblazing Gay Bookstore Giovanni's Room Is Closing." *Philadelphia Inquirer,* April 30, 2014.

Parthasarathy, Balaji. "India's Silicon Valley or Silicon Valley's India?" *International Journal of Urban and Regional Research* 28, no. 3 (2004): 664–85.

Patchett, Ann. "Owning a Bookstore Means You Always Get to Tell People What to Read." *Washington Post,* April 22, 2015. https://www.washingtonpost.com/opinions/theres-a-book-i-want-you-to-read/2015/04/21/doe5fd7a-e839-11e4-aae1-d642717d8afa_story.html?noredirect=on.

Pearson, Andrew. "A Cold Case and a Hotbed of Activism." *Independent Weekly,* February 23, 2011.

Pela, Robert. "A Different Fight: Like Gay and Lesbian Bookstores Everywhere, A Different Light Struggles to Continue Its Activist Mission in a World of Cyber Sites and Superstores." *The Advocate* 791/792 (1999): 117.

Pereira, Ivan. "East Harlem in Spotlight for NYC Tourism Push." *AM New York,* December 5, 2013.

Peterson, Andrea. "Gap between Those Who Use Internet and Those Who Don't Is Widening." *Washington Post,* November 13, 2013. https://www.washingtonpost.com/business/technology/gap-between-those-who-use-internet-and-those-who-dont-is-widening/2013/11/12/d9d8d002-4726-11e3-a196-3544a03c2351_story.html?noredirect=on&utm_term=.c8630324a03f.

Peterson, Melike. "Living with Difference in Hyper-diverse Areas: How Important Are Encounters in Semi-public Spaces?" *Social & Cultural Geography* 18, no. 8 (2017): 1067–85.

Pick, Grant. "Outward Mobility: Chicago's Gays and Lesbians Are Gaining Acceptance—and Power." *Chicago Tribune,* February 7, 1993.

Pickerill, Jenny, and Paul Chatterton. "Notes towards Autonomous Geographies: Creation, Resistance and Self-Management as Survival Tactics." *Progress in Human Geography* 30, no. 6 (2006): 730–46.

Pickett, Noella May. "Community Sustained Indie Bookstores through Tough Times." *Rutland Herald,* April 22, 2017. https://www.rutlandherald.com/news/community-sustained-indie-bookstores-through-tough-times/article_d09a186e-8fae-5707-82f1-80fb21fb62a1.html.

Piette, Hannah. "Right-Wing Protesters Attack Revolution Books 3 Times in 2 Days after Milo Yiannopoulos' Appearance at UC Berkeley." *Daily Californian,* August 3, 2019. https://www.dailycal.org/2017/09/27/right-wing-protesters-attack-revolution-books-3-times-in-2-days/.

Pine, B. Joseph, and James H. Gilmore. *The Experience Economy.* Cambridge, Mass.: Harvard Business Press, 2011.

Plummer, Kevin. "Historicist: Third World Books and Crafts." *Torontoist,* February 5, 2015. http://torontoist.com/2015/02/historicist-third-world -books-and-crafts/.

PM Press. "On the Ground: An Illustrated Anecdotal History of the Sixties Underground Press in the U.S." PM Press web page. Accessed 2017. http:// secure.pmpress.org/index.php?l=product_detail&p=368.

Polletta, Francesca. "Free Spaces in Collective Action." *Theory and Society* 28 (1999): 1–38.

Popper, Nathaniel. "Who's Buying the Bookstore?" *Wall Street Journal,* January 18, 2008.

Postelle, Brian. "Caffiend Closes: Firestorm Stokes the Fire." *Mountain Xpress,* June 24, 2008.

Potter, Chris. "Little Shop, Big Idea: Browsing through Pittsburgh's Most Political Bookstore." *Pittsburgh City Paper,* September 29, 2004.

Potter, Clair B. "The Other Amazon." *Chronicle of Higher Education,* March 27, 2016. http://www.chronicle.com/article/The-Other-Amazon/235810.

Prasad, Ritu. "It Takes Generations: The Women, Men, and Children of Chicago's Women's March." *Medill Reports Chicago,* January 25, 2017. https:// news.medill.northwestern.edu/chicago/it-takes-generations-the-women -men-and-children-of-chicagos-womens-march/.

Pratt, Mary Louise. *Imperial Eyes: Travel Writing and Transculturation.* Abingdon, U.K.: Routledge, 2007.

Price, Leah. *How to Do Things with Books in Victorian Britain.* Princeton, N.J.: Princeton University Press, 2012.

Quimby's. "FAQ." Quimby's web page. Accessed 2018. https://www.quimbys .com/faq.

Rafail, Patrick. "Protest in the City: Urban Spatial Restructuring and Dissent in New York, 1960–2006." *Urban Studies* 55, no. 1 (2018): 244–60.

Raff, Daniel MG. "Superstores and the Evolution of Firm Capabilities in American Bookselling." *Strategic Management Journal* 21, no. 10/11 (2000): 1043–60.

Rankin, Katharine N., and Heather McLean. "Governing the Commercial Streets of the City: New Terrains of Disinvestment and Gentrification in Toronto's Inner Suburbs." *Antipode* 47, no. 1 (2015): 216–39.

Reagon, Bernice J. "Coalition Politics: Turning the Century." In *Home Girls: A Black Feminist Anthology,* edited by Barbara Smith, 356–68. New York: Kitchen Table Women of Color Press, 1983.

Red Emma's. "About." Red Emma's Bookstore and Coffeehouse web page. Accessed 2017. https://www.redemmas.org/about.

Red Emma's. "A Few News Stories about Red Emma's from the Days of the #Baltimoreuprising." Red Emma's Bookstore and Coffeehouse web page. May 9, 2015. https://redemmas.org/posts/2016-02-a-few-news-stories -about-red-emma-s-from-the-days-of-the-baltimoreuprising.

Reich, Edward. "History Supports Big Box Regulation." *Wisconsin State Journal,* May 2, 2005.

Renz, Katie. "AK Press: A Tradition of Resistance." *Clamour* 32 (2005): 14.

Revolution Newspaper. "Four Fascist Attacks on Revolution Books Berkeley in Two Days." *Revolution Newspaper,* September 28, 2017. https://revcom .us/a/510/fascist-attacks-on-revolution-books-berkeley-en.html.

Rich, Meghan A., and William Tsitsos. "Avoiding the 'SoHo Effect' in Baltimore: Neighborhood Revitalization and Arts and Entertainment Districts." *International Journal of Urban and Regional Research* 40, no. 4 (2016): 736–56.

Richmond, Norman. "Leonard Oscar Johnson." *The Globe and Mail,* June 22, 1998.

Rios, Patrica G., and Austin Hoyt, dir. *Chicago—City of the Century.* DVD. Arlington: PBS, 2004.

Riverfront Times Staff. "Police Teargas Protesters in the Central West End after Vandalism to Mayor's Home." *Riverfront Times,* September 15, 2017. https:// www.riverfronttimes.com/newsblog/2017/09/15/stockley-protesters-march -through-central-west-end.

Roberts, Diane. "Seattle, by the Book." *Washington Post,* October 7, 2012.

Robinson, James. "An Abridged History of the Collective and the Store." Wooden Shoe Books web page. Accessed 2016. https://woodenshoebooks .com/history.html.

Roestone Collective. "Safe Space: Towards a Reconceptualization." *Antipode* 46, no. 5 (2014): 1346–65.

Rojas, James. "The Enacted Environment." In *Everyday America: Cultural Landscape Studies after J. B. Jackson,* edited by Chris Wilson and Paul Groth, 275–92. Berkeley: University of California Press, 2003.

Rønning, Helge, and Tore Slaatta. "Marketers, Publishers, Editors: Trends in International Publishing." *Media Culture and Society* 33, no. 7 (2011): 1109.

Rose, Damaris. "Rethinking Gentrification: Beyond the Uneven Development of Marxist Urban Theory." *Environment and Planning D: Society and Space* 2, no. 1 (1984): 47–74.

Rosen, Judith. "African-American Booksellers Look For a Turnaround." *Publishers Weekly* 261, no. 7 (2014).

Rosen, Judith. "Making Nonprofit Stores Pay Off." *Publishers Weekly* 260, no. 19 (2013).

Rosen, Judith. "Where Up Is the New Up: BEA 2012." *Publishers Weekly* 259, no. 18 (2012).

Rosen, Judith. "Women's Bookstores: Surviving in a Changing Retail Climate." *Publishers Weekly* 244, no. 17 (1997): 23–25.

Rosenbaum, Mark S., James Ward, Beth A. Walker, and Amy L. Ostrom. "A Cup of Coffee with a Dash of Love: An Investigation of Commercial Social Support and Third-Place Attachment." *Journal of Service Research* 10, no. 1 (2007): 43–59.

Rosenwald, Michael S. "Independent Bookstores Turn a New Page on Brick-and-Mortar Retailing." *Washington Post,* December 15, 2013. https://www.washingtonpost.com/local/independent-bookstores-turn-a-new-page-on-brick-and-mortar-retailing/2013/12/15/2ed615d8–636a-11e3-aa81-e1dab1360323_story.html?utm_term=.7cbff1f8edd9.

Rose-Redwood, Reuben. "Governmentality, Geography, and the Geo-coded World." *Progress in Human Geography* 30, no. 4 (2006): 469–86.

Rosol, Marit. "On Resistance in the Post-political City: Conduct and Counter-conduct in Vancouver." *Space and Polity* 18, no. 1 (2014): 70–84.

Ross, Andrew. "The New Geography of Work: Power to the Precarious?" *Theory, Culture & Society* 25, nos. 7–8 (2008): 31–49.

Ross, Andrew. *Nice Work If You Can Get It: Life and Labor in Precarious Times.* New York: New York University Press, 2009.

Rothstein, Richard. *The Color of Law: A Forgotten History of How Our Government Segregated America.* New York: Liveright Publishing, 2017.

Sabathia, Christine. "Only the Community Can Save Black Bookstores." *Sentinel,* October 11, 2007.

Sack, Robert D. *Human Territoriality: Its Theory and History.* Cambridge: Cambridge University Press, 1986.

Sadler, David. "Anti-corporate Campaigning and Corporate 'Social' Responsibility: Towards Alternative Spaces of Citizenship?" *Antipode* 36, no. 5 (2004): 851–70.

Salamon, Jeff. "Local Poet Hits Homer with Her First Swing." *Austin American Statesman,* July 25, 2004.

Salisbury, Stephan. "Gay Bookstore Battles British Law." *Philadelphia Inquirer,* November 7, 1986.

Samers, Michael. "The Myopia of 'Diverse Economies,' or a Critique of the 'Informal Economy.'" *Antipode* 37, no. 5 (2005): 875–86.

Sandercock, Leonie. "Cosmopolitan Urbanism: A Love Song to Our Mongrel Cities." In *Cosmopolitan Urbanism,* edited by Jon Binnie, Julian Holloway, Steve Millington, and Craig Young, 49–64. New York: Routledge, 2006.

Sanderson, Bill. "An Independent Bookstore Rises on the Upper West Side." *Wall Street Journal,* September 2, 2014. https://blogs.wsj.com/metropolis/2014/09/02/an-independent-bookstore-rises-on-the-upper-west-side/.

Sandford, Jason. "Firestorm Café to Close for Renovations." *Asheville Citizen-Times,* September 9, 2012.

Santos, Noëlle. "Meet the Owner." Lit Bar web page. Accessed 2017. http://www.thelitbar.com/owner/.

Sax, David. "What Barnes & Noble Doesn't Get about Bookstores." *The New Yorker,* October 21, 2016.

Schaller, Susanna, and Gabriella Modan. "Contesting Public Space and Citizenship: Implications for Neighborhood Business Improvement Districts." *Journal of Planning Education and Research* 24, no. 4 (2005): 394–407.

Scheer, Judith. "Berkeley Commercial Tenants Claim City Is a 'Bad Landlord.'" *Oakland Tribune,* June 6, 2014.

Schein, Richard, ed. *Landscape and Race in the United States.* New York: Routledge, 2006.

Schmidt, James. "How to Maintain an Alternative Library: The Civic Media Center Five Years On." *Counterpoise* 4, no. 2 (1998): 46.

Schmidt, James. "The Infoshop Is Not the Revolution, but It Sure Helps to Have One Around." *Counterpoise* 12, no. 1 (2008): 9–12.

Schneider, Mark, and Paul Teske. "Toward a Theory of the Political Entrepreneur: Evidence from Local Government." *American Political Science Review* 86, no. 3 (1992): 737–47.

Schulman, Sarah. *The Gentrification of the Mind.* Berkeley: University of California Press, 2012.

Schweers, Jeff. "UF Dream Defenders Chapter Key in Sustaining Capitol Protest." *Gainesville Sun,* July 23, 2013.

Scott, James C. "Domination, Acting, and Fantasy." In *The Paths to Domination, Resistance, and Terror,* edited by Carolyn Nordstrom and Joann Martin, 55–84. Berkeley: University of California Press, 1992.

Scott, James C. *Domination and the Arts of Resistance: Hidden Transcripts.* New Haven, Conn.: Yale University Press, 1990.

Scott, James C. *Seeing Like a State: How Certain Schemes to Improve the Human Condition Have Failed.* New Haven, Conn.: Yale University Press, 1999.

Scott, James C. *Weapons of the Weak: Everyday Forms of Peasant Resistance.* New Haven, Conn.: Yale University Press, 1985.

Scott, Ron. "Harlem Book Treasures." *New York Amsterdam News,* February 21, 2013.

Scutts, Joanna. "The Few, the Proud, the Independent Bookstores." *The Daily Beast,* February 27, 2015. https://www.thedailybeast.com/the-few-the-proud-the-independent-bookstores.

S. D., Trav. "Exit, Stage Lower East Side." *The Village Voice,* March 5, 2003.

Seajay, Carol. "Books: 20 Years of Feminist Bookstores." *Ms. Magazine* July/August (1992).

Sennett, Richard. "New Capitalism, New Isolation: A Flexible City of Strangers." *Le Monde Diplomatique,* February 2001. https://mondediplo.com/2001/02/16cities.

Sennett, Richard. *The Uses of Disorder: Personal Identity and City Life.* New York: Knopf, 1970.

Sessa, Sam. "New Page for Book Fair." *Baltimore Sun,* June 29, 2006.

Shaw, Kate. "Gentrification: What It Is, Why It Is, and What Can Be Done about It." *Geography Compass* 2, no. 5 (2008): 1697–728.

Shaw, Kate. "The Place of Alternative Culture and the Politics of Its Protection in Berlin, Amsterdam and Melbourne." *Planning Theory & Practice* 6, no. 2 (2005): 149–69.

Shaw, Kate, and Iris Hagemans. "'Gentrification without Displacement' and the Consequent Loss of Place: The Effects of Class Transition on Low-Income Residents of Secure Housing in Gentrifying Areas." *International Journal of Urban and Regional Research* 39, no. 2 (2015): 323–41.

Shih, Adrienne. "City Council to Examine Report on Telegraph Channing Mall." *Daily Californian,* March 5, 2015.

Shister, Gail. "Phila. Gay Bookstore Giovanni's Room Marks 35 Years." *Tribune Business News,* October 6, 2008.

Shryock, Andrew. "Other Conscious/Self-Aware: First Thoughts on Cultural Intimacy and Mass Mediation." In *Off Stage/On Display: Intimacy and Ethnography in the Age of Public Culture,* edited by Andrew Shryock, 3–28. Stanford, Calif.: Stanford University Press, 2004.

Shryock, Andrew, Nabeel Abraham, and Sally Howell. "The Terror Decade in Arab Detroit: An Introduction." In *Arab Detroit 9/11: Life in the Terror Decade,* edited by Nabeel Abraham, Sally Howell, and Andrew Shryock, 1–28. Detroit, Mich.: Wayne State University Press, 2011.

Siegel, Ben. "Rainbow Bookstore Faces the Future." *Isthmus,* April 25, 2014.

Simmel, Georg. "Group Expansion and the Development of Individuality." In *Classical Sociological Theory,* edited by Craig Calhoun, Joseph Gerteis, James Moody, Steven Pfaff, Kathryn Schmidt, and Indermohan Virk, 258–72. Malden, Mass.: Blackwell, 2002.

Simmel, Georg. "The Metropolis and Mental life." In *Classic Essays on the Culture of Cities,* edited by Richard Sennett, 47–60. New York: Appleton-Century-Crofts, 1969.

Singh, Preeti. "Making Sense of Dark Times." *NY City Lens,* February 7, 2017. http://nycitylens.com/author/psingh/.

Slater, Tom. "Gentrification in Canada's Cities: From Social Mix to 'Social Tectonics.'" In *Gentrification in a Global Context,* edited by Rowland Atkinson and Gary Bridge, 40–57. New York: Routledge, 2014.

Smith, Andrea. "Introduction: The Revolution Will Not Be Funded." In *The*

Revolution Will Not Be Funded, edited by INCITE!, 1–20. Durham, N.C.: Duke University Press, 2007.

Smith, Betty. *A Tree Grows in Brooklyn.* 1943. Reprint, New York: Harper Collins, 2006.

Smith, N. Craig. "Corporate Social Responsibility: Whether or How?" *California Management Review* 45, no. 4 (2003): 52–76.

Smith, Neil. *The New Urban Frontier: Gentrification and the Revanchist City.* London: Routledge, 1996.

Smith, Patricia. "Elegy Written in a City Square." *Boston Globe,* February 20, 1998.

Soja, Edward W. *Thirdspace: Journeys to Los Angeles and Other Real-and-Imagined Places.* Malden, Mass.: Blackwell Publishers, 1996.

Sommer, Mark. "Horsefeathers Market and Residences Adds Gourmet Touch to Connecticut Street." *McClatchy-Tribune Business News,* June 19, 2013.

Sorkin, Michael. *Variations on a Theme Park: The New American City and the End of Public Space.* New York: Hill & Wang, 1992.

Souccar, Miriam K. "Nonprofit Expansion in the Works." *Crain's New York Business* 27, no. 1 (2011): 1.

Spain, Daphne. *Constructive Feminism: Women's Spaces and Women's Rights in the American City.* Ithaca, N.Y.: Cornell University Press, 2016.

Spain, Daphne. "What Happened to Gender Relations on the Way from Chicago to Los Angeles?" In *The City Reader,* 5th ed., edited by Richard T. LeGates and Frederic Stout, 176–85. New York: Routledge, 2011.

Spikol, Liz. "Room with a Crew." *Philadelphia Weekly,* July 29, 2009.

Spratling, Cassandra. "Detroit's Shrine of the Black Madonna Faces Uncertainty." *Detroit Free Press,* February 5, 2014.

Spratling, Cassandra. "Drawing on Experience Local Residents Help Bring Diversity to Children's Books with Their Q.T. Pie and Applekids Characters." *Detroit Free Press,* December 16, 1999.

Staeheli, Lynn A. "Citizenship and the Problem of Community." *Political Geography* 27, no. 1 (2008): 5–21.

Staeheli, Lynn, Don Mitchell, and Caroline Nagel. "Making Publics." *Environment and Planning D* 27 (2009): 633–48.

Stanush, Michele. "The Poet's Voice." *Austin American Statesman,* May 27, 1991.

Stateside Staff, "Independent Bookstores Are on the Rise Despite Digital Competition." *RadioLab.* Michigan Radio, March 10, 2015. https://www.michiganradio.org/post/independent-bookstores-are-rise-despite-digital-competition.

Stein, Ruthe. "The Beatniks Are Back in San Francisco." *Plain Dealer,* February 11, 1993.

Stevens, Quentin. "The German 'City Beach' as a New Approach to Waterfront Development." In *Transforming Urban Waterfronts: Fixity and Flow,* edited by

Gene Desfor, Jennifer Laidley, Quentin Stevens, and Dirk Schubert, 235–56. Abingdon, U.K.: Routledge, 2011.

Stevenson, Iain. "'The Liveliest of Corpses': Trends and Challenges for the Future in the Book Publishing Industry." *Aslib Proceedings* 52, no. 4 (2000): 133–37.

Stewart, Sean, ed. *On the Ground: An Illustrated Anecdotal History of the Sixties Underground Press in the U.S.* Oakland, Calif.: PM Press, 2011.

St. Hope. "About Underground Books." St. Hope web page. Accessed 2018. https://www.sthope.org/about-us.

St. Martin, Kevin, Gerda Roelvink, and J. K. Gibson-Graham. "An Economic Politics for Our Times." In *Making Other Worlds Possible: Performing Diverse Economies,* edited by Gerda Roelvink, Kevin St. Martin, and J. K. Gibson-Graham, 1–25. Minneapolis: University of Minnesota Press, 2015.

Stone, Michael. "Wild Iris Books Seeks Nonprofit Status." *Gainesville Sun,* August 13, 2014.

Stratigakos, Despina. *A Women's Berlin: Building the Modern City.* Minneapolis: University of Minnesota Press, 2008.

Striphas, Ted. *The Late Age of Print: Everyday Book Culture from Consumerism to Control.* New York: Columbia University Press, 2009.

Swedberg, Richard. "The Cultural Entrepreneur and the Creative Industries: Beginning in Vienna." *Journal of Cultural Economics* 30, no. 4 (2006): 243–61.

Swerts, Thomas. "Creating Space for Citizenship: The Liminal Politics of Undocumented Activism." *International Journal of Urban and Regional Research* 41, no. 3 (2017): 379–95.

Swyngedouw, Erik. "The Antinomies of the Postpolitical City: In Search of a Democratic Politics of Environmental Production." *International Journal of Urban and Regional Research* 33, no. 3 (2009): 601–20.

Swyngedouw, Erik. "The Zero-Ground of Politics: Musings on the Post-political City." *New Geographies* 1 (2009): 52–61.

Swyngedouw, Erik, and Maria Kaïka. "The Making of 'Glocal' Urban Moderni-ties." *City* 7, no. 1 (2003): 5–21.

Tarrow, Sidney. *Power in Movement: Collective Action, Social Movements and Poli-tics.* Cambridge: Cambridge University Press, 1998.

Taurasi, Lynda-Marie. "Legacy of an Activist." *News & Observer,* February 20, 2011.

Taylor, Peter J. "The State as Container: Territoriality in the Modern World-System." *Progress in Human Geography* 18, no. 2 (1994): 151–62.

Teeman, Tim, and Kevin Fallon. "Want to Feel Gay Pride? Go Here." *Daily Beast,* June 26, 2015.

Thieme, Tatiana A. "The Hustle Economy: Informality, Uncertainty and the Geographies of Getting By." *Progress in Human Geography* 42, no. 4 (2017): 529–48.

Thoburn, Nicholas. *Anti-Book: On the Art and Politics of Radical Publishing.* Minneapolis: University of Minnesota Press, 2016.

Thompson, John B. *Merchants of Culture: The Publishing Business in the Twenty-First Century.* 2nd ed. New York: Plume, 2013.

Thompson, Marie. "The Discomfort of Safety." *Environment and Planning D: Society and Space* (2017): http://societyandspace.org/2017/02/14/the-discomfort-of-safety/.

Tilly, Charles. *Contentious Performances.* New York: Cambridge University Press, 2008.

Tilly, Charles. *Regimes and Repertoires.* Chicago: University of Chicago Press, 2006.

Tolia-Kelly, Divya P. "The Geographies of Cultural Geography III: Material Geographies, Vibrant Matters and Risking Surface Geographies." *Progress in Human Geography* 37, no. 1 (2013): 153–60.

Tonkiss, Fran. "Austerity Urbanism and the Makeshift City." *City* 17, no. 3 (2013): 312–24.

Torkildson, Sandra. "City Council Should Repeal Textbook Law." *Wisconsin State Journal,* May 15, 2007.

Torrance, Morag. "Forging Glocal Governance? Urban Infrastructures as Networked Financial Products." *International Journal of Urban and Regional Research* 32, no. 1 (2008): 1–21.

Trager, K. D. "Reading in the Borderland: An Ethnographic Study of Serious Readers in a Mega-bookstore Café." *The Communication Review* 8, no. 2 (2005): 185–236.

Trager, Louis. "Radical Reading S.F. Bookseller Doing a Capital Business on Left-Wing Titles." *San Francisco Examiner,* May 24, 1995.

Trimble, Lynn. "Palabras Librería/Bookstore in Phoenix to Celebrate Grand Opening on November 12." *Phoenix New Times,* September 27, 2016. https://www.phoenixnewtimes.com/arts/palabras-libreria-bookstore-in-phoenix-to-celebrate-grand-opening-on-november-12–8683040.

Trimble, Lynn. "Why Palabras Bilingual Bookstore Is Leaving Grand Avenue." *Phoenix New Times,* April 14, 2017.https://www.phoenixnewtimes.com/arts/palabras-bilingual-bookstore-phoenix-pablo-helguera-9243080.

Trucker, Elayna. "Bookselling in the 21st Century: The Perils of Shopping Locally." *LitHub,* December 15, 2016. https://lithub.com/bookselling-in-the-21st-century-the-perils-of-shopping-local/.

Turner, Fred. *From Counterculture to Cyberculture: Stewart Brand, the Whole Earth Network, and the Rise of Digital Utopianism.* Chicago: University of Chicago Press, 2010.

Uitermark, Justus, Walter Nicholls, and Maarten Loopmans. "Cities and Social

Movements: Theorizing beyond the Right to the City." *Environment and Planning A* 44 (2012): 2546–54.

Ukura, Kim. "Indie Bookstores Strive to Survive." *Madison Capital Times,* February 19, 2009.

Valentine, Gill. "Living with Difference: Reflections on Geographies of Encounter." In *Cities and Social Change,* edited by Ronan Paddison and Eugene McCann, 75–91. London: Sage, 2014.

Vorgna, Marc L., Julie Wood, Kimberly Spell, and Emily Mayrath. "Mayor Bloomberg and NYC & Company Announce 'Neighborhood x Neighborhood' Campaign Inviting Travelers to Explore New York City's Five Boroughs." NYC web page. March 13, 2013. http://www1.nyc.gov/office-of-the -mayor/news/092–13/mayor-bloomberg-nyc-company-neighborhood-x -neighborhood-campaign-inviting.

Wacquant, Loïc. *Punishing the Poor: The Neoliberal Government of Social Insecurity.* Durham, N.C.: Duke University Press, 2004.

Waterman, Tim. "Critique of Everyday Life Volume 1." *The Journal of Architecture* 20, no. 3 (2015): 566–73.

Watkins, Morgan. "Group Seeks Different Path to Healing for Domestic Abuse Victims." *Gainesville Sun,* December 5, 2015.

Whatmore, Sarah. *Hybrid Geographies: Natures Cultures Spaces.* New York: Sage, 2002.

White, Stuart. "Social Anarchism, Lifestyle Anarchism, and the Anarchism of Colin Ward." *Anarchist Studies* 19, no. 2 (2011): 92–104.

Whyte, William H. *The Social Life of Small Urban Spaces.* New York: Project for Public Spaces, 1980.

Willamette Week. "Best of Portland." *Willamette Week,* August 10, 2005.

Willett, Charles. "Alternative Libraries and Infoshops: The Struggle against Corporate and Government Indoctrination in American Schools and Universities, and in Daily Life." *Librarians at Liberty* 8, nos. 1–2 (2000): 11.

Willett, Charles. "Censorship in Libraries." *Counterpoise* 11, no. 3/4 (2007): 80–84.

Williams, Miriam J. "Care-full Justice in the City." *Antipode* 49, no. 3 (2017): 821–39.

Wilson, Elizabeth. *The Sphinx in the City: Urban Life, the Control of Disorder, and Women.* Berkeley: University of California Press, 1992.

Wilson, Helen F. "On Geography and Encounter: Bodies, Borders, and Difference." *Progress in Human Geography* 41, no. 4 (2017): 451–71.

Wilson, Janifer. "'Yah' Wilson Owner of Sisters Uptown Book Store." Video posted to Sisters Uptown web page. 2013. http://www.sistersuptownbook store.com/.

Woestendiek, John. "The ACLU Protests Prison's Denial of Gay Publications to Inmate in PA." *Philadelphia Inquirer,* January 24, 1985.

Wolch, Jennifer. *The Shadow State: Government and Voluntary Sector in Transition.* New York: Foundation Center, 1990.

Wood, Joseph. "Vietnamese American Place Making in Northern Virginia." *Geographical Review* 87, no. 1 (1997): 58–72.

Woolf, Virginia. *A Room of One's Own.* 1929. Reprint, New York: Mariner Books, 1989.

Wortham, Simon M. *Counter-institutions: Jacques Derrida and the Question of the University.* New York: Fordham University Press, 2006.

Wright, Scott. "From 'Third Place' to 'Third Space': Everyday Political Talk in Non-political Online Spaces." *Journal of the European Institute for Communication and Culture* 19, no. 3 (2012): 5–20.

Yaneva, Albena. "How Buildings 'Surprise': The Renovation of the Alte Aula in Vienna." *Science & Technology Studies* 21, no. 1 (2008): 8–28.

Young, Alfred F. *The Shoemaker and the Tea Party: Memory and the American Revolution.* Boston: Beacon Press, 2000.

Young, Iris Marion. "City Life and Difference." In *Readings in Planning Theory,* 2nd ed., edited by Scott Campbell and Susan Fainstein, 336–55. Malden, Mass.: Blackwell Publishing, 2003.

Young, Iris Marion. *Justice and the Politics of Difference.* Princeton, N.J.: Princeton University Press, 1990.

Yuen, Felice, and Amanda J. Johnson. "Leisure Spaces, Community, and Third Places." *Leisure Sciences* 39, no. 3 (2017): 295–303.

Zellar, Brad. "The ABA's New President." *Publishers Weekly* 249, no. 37 (2002): 21–22.

Zimmerman, Alex. "Aging Bluestockings Book Shop Launches Crowdfunding Campaign to Fund Rehab Efforts." *Village Voice,* October 2, 2015. https://www.villagevoice.com/2015/10/02/aging-bluestockings-book-shop-launches-crowdfunding-campaign-to-fund-rehab-efforts/.

Zukin, Sharon. "Whose Culture? Whose City?" In *The Urban Sociology Reader,* 2nd ed., edited by Jan Lin and Christopher Mele, 349–57. New York: Routledge, 2005.

Zukin, Sharon, Valerie Trujillo, Peter Frase, Danielle Jackson, Tim Recuber, and Abraham Walker. "New Retail Capital and Neighborhood Change: Boutiques and Gentrification in New York City." *City & Community* 8, no. 1 (2009): 47–64.

Index

Kimberley Kinder is a geographer and associate professor of urban and regional planning at the University of Michigan. She is author of *DIY Detroit: Making Do in a City without Services* (Minnesota, 2016) and *The Politics of Urban Water: Changing Waterscapes in Amsterdam.*

CPSIA information can be obtained
at www.ICGtesting.com
Printed in the USA
BVHW092232100621
609319BV00002B/39